A HISTORY OF POLICE
IN ENGLAND AND WALES

By the same author

The Civil Service Today (Gollancz 1951)

The Conquest of Violence: Order and Liberty in Britain
(Constable 1970)

The Maul and the Pear Tree (with P. D. James)
(Constable 1971)

T. A. CRITCHLEY

A History of
Police in
England and Wales

SECOND EDITION

1972

MONTCLAIR, NEW JERSEY

PATTERSON SMITH

First published 1967 by Constable & Company Ltd. as
A History of Police in England and Wales 900–1966

Second edition, revised and enlarged
published by special arrangement with Constable & Company Ltd.
by Patterson Smith Publishing Corporation
Montclair, New Jersey 07042

Library of Congress Cataloging in Publication Data

Critchley, Thomas Alan, 1919–
    A history of police in England and Wales.
    Bibliography: p.
    1. Police—Great Britain—History.   I. Title.
HV8195.C75 1972   363.2′0942   72–2666
            ISBN 0–87585–701–9

This book is printed on
permanent/durable paper

To Margaret

Carol, Barbara and Alan

'In England there has always been more liberty
but worse organisation, while in other countries there
is better organisation, but less liberty'

J. S. Mill, 'Representative Government',
in *Utilitarianism, Liberty and Representative Government*

Preface to the Second Edition

It was the interest shown by Americans in my *History of Police in England and Wales* that encouraged me to prepare this revision. The first edition had been completed before the riots in Chicago and Paris in 1968, before the publication of the thought-provoking report of the American National Commission on the Causes and Prevention of Violence, and before the imagination of the British people had been caught up, aghast, at the turmoil in Northern Ireland. It was written for British readers, and looking back over five years I am uncomfortably aware of a note of complacency running through it. I believe that, in their relatively mild, unoppressive system of police, the British have something to be modestly proud of, and I do not think that its growth has been due entirely to luck. In another book on a parallel theme—that of violence in society—I quoted a letter from a young American who was taking a postgraduate degree at Oxford, having graduated at Stanford University. Having noted the 'flexible and temperate efficiency' of the British police, she continued: 'Americans in England are instantly infected by the comfortable security on which your society seems to rest: they describe a new sense of freedom from fear they never knew they really had. I never knew what safety felt like till I came here.' This letter filled me with a sense of apprehension for the future as well as pride for the past. So far, by a combination of luck, our insular situation, and a tolerant, mature society well matched by a tolerant police force—trained in the concept of *service* rather than *force*—so far, we have got by. Five years ago I had no serious doubts that the traditional system in Britain would withstand the increasingly severe pressures of modern urban living. In 1972, as this book goes to press, I am less confident; but of one thing, at least, I am sure: the wider the interchange of ideas between the great democracies about our systems of policing, the better it will be for us all.

T.A.C.

London, February, 1972

Contents

Introduction

Total freedom is anarchy, total order tyranny. The police, who represent the collective interests of the community, are the agency which holds a balance somewhere between. Their standing is a rough index of society's own attitude towards the regulation of civilised living: regard for the police, which should not of course be uncritical, is regard for law and order. Patrick Colquhoun did not exaggerate when, writing at the end of the eighteenth century, at a time when the English were resisting the idea of paid professional police as being incompatible with liberty, he declared: 'Everything that can heighten in any degree the respectability of the office of constable, adds to the security of the state, and the safety of the life and property of every individual.'

Much of this is true of the police in any country, whether democracy or tyranny, but a crucial distinction has now to be drawn. The further purposes of policing (going, that is, beyond simple concern for the safety of life and property) touch the sensitive area of individual freedom, and resolve very differently according to the manner of a nation's government. Police action may be directed either to the promotion of personal freedom or to its eclipse. In a democratic state, where Parliament is supreme and the rule of law well established, a strong, highly respected police force is a condition, not a denial, of liberty within the restraints of law. This was well understood by Peel and the other pioneers of policing in England, but its truth has been obscured in recent years (just as it was imperfectly understood in the eighteenth century), owing to confusion between two quite different things: the beneficial purposes of strong policing in a democracy; and the despotism, deliberately destructive of freedom, of a so-called police state. For tyranny exercises arbitrary police power against which the citizen has no means, and therefore no hope, of redress. It is a priceless national heritage that the police system whose growth is described in this book combines the two virtues of all good policing. It sustains our civilisation; and, at the same time, it promotes the freedom under the rule of law without which civilisation is worthless.

A study of the history of police in England shows how these fundamental issues have influenced generations down to our own times to make occasional adjustments in the balance between liberty and order, by regulating the place of the police in the State. (The balance is also being constantly adjusted by means of the criminal law and the administration of justice.) The device which is most character-istically English has been to arm the police with prestige rather than power, thus obliging them to rely on popular support. Associated with this is the principle that every policeman is personally responsible to the courts for any wrongful act. These arrangements have worked well because they suit the English disposition to be law-abiding, but they are only likely to continue to work smoothly if the laws which the police enforce are themselves acceptable to public opinion. Similar ideas have also flourished in parts of the Commonwealth, and the experience of policing in England, and its lessons, have a world-wide interest.

A central purpose of this book is to attempt to trace the way in which this unique and valuable system has been fashioned by the needs and fears of society as they have been expressed from time to time in political currents. No grand design emerges, and there is no evidence of adherence to lofty constitutional principles. The empirical process about to be described gives little support to the common view that policing in England owes much of its excellence to attachment to the idea of local responsibility for law and order, or to a mystical fusion between the policeman and the ordinary citizen. The system has never been a tidy or logical one. It was built up with little regard to principle, but much concern, at the centre, for the political expedi-encies of the day, and the need for popular support for the police and a measure of technical competence. Nor can the growth of the system be understood if it is simply regarded from the centre. It was also built up (and the importance of this to the history of the police cannot be over-emphasised) out of the confluence of the vast number of complex local currents which contributed to the political and social histories of the towns and rural areas of England and Wales during the nineteenth century.

Even for this limited purpose, of describing the external pressures that moulded the English police system, a single volume would not be enough; and when to it is added the need for a coherent history of the system itself, a structure composed of many separate forces and, over the years, hundreds of thousands of policemen, the inadequacy of the present book will be apparent. A full history of police in England would, indeed, be compounded of many elements. Because policing has generally been regarded as a local function it would march in step with the history of local government, and of that most ubiquitous of offices, the justice of the peace. It would take account of the state of public order at significant periods, and show how rioting has stimulated fresh thinking about the need to strengthen the civil power. The history of the criminal law, crime and the administration of justice would be material to a study of the collapse of parish policing and the way in which, in the eighteenth century, the cause of penal reform eclipsed that of police reform. The influence of Continental thinkers, and of utilitarian radicalism, would need to be traced. Next might come the work of the early police reformers, the creation of the Metropolitan Police, the spread of the Victorian police system throughout the country, and its later evolution during the twentieth century into something like a national public service. The institution would have to be broken down into its component parts and the separate growth of each force examined in relation to the whole, and to local histories. A comparative survey would be needed to show how common characteristics emerged to invest the developing police service with a degree of unity, as conditions of service became standardised and smaller police forces disappeared. The influence of the Home Office, police authorities, local authority associations and chief constables would need to be evaluated. And still it would remain to deal with the history of police powers, changing methods in fighting crime, the growth of detective departments, and infamous crime and criminals. The roll of honour would be recited of men who died on duty. Chapters would need to be written on the history of police uniform and equipment, on policewomen, on the special constabulary, the Railway police, Tyne River police and other departmental forces, on the Police Federation, changing conditions of service, dogs, horses, the development of scientific aids and the way in which complaints against the police have been dealt with since Rowan and Mayne investigated them *in camera* in 1829, and Palmerston insisted, against Home Office advice, in referring one to the Durham Watch Committee in 1854. A volume or two might be added on the history of relations between the police and the public, and there would be a wealth of material left over for innumerable appendices.

Introduction

This book is therefore a wholly inadequate substitute for, or preface to, a history yet to be written. For this, abundant material exists in the Public Record Office, libraries, the British Museum, local archives, and the files of national and local newspapers. I have merely touched the surface of it all. In the meantime, however, an important start has been made by Professor Radzinowicz, in his *History of the English Criminal Law* (3 volumes, 1948–56), in drawing together the many strands which make up police history in London from about 1750 to 1829, and this may well set the pattern for future research.

Limitations of space have imposed severely restrictive principles of selection in the planning of this book. First, I have tried to include everything, in however summary a form, which seemed germane to the development of a theory about the nature and purpose of policing, to the status of the police under central and local government, and to the way in which a police institution has been reconciled with traditional English attitudes towards personal liberty. Second, I have aimed to describe the development of an organisation, by tracing the way in which upwards of 200 separate police forces were formed under political, social and economic pressures from more primitive local units, and how they subsequently evolved into the elaborate police system of today. Third, I have concentrated particularly on aspects of police history which help to illuminate or explain the working and problems of the police service of modern times, and its relation to the public, at the expense of incidents (as, for example, Cromwell's experiment with military police, which is relegated to a footnote) which have no long-term significance. The application of these principles explains why the first 800 years or so of 'police' history have been dealt with in a single chapter (which, however, anyone who visits the island of Jersey today can supplement for himself by observing the parish constable system still at work), while the next 200 years take up nine-tenths of the book.

Different weight has been placed on each of these principles according to the period under survey. The first, the development of the theory of policing, occupies much of the earlier chapters, but then ceases to be a dominant theme until the revival of interest in the constitutional position of the police at the time of the recent Royal Commission. The second and third principles, relating to the growth of the police as an institution, its practical working, and the relations between the police and the public, determine the scope of the later chapters. Somewhere in Chapter Six, however, a significant change of emphasis begins. During the third decade of the twentieth century the separate police forces of England and Wales began to operate with a sense of national as well as local purpose, as it came to be seen that the earlier system of largely autonomous local forces could no longer cope with modern problems. Before this integrating process started the pressures that moulded the shape of the police institution—local vested interests, the state of law and order, the prevalence of crime, and the changing pattern of local government—came from outside. But latterly those involved in the administration of the police have been able to review its problems with the authority and breadth of vision available to a national or quasi-national organisation, and the earlier, external pressures have been matched by pressures from within. Consequently, the emphasis in dealing with the last forty years shifts from the external influences that moulded the earlier institution towards the internal, administrative measures that marked out its more recent course towards unity and higher efficiency. In other words, an outline of part of our social and constitutional history must to some extent give way to chapters of administrative history. The drawback of this is that as one looks back over the years it is the institution that takes shape rather than the lives of the men and women who composed it—a warped and unworthy way of treating generations of men to whose moral and physical courage English civilisation owes so much. In the hope of redressing the balance, however slightly, by imparting at least the flavour of humanity to the story, I have attempted, in Chapter Five, to recapture something of the way of life of Queen Victoria's policemen, though at best it can only be a very faint shadow of the truth.

Sources

As this is to some extent a pioneer attempt to outline the complete history of the police from earliest times until the present day, I have sprinkled the text with references to leading authorities and original documents to an extent which may be irksome to some readers, but which I hope may be justified by the help it is intended to give to other students in this field. In addition to the Select Bibliography of printed sources, specific references will be found at the end of the book. The principal sources on which I have drawn are as follows:

For *Chapter One* I have leaned on Holdsworth's *History of English Law*, several recent scholarly works on the medieval period, and Sidney and Beatrice Webb's great work, *English Local Government*

Introduction

(Vols. 1–4, 1906–22). Professor Radzinowicz's work I have already mentioned: I am heavily in his debt for a number of the facts contained in *Chapter Two*, and for this chapter I have also drawn on some books by Charles Reith and Douglas G. Brown, which are mentioned in the Bibliography. These take account of documents in the library at New Scotland Yard, and also of some Home Office papers, which I have also consulted. For material about the early history of policing in the City of London I have relied on an article in *The Police Journal* (Vol. IV, 1931).

Chapter Three breaks some new ground. Much of the material has been drawn from parliamentary papers and debates, together with Home Office documents now in the Public Record Office. Searching the volumes of *Hansard* for the debates on the County Police Bill, 1839, I was struck by the much greater space devoted to the Birmingham, Manchester, and Bolton police, and thus stumbled on a revival of the argument about first principles, ten years after Peel's Act, which this time resulted in the formation of three further police forces on the Metropolitan model under Crown-appointed police commissioners. It was only after preparing this chapter, much of which is concerned with the influence of Chartism on the growth of policing, that I came across F. C. Mather's valuable *Public Order in the Age of the Chartists* (1959), from which I discovered that I had been anticipated in exploiting some of the Home Office papers which deal with the formation of the centrally controlled forces. Apart from adding a few footnotes, however, I have thought it best to leave this part of the chapter as originally drafted. In dealing with the development of municipal police forces after 1835, I have drawn on research by Jenifer Hart embodied in an article 'Reform of the Borough Police, 1835–1856' in the July, 1955, issue of the *English Historical Review*.

Chapter Four also breaks a certain amount of new ground. In preparing it I have rummaged Home Office documents in the Public Record Office, and also made extensive use of Parliamentary papers and debates, together with the early reports of the inspectors of constabulary. I am also indebted (once again) to Jenifer Hart for an article 'The County Borough Police Act, 1856' in the Winter, 1956, issue of *Public Administration*; and, for some facts about the early development of police forces, to an article by Henry Parris, 'The Home Office and the Provincial Police in England and Wales, 1856–1870', in the Summer, 1961, issue of *Public Law*.

The source material for much of *Chapter Five* is of a different category. Here I have turned to the forty or so local police force histories, many of which were prepared to mark the centenary of the foundation of the force. Some of these make valuable use of local records which usefully supplement material available in Home Office and Parliamentary papers.

These five chapters complete the story of the growth of the police institution up to the beginning of the First World War. In dealing with the next period, which describes the way in which a series of separate local police forces evolved into something like a national police service, and the influence on the service of the Second World War, I have had the great privilege of being permitted to make use of two unpublished works by Sir Arthur Dixon, C.B., C.B.E., entitled *The Home Office and the Police between the two World Wars* and *The Emergency Work of the Police Forces in the Second World War*. As the head of the Police Department of the Home Office for many years, Sir Arthur Dixon made an outstanding contribution to the development of the police service, and his labour, after his retirement, in documenting from Home Office files the history of the police during the formative period from 1919 to 1945 has immensely lightened my task.

The remaining chapters deal with more recent events, with some of which I have been privileged to be involved personally.

Acknowledgments

In addition to the works already mentioned, I gratefully acknowledge help from many of the books listed in the bibliography, and numerous official publications; for permission to quote from Crown copyright material I am indebted to the Controller of H.M. Stationery Office. I am grateful to Mr. G. W. Reynolds, M.P. and Mr. A. R. Judge, for generously allowing me to read, in advance of its publication, their forthcoming history of the police strikes of 1918 and 1919, which has been of the greatest value in dealing with this episode in Chapter Six; and to Lord Tenby for supplying me with an eyewitness account of the way in which his father, David Lloyd George, dealt with a deputation of police strikers at 10 Downing Street. Sir Arthur Dixon has very kindly read a first draft of Chapters Six and Seven, and discussed many valuable suggestions with me; my debt to him is immense, and I gratefully acknowledge permission to quote several passages from his works. Mr. Peter Harvey, Assistant Legal Adviser to the Home Office, was good enough to read and comment on a first draft of Chapters

Introduction

One, Three and Four, and to him and to several other of my colleagues at the Home Office who have read parts of the book in draft I am deeply grateful. My thanks are also due to Miss A. A. Gough, M.B.E., the Librarian at the Home Office; Mr. D. T. Brett, the Librarian of the Police College (who very kindly prepared a bibliography to guide my reading at an early stage); the staff of the London Library, and various members of the staff of the Home Office and Public Record Office, who have willingly responded to what must at times have seemed insatiable demands. I especially wish to express my thanks to Mr. Miles Huddleston, of Constable and Company, for an invitation to write the book, and to Sir Charles Cunningham, K.C.B., K.B.E., C.V.O., then Permanent Under-Secretary of State at the Home Office, for permission to accept his invitation.

Finally, it is a pleasure to express my deep gratitude to Miss Marjorie Scotcher, who prepared the bulk of the final typescript, to my daughter, Carol Mathieson, who shared part of the burden, and above all to my secretary, Mrs. Doris Wright, whose heroic spare-time labours, in typing the whole of the first draft and lending an always willing hand with the final copy, have sustained me throughout, and advanced the completion of the book by many months.

As a civil servant I have obtained official permission to publish this book, but I wish to make it clear that no one but myself is responsible for any errors it contains. Any judgments and expressions of opinion are, similarly, my own responsibility, and must not be taken in any way to represent the views of the Home Office.

T.A.C.

January, 1967

A History of
Police in
England and Wales

Chapter One

The Era of
the Parish Constable 900-1750

The origins of the English police system are to be found in the tribal
laws and customs of the Danish and Anglo-Saxon invaders, and the
seeker after them is consequently apt to lose his way in a jungle of
archaic terms. The nearest equivalent to the modern policeman is the
Saxon tythingman, otherwise borsholder or headborough. Above
him was a hundred man and then the shire reeve or sheriff. Collective
fines levied on a community as punishment included fightwitt,
grithbryce, and frithbrec; and territorial divisions in which policing
operated were variously known as hundreds, wapentakes, rapes, and
lathes. With the coming of the Normans the verbal jungle thickens as
French institutions are heaped on top of the ancient ones, and local
variations multiply. When the term 'constable' appears on the scene
after 1066 it seems at first sight a welcome and familiar landmark, but
examination shows it not to have been a civil office at all, but a high
military one associated with the royal court.* The early Norman
constable thus bore no relationship to the Saxon tythingman. Nevertheless, a century or so after the Conquest, we find a more lowly race
of persons designated by the title 'constable' taking over the tythingman's duties; and from the marriage of Saxon tythingman and
Norman constable, and with the assimilation of Norman and Saxon

* The constable, according to Helen M. Cam (*The Hundred and the
Hundred Rolls* (1930), p. 193), represented the fusion of popular and royal
government more completely than any other local government official.
Elected by the township, he was the embodiment of communal responsibility; but he was also the embodiment of royal authority. The first statutory
mention of the title 'constable' is in 1252. The derivation of the term is
generally regarded as being *comes stabuli*—Master of the Horse. The
holder of the office enjoyed high status. In Jersey, whose system of government is still founded on the original Norman, there are no justices of the
peace, and the constable remains the principal officer of the parish or township, where his functions are analogous to those of the *maire* of the French
commune.

1

titles and offices, the verbal jungle thins out, and the English parish constable of the Middle Ages emerges as the direct lineal descendant of the ancient tythingman.

And lastly, the advent of the justice of the peace in the fourteenth century gives the final shape to what the early Victorians contemptuously wrote off as 'the old police', a working partnership of parish constable and justice which by then had endured with remarkable stability for almost 500 years. Here it is possible only to give a sketchy and inadequate outline of the intricate development, extending over so long a period of time, of the legal and administrative framework within which the office of constable thus evolved.

Frankpledge

From very early times, certainly from the reign of King Alfred, the primary responsibility for maintaining the King's peace[1] fell upon each locality under a well-understood principle of social obligation, or collective security. It has recently been suggested that the ancient roots of this system may be found in voluntary associations or frith-guilds, formed in Wessex for mutual protection against theft.[2] In Saxon times the tun or vill was the smallest unit of local government (approximating, very roughly, to the modern parish), and, as Professor Sayles puts it, 'the primary importance of the vills in governmental life lay in the police duties which came to be imposed upon them. The most serious problem of everyday administration was to discover and punish those evildoers whose deeds struck at the roots of an orderly society'.[3] Every male person, unless excused through high social position or property, was enrolled for police purposes in a group of about ten families known as a tything, and headed by a tythingman. If any member of the group committed a crime, the others had to produce him for trial; if they failed to do so they could be fined or called upon to make compensation. In addition, all members of the tything had to find a security who would appear to answer any charge preferred against them. In essence, therefore, the system relied on the principle that all members of a community accepted an obligation for the good behaviour of each other. Groups of tythings were formed into a hundred, the head man of which was known as a hundred man or royal reeve, who exercised administrative and judicial powers through a hundred court; and overall, the shire reeve, or sheriff, had a general responsibility under the King for the conservancy of the peace in the shire. He was thus able to muster the *posse comitatus*—namely, the whole available civil force of the shire—in case of emergency. Linked with these arrangements was an obligation on all members of a community to join in pursuit of a felon by means of hue and cry. A picture of the system at work is contained in the laws of Edgar, passed at the end of the tenth century: 'If there be present need, let it be made known to the hundred man and let him make it known to the tythingman and let all go forth to where God may direct them to go. Let them do justice on the thief, as it was formerly the enactment of Edmund.' Canute ordained that enrolment in a tything was compulsory: 'And we will that every freeman be brought into a hundred and into a tything . . . as soon as he is twelve years old.'

These simple arrangements were taken over by the Normans, modified, and systematised under the description 'frankpledge'—the most important police institution of the Middle Ages[4]—which has been authoritatively defined in modern times as 'a system of compulsory collective bail fixed for individuals, not after their arrest for crime, but as a safeguard in anticipation of it'.[5] In the early period after the Norman Conquest the juxtaposition of two alien cultures, with a master race holding its defeated enemies in subjection and attempting to impose a new language and foreign manners, strained the primitive means of law enforcement beyond their capacity. The Normans tightened up observance of the old system and required the sheriffs, who were royal officers, to supervise its working by holding a special hundred court, which sat twice a year, to ensure that all who ought to be enrolled in a tything, and thus pledged for their good behaviour to one another, were in fact enrolled. This court of scrutiny, which came to be known as the 'view of frankpledge and sheriff's tourn', also served the ends of savage repression, for the Norman sheriffs were men of great power and little scruple. They extorted the payment of fines at the least opportunity or none. If a Norman were murdered (and the onus of proof of race lay on the conquered Saxons), the penalty on a community could be ruinous. Moreover, many sheriffs behaved with a degree of barbarity uncommon even in that period. The *Anglo-Saxon Chronicle* records pitifully: 'A.D. 1124. This same year after St. Andrew's Mass and before Christmas, held Ralph Basset and the King's thanes a "gewitenemote" in Leicestershire, at Noncothoe, and there hanged more thieves than ever were known before, that is, in a little while, four and forty men altogether; and despoiled six men of their eyes and multilated them. Many true men said that there were several who suffered very unjustly; but our Lord

3

God Almighty, who seeth and knoweth every secret, seeth also that the wretched people are oppressed with all unrighteousness. First they are bereaved of their property and then they are slain. Full heavy year was this.'

Worse was to come. Under the early arrangements, the members of tythings were only required to produce one of their number when he was wanted by the authorities. By the Assize of Clarendon, 1166 (enacted to celebrate the centenary of the conquest?), the villagers were required to report to the sheriff's tourn any suspicions they might harbour about one another, together with any other matter affecting the affairs of the district.[6] These reports, or 'presentments', as they were known, were made by the tythingman (or chief pledge, as he was now sometimes called in his progression towards becoming a constable) to a jury of twelve free men of the hundred, who forwarded serious accusations to the sheriff. In this is to be seen an early use of the jury system. Information would be required not only about felons, but also about any suspicious character 'such as sleep by day and watch by night, and eat and drink well and have nothing'.

Revulsion from barbaric practices and the closer integration of the community as a result of intermarriage between the Normans and Anglo-Saxons contributed, towards the end of the twelfth century, to a reversion to renewed emphasis on the old principle of local, rather than central, law enforcement. Arrangements were relaxed. The unpopular sheriff's tourns, which were royal courts of the hundred, gave way to local manorial courts, or courts leet, which under the steward of the lord of the manor took over the sheriff's jurisdiction. They also added administrative functions to it. And somewhere about this time of general relaxation the Norman title of 'constable' acquired the local significance it has held ever since. It had descended the social scale from its zenith as an office of the royal court, down to the constable of a castle, to the head constable of a shire (during the reign of King John), to the high constable of a hundred, and finally to the petty constable of the vill, tything, or manor: a ubiquitous office, whose 'military' and 'police' functions were for many years barely distinguishable.

Emergence of the office of Constable

There was, of course, no complete break with the past. The old Saxon principle of collective obligation to maintain the King's peace continued to be active. But the unit of responsibility under feudalism, formerly the tything, became the feudal manor. And the manorial court, or court leet, not only took over from the sheriff's tourn the supervision of frankpledge (the 'view of frankpledge'); it also elected annually the officers who were to serve their turn in assisting the lord of the manor to regulate the affairs of the community. Hence the court came to exercise three functions: it ensured that frankpledges were working properly, it awarded punishment, usually by way of a fine, against either an individual or the whole community, and it appointed the principal officers of the manor. Among these officers, the titles of whom attest the special purpose for which each was appointed—ale-taster, bread-weigher, swine-ringer—the constable was pre-eminent, carrying (and inheriting from his Saxon predecessors) a special responsibility, as the principal representative of the manor, for making the periodical reports, or presentments, to the court leet. These dealt with the local affairs and suspicions which had formerly been reported to the sheriff's tourn. The superior position of these local leaders-cum-common-informers was acknowledged by the court lawyers of the time in dignifying them, in a statute of 1252, with the honourable Norman title of 'constable'—having equal authority with mayors and bailiffs—a title which had no doubt been in general use for many years earlier.

Thus by the end of the thirteenth century the constable had acquired two distinct characteristics: as the annually elected representative of the manor, or parish, he was its executive agent, embodying the principle of collective responsibility established by the Saxon tythingman, and duly making his presentments at the court leet; but he was also an officer recognised by the Crown as having a particular responsibility for the keeping of the King's peace by hue and cry and other means, and the use of the designation 'constable' gave his authority a royal flavour which, marking him out from other local officers, would have established his ascendancy in the manor or parish. In some such way, it seems, the common-law duties and privileges of the constable emerged, and from this early time the titles tythingman, borsholder, headborough, and constable, all still in common use for many years as synonyms for the same office, are nevertheless distinguishable for the inflexion of superiority.the Norman designation alone carried until its degradation in late Tudor times.

Statute of Winchester, 1285

The next milestone in the development of early ideas about law enforcement is the Statute of Winchester, 1285, the preamble to which described its object as 'to abate the power of felons'. This, of first importance, is nevertheless to be seen largely as a consolidating measure. It preserved and codified well-tried features from earlier systems, and in particular it reaffirmed the principle of local responsibility for policing a district, underlining this principle by introducing, or reviving, three practical measures by which it was to be carried into effect.

The first of these, the system of watch and ward, is of particular interest in that it introduced the idea of town watchmen as a means of supplementing the traditional duties of the constable, and marks the emergence of a distinction between town and rural policing. A watch of up to sixteen men, depending on the size of the town, was to be stationed at every gate of a walled town between sunset and sunrise, and the watchmen were given power to arrest strangers during the hours of darkness. All the men of the town were placed by the constable on a roster for regular service, and refusal to obey a summons to serve resulted in committal to the stocks. Arrested persons were handed over to the constable in the morning, and they too would be placed in the stocks. The second measure dealt with by the Statute of Winchester was the ancient Saxon practice of hue and cry, now revived as a means of dealing with strangers who resisted arrest by the watchman: 'hue and cry shall be levied on them, and such as keep the watch shall follow with hue and cry, with all the towns near'. In effect this meant that a fugitive was to be pursued by the whole population. Work had to be laid aside, and anyone who failed to respond to the call was regarded as siding with the fugitive, and was himself hunted down. To back up these measures the Statute provided for the maintenance of what was termed an 'assize of arms'. This required that every male between the ages of fifteen and sixty was to keep in his house 'harness to keep the peace'. Those of a superior rank were to maintain 'a hauberke and helme of iron, a sword, a knife and a horse', while the poor people were to have available bows and arrows. In each hundred two high constables were to be appointed by the hundred court to make a half-yearly inspection of arms. These high constables, whose later career is traced briefly below, may be loosely regarded as the successors of the Saxon hundred men. The line dividing their military and police functions was narrow: under the sheriff of the county they supervised the activities of petty constables and watchmen, not only against thieves, but against rebels and outlaws also.

The Statute of Winchester was the only general public measure of any consequence enacted to regulate the policing of the country between the Norman Conquest and the Metropolitan Police Act, 1829, so that for nearly 600 years it laid down the basic principles. (The Justices of the Peace Act, 1361, described below, affected the manner in which these principles were applied, but did not disturb them.) These principles can now be summed up. First, it was a duty of everyone to maintain the King's peace, and it was open to any citizen to arrest an offender. Second, the unpaid, part-time constable had a special duty to do so, and in the towns he was assisted in this duty by his inferior officer, the watchman. Third, if the offender was not caught red-handed, hue and cry was to be raised. Fourth, everyone was obliged to keep arms with which to follow the cry when required. Finally, the constable had a duty to present the offender at the court leet. The Statute made no mention of frankpledge, and it can be assumed that compulsory enrolment of the population in tythings as surety for each other had by this date become obsolete. The preventive aspect of policing was secured by the watch by night and the ward by day, the repressive by hue and cry, and the punitive by presentment. There is no reason to suppose that, in the stable conditions of England in the Middle Ages, these arrangements were other than effective. At bottom, they enlisted the whole community in what today would be called the fight against crime, and penalised laxity by the imposition of a collective fine.

The Statute of Winchester, embodying a fusion of Saxon and Norman ideas, may thus be conveniently regarded as marking the end of the first police 'system' in England, which can be seen to pivot largely round the part-time constable, a local man with a touch of regal authority about him, enshrining the ancient Saxon principle of personal service to the community and exercising powers of arrest under the common law.

Advent of the Justice of the Peace

Taken together, the Statute of Winchester, 1285, and the Justices of the Peace Act, 1361, mark the transition from frankpledge, the early feudal means of law enforcement, into a rudimentary police system based on a working partnership of constable and justice. This system reached its zenith under the Tudors and progressively disintegrated during the seventeenth and eighteenth centuries, although tattered remnants survived until mid-Victorian times. In all it lasted, in various stages of evolution and decay, for nearly 500 years. Here it is possible only to attempt, in brief outline, to show how the advent of the justice of the peace influenced the constable's office, the way in which the status of the office declined, the nature of the constable's duties in the time of the Tudors and Stuarts, the manner in which, a little later, the status of the high constable of the hundred shrank to that of a rate-collector, the shroud of legal obscurity which enveloped the whole disjointed system in its last stages of dissolution, and the causes which led to its final collapse.

Like the Statute of Winchester, 75 years earlier, the Justices of the Peace Act, 1361, gathered up elements from earlier systems and cast them into a statutory mould that gave them a new meaning and a new usefulness, but the two statutes were based on contrary principles: that of Winchester was directed to localising the means of law enforcement; that of 1361 tended to centralise these means.

The ancestors of the justice of the peace were certain knights commissioned by Richard I in 1195 to take security to keep the peace from everyone over the age of sixteen. This idea developed in the succeeding century, and the knights came to be known as *custodes pacis*, or keepers of the peace. Their authority was gradually enlarged, and by the fourteenth century they were empowered to deal with minor offences. The first statutory recognition of them came in an Act of 1327, which provided that 'in every county there shall be assigned a good and lawful man to keep the peace'. This statute is still in force. In due course the judicial authority of the keepers of the peace was widened, and the Act of 1361 formally recognised them as justices. At the same time it defined their responsibilities in a way which led to their unique position in the shires as holders of a mixture of police, judicial, and administrative authority. They were appointed by the sovereign and derived their authority from him, and their primary duty was to maintain the King's peace. Their coming, as Professor Vinogradoff puts it, 'marks the end of the feudal federations of local potentates endowed with franchises in manors and boroughs. . . . The class rule of the gentry, constituted in county groups, was substituted for feudalism by a definite concentration of judicial and administrative functions in the hands of the justices of the peace.'[7]

8

From early times the justices superseded officers of a merely local origin. Their higher social status marked them out as the constable's natural mentor, and for many years the justice was regarded as the superior, the constable as the inferior, conservator of the peace. Commonly the justice would be the lord of the manor, and he or his steward would preside over the leet court, by which the constable, as a principal officer of the manor, was appointed. Thus the constable was the justice's man, 'the lowe and lay minister of the peace',[8] a general factotum in carrying out, under the authority of the justice, the affairs of the manor. He became the executive agent of the justice in much the same way that he remained the agent of the manor, or parish. In common with all other parish officers, he was unpaid, although he was allowed certain customary fees and expenses. As in ancient times, the office was filled in rotation by house-row among all parishioners qualified according to local traditional requirements or customs, or sometimes, in rural areas, according to the tenure of ancient farms; and refusal to accept office was punishable by fine. His staff, or baton, was his symbol of authority, which he might hang outside his cottage door. It was also available as a defensive weapon. He wore no distinctive uniform of any kind.

Some explanation is necessary of the way in which the constable of later medieval times obtained his prefix 'parish'—how he changed, in other words, from being an officer of the tything, or manor, into an officer of the parish. The reason is to be found in the growth of the parish as a unit of local government. Originally an ecclesiastical community, it was beginning by the reign of Henry VIII to acquire civil functions, and in late Tudor times this process was far advanced—the parish, controlled by its vestry, had become an important unit of local administration. It was natural to this development that the parish should attract and take over some of the functions of the obsolescent remnants of feudalism, and in this way the constable came to be associated with it. Hence in the final stage of the process we find the constable, as the most important official of the parish, appointed by the court leet (or sometimes, later on, by quarter sessions) on the nomination of the parish vestry; and it was through the constable that 'the activities of this new civil unit [the parish] were linked up and subordinated to the organised rule of the justices of the peace'.[9]

Degradation of the office of Constable

Inevitably the advent of the justice of the peace degraded the constable's office, but even so it was slow to lose its feudal dignity. During the fifteenth and for much of the sixteenth centuries he was still (at least in many areas) pre-eminent among the four principal annually elected officers of the parish—constable, churchwarden, surveyor of highways, and overseer of the poor; and he held this position in some small towns right into the eighteenth century, just as he still does in the island of Jersey today. An authority writing in Queen Elizabeth's reign commented that 'It may appear there was a credit given unto them, not altogether unlike to that which is now given to justices of the peace'. In most areas, however, a decline had set in by the Tudor period, although the author of a book on *Degrees of People of England,* published in 1586, suggests that this decline had not then gone very far. In commenting that 'the fourth and last sort of people in England are daie labourers, poore husbandmen . . . tailors, shoe-makers, carpenters [who] are to be ruled, and not to rule others', he observes that 'in villages they are commonlie made churchwardens, side-men, ale-conners, now and then constables . . . '.[10] Here is a clear inference that the constable was still held in higher esteem than the other parish officers. Yet within a short period the office was commonly regarded as appropriate only to the old, idiotic, or infirm.

The reason for this change is to be found in the reluctance of the wealthier merchants and tradesmen and farmers of the sixteenth century to serve their turn in undertaking the onerous and unpaid duties of the office, and their general resort to the practice of paying deputies to act in their place. The deputies themselves would often pay deputies in turn, with the result that the office came to be filled by those who could find no other form of employment, and so served more or less permanently as parish constable from year to year at a menial wage. Hence the office sank lower and lower in public esteem as the old principle of personal service died out. The deputies, according to Bacon (1561–1628) were 'of inferior, yea, of base condition, which is a mere abuse . . . for the petty constables in towns ought to be of the better sort'. The contrast between the lingering high status and dignity of the lawyer's conception of the ancient office and the nature of the men who now filled it was acute. At the same time that Coke (1552–1634) was loftily laying down the qualifications—'*Honesty:* to

10

execute his office truly without malice, affection or partiality; *Knowledge:* to understand his duty what he ought to do; *Ability:* as well in estate as in body . . . therefore they ought to be chosen out of the better sort of parishioners, and not either by the house or other custom' —Shakespeare was drawing contemptuous laughs out of Dogberry and Verges and Constable Elbow ('As they are chosen, they are glad to choose me for them; I do it for some piece of money'—*Measure for Measure*, Act II, Sc. 1): a picture engagingly filled out by a real-life constable in Wiltshire, who in 1616 prayed successfully to be relieved of his office, being unable, presumably, to afford to pay a deputy, on the grounds that 'I am unlearned, and by reason thereof am constrayned to go two miles from my house to have the help of a scrivener to read such warrants as are sent to me'.[11]

Duties of the Parish Constable

To understand the reason why all who could afford to do so paid their way out of serving their turn in the formerly honourable office of constable, it is necessary to appreciate the onerous nature of the work involved, which took up time which otherwise could be turned to profit.

A constable's duties, originally based on the common law, were later extended by Acts of Parliament; and a typical oath (the details varied from place to place) quoted in the *Liber Albus* ran as follows:

'You shall swear that you shall keep the Peace of our Lord the King well and lawfully according to your power, and shall arrest all those who shall make any contest, riot, debate, or affray, in breaking of the said peace, and shall bring them into the house or Compter of one of the Sheriffs. And if you shall be withstood by strength of such misdoers, you shall raise upon them hue and cry [and] shall follow them from street to street and from ward to ward until they are arrested. And also you shall search at all times when you shall be required by scavenger or Bedel, for the common nuisances of the ward; until they are arrested. . . . And the faults you shall find, you shall present them unto the mayor and to the officers of the said City. . . . So God help you and the Saints.'

In practice this meant that the constable had to set the nightly watch in the towns, take over prisoners from the watchmen and put them in the stocks or a lock-up, or keep them in his own cottage until he was able to deliver them over to a justice. Staff of office in hand, he was to initiate the hue and cry after a fugitive offender for which, in Tudor times, he would sometimes ask the justice to 'grant a hue and cry', a document that by the eighteenth century, and ever since, has been more commonly known as a warrant.[12] The dissolution of the monasteries created a huge army of vagrants whose only alternative to starvation was plunder, and under the barbaric laws of the Tudors the parish constable was the principal agent in maiming, burning with hot irons and other refinements of torture, before whipping the vagabond, 'until his or her body be bloodie', out of the village or town. It is surely fair to suppose that many men refused to have anything to do with such practices. Much the greater part of the constable's unpaid work, however, was that connected with presentments; and it is in carrying out these duties that he is still seen, characteristically, as the representative of the parish.

The constable was under a legal obligation of great antiquity to bring before the jury of the court leet which appointed him (or, later, before the court of quarter sessions) reports, or presentments on oath, of all who had offended against the law—whether common or statute —just as in the heyday of feudalism the chief pledge had brought matters to the sheriff's tourn. The offender might be an individual or the whole parish. The offence might be what would today be called a crime (comprising 'all bloodsheddings, affrays, outcries, rescues, and other offences, committed or done against the King's Majesty's Peace'), or it might be the failure on somebody's part to maintain a road or a bridge. It might be the refusal of somebody to serve his turn in one of the parish offices, or negligence in doing so. It might relate to 'such as are idle and will not labour, and can give no account how they get their living', 'suspicious persons, whores, notivigants or nightwalkers, and mothers of bastards', 'such bakers as put light bread for sale', or 'such persons as keep any hogs to the common annoyance of His Majesty's subjects'. Such presentments were made long before the institution of Parliament, and statutory enactments later extended their range. The presentment procedure was all-embracing. Private and public complaints of every kind were reported. Administrative, criminal, and judicial issues—all were indiscriminately brought to the court by the parish constable, and presented as criminal offences, or public nuisances, or offences against the community. Four times during his year of office he would be required to make his way to the market town to attend the quarter sessions (or twice a year to the court leet), and there produce several dozen, and sometimes upwards of a hundred, separate pieces of paper of all shapes and sizes on which he had written down, more or less literately, the affairs of the parish: 'Our hyghe Wayes are all well according to the Statute . . . '; 'Arthur Moore keepeth a vytelling house being not licensed, and the parsonage sprynge is destroyed . . . '; 'We presente Geo. Mann vacabonde, punished the 22nd July and delivered to the constable at White Notley . . . '; 'And this Newcombe and she have continewde to live together—whether she be wyffe or no we cannot tell'.[13] Sidney and Beatrice Webb, in their monumental *English Local Government*, give a vivid picture of 'innumerable tattered, dirty, and half-illegible scraps of paper' which they examined all over the country, that still survive to tell the stories, in the words of the parish constable, of life in the villages of England centuries ago. The offence might be 'not coming to church', 'not hanging out a lantern with light', 'selling ale without licence', 'the nuisance of muck', 'cutting turf off the commons', 'not mending the wall', 'not mending the bridge', 'refusing to keep nightly watch when ordered by the constable', and so on. A typical presentment, as late as 1736, shows the constable still acting in the most ancient office of all, as representative of the people of the vill or tything, and echoing the terms of the Statute of Winchester: 'The Return of the Tythingman of the parish of Markham in the County of Berks. . . . The poor are provided for, the stocks and whipping post in good repair, warrants executed, watch and ward duly kept, and all things belonging to my office are in good order to the best of knowledge.'[14]

This system was buttressed by penalty provisions without which it could scarcely have worked at all, so reluctant were men to serve, in effect, as unpaid public accusers. The principal of these was the obligation, traceable to the Assize of Clarendon and attaching to the parish as a whole, to disclose and bring to punishment every breach of the laws and customs by which the community was bound, any failure in which rendered the inhabitants liable to amercement, or collective fine payable to the Crown, in addition to a further payment to the injured party. A second sanction lay against the constable himself, who could be presented (usually by the high constable of the hundred) and punished for negligence—a further inducement, if any were needed, to pay somebody else to do the unpleasant work and incur the risk.

It is easy to see how, as the status of the constable sank lower and lower, with paid deputies taking over, the system fell into general disrepute. Yet until the nineteenth century there was little to put in its place, and as late as 1806 the high constables of Surrey were being

13

threatened with a fine of £5 if they neglected to present any 'decayed road, bridge or other nuisance'. Then, 'at one fell swoop', in the words of the Webbs, 'and with characteristic disregard for history, custom, and tradition, an Act of 1827 abolished all obligation of high or petty constables to make presentments of "popish recusants", persons not attending church, rogues and vagabonds, forestallers and regrators, profane swearers, servants out of place, false weights and measures, highways and bridges out of repair, riots and unlawful assemblies and "whether the poor are well provided for and the constables legally chosen" '.[15] It was as though Alice's pack of cards had fallen about the ears of tythingmen, headboroughs, borsholders and lords of the leet—except that many of them still managed to survive, at least nominally, for a number of years.

The High Constable

In carrying out his duties, the constable was supervised not only by the justices, but also, in later times very loosely, by the high constable, to assist whom he had to make oath: 'In the presence of the High Constable you shall be aiding and assisting unto him, and in his absence you shall execute his office and do all things belonging to your office, according to your knowledge and power.' The duties of the high constables as inspectors of the arms which householders were required to keep was mentioned in the Statute of Winchester. Just as the petty, or parish, constable represented, and acted as the executive agent of, the township, so the high constable represented, and acted as the executive agent of, the hundred. Formerly appointed by the hundred court, they came in later times to be appointed, still as high constables for the hundred, by quarter sessions—under a statute of Henry VIII the justices in Wales were authorised to select two 'substantiall gentlemen, or yeomen, to be chiefe constables of the hundred wherein they inhabit, which two constables in every hundred shall have a speciall regard to the conservation of the King's peace'.[16] In the sixteenth century they seem to have been exercising some of the functions of the justice in giving instructions to parish constables, but their office suffered a corresponding degradation, though for different reasons.

In earlier times the high constable's social position, like his duties, was intermediate between that of the justice and the parish constable. In rural areas he would be found from the lesser gentry or yeomanry;

14

in the towns from the ranks of the manufacturers or more prosperous tradesmen. It was his duty to supervise the parish constables in his hundred in making presentments, and in particular to present any constable he considered to be negligent. He would from time to time be urged by the justices to stimulate the parish constables to greater activity, but any analogy with the modern chief constable would be totally misleading: there was no question of day-to-day supervision over, or general instruction of, the unfortunate cobbler or carpenter during his twelve months' stint of office as village constable. There could have been little enough scope for the high constable once justices of the peace had firmly established their ascendancy over parish constables, and during the seventeenth century, as the importance of the hundred as an administrative unit declined, the duties became nominal. Alehouse-keepers, petty tradesmen, and small farmers succeeded the yeomanry in filling the office, many of whom were probably little better educated than the parish constables under them. In the eighteenth century, however, when the early stages of the Industrial Revolution underlined the inadequacy of local government to cope with the problems of new roads and houses and expanding farms, the high constable was at last given a job of work. He became a general factotum, inspecting weights and measures and roads and bridges (a sad descent from the feudal duty of inspecting arms under the Statute of Winchester), but spending most of his time as a collector of the county rates. This came about through the working of the system of presentments, already described. When an offence against the community was presented, such as failure to repair a bridge or road, the result of the 'trial' was commonly to fine the parish collectively, and the high constable was responsible for seeing that the money was duly paid over. From here it was a short step to the introduction of community rating to pay for essential public works, and the high constable of ancient times, still bearing his proud Norman title, shrank, in consequence, to the petty salaried official who testified before a select committee of Parliament in 1853 that his duty as High Constable of the Hundred of Aveland was to collect the county rates, for which task he was paid £24 a year.

Legal obscurity of the Constable's office

Looking as a whole at this slow, evolutionary process over a period of 500 years, during which the office of constable was gradually going downhill, it is manifest that the changes were neither willed from below nor, until latterly, imposed from above. For the most part the system simply adjusted itself, with local variations, to meet the pressures and needs of changing economic and social conditions. One consequence was that titles of offices, persisting long after the original function had lapsed or altered out of recognition, gave an illusion of permanence: right up to the early years of the nineteenth century the old Saxon names of tythingman, headborough, and borsholder were indiscriminately employed as synonyms for 'constable', and presentments almost everywhere spoke of watch and ward and hue and cry in the terms of the Statute of Winchester. A more far-reaching consequence was that, just as the titles and outward forms lost their original meanings and became confused, so the nature of the office of constable itself became a matter for learned dispute. Successive edicts of the royal courts and, in more recent times, Acts of Parliament, had largely obscured its remote antiquity, and the new situation was full of riddles. Was it a local office, or an office under the Crown? What powers attached to it, and whence was its authority derived?

In Tudor times such questions were scarcely admissible. To their authoritarian and personal form of government the system would seem well adapted. With Crown-appointed justices of the peace exercising authority over the parish constables, the whole stemmed ultimately from the sovereign, and the periphery derived authority from the centre. A local system of policing was seen to be compatible with the recognition that maintenance of the King's peace must ultimately be the concern of the Government itself—a point which a contemporary observer seems to hint at in remarking that 'when there be many tythingmen in one parish there only one of them is a constable for the King, and the rest do serve but as the ancient tythingmen did'.[17] But in the seventeenth century the pattern of policing became even more confused, owing to the advanced state of decay into which many courts leet had by then fallen, and questions were asked with renewed insistence. What kind of creature under the law was the constable, and what was his authority?

The courts leet, or manorial courts, it will be recalled, had appointed the constable from very early times, and while they continued to do so it was arguable that the office was a purely local one. But by the turn of the sixteenth century the court leet had largely outlived its usefulness—and the sheriff's tourn, which it had replaced 400 years earlier, was virtually defunct. Both had been superseded by the justices of the peace. Many courts leet had accordingly simply contracted out of their obligation to appoint a constable: in Hampshire, for example, there were in 1612 no fewer than thirty-one such omissions, remedied in each instance by the justices making the appointments.[18] As a result, the choice was, by a statute of Charles II[19] in 1662, transferred, 'until the Lord of the leet should hold his court', to any two justices of the peace. The nostalgic and euphonious language of this statute did nothing to arrest the decay of manorial courts, and its significance is open to argument. On one view, it, and in particular the swearing-in of constables by justices, was far-reaching: 'Perhaps the administration of the oath to constables by justices of the peace may be fairly considered as the characteristic mark of the final subordination of local to central government in rural districts, of the conversion of a local administrative officer into a ministerial officer of the Crown.'[20] On another view, it could be seen as no more than a rationalisation of earlier practices, made necessary by the failure of the courts leet—nor, probably, would most modern opinion accept that the seventeenth-century justice was very subservient to the Crown. In any case, as the lord of the manor and the justice was generally the same person, it is doubtful whether contemporary people saw any significance in it at all. However this may be, the legal theorists tried to make sense of the position of the constable, but, according to the authority already quoted, they were in difficulty: 'He possessed an undoubted though somewhat vague authority, but it was not derived from the sovereign: he was by common law a conservator of the peace, but he was no longer vested with any of those magisterial functions which justices, coroners and other conservators exercised by virtue of their office; his person was surrounded with a good deal of traditional sanctity, but when the law was more closely examined it was found that his actual powers for the preservation of the peace differed very slightly from those of the lieges who were not endued with the authority of office.' Perhaps, this authority suggests, the constable's position at this time can best be explained if he is regarded not merely as an officer appointed for the preservation of the King's peace, nor as the mere officer of the parish, but as the direct representative of the old vill or township. 'As the powers which might have grown by exercise more definite and more extensive generally passed away to the local justice, the responsibilities remained and became attached to the office.' Nevertheless, the parish constable still retained enough powers to worry Sir William Blackstone: 'of the extent of which powers, considering what manner of men are for the most part put upon these offices, it is perhaps very well that they are generally kept in ignorance'.[21]

Collapse of the old system: (1) *The corruption of Constables*

The era of parish constable and justice as an effective police system did not long survive the Restoration,* and from about 1689 onwards its decline in urban areas was rapid. There were three main causes of this: first, the contempt into which the office of constable had fallen; second, the contempt in which many justices of the peace came to be held, as the 'trading justice' or 'justice of mean degree' superseded the relatively honest holders of the office during Tudor and early Stuart times; and, third, the growth in population and wealth, and the expansion of towns, which marked the early stages of the Industrial Revolution, multiplying the opportunities for crime, while at the same time undermining the stability of society and hence destroying the principle (of the universal obligation to serve as constable) on which the only available means of maintaining law and order still relied.

Little further need be said about the first of these causes. No man who could afford to pay his way out of serving as constable in the reign of King George I neglected to do so. Daniel Defoe, writing in 1714, spoke of 'the imposition of the office' of constable as 'an unsupportable hardship; it takes up so much of a man's time that his own affairs are frequently totally neglected, too often to his ruin'.[22] When the admirable principle of personal service died out, the office sank to its lowest grade, and men paid deputies who were 'scarcely removed from idiotism'. Alternatively, it was possible to escape service by paying a fine to the parish funds according to a scale customary in the locality, and in many crowded parishes, particularly in London, these fines became an important source of income. Defoe himself paid £10 in 1721 'to be excused from serving parish offices' in Stoke Newington. Yet again, the obligation could be evaded by acquiring what was known as a 'Tyburn ticket'. An Act of 1699 provided that a person who prosecuted a felon to conviction should enjoy lifelong exemption from all parish offices, and these certificates changed hands for substantial sums of money, their sale or auction occasionally being advertised in the newspapers. Hence by the end of the eighteenth century many of the men who served as parish constables, whether in

* Cromwell's system of military police, a brief interruption in the traditional arrangements, lasted for two years, from 1655–7. England and Wales were divided into twelve administrative districts, each under the command of a military officer appointed by Cromwell personally. The system was directed to the repression of frivolity rather than towards the ordinary ends of civil policing.

18

London, in the new industrial centres in the Midlands and North, or in areas still largely rural, were at best illiterate fools, and at worst as corrupt as the criminal classes from which not a few sprang.

Collapse of the old system: (2) The corruption of Justices

The second cause of the collapse of the old system, the corruption of many justices of the peace, touches more closely the history of criminal law, local government, and justice than that of the police; it can therefore only be mentioned briefly here.

The seeds of the decline in the standards of integrity of many magistrates can be seen in the disaffection from the Crown, in the years following the revolution of 1689, of a number of county families who for generations had filled the office of justice. The term employed to describe their successors, the 'justice of mean degree', speaks for itself. Tradesmen and shopkeepers, often needy adventurers, looked to the law, as to all else, for profit. The notorious 'trading justice' of the first half of the eighteenth century emerged as the product of a system which aimed at making the administration of justice self-supporting by exacting a fee for every act performed. The potential for evil in the system is obvious. The magistrate rewarded in proportion to the number of persons he convicted had little incentive to resist the corruption of the times, and many submitted to it. Then, to quote the Webbs, 'the transition from "encouraging business" to a corrupt or oppressive use of the magisterial authority in order to extort fees or levy blackmail was, to a trading justice, seldom perceptible. . . . The plays of Gay and Fielding, and the novels of Fielding and Smollett, abound in vivid and scarcely quotable scenes, in which the trading justice commits acts of turpitude which would be incredible if these romances could not be authenticated by official documents and contemporary descriptions of actual cases.'[23] To fall into the clutches of such men meant ruin to honest citizens, and the cupidity of the justices and their notorious relationship with known criminals brought the law into the utmost contempt.

Ingenious criminals were able to exploit this state of affairs in such a way as to enjoy virtual immunity from prosecution. The outstanding example is the notorious Jonathan Wild, who, for a number of years until his execution at Tyburn, obtained single-handed control over the bulk of London's criminals, acted as a receiver on such a scale that he found it necessary to charter ships to transport booty to warehouses abroad, and, publicly advertising his office as 'Thief-taker General', established himself as a much-feared but well-respected man-about-town. Although by manipulation and blackmail he later devised elaborations, Wild's basic method was simple. Having ordered his men to commit a burglary, he would receive the victim courteously in a sumptuous office, take particulars of the missing goods, and restore them to their grateful owner on payment of a commission. That he should have been able to carry on in business for seven years is a sufficient commentary on the state into which law and order, and the administration of justice, had fallen. Another result of the advent of the 'trading justices' was, however, of much greater significance to the history of the police than the colourful career of Jonathan Wild and his henchmen. This was the recognition by the Government that London had to be delivered out of the hands of corrupt justices; and out of this emerged two ideas of great importance. One, slow to develop, was the idea of appointing a stipendiary magistrate whose administration of justice would be uninfluenced by personal avarice; the other was the idea of recognising in London what was called a 'court justice', as a semi-official magistrate who could be relied upon to act on the instructions of the Government in an emergency.

In the combination of these two ideas is to be found the germ of the office of Chief Magistrate of Bow Street. The first to occupy the office was a Metropolitan magistrate named Thomas De Veil. Of a resourceful character and unpromising background, he seems to have been rather less corrupt than his fellow magistrates, and more energetic. As was the fashion, he amassed a fortune in trading in justice, and his services were duly recognised by the Government by a grant of a knighthood and a sum of money. Then for seventeen years, from 1730 until 1747, he became the leading Metropolitan magistrate. He transferred his office to Bow Street; and when, two years after his death, the novelist Henry Fielding succeeded him, the office was already recognised as 'The First Magistrate for Westminster'.[24] Fielding, having railed for years in plays and books about the corruption of justice, very properly refused to touch what he described as 'the dirtiest money on earth', and was helped in this decision by a grant from the Government from the secret fund of £200 a year. In this way he, and after his death his blind half-brother John, was able to consolidate the reputation for fair dealing by the Chief Magistrate, and at the same time to exploit the office for the introduction of the pioneer reforms in policing London to be described in the next chapter.

Collapse of the old system: (3) The breakdown of law and order

The third cause of the collapse of the old police system was sheer inability, in its debilitated and corrupt state, to cope with a social and economic upheaval which in the course of the eighteenth century doubled England's population from 6 to 12 millions, transformed the Metropolis from two overgrown cities into a massive conurbation, and turned vast rural areas into agglomerations of slum, mine, and factory, which lacked the elementary conditions of civilised living.

First to suffer in point of time was London, and the extent of criminality in the capital at the end of the seventeenth century and during the first half of the eighteenth, defies description. Even the Webbs confessed to 'despair of conveying any adequate picture of the lawless violence, the barbarous licentiousness, and the almost unlimited opportunities for pilfering and robbery offered by the unpoliced London streets'.[25] Whole districts were regarded by immemorial custom as sanctuaries in which thieves enjoyed complete immunity. To Henry Fielding the vast growth of London, with its lanes, alleys and courts, and labyrinthine warren of cellars appeared 'as a vast wood or forest, in which a thief may harbour with as great security as wild beasts do in the deserts of Africa or Arabia'. Shenstone commented in 1743 that London was 'really dangerous at this time; pickpockets, formerly content with mere filching, make no scruple to knock people down with bludgeons in Fleet Street and the Strand'. The Council of the City of London declared in the following year that 'divers confederacies of great numbers of evil-disposed persons armed with bludgeons, pistols, cutlasses and other dangerous weapons' were infesting the streets, while Horace Walpole wrote in 1752: 'one is forced to travel, even at noon, as if one were going to battle'.

Over the remainder of urban England the breakdown in law and order marched in step with the progress of the Industrial Revolution, so that its worst effects were not apparent until the fifty years that straddled the turn of the eighteenth century. The England of the start of the century, outside London, differed little from that of the Middle Ages. Most people still lived in small hamlets or villages surrounded by vast acres of open country, islanded here and there by ancient city or market town which was little more than an overgrown village, where the old-established tradesman and master-craftsman enjoyed the good life his predecessors had lived for centuries. The rulers lived remotely in London or in the big country houses, and their chief confederates in local affairs were still the justices of the peace, who were commonly also lords of the manor. One hundred years later the old pattern had disappeared in many areas as the destructive forces that made havoc of law and order in London worked themselves out in the Midlands, the cotton towns of Lancashire, and wool towns of Yorkshire, or wherever else men's ingenuity had replaced green fields by mine and factory and insanitary slum. In areas such as these the honourable old principle of gratuitous personal service in the office of constable, or any other parish office, was simply forgotten or swept aside as irrelevant, just as it had been in London; so that, at the very time when incitements to crime and licentiousness multiplied, the means for dealing with them sank to their lowest ebb.

Ideas to cope with this situation were not lacking. Towards the end of the seventeenth century a campaign for moral regeneration had achieved astonishing vigour under the leadership of the King and the Archbishop of Canterbury. Royal proclamations called for an end to drunkenness and debauchery, and societies were promoted to lay information against profane cursers and swearers, prostitutes, adulterers, Sabbath-breakers, and many others. Common informers multiplied, and zealots of the worst type brought great misery to multitudes of the poor: for it was fashionable to view crime as a by-product of poverty, debauchery, and sexual irregularity; and an influential school of thought insisted on drawing a distinction between the dissolute ways of the wealthy, which harmed no one but themselves, and those of the poor, which if persisted in deprived the nation of the produce of their toil. However, societies for the suppression of vice and the promotion of virtue achieved little in the long run, and the reformers accordingly turned their bewildered attention to the state of the criminal law, which, they concluded, was too lax to provide an effective deterrent. The death penalty was extended to, and implemented in, an increasing number of cases, but still there was criticism of excessive leniency, and voices spoke up in favour of breaking men on the wheel, castration, hanging in chains alive, and other refinements of cruelty.

The search for a substitute

It is against this deteriorating background, with the danger of a total relapse into barbarity, that the pioneer efforts of the Fieldings, from their office at Bow Street, must be evaluated. When it came to talk of reforming human nature, they could be as good Puritans as any, and as magistrates they administered the criminal law with due severity. But they also held that preaching and punishment alone were not enough. To restore the King's peace to the streets of London, the law itself had to be reformed, and the agency for enforcing it, the parish constables and night-watchmen, had to be re-examined from first principles. As a result of the public discussion they stimulated, successive governments, apathetic to affairs outside London, were nevertheless cajoled during the next eighty years into supporting a series of modest ventures aimed at strengthening the policing of the Metropolis, until finally Peel brought matters to a head.

But the Fieldings, like all police reformers from their time (*c.* 1750) until Peel, were concerned exclusively with the problems of policing London and the highwayman-infested areas surrounding the capital, and they were largely indifferent to the state of law and order in the new industrial areas elsewhere. Hence, from the middle of the eighteenth century efforts to remedy the deficiencies of the old police system followed divergent paths in London and in the provincial towns. In addition to the cause mentioned, there are three reasons for this. The first is that the later reformers in London were searching for means of dealing with the Metropolitan conurbation as a whole, thus bringing the City, Westminster, Southwark, and all the outlying parishes for several miles around under a single police system with unified control. No such problem arose anywhere else in the country. The second is that, from the start, the new thinking in London owed as much to principle as to expediency, and the course of reform was accordingly influenced by cross-currents of philosophical thought contributed by the utilitarians and self-appointed guardians of the Constitution, as well as by the urgent needs of the time. Elsewhere, on the other hand, the new race of iron-masters, mill-owners, and other industrial aristocrats who were sapping the authority of the justices, were concerned less with philosophy than with value for money in getting things done. Finally, the Government itself was interested in police reform in London, but was indifferent to local affairs outside the capital.

For all these reasons, the direction which the reform of the police took in the provinces, although it marked a notable break with the past, nevertheless evolved more naturally out of the old system than did that of the London police. It will therefore be convenient to deal first with the steps taken to supplement the old parish constable system outside London before going on to describe the way in which, in the capital, the early idealism contributed by the Fieldings, and sustained throughout a long period of hesitation and misgiving, at length culminated in the first of the New Police in 1829, thus replacing the old system altogether.

Self-help outside London

In order to understand the nature of the measures taken to patch up the police system outside London during the eighteenth and early nineteenth centuries ('reform' is too grand a word for the faltering process about to be described), it is necessary to bear in mind two facts. The first is that throughout the whole of this period the Government not only remained indifferent to local affairs, but, as the Webbs put it, 'deliberately abstained from any consideration of them'.[26] The second is that nothing resembling modern units of local government existed. About 170 municipal boroughs were inefficiently self-governing under the authority of ancient charters,* but much of the new urban sprawl that came in the wake of the Industrial Revolution, together with the whole of rural England, continued to rely on the elaborate and decaying paraphernalia of institutions inherited from bygone times. These constituted by now an infinitely complex and confused network of parish vestries and courts leet in various stages of obsolescence, alongside hundred and county courts, to all intents and purposes self-regulated in their rich variety by custom, ancient charter, manorial privilege, and common law, rather than by any statute of Parliament. And 'the axle round which revolved all the old established local institutions', in the words of the Webbs,[28] remained, far into the eighteenth century, the ancient principle of universal obligation to render unpaid personal service to the community in the office of constable, churchwarden, and so on. Thus, over much of England, King Alfred's foundations had weathered every storm.

The incongruity of this situation needs no emphasis. The busy, sweating working classes of the new industrial areas, living in conditions of indescribable squalor and enraged from time to time by the desperate and starving mobs that characterised the latter part of the century, were left to police themselves on principles removed only by

* In some of the larger municipal boroughs, such as Bristol, Liverpool, and Leicester, where the corporation had virtually replaced the court leet, the mayor and aldermen appointed night-watchmen, and occasionally day police.[27] These watchmen are to be seen as lineal descendants of the town watch which was made obligatory by the Statute of Winchester.

a hair's breadth from frankpledge and the Statute of Winchester. After twelve hours in factory or mine, they ought, for all the law cared, to serve in rotation as night-watchmen, and forgather twice a year at the court leet to appoint a constable. Presentments still survived, and Staffordshire miners and Manchester cotton-spinners were still under an obligation to follow the hue and cry after a fugitive offender. In practice, of course, the old principles, devised for a stable, unchanging community, simply broke down; and there was often no one to keep order, or mend and pave the streets, or light them, or even to clear away the accumulating filth and refuse.

In default, therefore, of guidance or aid from the Government, most local communities set about putting their own affairs in order in their own way. One form which this self-help took was the foundation of numerous voluntary societies to provide funds for the capture and prosecution of felons. A more important development, however, was a stream of Improvement Acts which passed through Parliament during the second half of the eighteenth century.

From about 1750 onwards town after town promoted its own local Act to obtain from Parliament power to levy a local rate for watching, lighting, paving, and cleaning the streets. In all, some 200 towns obtained powers in this way, together with another 100 parishes and municipalities in the Metropolis, usually under the title 'Street Act', 'Paving Act', or 'Police Act'. The local authority thus created would be composed of street commissioners, paving commissioners, or police commissioners, all of which, however, were authorised to exercise the whole range of permitted functions—a point which explains the otherwise confusing fact that (for example) the Birmingham street commissioners employed watchmen as well as street-cleaners, while the Manchester police commissioners employed lamp-lighters as well as watchmen. (In any case, the term 'police' was at that time almost synonymous with the later term, 'local government'.) These improvement commissioners, as it is convenient to call them collectively, employed salaried staffs, and their clerk was to all intents and purposes equivalent to a town clerk. A principal task was to allocate, among the various public services which had been so grossly neglected for so long, the slender resources from the limited rate they were empowered to levy. Most, understandably, gave first priority to paving, lighting, and cleaning the muddy and defiled streets they had inherited from the Middle Ages, worsened beyond description in areas of jerry-built slum; but almost all sooner or later appointed and paid a nightly watch, while a minority of the wealthier

25

appointed a few day constables as well. Sometimes local residents were persuaded to act as amateur inspectors of these 'police', and if the resources permitted a senior man might be paid to take charge of a group of services, and he would then enjoy, *inter alia*, some such imposing title as Superintendent of the Night Watch. The paid night-watchmen, successors to the nightly watch ordered by the Statute of Winchester, would, it seems, have been sworn in as constables. Many were old and ailing. Some were employed out of motives of charity; some as an alternative to making them a charge on the poor rate. They carried lanterns and rattles and called out the passing hours—if they kept awake. An alderman from Romsey told a select committee of Parliament many years later: 'the old police was formed under the paving commissioners. . . . There were four watchmen who, as far as my recollection goes, were appointed, not for their efficiency, but for their being willing to watch for 1*s*. 6*d*. a night.' They had been hard at work all day and were seen sleeping under the gateways at night.[29]

It is debatable how far the employment of these Improvement Act police marks a significant stage in the transition from the ideas underlying the 'old police' to those to be adopted, some half a century later, in establishing the new. On one view the towns were merely taking powers to enable them to discharge more effectively their ancient duty under the Statute of Winchester to provide a nightly watch, and in most of them the police arrangements, on the eve of the Municipal Corporations Act, remained chaotic and wretched: a table compiled by Sir J. Somers Vine in 1879 from information supplied from local records shows a heavy preponderance, as late as 1835, of 'leet constables', with a sprinkling of tythingmen, headboroughs, bellmen, beadles, borsholders, sergeants-at-mace, and others.[30] On another, and perhaps better, view, the Acts represent the first major change of principle in the police system outside London since the Statute of Winchester was enacted, in that reliance on the principle of obligatory personal service was largely abandoned in favour of the employment of paid police. The two principles, in fact, continued to operate side by side. In Manchester, for example, the court leet (admittedly an exceptionally vigorous survival) was still electing the constable, who, a leading industrial aristocrat, enjoyed high civic status and seems to have had nominal control over the day constables, while the improvement commissioners were running an entirely separate nightly watch. The two rival authorities thus contended side by side in the exercise of good works, and for many years right into the nineteenth century the improvement commissioners were completely dominated by the officers of the 'court leet and view of frankpledge', as it was still called. It is difficult, indeed, to discern any clear trends during this confused transitional period, but those who like to see an unbroken thread in police history from Saxon to modern times may take comfort from the knowledge that in Manchester (and the same may well have occurred elsewhere) one of the two constables annually elected by the court leet was until 1839 appointed by the improvement commissioners to be chairman of the watch committee that controlled some thirty day police and about 150 watchmen.[31] By such compromises and fusions the spirit of the old no doubt informed, in some fashion, the new.

In the long run, however, the extent of the break from the old is less significant than the link which was being forged with the new thinking now going on in London. Everywhere the idea of employing regular paid policemen in substitution for part-time amateurs was gaining ground, and in these pockets of Improvement Act police in every town of any consequence in the country, decrepit and inefficient as many watchmen undoubtedly were, are to be found the direct lineal ancestors of the municipal police forces set up under the Municipal Corporations Act, 1835. The improvement commissioners were 'the starting point of the great modern development of town government . . . the progenitors of nearly all the activities of our present municipalities'.[32] As will be shown in Chapter Three, many of the Improvement Act watchmen and constables simply continued in office under the authority of the newly formed watch committees. Some towns which did not receive charters of incorporation until late in the nineteenth century continued to run police forces under Improvement Act powers for many years, a situation which caused Parliament, by means of the Towns Police Clauses Act, 1847, to prescribe model provisions for adoption in local Acts by reference.

This willingness to patch up the policing of the towns left rural England untouched. Here the vestiges of court leet and presentment and the ghost of frankpledge slumbered on in a seemingly undying sunset, unclouded by the Industrial Revolution and the Napoleonic Wars. Lords of the manor and justices of the peace held unchallenged and unchallengeable sway over parish constables, and the race of borsholders and tythingmen was not yet wholly extinct. Incentive to reform was totally lacking. According to the Webbs' study of contemporary sources, crime presented no serious problem in rural England before the middle of the eighteenth century, but at its conclusion the effect of new roads and canals, the emergence of professional highwaymen, and the increase in vagrancy which resulted from lowered standards of living caused by land enclosure, had created the shocking conditions described by the Royal Commission on the Police of 1836–9. Meanwhile, the wealthy paid gamekeepers to protect their property and slept with arms near to hand, and the middle-class tradesmen formed voluntary protection societies. The poor simply managed as best they could until the reform of rural police was at last put in hand.

Chapter Two

The New Police in London
1750-1830

The history of the first 1,000 years of police in England, up to, say, 1729, is mainly the story of how the tythingman changed into the parish constable, and latterly of the constable's slow decline; that of the next 100 years, in London at least, is the story of the way in which a medley of local parish officers and watchmen came to be replaced by a single body of constables embodied into a police *force*, the governing principles of which were unity of control and professional excellence.

Enough has been said in the previous chapter about the frightening breakdown of law and order in London during the first half of the eighteenth century. Some saw a remedy in increasing the severity of the penal code; societies for the reformation of manners proliferated; all who could afford to do so formed mutual protection societies, paying annual subscriptions towards the cost of capturing and prosecuting thieves; and the commonplace offer of rewards and free pardons for information leading to the capture of felons seemed to practical men a more worthwhile form of insurance than pinning their faith to the discredited system of justices, parish constables, and night-watchmen. Even so, the need to put fresh life into the well-tried principles of the Statute of Winchester was constantly reiterated, and for many years it does not seem to have occurred to Parliament that these principles might have grown obsolete. The old idea of collective responsibility was reaffirmed by the Riot Act of 1715, which made the inhabitants of a hundred liable to make amends for certain offences committed within their boundaries; and an Act of 1735 likewise attempted to revive the institution of hue and cry by providing that a constable who neglected to raise it, or failed to join in the pursuit, should be liable to a fine of £5, and any person who apprehended the offender within forty days should receive a reward of £10, levied on the hundred responsible. In keeping faith with the ancient principles, however, the various Metropolitan authorities attempted from early times to remedy their limitations by increasing the number of paid night-watchmen.

Of these authorities, the City of London was pre-eminent in importance and in having the most highly developed form of government, based on a series of ancient charters and enactments. When the Statute of Winchester became law in 1285, the City received its own separate statute, as a result of which the area was divided into twenty-four wards, each containing six watchmen supervised by an alderman. In addition to this 'standing watch', there was also a 'marching watch', which was called out on special occasions.* The curfew one hour after sunset and the nightly closing of the City gates and taverns completed the arrangements for keeping the peace, the whole of which were under the authority of the Mayor and City aldermen. In 1663, an Act passed by the Court of Common Council provided for the employment of 1,000 watchmen, or bellmen, to be on duty from sunset to sunrise. The effectiveness of these 'Charlies' (so called in memory of King Charles II, in whose reign they were instituted) was improved by an Act of 1737, which also established a system of day police. But the wages paid to Charlies were derisively low: for the most part they were contemptible, dissolute, and drunken buffoons who shuffled along the darkened streets after sunset with their long staves and dim lanterns, calling out the time and the state of the weather, and thus warned the criminal of their approach, while attracting to themselves the attention of ruffians and practical jokers. Even so, the City was probably better policed than any other part of the country during the eighteenth century, and a Parliamentary committee of 1812 considered that it afforded 'an example of that unity, and of that dependence of parts on each other, without which no well-constructed and efficient system of police can ever be expected': a similar system, they concluded, would bring great benefit to Westminster and its adjacent parishes.

For conditions in the remainder of the Metropolitan area were, by comparison, chaotic. The agglomeration of houses and shops and streets, comprising some 152 separate parishes with an aggregate population, towards the end of the eighteenth century, of upwards of a million, lacked any unitary control or corporate being. Westminster itself was until 1584 under the control of the Abbey authori-

* A picturesque description of the watches garlanded and in 'bright harness' marching for 'three thousand two hundred tailor's yards' is contained in Stow's *Survey of London* (1598), Everyman edn. (1912), pp. 92–3.

ties, and stretching out in every direction was a diverse and growing collection of townships, manors, parishes and villages without coherence of any kind. During Elizabeth's reign an Act of Parliament provided a form of government under which the city was divided into twelve wards, but for policing reliance was still placed on the ubiquitous system of parish constables. A medieval hierarchy of Lord High Steward, High Bailiff, Burgesses, Court of Burgesses, Court Leet, Annoyance Jury, and others survived until the nineteenth century, so that it is not surprising to find that, staggering under this confusion, Westminster was the first authority in the whole of England to promote, in 1662, a local Improvement Act. This established a new local authority with powers in both the City of London and Westminster itself, and, as the commissioners who comprised it (one of whom was the diarist Evelyn) had their office in Scotland Yard, they were known as the 'Commissioners of Scotland Yard'—although, curiously enough, it seems that they exercised no police functions. Most of the 152 parishes outside Westminster followed suit during the eighteenth century, and under the authority of their own local Improvement Acts employed small bodies of watchmen. These watchmen confined their activities, such as they were when they were not dozing in their watch-boxes, to their own small parish; co-operation between parishes was virtually non-existent; local jealousies were intense; and there was, naturally, no pooling of information. Such were the arrangements for policing London which challenged the ingenuity of the straggling line of police reformers that started with Henry Fielding and ended, three-quarters of a century later, with Peel. Midway through the period, in 1797, they were well summed up by Patrick Colquhoun, the first man ever to carry out a systematic survey of London's policing: 'The watchmen destined to guard the lives and properties of the inhabitants residing in near eight thousand streets, lanes, courts, and alleys, and about 162,000 houses . . . are under the direction of no less than above seventy different Trusts; regulated by perhaps double the number of local acts of Parliament (varying in many particulars from one another), under which the directors, guardians, governors, trustees, or vestries, according to the title they assume, are authorised to act, each attending only to their own particular Ward, Parish, Hamlet, Liberty, or Precinct.'[1]

The influence of the Fielding brothers

The manner in which Henry Fielding succeeded to the office of Chief Magistrate of Bow Street in 1748, and set about rescuing the administration of justice from the corrupt state into which it had fallen, was described briefly in the last chapter. But Fielding was not content merely to challenge the judicial processes. From his vantage-point at Bow Street, he soon turned the abundant genius, compassion, and understanding of human nature that had filled his novels to no less a task than the reformation of a whole society whose sense of security had been shaken by the rebellion of 1745, and whose morals were being corroded by alcoholism aided by cheap gin. Within three years of taking office he published a pamphlet, *An Enquiry into the Causes of the Late Increase of Robbers*, with the declared intention 'to rouse the civil power from its present lethargic state'. At the outset he defined the delicate poise whose attainment was to baffle thinkers on the subject of police reform for three-quarters of a century: his was a design which 'alike opposes those wild notions of liberty that are inconsistent with all government, and those pernicious schemes of government which are destructive of true liberty'. Four more pamphlets followed, in which Fielding established himself as a pioneer thinker on questions of penal policy and criminology, resourceful in remedies to deal with what he conceived to be the social causes of crime—drunkenness, gambling, obscene literature, sexual laxity, vagrancy, and others—and with the over-severity of the criminal law and the administration of justice.

As a police reformer, however, Fielding was less radical. He influenced the first of a long series of Parliamentary committees, set up in 1750, to recommend a strengthening of the nightly watch in Westminster, but he sought no change in the traditional system of parish constables. He did, however, embark on two cautious initiatives which showed his awareness of the police problem, and established a slender foundation on which others were to build. The first was to publish *The Covent Garden Journal*, which appeared twice a week during the course of 1752. Fielding wrote the greater part of it himself, giving accounts of cases that had come before him as a magistrate, with the object of educating public opinion to a greater sensitivity to penal problems; he also used the journal to advertise descriptions of robbers. His other main initiative resulted in the formation, in 1750, of a small body of 'thief-takers' attached to his office at

Bow Street. For this purpose he recruited six or seven householders 'actuated by a truly public spirit against thieves', who undertook to continue as constables after their year of office had expired. This nucleus, drawn from the area of Bow Street, he placed under the joint leadership of himself and the High Constable of Holborn, a man named Saunders-Welch, who became a friend of Dr. Johnson. They had several early successes in breaking up gangs of criminals, and the men received the rewards, (or 'blood money', as they were known) offered for the apprehension of criminals. They had no uniform other than the distinctive staff of a parish constable. The enterprise was continued temporarily with the aid of a Government grant of £600. It evolved, many years later, into the Bow Street Runners; but the scheme marked no major departure from the past, and Fielding seems to have intended none.

Henry Fielding died at the early age of forty-seven, and was succeeded, in 1754, by his blind half-brother John who, in the course of twenty-five years as Chief Magistrate at Bow Street, carried Henry's ideas forward. John, like Henry, received £200 a year (later increased to £400) from secret Government funds; and after his retirement in 1779 the payment of a salary to the Chief Magistrate was openly acknowledged. As Professor Radzinowicz puts it, the greatness of the brothers 'as educators of public opinion, lies in the single-minded determination with which, over a period of nearly thirty years, they strove to demonstrate to their contemporaries how serious were the dangers which threatened to engulf the nation and how pressing was the need for discarding fragmentary remedies in favour of a larger plan'.[2] John Fielding published several pamphlets, the most notable of which was *A Plan for Preventing Robberies within Twenty Miles of London*, containing the suggestion that householders should combine in bands of twenty for the purpose of supplying Bow Street with information about criminals. He also described the work of his brother's band of 'thief-takers', and elaborated the idea of disseminating quick and accurate information about known criminals among magistrates and constables throughout the country. Under his guidance Bow Street became a clearing-house of crime information, and he published regular broadsheets entitled *The Quarterly Pursuit of Criminals* and *The Weekly Pursuit*, with an occasional supplement, *The Extraordinary Pursuit*, which were the forerunners of the *Police Gazette*. These sheets were widely distributed, and the detailed descriptions of offenders which they contained were fixed to church doors, inns and other public places. Meantime, John Fielding was extending the corps of Bow Street semi-regulars started by his brother, and he obtained a grant of £400 a year from the Treasury to enable him to pay four 'pursuers' who were available to act anywhere in the country, together with ancillary staff at Bow Street. The grant also covered the cost of printing his handbills and broadsheets, and the maintenance of two horse patrols. By these steps what had started as 'Mr Fielding's men' had, by about 1785, become the Bow Street Runners. A further temporary Treasury grant in 1763 enabled Fielding to establish a night horse patrol of eight men to guard the roads leading into London against highwaymen, but the Government had little enthusiasm for the plan: in the following year the grant was withdrawn, and the horse patrol was not revived for another forty years.

Thus the actual achievements of the Fielding brothers after thirty years of sustained effort were meagre: for the last sixteen years of his life John Fielding was able to maintain only the four 'pursuers' and two horsemen of the original scheme. But their influence was out of all proportion to their achievements. In 1761 John Fielding was knighted, and in 1770 he was the principal witness before the first of a long series of Parliamentary committees set up to consider the policing of London after a particularly serious breakdown in law and order caused by Wilkes. Fielding pleaded that, in the interests of unity of command and co-ordination, the Bow Street magistrates should be entrusted with 'the whole direction' of all Westminster constables and watchmen. The committee, however, faithful to the old principles, contented itself with a series of recommendations designed to enforce more rigorously the obligation of householders to serve as constables, to encourage parishes to recruit better men as night-watchmen, to transfer control of watchmen from the parish vestry to the magistrates, and to establish closer supervision over pawnbrokers, public houses, prostitutes, and other encitements to crime. This committee is of permanent interest, however, in recording the discovery that the parishes which formed part of the Metropolis were 'under no particular Act of Parliament, but exercised their authority under the Statute of Winchester [which], being very obsolete, is a very improper regulation'. They did not, however, seek to correct its impropriety or to replace it by something more attuned to the times. The only outcome of the inquiry was an Act of 1774 designed to regulate the nightly watch in Westminster, which, however, had little effect.

The outlook of this committee, and of others which succeeded it, is typical of the apathy towards any radical reform of the police which marked the end of the Fieldings' early initiatives. Everywhere enthusiasm ebbed; for, to quote Professor Radzinowicz again, 'During this long period of more than three-quarters of a century, from 1750 to 1828, there was no section of public opinion, no group in Parliament or outside, no leading newspaper or periodical which would advocate a reform in the traditional machinery for keeping the peace'. The partnership of the justice and parish constable 'had acquired an almost constitutional validity'. For many years the English people had no desire for a police institution; 'indeed, with few exceptions, they regarded its non-existence as one of their major blessings'.[3] The reasons for this hostility to the police idea must now be examined.

Pitt's abortive Bill of 1785

At about the time when the Fieldings were initiating their cautious reforms in the face of a largely apathetic or hostile public opinion, the term 'police' was coming into common usage, and to most people it had a sinister ring. John Fielding was complaining in 1761 that the term had been 'greatly misunderstood and misrepresented', but distrust of the police idea in no way abated as the century advanced. Dr. Johnson recognised the French origin of the word, and defined it in his dictionary as 'The regulation and government of a city or country, so far as regards the inhabitants'. To most people the French origin was enough to damn the idea of something like a *gendarmerie* from the start, and the more the reformers argued for its acceptance as a means of maintaining law and order, the more the emotive power of the term 'police' darkened men's minds to any advantage its introduction might bring to this country. In France, it was popularly held—and with some justification—there were spies and informers everywhere; once admit a police force into England, and the long-cherished liberties of Englishmen would be swept away in a régime of terror and oppression.

So persistent was this attitude that it survived the shock of the Gordon Riots, when for nearly a week in the summer of 1780 London was abandoned to mob violence, from which it was rescued only by the Army, following the personal intervention of the King. Ironically, John Fielding lay dying as London blazed and the rioters sacked Bow Street and made a bonfire of his papers and Henry's manuscripts. The state of impotence to which parish constables and watchmen had been reduced was ludicrous. At one time, near the spot where fires

35

were burning fiercest, a watchman was seen passing with a lantern in his hand 'calling the hour as in a time of profound tranquillity'.[4] Shelburne, who two years later became the first Home Secretary, spoke up boldly on the second day of the riots in praise of the French police system, which was 'wise to the last degree' in its construction, and only abominable in 'its use and direction'. A similar organisation ought, he urged, to be adopted in England. His, however, was virtually a lone voice. The riots shocked public opinion into questioning the evident weakness of the forces of law and order, and a welter of suggestions poured into the Home Office, some well-considered, many silly. The most favoured were for a further strengthening of the already savage criminal law, reliance on mobilisation of the ancient *posse comitatus* with the hue and cry, and the creation of voluntary associations of armed citizens who would act, in effect, as a 'people's police'.

Pitt's Government, however, took the lesson of the Gordon Riots to heart, and in 1785 Sir Archibald Macdonald, his Solicitor-General, introduced into Parliament a radical Bill, prepared with the help of the Bow Street magistrates. The Bill owed much to the influence of the Fieldings, but went a great deal further. They, in common with everyone who had ever concerned themselves with the police problem since the fourteenth century, had held that the proper authority to control the police were the justices. Pitt's Bill proposed to sever this ancient link. It embodied all the major proposals of the last thirty years and, presenting them in an imaginative sweep, anticipated Peels' Metropolitan Police Act by nearly half a century. The Bill provided for the establishment of a strong police force to act throughout the whole of the Metropolitan area (including the City), which, for police purposes, was to be a unified 'District of the Metropolis'. The Crown was to be empowered to appoint a board of three salaried commissioners of police, who would be deemed to be justices of the peace. The Metropolitan area was to be divided into nine divisions, in each of which was to be a force of 'petty constables' under the command of a chief constable and, ultimately, of the police commissioners. The constables, who were to be regarded as 'ministerial officers of the peace', were to patrol on foot and on horseback, and to be armed with powers of search and arrest. They were to be forbidden to receive tips or other rewards. The existing parish constables and watchmen were to be retained, but their duties were to be co-ordinated with those of the regular police. Existing Metropolitan justices were to be stripped of their executive police duties and confined to the exercise of judicial functions only.

This advanced measure was greeted with widespread dismay by the Press and in the City of London, and it was bitterly opposed by the justices. Predictably, the City saw it as a violation of their corporate dignity and right to self-government—'if a torch had been applied to the buildings there it could not have created greater alarm', according to one City alderman whose memory of the Gordon Riots was short. The benches of the Middlesex and Surrey justices regarded it as 'a dangerous innovation and an encroachment on the rights and security of the people'.[5]

Pitt bowed before the storm. Perhaps, like Peel, he should have had the political sagacity not to interfere with the City. Admitting that he was not 'perfectly master of the subject', he allowed the Bill to be withdrawn, and the opportunity to establish a Metropolitan police force was lost for over forty years. Thereafter what little enthusiasm there had been for police reform disappeared, and the establishment of the tyranny in France, three years after the outbreak of the Revolution in 1789, served further to alienate most Englishmen from an institution which, always regarded with suspicion, was now plainly exposed to the world as an instrument of terror. When, therefore, a private Member introduced a modest reforming measure into Parliament in 1792 (three months before the September massacres), the proposals it embodied were timid in comparison with Pitt's abortive plans. They were accordingly acceptable to Parliament.

The Middlesex Justices Act, 1792, as this measure is entitled, was primarily an attempt to reform and purify the London magistracy, and as such it was of far-reaching importance; it was only secondarily concerned with providing a more effective means of policing. The Act created seven magistrates' offices in the Metropolitan area, additional to the Bow Street office, to each of which three stipendiary magistrates were appointed at salaries originally fixed at £400; each of the seven offices was to employ six full-time constables at a weekly wage of 12s. A controversial clause subsequently added to the Bill authorised the constables to arrest on suspicion. Originally enacted only for a period of three years, the Act was subsequently made permanent in 1812. Admittedly a step forward in the recognition of the need for a paid constabulary force in London, it was of little long-term significance, for its tendency was reactionary—reverting to the principle of placing separate groups of constables under the control of justices—and it was conceived on too paltry a scale to have much effect.

Including the Bow Street Runners, which by 1797 had been expanded to a force some seventy strong, London at the turn of the century had a total of about 120 full-time police officers, and the main burden of maintaining law and order still rested on the elderly, ailing, or indifferent shoulders of isolated pockets of parish constables and watchmen, whose attitude to the newcomers was one of deep suspicion and hostility.

But Pitt's Bill of 1785 had not been entirely lost. The bold plans that England rejected, Ireland was quick to seize. The abortive Bill was enacted, substantially in its original form, by the Dublin Parliament in the following year, 1786, and thus laid the first slender foundations for the Royal Irish Constabulary. As a result, Robert Peel, who was Chief Secretary for Ireland between 1812 and 1818, introduced police reforms in that country, but it was not until 1838 that a Metropolitan force was established in Dublin on the lines of Peel's London police. Nevertheless, Maitland makes an interesting point in suggesting that 'A full history of the new police would probably lay its first scene in Ireland, and begin with the Dublin Police Act passed by the Irish Parliament in 1786'.[6]

Policing as a new science

One of the successful applicants for a post as magistrate in the new offices established by the Middlesex Justices Act 1792 was a Glasgow merchant named Patrick Colquhoun. A self-made man who had been appointed Lord Provost of Glasgow at the early age of thirty-seven, he turned his immense energy selectively to a wide variety of social problems; but his dominating interest, throughout twenty-five years as a Metropolitan magistrate, was in the reform of the police. In 1797 he published *A Treatise on the Police of the Metropolis*, which was widely acclaimed and went through no fewer than seven editions in the course of ten years. Its language was revolutionary: 'Police is an improved state of Society. . . . Next to the blessings which a Nation derives from an excellent Constitution and System of general Laws, are those advantages which result from a well-regulated and energetic plan of Police, conducted and enforced with purity, activity, vigilance, and discretion.'

The treatise broke new ground. In the painstaking manner in which he marshalled statistics relating to crime and criminals, and in relying on this systematic evidence as a basis for drawing up wide-ranging plans, Colquhoun adopted a technique which is common-place in our own times, but was then virtually unknown. He threw down a challenge to the traditionalists in declaring that a well-regulated police, whose primary aim should be the prevention of crime, was 'perfectly congenial to the principle of the British con-stitution', and proceeded to develop sweeping proposals embracing the reform of the criminal law and the magistracy, projects for the moral reformation of society, and a system of preventive police which owed much to an acknowledged admiration of the French—which had reached 'the greatest degree of perfection'—a fact which so delighted our enemies that at the height of the Napoleonic War Colquhoun's treatise was translated and published in France. Fascinated by the novelty of his subject, Colquhoun wrote in the Preface to the sixth edition of his *Treatise* (published in 1800) that 'police in this country may be considered as a new science; the properties of which consist not in the judicial powers which lead to punishment and which belong to the magistrates alone; but in the prevention and detection of crimes; and in those other functions which relate to internal regulations for the well order and comfort of civil society'. This science 'was not yet perfectly understood'.

Colquhoun followed the abortive proposals of 1785 in insisting on the complete separation of judicial and police powers. He proposed the creation of a central police board, consisting of five commissioners, who were to be 'able, intelligent, prudent and indefatigable' men. The Home Office itself had too many other tasks to enable it to give the 'strength, vigour, and energy' to a police system, but the board should be under the general control of the Home Secretary. A nucleus of professional police should be established in every parish, at the head of which should be a 'high constable of the division', who would be assisted by a parochial chief constable. These officers would be paid and controlled by the central police board, and they would take charge of the local constables elected by the court leet or the magis-trates without the option of employing deputies. To reap the full benefit of centralisation, Colquhoun carried forward three ideas borrowed from the Fieldings, to whose pioneer work he justly paid tribute: the central police board should organise an intelligence service; it should maintain a register of known offenders, with classified information about particular groups; and it should publish a *Police Gazette*, not only for the purpose of aiding in the detection of crime, but also as a vehicle of moral education—'with commentaries suited to the comprehension of the vulgar, tending to operate as warnings, and to excite a dread of crimes', with 'occasional observations on the horrors of a gaol; on punishments—whipping, the pillory, the hulks, transportation and public execution'.

Colquhoun's proposals thus represent an important link between the old and the new ideas. In essence, his plan was put forward as a means of revitalising the parish constabulary and superimposing over it a meed of professional direction and co-ordination deriving authority from the Home Secretary. This balance was nicely adjusted to the spirit of the times. Colquhoun's ideas were enthusiastically received by the Press and in Parliament, but not in the City, where the proposed police board was seen as 'a new Engine of Power and Authority so enormous and extensive as to threaten a species of despotism and inquisition hitherto without a parallel in this country'.[7] In the same year that he published his treatise, Colquhoun was one of only three witnesses (another of whom was his close friend and associate, Jeremy Bentham) to be called before a Select Committee on Finance, etc., appointed by Pitt to consider particularly police, including convict establishments. For a time Colquhoun carried all before him. In a closely reasoned and well-documented report, this committee, in its *Twenty-eighth Report*, published in 1798, substantially endorsed his plans. The Government prepared a Bill, and the moment seemed ripe at last for the establishment of a modern police system in London. Then, for reasons which remain a mystery, the whole project was abandoned. For the next ten years interest in general police reform died away, until a shock to public confidence even greater than that caused by the Gordon Riots allowed the voice of reform to be heard once again.

In December, 1811, two whole families in the East End of London were silently exterminated in macabre circumstances which created a wave of public panic. One, consisting of a linen-draper named Marr, his wife, child and shop assistant, were savagely butchered with a ripping chisel and maul. The sense of horror had not abated when, a week later, a man named Williamson and his wife and servant were found with their skulls fractured and their throats cut; a bloodstained iron crowbar and maul lay beside the bodies. De Quincey later treated the 'Wapping murders' with light irony in his essay, *Murder considered as One of the Fine Arts*, but no one treated them lightly at the time. Complacency about the need for reforming the police vanished overnight. The watchmen in the area were instantly discharged. Special armed patrols were appointed, and several neighbouring parishes volunteered to supply additional men for night-patrolling. Public concern mounted throughout the whole country, and just as after the Gordon Riots, so again a welter of suggestions poured into the Home Office from all over the country. Some even favoured radical reform of the parish constable system, but most seem to have looked no further than an improvement in the quality of the parish police and the nightly watch. Even Colquhoun now contented himself with a series of minor suggestions designed to improve the quality of watchmen.

The Home Secretary acted in two ways. The murderer, a man named Williams, was at length caught; but he evaded justice by hanging himself from a beam so low that, as the *Morning Post* commented, he must have been obliged 'to sit down as it were to accomplish his purpose'. The Home Secretary accordingly satisfied public opinion by authorising the body to be displayed, along with the ripping chisel and maul, in a high, open cart which, driven slowly along the crowded streets, at length paused outside the Marrs' house and then drove on to where a hole had been dug in the ground. The body was flung in and a stake driven through it, the instruments of murder being consigned to Bow Street. Secondly, the Home Secretary moved Parliament to set up a committee of enquiry into the state of the nightly watch and the effectiveness of the various local Acts within the Metropolitan area, but made it clear that he did not expect or desire any radical recommendations from the committee. Pitt's abortive Bill of 1785 seems to have been entirely forgotten, although the report of 1798 embodying Colquhoun's proposals was specially reprinted for the use of the new enquiry. The committee, however, disregarded it. They produced a hasty, ill-informed, and disappointing report, the principal recommendation of which was to introduce arrangements by which the state of the watch should be regularly inspected by officers paid to make rounds during the night. By these means it was thought that elderly and unfit watchmen could be weeded out. The committee proposed better arrangements for supplying information to the eight 'police offices', as the magistrates' offices were now generally called, and Bow Street was to be recognised as a clearing-house for crime under the direct authority of the Home Secretary. A Bill embodying these recommendations was introduced into Parliament in July, 1812, but by then the shock of the Wapping murders had faded. The Bill was quietly dropped. In the calm light of reason, men argued that no police system, however perfect, could ever prevent murders from being committed. The most that could be hoped for was to prevent a murderer's escape or to detect him more speedily, and these considerations pointed to the need to strengthen the nightly watch. With such agreeable and stoical reflections, rate-payers were relieved at being spared the burden of a costly police system which nobody wanted, and the zealots for personal liberty achieved a further triumph. Colquhoun's 'new science of police' was not merely imperfectly understood. Nobody wanted to understand it.

River police and Bow Street Runners

In the meantime, the stagnancy of the long debate about the theory of policing had not held up some useful reforms that were gradually providing London with a nucleus of professional police—offensive to constitutional principles as they might be.

In two chapters of his *Treatise*, Colquhoun called attention to the extent to which the vast wealth which poured into the Port of London was a prey to thieves, and he later dilated on this in a *Treatise on the Commerce and Police of the River Thames*, published in 1800. With characteristic precision, he estimated that there were no fewer than 10,000 thieves, footpads, prostitutes, and pilferers at work on the jetties and quays that lined the riverside, and that the plunder and pillage represented an annual loss of over half a million pounds. This argument for the establishment of a preventive police for the river appealed instantly to the shipping interests, and a Marine Police Establishment was set up in June, 1798 (four-fifths of the cost being borne by West Indian merchants), consisting of some sixty salaried officers—considerably more full-time men than in all the police offices put together. The men were given careful instructions to 'spurn with indignation' any attempt to corrupt them, and at all times to display 'the utmost zeal, vigilance, prudence, discretion, and sobriety' Colquhoun had associated himself with a man of buccaneering propensities named John Harriot in recommending the scheme to the Government, and the new force was placed under Harriot's im-mediate command, with Colquhoun as its superintending magistrate. The experiment met with striking success; and two years later, in July, 1800, the Thames River Police Act, which owed much to the joint efforts of Colquhoun and Bentham, converted the private venture into a public concern. A ninth police office was created on the lines of that of Bow Street and the seven set up by the Middlesex Justices Act, 1792, and the justices of the new Thames Police Office were empowered to appoint and dismiss constables. The Thames magistrates acted directly on the detailed instructions of the Home Secretary; and the Thames river police thus became the first regular professional police force in London.

It was followed, before long, by a rapid expansion of the Bow Street foot and horse patrols founded half a century earlier by the Fielding brothers. The seven police offices created by the Middlesex Justices Act had been authorised to employ not more than six constables each, but this limit was increased in 1811 to twelve. The magistrates office at Bow Street, however, which had existed from much earlier times, enjoyed a prestige and a freedom from statutory regulation which provided the Chief Magistrate, with the Home Secretary's support, unlimited scope for experiment. The holder of the office in the early years of the nineteenth century, Sir Richard Ford, was an enterprising man. Dividing his time equally between the Home Office and Bow Street, he was ever ready to act on the Home Secretary's directions in appointing his constables as spies and informers to deal with enemy aliens during the Napoleonic Wars. He also took vigorous steps to combat crime. In 1805 he revived John Fielding's idea of a horse patrol and stationed some sixty men on the principal roads within twenty miles of London. They were carefully selected, preference being given to applicants who had served in a cavalry regiment. This roisterous body of men, some of whom made substantial fortunes out of their shady business in trafficking in crime, undoubtedly formed something of a *corps d'élite*, creating in their own lifetime the myth of the Bow Street Runners, a body well summed up by Professor Radzinowicz, taking a cue from Sir John Moylan, as 'a closely knit caste of speculators in the detection of crime, self-seeking and unscrupulous, but also daring and efficient when daring and efficiency coincided with their private interest'.[8] They undertook missions all over the country and even abroad, but also contrived to clear such notorious places as Hounslow Heath of highwaymen. Their routine duty was to patrol the main roads as far out as Enfield, Epsom, Windsor and Romford, giving confidence to travellers with their greeting, 'Bow Street Patrol'.

In 1821 a second echelon, 100 strong, was established. This, curiously known as the 'Unmounted Horse Patrol', served to train men for promotion to the mounted branch, and operated in the suburban areas within a radius of five or six miles from London. Elaborate arrangements for conference points between the two branches of the horse patrol were worked out. The men were sworn in by the Chief Magistrate of Bow Street to act as constables throughout

Middlesex, Surrey, Essex, and Kent and they acted under the direct authority of the Home Secretary: both branches of the Horse Patrol were commanded by a Home Office official named William Day, who, as Keeper of the Criminal Registers in the Department, had helped to organise the first patrol in 1805; he later set up office in Cannon Row. These patrols became the first uniformed police force in the country (the river police had no distinguishing uniform). They wore blue coats with yellow metal buttons, a scarlet waistcoat, blue trousers, Wellington boots, and black hats. To the scarlet waistcoats they owed the nickname 'Robin Redbreasts'.

The foot patrol, in the meantime, had been considerably strengthened. Like the horse patrol, it also split into two branches. The first in point of time was a night patrol, about 100 strong, which came to be organised in an increasingly sophisticated manner. By 1818 one body, known as the 'country party', would start their beats between four and five miles from London, patrolling inwards along the main roads leading into the capital, while a 'town party' would set out from the centre to meet them. In 1821, however, the increase of crime in central London led to the withdrawal of the 'country party' into the inner area, their place in the outer suburbs being taken by the unmounted horse patrol mentioned above. The foot patrols were given a measure of local discretion, generally starting off at about dusk and remaining out until one o'clock in the morning. They wore no uniform, but carried a truncheon, a cutlass, and occasionally a pistol. They were heartily detested by watchmen, who regarded them as spies set on themselves, but they co-operated with the horse patrols.

The fourth and last of these special Bow Street patrols was an outcome of a recommendation by a Parliamentary committee of 1822 under Peel's chairmanship. This was a special foot patrol by day, consisting of twenty-seven men, designed as a preventive force against daylight robbery, and instructed to watch for suspicious activities which might suggest plans for night burglaries. The men, mostly old soldiers, appeared in the streets for the first time in August, 1822, wearing a uniform (in contrast to the plain-clothes night-patrol) which consisted of a blue coat and trousers and a red waistcoat, which, Peel thought, would make them 'proud of their establishment'.

Hence by 1828, on the eve of the formation of the Metropolitan Police, a substantial corps of professional full-time officers already existed in London: the constables employed by the seven police offices, the various Bow Street patrols, and the Thames river police totalled some 450 men directly under the control of the Home Secretary. It was a meagre force to serve a population of nearly one and a half million, and at the best it could do little more than attempt to catch a few criminals and bring them to justice. As a preventive force it was negligible. In addition, there were upwards of 4,500 watchmen employed by the City of London or, in the Metropolitan district, by various parishes, often under Improvement Act powers.[9] The total cost to London of the old police during its last years amounted to the not inconsiderable sum of about a quarter of a million pounds.

The Utilitarians

By the 1820s the agonising struggle to avoid introducing a police system into London was entering its concluding stages, though few could have suspected it, for the currents of fresh thinking that helped to bring matters to a head flowed deeply below the surface of public affairs.

Sixty years earlier, when the Fieldings were striving to educate public opinion, they had ranged indiscriminately over the whole field of criminal law reform and police reform; but as the century advanced the two movements followed divergent paths, each attracting its own, largely separate, protagonists. Professor Radzinowicz has pointed out that most of the early thinkers in this field—Blackstone (1723–80), Adam Smith (1723–90), and Paley (1743–1805)—were hostile to the idea of a preventive police, holding, to put it in Utilitarian terms, that the greatest happiness for the greatest number was unlikely to be advanced by an elaborate system calculated to interfere with individual liberty: an admittedly imperfect police system was part of the price of freedom. Thus they assumed a position directly contrary to that of the police reformers, who held that without an efficient police the happiness of both State and individual was constantly at risk. The argument, therefore, involved one of the greatest of all human issues—namely, the responsibility of the State in relation to the rights of the individual. To this argument there could (and can) be no finality, but an escape from the logical dilemma was available to those who saw in the reform of the criminal law a preferable alternative to the creation of a civil force of police. Hence the cause of penal reform drew support from that of police reform, for it faced none of the obstacles that stood in the way of the latter: its objects were attainable without significant public expense, and it offered no threat

45

to personal liberty. It thus became possible to argue that the more dangerous ideas should be shelved until the effect on society of such humanitarian measures as the abolition of public executions and the amelioration of prison life had been evaluated. While, therefore, for many years the police reformers supported the reform of the criminal code, the law reformers were generally hostile to the cause of police reform.

After the turn of the eighteenth century, however, under the influence of Jeremy Bentham (1748–1832), the two movements began to draw together once more. A man of catholic learning, liberal principles and incalculable influence in many branches of public affairs, Bentham had early been impressed by the work of the Italian Marquis Beccaria, whose *Essay on Crime and Punishments*, with a commentary by Voltaire, had been published in an English translation in 1767. Beccaria, in a passage which, in Professor Radzinowicz's words, had all the force of a new concept, wrote: 'It is better to prevent crimes than to punish them. This is the chief aim of every good system of legislation, which is the art of leading men to the greatest possible happiness or to the least possible misery, according to calculation of all the goods and evils of life'.[10] Beccaria pleaded for the revision of traditional attitudes towards crime and punishment, but was himself lukewarm towards the French idea of policing. Bentham, working out his vast and labyrinthine philosophies of Utilitarianism over a period of many years, espoused both causes and attracted disciples to further each—Romilly, the criminal law reformer, whose influence did much to purify the criminal code from its medieval barbarity; and Colquhoun, the pioneer police reformer, whose work has already been mentioned. And then, towards the end of his long life, Bentham proposed in his *Constitutional Code* the creation of a completely centralised preventive police system under the control of the Government. These views came to the attention of a young lawyer, Edwin Chadwick, who was to play a notable part in gathering up the thinking of three-quarters of a century and complete the Utilitarians' theoretical study of the 'science of police', without which Peel's political skill could have achieved little.

But these powerful currents of thinking caused few surface ripples. Parliament continued to regard the police idea with disfavour. Three more Parliamentary committees, in 1816, 1818, and 1822, rejected it as incompatible with British liberty. The first published copious evidence, but made no proposals. The second at last recognised the weakness of a system of parish constables and watchmen, and proposed to rescue the office of high constable from oblivion by attaching a salary to it and giving the high constable effective control over the parish constables, who themselves should be more carefully selected; a reliable certificate of character should be required from the deputies, and a limit put to their period of service. On one point, however, this committee was emphatic: a system of police on the Continental model would be 'odious and repulsive, and one which no government could be able to carry into execution . . . it would be a plan which would make every servant of every house a spy on the actions of his master, and all classes of society spies on each other'. The third committee, of 1822, set up on the motion of the newly appointed Home Secretary, Peel, similarly contented itself with proposals for minor reform designed to strengthen the traditional system, recommended the formation of the Bow Street day patrol, and took the conventional line (warmly endorsed by *The Times*) about the dangers of any new-fangled system of police. In a much-quoted passage they declared:

'It is difficult to reconcile an effective system of police, with that perfect freedom of action and exemption from interference, which are the great privileges and blessings of society in this country; and Your Committee think that the forfeiture or curtailment of such advantages would be too great a sacrifice for improvements in police, or facilities in detection of crime, however desirable in themselves if abstractedly considered.'

The Metropolitan Police Act, 1829

The Chairman of this thoroughly reactionary committee was, of all men, the Home Secretary, Robert Peel, who nevertheless in the same year was speaking in Parliament of a project for 'a vigorous preventive police, consistent with the free principles of our free constitution'.[11] A politician of exceptional genius, Peel was clearly not prepared to commit his reputation too swiftly or too deeply to so controversial a public issue as police reform, although there is no doubt that he had set his heart upon it from the beginning of his term at the Home Office. Instead, he devoted his early years as Home Secretary to the cause of the reform of criminal law. So passed several years, during which Peel seems to have been preparing himself, by discussion with authorities abroad as well as at home, to re-enter the struggle for police reform when he judged the moment ripe. By 1826 he had drawn up a plan for setting up a single police system within a radius of ten miles of St. Paul's with the exception of the City, 'with which', he told a correspondent, 'I should be afraid to meddle'.[12] Then in the following year, 1827, he found himself a fellow member with Lord John Russell of yet another Parliamentary committee on criminal matters. The second report of this committee, published in July, 1828, struck a modern note in asserting that 'the art of crime, if it may be so called, has increased faster than the art of detection'. For the counties, the committee rather lamely saw a means of salvation once again in the office of high constable, but significantly commented that there was ground 'for instituting inquiry into the management of the Police of all our great towns'.

The recommendation came too late, for six months earlier the stage had been set for the last of this wearisome procession of Parliamentary inquiries. In February, 1828, Peel moved for the appointment of an inquiry with disarming terms of reference: 'to enquire into the cause of the increase of the number of commitments and convictions in London and Middlesex for the year 1827; and into the state of the police of the Metropolis and the district adjoining thereto'. Having thus adjusted priorities to a realistic assessment of the state of public opinion, he proceeded in all that followed to display consummate Parliamentary skill. His latest biographer has suggested that he was deliberately dull and unemotional.[13] He delivered some unexciting statistics about crime and, playing the whole matter down, declared, 'I must confess that I am not very sanguine with respect to the benefits to be derived from this committee'. He despaired of persuading the City of London to co-operate in any general system of policing. He described the defects of the existing arrangements, but did not 'believe that any effectual remedy can be devised by which the evil can be cured'. Nevertheless, he did not wish to disguise the fact that 'the time is come, when, from the increase in its population, the enlargement of its resources, and the multiplying development of its energies, we may fairly pronounce that the country has outgrown her police institutions and that the cheapest and safest course will be found to be the introduction of a new mode of protection'. Addressing himself now to 'those who live in agricultural districts', he demanded: 'Why, I ask, should we entrust a grocer, or any other tradesman, however respectable, with the direction and management of a police for 5,000 or 6,000 inhabitants? Why should such a person, unpaid and unrewarded, be taken from his usual avocations and called upon to perform the laborious duties of a night constable?' He apologised for speaking for so long, observing that, although the select committee would be concerned only with London, 'the subject matter of the inquiry is connected with objects of such deep importance, not merely as they regard the security of individual property, but also as they regard the morals and habits of the entire population'.[14] There is little doubt that Peel saw as his ultimate objective the creation of a police system throughout the country.

The committee reported within six months, in July, 1828. Among the witnesses was Edwin Chadwick, who, with Bentham and Colquhoun made up the trinity of Utilitarians whose school of thought finally reconciled the English ideal of liberty with the French idea of police. Chadwick, 'the heir of Bentham's doctrine of police',[15] and his devoted friend and admirer during the last years of the philosopher's life, played a valuable part in representing to the committee the Utilitarians' insistence on the primary importance of the preventive nature of police work. The report of the committee[16] gave Peel all he wanted. It noted that the existing police system in London had been almost uniformly condemned by all previous inquiries, and recommended the creation of an Office of Police under the direction of the Home Secretary, who should have unified control over the whole police in the Metropolitan area, including the nightly watch. Specially appointed justices should be in charge of the Police Office, but the committee abstained from advising on the detailed management of the force. The cost should be met partly from public funds and partly by a special rate levied on the Metropolitan parishes. Probably in fulfilment of a bargain struck behind the scenes, the committee recommended that the City should be excluded from the arrangement, but refrained from offering convincing reasons for doing so.

In April of the following year, 1829, Peel introduced his 'Bill for Improving the Police in and near the Metropolis'. The circumstances could not have been more favourable. In the Duke of Wellington he now had a Prime Minister who, ever since the shock of Peterloo, had preferred to entrust the maintenance of law and order to professional police rather than soldiers; influential public opinion had been educated by the work of Bentham and Colquhoun; confidence in parish constables and watchmen had largely disappeared; and political opposition had been bought off or conciliated. The Bill largely followed the recommendations of the committee, defining the area for which the new Police Office was to be responsible as the 'Metropolitan police district', a district extending over roughly a seven-mile radius from central London. The 'two fit persons' who as justices were to take charge of the Police Office were authorised to create and administer a police force composed of 'a sufficient number of fit and able men'. The men were to be sworn in by one of the justices as constables, and to have the powers and privileges of a constable at common law. The justices (or commissioners, as they were called later) were to exercise their powers to direct and control the force under the authority of the Home Secretary, and their power to frame orders for the government of the force was likewise subject to his approbation. A Receiver was to be appointed by the Crown with a duty to control the revenue required for the force and manage its property and legal business, and power was given to levy a police rate, not exceeding 8*d.*, throughout the Metropolitan police district. Thus the Bill provided for a complete separation of police administration in London from its centuries-old link with the magistracy and the parishes. In introducing the Bill, Peel declared that 'the chief perquisites of an efficient police were unity of design and responsibility of its agents'. He intended to proceed slowly in establishing a police force, with a 'cautious feeling of his way and deriving aid from experience, essential to the ultimate success of all reforms'. He would apply the Bill to a few districts in the vicinity of the Metropolis at first and then gradually extend it to the others as 'its advantages unfolded themselves'.[17]

It is one of the most remarkable facts about the history of police in England that, after three-quarters of a century of wrangling, suspicion, and hostility towards the whole idea of professional police, the Metropolitan Police Act, 1829, was passed without opposition and with scarcely any debate. Part of the explanation no doubt lies in the adroitness Peel showed in excluding the City from his plans, in return for which it seems probable that the Whigs undertook to give the Bill an easy passage. 'Pray pass the bill through this session', Peel wrote to the Duke of Wellington when it was to go up to the House of Lords, 'for you cannot think what trouble it has given me.'[18] Another remarkable fact is that Peel's Act remains the governing statute of the Metropolitan Police to this day. Recognition of Peel's genius ought not, however, to obscure his own want of originality of thinking about police reform. Regrettably, in harvesting the corn he failed to acknowledge his debt to those who had long prepared the way: Henry and John Fielding, who sowed the seed three-quarters of a century earlier, Patrick Colquhoun, who raised the crop, and Bentham, who tilled the soil in which it grew.

The first policemen

The story has too often been told[19] to need retelling here, even if space allowed, of the events which followed. A brief outline must suffice.

The Metropolitan Police Act became law on July 19th, 1829, and Peel at once set about appointing the first commissioners of police (as the two justices soon came to be called). For one he sought an ex-soldier able to enforce discipline, and for the other he hoped to find a practical and efficient lawyer. His appointments could not have been more successful. Colonel Charles Rowan was a retired officer of forty-six who had fought with the Light Brigade under Wellington at Waterloo; his colleague, Richard Mayne, to whom he was introduced in a room at the Home Office within a fortnight of the Act receiving the Royal Assent, was a young Irish barrister thirteen years Rowan's junior. The partnership was a famous one. The newly appointed commissioners found accommodation at 4 Whitehall Place, which backed on to a narrow lane to the east of Whitehall known as Scotland Yard. This rear entry gave a name to the new office which has been inherited by successive buildings.

Planning proceeded apace. While alterations were going on in the Scotland Yard building, the new commissioners occupied a room at the Home Office, and were given a small staff of civilians. The Act was largely an enabling measure, which sensibly left the details of the organisation to be worked out in the light of experience. It was decided to divide the Metropolitan district into seventeen police divisions, each containing 165 men, making a grand total of nearly 3,000. The limits were roughly those of the Bow Street foot patrols, with a radius up to seven miles from Charing Cross. Each division was to be put in charge of an officer entitled 'superintendent', under whom were to be four inspectors and sixteen sergeants. The title 'inspector' was borrowed from the Bow Street patrols, and that of 'sergeant' was taken from the Army. Each sergeant had control of nine constables. After some hesitation, the decision was taken to clothe the men in a non-military uniform consisting of a blue tailed coat, blue trousers (white trousers being optional in summer) and a glazed black top-hat strengthened with a thick leather crown, which, in Melville Lee's happy phrase, 'was just just homely enough to save the situation'.[20] A rattle was to be carried, together with a short truncheon concealed beneath the long tails of the coat. The Receiver embarked on the prodigious task of finding accommodation all over London for housing the men and providing the first station houses—the term 'police station' came later.

During August the commissioners set about the task of recruiting nearly 3,000 men. A ready-made source of volunteers was the Bow Street foot patrol (the unit continued an independent existence until 1839), and parish vestries were invited to supply lists of parish constables or watchmen who might wish to be considered for appointment. Few were found to be qualified. The regulations demanded that men should be under thirty-five, of good physique, at least five feet seven in height, literate, and of good character. From the outset it was a deliberate policy to recruit men 'who had not the rank, habits or station of gentlemen'.[21] There was to be no caste system as in the Navy or Army, and ranks up to that of superintendent were to be drawn, typically, from ex-warrant officers and N.C.O.s. When vacancies occurred, promotion to higher rank was to be given to men from within the force. The wage of a constable, at a guinea a week, was deliberately fixed at a level to deter ex-officers, and at the same time to keep down the cost of the force. Among the flood of applications which poured into Scotland Yard, those from military men of senior rank and from people with influence in the Government were generally turned down. From the start, the police was to be a homogeneous and democratic body, in tune with the people, understanding the people, belonging to the people, and drawing its strength from the people. A former sergeant-major named John May was appointed superintendent of 'A' Division at Scotland Yard, and he undertook the preliminary interviewing of applicants, passing the more promising on for final selection by the two commissioners.

Next came the important task of framing the instructions for the new force. Peel knew only too well how unpopular had been the decision to establish it; if it were to succeed, it must rely on public co-operation and goodwill. Hence the principles embodied in the first enlightened instructions (which remain valid to this day) exactly reflect the circumstances of 1829:

'It should be understood at the outset, that the* object to be attained is the prevention of crime.

'To this great end every effort of the police is to be directed. The security of person and property and the preservation of a police establishment will thus be better effected than by the detection and

* In a second draft of the instructions, Peel inserted the word 'principal'.

punishment of the offender after he has succeeded in committing crime. . . .

'He [the constable] will be civil and obliging to all people of every rank and class.

'He must be particularly cautious not to interfere idly or unnecessarily in order to make a display of his authority; when required to act, he will do so with decision and boldness; on all occasions he may expect to receive the fullest support in the proper exercise of his authority. He must remember that there is no qualification so indispensable to a police-officer as a perfect command of temper, never suffering himself to be moved in the slightest degree by any language or threats that may be used; if he do his duty in a quiet and determined manner, such conduct will probably excite the well-disposed of the bystanders to assist him, if he requires them.

'In the novelty of the present establishment, particular care is to be taken that the constables of the police do not form false notions of their duties and powers.'

By Saturday, September 26th, 1829, the planning was virtually completed. Substantial numbers of men had been enrolled and recruits were flowing in daily. That day the men paraded in the grounds of the Foundling Hospital in Holborn to be sworn in by Rowan and Mayne. They formed ranks, their conditions of service and instructions were read out, and each man was given a parcel of uniform. On the Monday they were told where they were to be lodged and fed, and that evening they were shown their beats. And then, at 6 p.m. on Tuesday, September 29th, the first parties of the 'new police' marched out from a still only partly converted 'station house' at Scotland Yard and five of the old watch houses. Londoners regarded them with hostility or derision, and coined nicknames—'peeler' or 'bobby'. Considering the novelty of the experiment, and the astonishing speed with which the whole unprecedented operation had been conducted, all went smoothly; and on October 10th Peel was able to report to his wife: 'I have been again busy all the morning about my Police. I think it is going very well. The men look very smart and a strong contrast to the old Watchmen.' He had, he said, been laughing at a cartoon 'called "Peeling a Charlie", in which I am represented stripping one of the old watchmen of his great-coat, etc.'. Next month the Duke of Wellington told Peel, 'I congratulate you upon the entire success of the police in London. It is impossible to see anything more

53

respectable than they are'[22]; to which Peel replied in the memorable sentence: 'I want to teach people that liberty does not consist in having your house robbed by organised gangs of thieves, and in leaving the principal streets of London in the nightly possession of drunken women and vagabonds.'

By May, 1830, the Metropolitan Police was a force about 3,300 strong, with many names on a waiting list—who did not, however, have to wait long, for the turnover in manpower, mainly on account of dismissals for drunkenness, was extremely high. The force's testing time was about to come.

The early 1830s saw the Reform Bill Riots in London, and the growth of subversive activities which provided endless opportunities for the police to perfect techniques of crowd-control and practise the newly acquired art of baton charges. The London parishes, on whose shoulders the whole cost of the force was to be borne, were not so easily mesmerised by Peel as Parliament had been, and during 1830 meetings of vestries all over London passed resolutions denouncing the new police as an 'outrage and an insult' to the people. A typical pamphlet (preserved in the Public Record Office) came to the attention of Peel. Insisting on the restoration of parish policing, it concluded with the brave exordium, 'Join your Brother Londoners in one heart, one hand, for the ABOLITION OF THE NEW POLICE'. Peel minuted: 'Here is another proof of the necessity of a clear, detailed, and authorised explanation in the public Papers of the Metropolitan Police, and in so far as Rates are concerned. We are run down by the Press when we have truth completely on our side.' But the parishes, Press, and public continued to fulminate against the new police. Wild rumours circulated. It was said that the police were being drilled in order to put the Duke of Wellington on the throne, and placards appeared in the London streets carrying inflammatory exhortations to Englishmen to get rid of 'Peel's bloody gang', who were alleged to be arming themselves with cutlasses. Policemen attempting to control traffic were ridden down and lashed with whips. In August, 1830, the first Metropolitan policeman to be killed on duty, John Long, was stabbed in Gray's Inn Road. Complaints about police poured into Scotland Yard, and Rowan and Mayne, carefully investigating each personally, were accordingly accused of constituting a sinister 'police court'; outrage and insult could go no further.

Peel worked loyally with the commissioners in riding out these storms, but he was succeeded in November, 1830, by Melbourne. The new police had lost their creator and mentor; and their worst months were still to come when, in the summer of 1833, a conjunction of events led to the setting up of two Parliamentary committees of inquiry into their conduct. The first concerned a sergeant named Popay, who had been a schoolmaster before joining the police. Popay was discovered to have insinuated himself in the guise of a poor artist into a subversive movement, where for some months he acted as a double agent. In the sensitive state of public opinion about the new police, the discovery fed renewed outcries against tyranny, for now there was triumphant evidence that at least one policeman had been used, or had chosen to caste himself, as a spy. A Parliamentary committee exonerated the authorities from connivance in Popay's conduct, which they condemned as 'a practice most abhorrent to the feeling of the people and most alien to the spirit of the constitution'. Popay was dismissed, but the damage had been done. Later in the same year came the first major clash between the Metropolitan Police and the London mob. This was a public meeting organised by the National Political Union in Cold-Bath Fields. Melbourne instructed the police commissioners to have the ringleaders arrested if, despite warning, the meeting were held. Rowan himself directed operations, in the course of which the police were stoned, baton charges ensued, and three policemen were stabbed, one of whom was killed outright. Such was the public feeling against the police that at the inquest on the dead man the jury, against all the evidence, brought in a verdict of 'justifiable homicide'. The Government indignantly and successfully applied to the Court of Kings Bench for the verdict to be quashed. A Parliamentary committee heard some 'buck passing' between Melbourne and the commissioners about what instructions had been given to whom, but in the result upheld authority. Public opinion, fickle as ever, veered in favour of the police.

Such were the intolerable conditions in which the Metropolitan Police forged the reputation which, within a few years, was to make the force world-famous. Their imperturbability, courage, good humour, and sense of fair-play won first the admiration of Londoners and then their affection. Henry Fielding, nearly a century earlier, had set out to reconcile order with freedom in the streets of London. The sensible principles which governed the force in the early testing years effected the reconciliation in characteristically British fashion. It may well be that the long public debate over the theory of policing, and the instinctive obstinacy with which the police idea had time and time again been repudiated, paid dividends in the 1830s in the way in which 3,000 unarmed policemen, cautiously feeling their way against a hostile public, brought peace and security to London in place of the turmoil and lawlessness of centuries. The process of settling down was also no doubt aided by the fact of the Home Secretary's account- ability for the force, which must have provided a valuable Parlia- mentary check during the formative years. Above all, however, credit for the successful transition from the era of parish constables and watchmen to that of professional policing belongs to Rowan and Mayne. London was admirably served by its first commissioners of police. Praising the conduct of the police, a Parliamentary committee which sat in 1833 and 1834 declared: 'Much, in the opinion of Your Committee, is due to the judgement and discrimination which was exercised in the selection of the individuals, Colonel Rowan and Mr. Mayne, who were originally appointed, and still continue to fill the arduous office of Commissioners of Police. On many critical occasions and in very difficult circumstances, the sound discretion they have exercised, the straightforward, open, and honourable course they have pursued—whenever their conduct has been questioned by the Public—calls for the strongest expression of approbation on the part of Your Committee.' The committee reported that complaints against the police 'have not been well founded'. And now at last the old bogy that had haunted men's imagination for so long was laid: 'It appears to your committee that the Metropolitan police has imposed no restraint, either upon public bodies or individuals, which is not entirely consistent with the fullest practical exercise of every civil privilege, and with the most unrestrained intercourse of private society.' English liberty had survived.

It remained to mop up. Peel's Act isolated the decrepitude of the City's Charlies, Colquhoun's old-established Thames river police, the scattered groups of constables employed in the police offices set up by the Middlesex Justices Act, 1792, and the legendary Bow Street Runners, who for several years yet were able to pursue their profitable line of business in undertaking missions on behalf of wealthy and influential clients. In 1832, and again in 1838, the City police system was reorganised; and in the following year, threatened by Lord John Russell, the Whig Home Secretary, with a Bill to amalgamate the City and Metropolitan police districts—which caused the Corporation to address an urgent petition to Queen Victoria—the Corporation promoted a City of London Police Bill which established a force, some 500 strong, under the command of a commissioner appointed by the Corporation. In the same year a second Metro- politan Police Act converted the River Thames force into the Thames

Division of the Metropolitan Police, put an end to the anachronism of the constables employed in magistrates' offices, and absorbed the Bow Street foot patrol. (The horse patrol had already been amalgamated with the Metropolitan Police by an Act of 1836, and thus formed the nucleus of the mounted branch.) Finally, the Act of 1839 enlarged the boundaries of the Metropolitan police district to cover an area, encompassing a radius some fifteen miles from Charing Cross, which remained unaltered until minor adjustments were made by the Police Act, 1946. Thus Lord John Russell, who had early been associated with Peel in the series of Parliamentary committees of the 1820s which paved the way to reform, set the seal on his political opponent's work, while at the same time, in ways described in the next chapter, carrying it into the provinces.

From this point onwards the history of the Metropolitan Police—the formation of the Detective Department (forerunner of the C.I.D.) in 1842, the sad last years of Richard Mayne, who reigned too long alone after Rowan's retirement in 1850, (a successor to Rowan was appointed, but by an Act of 1856 the force was placed under a single Commissioner) the quarrel between a high-handed commissioner, Sir Charles Warren, and the Home Secretary in 1888 which led to the former's resignation, the Battle of Sidney Street, finger-printing, and an endless succession of notorious murders —all belongs properly to the story of Scotland Yard; and in subsequent chapters developments in the Metropolitan Police can be mentioned only where they have a bearing on the more general history of police in England.

Chapter Three

The First Provincial Police 1830-53

The decade that began with the creation of the Metropolitan Police in 1829 was one of the most important in the history of the police in the remainder of England and Wales also, for it saw provision made, by a series of somewhat hesitant steps, for the establishment of regular forces throughout the country.

It has sometimes been suggested that these steps followed a logical sequence: that the early success of the Metropolitan Police drove criminals out of London, with the consequence that provision was made, in the Municipal Corporations Act, 1835, to create police forces in the towns; and the borough forces in turn (on this theory) harried criminals into the rural areas, with the final result that, four years later, the Government completed the task by means of the County Police Act, 1839. This attractive theory bears no relation to the facts. Determination to suppress crime was undoubtedly one, but probably not the major or most urgent, of the causes that led, first, to the reform of the borough police, and, second, to an enabling Act that permitted magistrates to reform the rural police; and there is no evidence that a policy of hounding criminals from one area to another, until finally the trap closed in the counties, actuated either measure.

Early steps to reform

The long debate over the policing of London aroused only faint echoes elsewhere. During the early decades of the nineteenth century almost every provincial town had supplemented its parish constables by a body of paid night-watchmen, and occasionally day constables who earned fees; and it is probable that, during the unsettled times following the end of the Napoleonic Wars, the quality of the embryo police forces in such towns as Bristol, Liverpool, and Manchester was steadily rising. But there was no movement for the general reform of borough police forces on the London model, and it would have been surprising if there had been. No other area demanded the unitary treatment, spanning and overriding the interests of numerous separate local authorities; and nowhere else, by the same token of size, was the breakdown of law and order so persistent. Consequently, *laissez faire* by the Government and self-help locally left it open to the prominent citizens of every town to augment their corps of watchmen so far as a threat of local disorder warranted an increase in the local rate; and many tradesmen and farmers still preferred to rely on membership of voluntary protection societies, enlisting the self-interest of others by offering rewards for the capture of thieves. The Luddite riots in 1811–12, when frame-breaking was fanned to violence by Irish trouble-makers, were suppressed with the aid of soldiers; but the Government was sufficiently concerned to promote permissive legislation (Geo. III, xvii, 1812) aimed at strengthening, in Nottingham and the surrounding areas, 'the Duties of Watching in the Night-time and Warding in the Day-time', by conscripting virtually the whole male population for police work. In any area where the justices adopted the Act, the constables (or 'every headborough, borsholder, or tythingman') were required to compile lists of all ratepayers over the age of seventeen, who were to be placed on a rota for regular day and night duty, with powers of arrest. Under the supervision of the high constable, each parish constable was required to 'enter in a Book to be kept for this Purpose' the name of each watchman, 'with Remarks upon his conduct, specifying whether he has been attentive and diligent, or disobedient and remiss in the Duty of Watching and Warding'. This measure, however, was exceptional and temporary: it was enacted for two years, and later extended for a further twelve months. The important point is that it still left entirely to local discretion the scale of local policing. In the view of the Government, at least until about 1830, if any town felt itself in-adequately protected the remedy was largely in its own hands.

Consequently, it was to the rural areas, not the towns, that Peel turned his attention in 1829, at the same time that he was creating the Metropolitan Police. His concern about them, expressed in moving for the appointment of the select committee of 1828, was mentioned in the previous chapter; and in April, 1829, he told the House of Commons that he was contemplating a general police measure for the English counties. In co-operation with the local Members of Parliament, however, he secured the enactment of a Cheshire Police Bill, which, it was thought, might serve to create a prototype system of policing which could be extended to the whole country.[1] Under this Act,[2] which received the Royal Assent on June 1st, 1829 (a month before the Metropolitan Police Act) a new and final lease of life was given to the ancient office of high constable. Each hundred in the county was to have a stipendiary deputy high constable—'for it is vain to expect that high constables of hundreds . . . will exert themselves to the extent that is in many cases rendered absolutely indispensable to the preservation of life and property', as the local newspaper, the *Chester Courant*, put it.[3] These officials, nine of whom were appointed, were to receive annual salaries of £80 to £100, and each, under the authority of the local magistrates, was given control of several paid petty constables. Hence Cheshire became the first area outside London (and perhaps a few other large towns) to maintain a regular paid constabulary, and Peel watched to see how far the experiment might be applicable generally in other counties.

Meantime, events in the towns moved swiftly. Continuing threats of riot and disorder—notably the calamitous Reform Bill riots in Bristol in 1831, with similar outbreaks of rioting in Nottingham, Derby, Worcester, Exeter, Coventry, and Preston—fed the Tory Government's concern about the inadequacy of the means of maintaining law and order in those towns governed by ancient charters. A Special Constables Act of 1831 empowered justices to conscript men as special constables on the occasion of a riot or a threat of riot (the first statute to deal with special constables was the Act of Charles II which authorised the appointment of parish constables by justices: p. 17); and later that year, and in the following year, 1832, Peel was pressing on the succeeding Whig administration the urgency of implementing a promise in the King's Speech at the opening of the session to bring in a 'measure for the establishment of a municipal police in the cities and towns of the kingdom', which 'called for all the energy and attention of government'.[4] But the Government refused to be rushed. The Royal Commission on Municipal Corporations, which paved the way to the historic Act, was appointed in July, 1833. In the same year Parliament enacted a stop-gap measure, the Lighting and Watching Act,[5] which was the first statute to deal with the establishment of paid police forces in the country generally. As the Parliamentary proceedings on it were not recorded, it is impossible to say what hopes were entertained of the Act, but its intention is clear enough. It enabled a quorum of ratepayers to adopt its provisions for their parish, appoint several of their number to be 'inspectors', and levy a rate for the employment of 'watchmen, sergeants of the night, patrols, street-keepers', and others, who were to be sworn in as constables. Thus the Act filled a gap where Improvement Act powers were lacking or unused. It is of interest in marking a reaction towards the traditional use of the parish as a unit for policing, or perhaps a failure, understandable, however, as the Royal Commission was then sitting, to grasp an opportunity to break away from it. The Webbs portray it as a means of propping up the tottering structure of parish government, and point out that it marked a significant rejection —consistent with their exclusion from the new arrangements for policing London—of the role of the justices in police matters, a trend followed by a similar diminution of the justices' functions in other branches of local government as the century progressed.[6]

It has not been possible to ascertain what use was made of the Lighting and Watching Act, but there is reason to think that it was adopted more extensively than has hitherto been suggested.* However, this Act, and all the minor reforms and expedients that had preceded it, were rapidly overtaken by fresh and very much more powerful political currents which far transcended in their sweep the arrangements for policing. To the Tories' concern about the break-down of law and order in the towns was now added the determination of the Whigs, directly the Municipal Corporations Commission had reported, to give them democratic forms of government; and it was this confluence of political currents—above all, the new tide of radicalism—that shaped the mould in which the first of the new provincial police forces were cast. In two surges it loosened the foot-holds of privilege in Parliamentary government (by the Reform Act, 1832) and soon afterwards in local government (by the Municipal Corporations Act, 1835). Then, working itself out among the masses under the banner of Chartism, it led to a spate of legislation urgently rushed through Parliament in the closing weeks of the session of 1839 by a Whig Government nervous at what it had unleashed, and resolved to provide police to quell the popular riots its liberal policies had done much to encourage. It would not therefore overstrain the truth to say that, while the regular borough police came into being on a side-wind of Parliamentary and municipal reform, the first county constabularies were a reaction to the further fair promises which that reform appeared to hold out. The success of the Metropolitan Police and the desire to suppress crime were undoubtedly relevant factors;

* Histories of several local police forces show it to have been adopted in both county and borough areas. An article in *The Police Journal* for June, 1966, describes its operation in Ulverston, Lancashire.

but politics rather than policies provided the sharper and more immediate spurs to action.

Police reform in the boroughs

The instrument by which regular police forces were required to be established in the boroughs of England and Wales was the Municipal Corporations Act, 1835, but that statute was not exclusively, or even primarily, promoted for police purposes. It was as much a product of the fresh breeze of radical thinking that was blowing through the England of William IV as the great agitation for Parliamentary reform which paved the way for the Reform Act of 1832, and the motive behind each measure was basically the same: to extend the franchise to the new middle classes, and so bring fresh blood into the business of both national and local government. Indeed, Trevelyan regards the Municipal Corporations Bill as the direct sequel to the Reform Bill.[7] The rotten town governments survived by only three years the Parliamentary rotten boroughs. Dissenters and tradesmen once and for all ousted the last of the generations of Tory lawyers and churchmen and noblemen's agents who had long ruled the courts leet and the old town corporations by virtue of their caste, and instituted the age of municipal enterprise and local self-government. And it was to these novel, democratic forms of town administration that the Act assigned, among other duties, that of maintaining a police force. So far as its police provisions are concerned, it is probably best regarded as an attempt to rationalise and modernise, somewhat on the lines of the Metropolitan Police, the confused pattern of Improvement Act watchmen and constables which already existed in many towns. At the same time it placed the force of 'new police' under the democratic town councils, which themselves took over the functions of the improvement commissioners and the ancient corporations.

There is no question here, as has sometimes been suggested, of deliberately putting new life into the old principle that responsibility for maintaining the King's peace lay on each locality, for that principle had in practice long been disregarded. A Royal Commission appointed in the following year, 1836, had no hesitation in declaring that the old function of watch and ward had entirely fallen into desuetude, 'which is ascribable to the dereliction of the constitutional principle of local responsibility to the supreme executive for the prevention of crime'.[8] It is true that the Municipal Corporations Act had the effect of once more reaffirming the responsibility for the maintenance of law and order of convenient bodies of local citizens, and it is also true that the old principle had never been formally repudiated—as it has not been to this day. But it would be a falsification of history to credit the legislature of 1835 with any intention to preserve the mystique of frankpledge. All that happened was that the opportunity was taken of the general reform of local government in the towns to provide machinery for law enforcement to replace that which had broken down under the social and economic pressures of the Industrial Revolution. Nor were the men who pioneered the work of the new town councils the kind of people who would look back sentimentally into the mists of history.

The Act applied, initially, to 178 boroughs in England and Wales which had been granted charters of self-government by successive sovereigns. It also enabled new charters to be granted under its provisions.* Municipal corporations were to be established in the boroughs, and a town council was to be elected by popular franchise. Immediately after their first election, the council were required to appoint a sufficient number of their own body (subsequently restricted by the Municipal Corporations Act, 1882, to not more than one-third of the council) to form a watch committee, together with the mayor, who was declared to be a justice of the peace. The watch committee, within three weeks of its first formation, was to appoint a 'sufficient number of fit men' to be sworn in to act as constables, for preserving the peace by day and night and preventing robberies. The committee was given power to dismiss as well as appoint the constables, and to frame regulations for them. The Act preserved the powers of the constable under the common law, and it also gave statutory force to the old convention that he was to obey the lawful commands of a justice. It extinguished the police powers of improvement commissioners in any area to which it applied, and also superseded, in these areas, any police maintained under the Lighting and Watching Act.

There were resemblances here to the Metropolitan Police Act of 1829, but there were also important differences, both in the statutes and in the way in which they were applied. From the start, Metropolitan policemen were given a regular rate of pay, in return for which

* Many rapidly growing industrial towns, including Birmingham, Manchester, Bolton, Bradford, and Middlesbrough, had not been granted charters of incorporation by 1835. The Act did not therefore apply in these areas, and the towns were under no obligation to create a police force until in due course a charter was granted.

they were required to give their whole time to police work, and they were strictly forbidden to accept gratuities. None of these conditions applied to a borough force unless the watch committee chose to form rules to impose them. Some did and some did not. But perhaps the most vital difference lay in the treatment accorded to the old gang of night-watchmen, day constables, beadles, and the like. In London the slate was scrubbed clean; all former watchmen and constables were dismissed, and while a few were subsequently admitted to the new force in 1829, most of the recruits came freshly to police work. In the towns to which the Municipal Corporations Act applied, on the other hand, many watch committees saw in the old hands a convenient, cheap, and ready-made source of labour, which loyalty to past employees of the borough would in any case encourage them to retain; and there were no new brooms of commissioners to sweep away the debris of centuries. If they could fulfil their obligations under the Act by simply taking over the old night-watchmen and day police, who for years had been employed under Improvement Act powers (or in some cases under the more recent Lighting and Watching Act), many watch committees must have argued, why embark on more elaborate and costly arrangements?

The larger towns advertised publicly for recruits for their forces and considered the former watchmen and constables along with new applicants, and some—Bristol,[9] the largest city outside London, is an example—probably made as clean a sweep as was made in London. Some applied to the Metropolitan Police Commissioners for an officer to take charge of the force, but it seems doubtful whether many of the smaller towns took much trouble to look beyond their own resources. Systematic research into local records, beyond the resources of the present work, would be required to support any confident assertion of the extent to which the new police forces of 1835 and 1836 were composed of members of the old gang reconstituted under a new authority, but the evidence of the several local-force histories which bear on the matter provides a fairly common pattern. Thus the new Leeds force of twenty men, which was created in 1836, had as its head constable the former superintendent of the night-watch (a body set up under a local Improvement Act), and the four inspectors in the new force had, similarly, served as constables in the old. In January, 1836, the new watch committee of Chester took over a few men formerly employed under Improvement Act powers. Three years later one was still described as superintendent of the watch and another as superintendent of police; and the latter served on as head constable of the force until 1864. Something of the same sort happened in Newport. In 1830 the improvement commissioners appointed four night-watchmen, and some years later it seems that two bailiffs and twelve day constables were being appointed by the mayor, and paid by fees for work done. In 1834 the local Member of Parliament persuaded Mayne to 'release an intelligent officer to be appointed chief constable of Newport at a yearly salary of £90' to take charge of them. When the Watch Committee first met they discovered the ex-Metropolitan policeman to be the only paid officer, and he stayed on as head constable, together with one other paid constable (who received £25 a year, plus fees) and twelve part-timers. A final example shows the birth of a borough force through every antecedent stage. Under a Swansea Improvement Act of 1809 seven night-watchmen were appointed, and these were supplemented in 1821 by a day constable, who was paid for duties actually performed. The inadequacy of these arrangements led to the formation, in 1829, of a private society for apprehending and prosecuting thieves, and this enrolled special constables. In the following year a Bow Street Runner was employed temporarily to co-ordinate the activities of night-watchmen, day constables, and specials, but in 1833 the whole arrangements were scrapped when three regular full-time policemen were appointed under the Lighting and Watching Act and placed under the command of the head of the special constables, who was styled 'chief constable'. In 1835 the newly formed Watch Committee appointed the 'inspector' under the Lighting and Watching Act (who, however, was illiterate) to this new force. Thus old traditions survived, and the majority of the new borough forces were much inferior bodies to the Metropolitan Police. They were in no position to compete in recruiting or in their arrangements for training recruits, for their size imposed on them in these and in almost every other respect disadvantages which had never hampered developments in London. Part-timers and fee-earners, as in the days of the parish constable, were still commonly employed by the reformed municipal corporations.*

---

* Misgivings about the adequacy of the provision likely to be made by many towns may well be the reason why the Act strengthened the arrangements for appointing special constables in the boroughs: by section 83 the justices were required to appoint, in October every year, as many special constables as they thought necessary, with powers to act on a warrant declaring that the regular force was insufficient to maintain law and order. This provision (re-enacted in 1882), though long disregarded, was not repealed until 1964.

One of the causes of this disappointing outcome is to be discovered in the very different circumstances in which the parent statutes were enacted. The one, a child of Peel's own creation, concentrated exclusively on the single problem of establishing an efficient police force in London. The other was a by-product of the movement for Parliamentary and municipal reform. It was hastily prepared, hastily rushed through Parliament, and woefully incomplete; and on the most crucial question of all Parliament simply failed to legislate. The Metropolitan Police Act established beyond doubt that the force was placed under the authority of the Home Secretary. But who was to control the borough police forces? The Municipal Corporations Act, like the earlier Improvement Acts, was silent. It made no mention of the Home Secretary, other than to require watch committees to send quarterly reports to the Home Office giving information about the number of constables appointed, their rates of pay, and the rules governing the force. Nor was any mention made of a chief constable, superintendent, or any other rank to take charge of the 'fit men' who were to 'act as constables'. They were thus banded together in the smaller towns much as they had been for years—as a body of watchmen rather than an organised force. They were required to obey the lawful commands of justices, but it was evident that the justices were not organised or professionally qualified to act as section commanders. Perhaps the watch committee was meant to do so? The Act was silent. The committee's powers to appoint, or suspend or dismiss the constables appeared to establish a kind of master-and-servant relationship, but whether this gave the committee power to give orders to the force was, and remained until the early legislation was repealed by the Police Act, 1964, an unresolved question, for it was never tested in the courts of law. It has therefore been open to anyone, according to his interests, from the time of the enactment of the Municipal Corporations Act in 1835 until the law was clarified in the Police Act, 1964, to assert that the force was under the control of the watch committee, whatever that might mean;* or under the control of the justices, which it demonstrably was not; or under the control of the chief or head constable, which was undeniable so far as it went,

---

* It probably meant a great deal in the early days, particularly in the small boroughs where only a handful of policemen were employed, and the head constable was only paid marginally more than his men. There is evidence that control in some larger boroughs was also very close: in Swansea in 1844 the inspector in charge was required to report to the whole council, sitting as a watch committee, every Friday morning.

but simply shifted the question one remove. Who controlled the chief constable?

These questions do not seem to have come to a head for several years, but when they did they resulted in sharp clashes which continued until modern times, culminating in a head-on collision between the Watch Committee and the Chief Constable of Nottingham as recently as 1958.* The immediate task was to get the new borough forces established. The first town councils were elected in December, 1835, and in most places they appointed watch committees in January or February, 1836.[10] Two years later, however, only about half the boroughs had established police forces, and even ten years afterwards, in 1845, there remained upwards of thirty boroughs which had not done so. As late as 1856, when the first inspectors of constabulary were appointed, they discovered that thirteen boroughs had simply ignored the Act. This reluctance to spend the ratepayers' money was also manifested in another way: of the boroughs which did establish police forces, some, and probably the majority, failed to appoint a sufficient number of policemen. Mrs. Hart has shown that, taking the whole country throughout the period 1836 to 1856, the municipal corporations which maintained separate police forces had only about half as many police in proportion to their population as London. An example of dilatoriness in acting on the new law came to the attention of the Royal Commission appointed in 1836, which found that the borough of Stockport 'does not appear to have been strong enough to supersede by one uniform, well appointed and complete force, the various private watches'. Four policemen had been appointed to share the work of patrolling the town by night, but they were greatly outnumbered by the thirty-three or thirty-four watchmen still paid by private subscriptions, the majority of whom were thought to be corrupt. This situation, or something like it, must have continued for a long time, for while in London the ratio of

* This incident is described on pp. 270–2. Another clash between a watch committee and its chief constable is mentioned on p. 131. But sometimes it was the justices and the watch committee who were at loggerheads. An early illustration of the general inadequacy of the law appears from a letter of January 30th, 1843, in *H.O.* 43/63. Referring to the legality of the appointment of a police superintendent, the Home Office told a complainant that the Home Secretary 'regrets that such a collision and difference should have arisen between two magistrates and the watch committee of the Borough of Newport, and he would be glad if he could by his mediation and advice restore a good understanding; but of this he has no hope'. The parties were invited to test the issue before the Court of the Queen's Bench.

police to population in the 1850s was one policeman for 461 inhabitants, in Stockport it was one policeman for 3,620 inhabitants—
the worst ratio of any borough in the country. In Northampton it was
not until 1848 that the day and night police were amalgamated to form
one body and converted into full-time policemen. Such examples
could be multiplied, and fully bear out Mrs. Hart's comment: 'It
seems probable that in most boroughs the reform of the police was
gradual and not spectacular as in London, and that the level of
efficiency was still low in the eighteen-fifties. The impression gained
from looking at the evidence is often that in the boroughs one is much
nearer to the old world of early nineteenth-century watchmen earning
a few shillings by casual police work than to the new world of professional, full-time, carefully recruited, and supervised Metropolitan
Police officers. 1835 is no doubt an important date in the history of the
borough police, but there are some grounds for thinking that 1856
was more of a landmark.'[11]

First Report of the Constabulary Commissioners, 1839

The Government decided not to await the results of the Municipal
Corporations Act before reviewing the needs of the rural areas.
Edwin Chadwick, the Secretary of the Poor Law Commissioners,
whose influence in the events which preceded the creation of the
Metropolitan Police was mentioned in the last chapter, had for some
years been pressing the Home Secretary to take steps to improve the
rural police, not least in order to deal with 'the suppression of tumults
connected with the administration of relief'.[12] In July, 1836, as the first
watch committees were organising their first policemen in the towns,
the Home Secretary, Lord John Russell, was saying that he had 'given
his attention to the subject of rendering the constabulary force of rural
parishes more efficient, but that a great press of business had prevented the introduction of a Bill'. Nevertheless, in the following
month the Home Office were expecting that a measure would be
proposed to Parliament in the next session 'for the establishment of a
rural police generally'.[13]

Now, however, Chadwick stepped forward again, proposing the
appointment of an inquiry to recommend what arrangements should
be made, and Russell responded warmly: 'I very much approve of
your plan of having a Commission respecting the Rural Police', he
wrote on September 1st. 'I do not apprehend however much difficulty

in introducing them, if they are not clothed in uniform. If that is essential, I am afraid we should have to meet many obstacles. I think three Commissioners should be quite sufficient. Yourself, and Colonel Rowan should be two.' The third, he thought, should be 'a Country Gentleman' whose attendance would hardly be required for 'more than a few days, as the labour would in fact fall upon yourself and the paid clerk'. The Home Secretary concluded by claiming that he had given some thought to the problem. He had 'already got the outline of a plan for the purpose which was chiefly drawn by the Duke of Richmond. . . .* In the event of Constables not being appointed by Boards of Guardians the Justices should name them.'[14]

The Royal Commission, 'for the purpose of Inquiring as to the best means of establishing an efficient constabulary force in the counties of England and Wales', spent nearly three years on its task. It amassed much colourful evidence about the state of crime, the careers of habitual delinquents, the nature of their depredations, the degree of insecurity of travellers on the roads, and the increasing risks opened up in rural areas by the conveyance of valuable cargoes by canal and railway. A commercial traveller with interests throughout the south of England said that it was only on very rare occasions that he dared to travel after dark. 'Occasionally in a moonlight night I may; but it would be contrary to prudence for any person who travels about the country with much money in his pocket to be out after dusk.' This was the almost universal habit among travellers. A straw-hat manufacturer agreed, and said that he had himself been shot at near Harpenden, while on his way to Luton Market to buy straw, and a third traveller testified that farmers in northern towns commonly waited for hours to make up parties for their return home after dark from the markets, rather than risk the journey alone. Asked (no doubt by Rowan) what kind of force would give confidence to travellers, the witness predictably replied, 'A police like the Metropolitan, on which one might rely in case of need.' The local and municipal police, he said, could not be relied on.

The Commission was an enterprising body. Not content to rely

---

* A member of Melbourne's Cabinet—'prejudiced, narrow-minded, illiterate and ignorant, good-looking, good-humoured and unaffected, tedious, prolix, unassuming, and a duke'—he had personal experience of the need for rural police in 1830, when he fought a battle against a mob of 200 labourers in Sussex whom he beat with the aid of fifty of his tenant farmers. He afterwards harangued the rioters and sent them away in good humour (*Dictionary of National Biography*). No trace of Richmond's rural police plan has come to light.

solely on the evidence of respectable citizens, its members interrogated many convicted prisoners, and in an account of 'Confessions of Delinquents' they painted a rogues' gallery of Fagins and Sykeses. One, aged twenty-two, 'the son of respectable parents', took advantage of his career to satisfy a tourist's curiosity: 'I thought myself secure when I got to Robert Burns' cottage, about three miles. I looked about it; admired the scenery . . . crossed the water to Donaghadee . . . went to see the monument "to King William of the Boyne".' He put an extensive knowledge of criminal practices at the disposal of the Commission: robbery in the streets with violence was often carried out by hitting the victim on the head with a stone in a stocking, but a more refined method was to 'take fast hold of the nose, and pushing it quite flat towards the mouth, so as almost to break the gristle of the nose, this will take away a man's senses nearly'. Obligingly, the witness offered hints on crime-prevention: 'The strongest chain is soon smashed . . . inside bolts should be top and bottom, and, to be good for anything, should, when shot, be locked in that position by one of those patent locks. The main door-key is best left in the lock.' However, 'in London or Liverpool, or such places as have got the new police, there is little to be done, unless it be picking pockets'.

Around the coasts, too, the 'new police' were beginning to show their worth—but only in the very few places where they were available. From elsewhere, the Commission heard of barbarous practices. Whole villages were alleged to consist very largely of men 'calling themselves fishermen, but who in fact, live by plundering wrecks. They intermarry . . . a most determined set of villains; it matters not what comes in their way, they will have it.' A few years earlier a ship had been wrecked off the Cheshire coast. Her captain's body was washed ashore, where the wreckers were massed like vultures. They stripped it naked, and while the corpse lay waiting to be taken off for the inquest someone cut off a finger to secure a ring. A woman bit the ears off a female body to secure the earrings. From all round the coasts the story of plunder was the same. Coastguards were powerless against the determined villagers, often drunk from the liquor they seized. Regardless of compassion for the drowning, they would wade or swim out in a foray to be the first to touch a floating cask or case, and thus by ancient custom lay claim to ownership. While the Commission was sitting a force of twenty-five coastguards held a crowd of between 4,000 and 5,000 people at bay, firing over their heads and drawing their swords in an attempt to protect the cargo of a French brig wrecked between Sennan and Priest Coves, near Penzance.

But the Commission also heard striking evidence of the efficiency and determination of the 'new police' in giving 'that protection which all humanity and civilisation demands for strangers and property cast on the shore by shipwreck'. One weekend early in January, 1839, a storm wrecked a large number of ships on the Cheshire and Lancashire coasts. For two days the plunder proceeded on a vast scale, and the local constables made no effort to interfere. But on the second night the chief officer of the newly formed Liverpool City Police sent a force of about twenty men, under Superintendent Quick, to the Cheshire coast 'with a view to assisting in saving life and property'. Quick had formerly served in the Metropolitan Police, and knew his business. About twenty-five prisoners were taken in the act of plundering bales and cases, and they were duly produced before the Cheshire magistrates. Nothing like it had ever happened before, and the magistrates were furious that the Liverpool police should dare to interfere in Cheshire. They ordered Quick and his men to go about their business, but Quick stood his ground. 'Sir', he said, 'these persons were caught in the act of plundering, and I believe you will find, if you will refer to the Municipal Act, that we have, as constables of Liverpool, authority in Chester in consequence of its being within seven miles of the borough.' The magistrates angrily repudiated this view of the law and appealed to the clerk of the court, who upheld them. Quick, however, was familiar with his statutes. He persuaded the magistrates to remand the prisoners in custody, and next day the Town Clerk of Liverpool sent over an extract from the Act. The magistrates reluctantly committed the men for trial.

Having thus graphically described the 'nature and extent of the chief evils to be prevented or repressed', the Commission proceeded to show the inadequacy of the existing means of dealing with them, and its findings are hardly surprising. It quoted extensive evidence of the incompetence of local constables in preventing or detecting crime. It reported that the principle of watch and ward had fallen into abeyance, and the leisure that had enabled the gentry of an earlier generation to follow the call of hue and cry was not available to the new middle-class businessmen. Reliance therefore had to be placed on the parish constables, but they were totally unfit for their job, being generally drunken, dissolute and shiftless. 'We desire to express our opinion', said a body of Glamorganshire magistrates, 'that the present constabulary force of this part of the country cannot by any possibility be worse than it is. . . . All the constables in rural districts, with very rare exceptions, are perfectly illiterate.' The Durham

71

magistrates ascribed the failure of the rural constables to bring offenders to justice to three main causes:

'(1) To a natural dislike on the part of the constables to make exertions, for which they receive no adequate remuneration.

'(2) To a dread of retaliation on the part of the offenders, should any active measures be taken for their discovery.

'(3) To the natural sympathy between the culprits and officers as acquaintances and fellow-townsmen.'

Corroborating all it had heard from the magistrates, the Commission next heard evidence from convicted delinquents, all of whom testified to their fear of the new paid police in the towns, but professed total indifference to the activities, such as they were, of parish constables. All the evidence was pointing the same way: there could be no security in the country districts without a trained, full-time police force. Others had already drawn the same conclusion, and acted on it to the best of their abilities—or, as the evidence proceeded to show, taken advantage of it. The Commission learned that upwards of 500 voluntary associations existed for purposes of self-protection, with rules providing for mutual insurance and for mutual action to apprehend delinquents. The Home Office had encouraged the growth of these associations, and were actually recommending them in August, 1836, on the eve of the Royal Commission's appointment, as an interim measure pending legislation.[15]

However, the Commission discovered that many of the associations, unknown to their sponsors in the business community, were carrying on, under a cloak of respectability, a profitable line in crime. Lacking any organisation, discipline, authority or even regular pay, they attracted many of the most cunning criminals to their ranks, and organised brothels and receivers on a large scale. 'Hereafter,' the Commission commented soberly, 'such associations and such rules may be cited to prove that the community in which they arose was relapsing into a state of barbarism.' However, not all the voluntary associations were corrupt. Some communities, notably Barnet in Hertfordshire, starting with an association in 1784 designed simply to offer rewards for the apprehension of persons who committed offences against any of its members, later employed two paid officers (subsequently increased to six) to prevent crime by patrolling the district. This experiment met with great success, and was far-famed.

Finally, the Commission made a special point of inquiring into the results of Peel's experiment with the only existing paid constabulary force for a county—the Cheshire constabulary—and they were not impressed. The experiment had suffered, they thought, from the fragmentation of the force into separate small constabularies, each maintained by its own body of local magistrates, and hence the county constabulary lacked the unity which was one of the principal achievements of the Metropolitan force. Moreover, magistrates, in the Commission's opinion (as in that of Pitt, Colquhoun, and Peel), were an inherently unsuitable body to maintain police forces.

The last finding was important, for if it had been acted upon it would have led to the severance of the centuries-old association between police and magistracy in the counties and, since the magistracy constituted the local government, between the police and local government also. The Commission, aware no doubt of the controversial nature of its view, was at pains to set out the reasons which had led to it. They may be summarised as follows: first, being country gentry, the magistrates were too remote from the working classes from whom most criminals came and so, lacking knowledge and a just appreciation of the gravity of the problem, they failed to appoint enough constables to grapple with it; second, being generally wealthy men, they were in a position to protect their own property and had little interest in protecting that of others, particularly the valuable property in transit through Cheshire on railways and canals; third, the Commission insisted that, whatever the position might have been in the past, the judicial and executive functions of the magistrates were constitutionally distinct and essentially incompatible. To these arguments the Commission added the further practical point that, as one police witness put it, the magistrates 'are of too high a station in life to be acquainted with the necessary technicalities connected with thief-taking'. At present, this witness pointed out, the ignorance of the unpaid constables made it necessary for the magistrates to supply their deficiencies by giving them instructions; but if a paid constabulary were to be set up the magistrates ought not to be put in the position of doubling the role of magistrates and superintendents of police.

The principal lesson which the Commission drew from the Cheshire experiment was consequently that the long association between the magistracy and the police ought finally to be brought to an end throughout the country. 'One of the first and most important steps in the improvements of the Metropolitan Police consisted in the separation of these functions . . . the completion of the separation is essential to the completion of the improvement. The demands of time requisite for the performance of the executive duties involved in the efficient superintendence of any well-regulated constabulary, which require an uninterrupted daily attention, are now so great as to be compatible only with the performance of the duties as a profession. ... The first and only important improvement of the Metropolitan Police consisted in its organisation upon a large scale, and in subjecting it to unity of action.'

Consistently with these radical views, the Commission seems to have had no difficulty in arriving at the conclusion that a single professional police force should be created for the rural areas on the same principles of training and management as had been applied to the Metropolitan Police. The Metropolitan Police Commissioners should regulate the force, under a code of rules approved by the Home Secretary. One-quarter of the cost should be borne by the Exchequer, and three-quarters should be met from county rates. The new force, numbering not more than one policeman for every 2,000 of the population, should not be imposed on the country by direct government action, but magistrates in quarter sessions should be empowered, by a majority vote, to apply to the Metropolitan Police Commissioners for an allotment of police to them. The magistrates should have power to dismiss officers found unsuitable. In effect, therefore, the Commission was recommending the extension of the successful experiment in London to the whole of the remainder of the country—including the boroughs, according to Chadwick's evidence to the Parliamentary Committee of 1853.

In reaching this conclusion (which, from the bias of many of the questions to witnesses, it seems probable they had reached at the outset), the Commission was also influenced by the belief that the strengthening of police forces in the towns had caused many criminals to migrate to rural areas. It is doubtful how far this belief was valid, and it has been authoritatively challenged in recent times.[16] That some criminals preferred to work outside London after the Metropolitan Police were established is beyond dispute, and it seems equally probable that police activity in those boroughs which were quick to set up efficient forces after 1835 drew criminals elsewhere, but how many of them found sufficient scope for business in rural areas is open to question. In any case, these rural areas had for many years suffered severely from crime, particularly that committed by migrant criminals. The Commission heard much evidence about criminality among vagrants, and cited instances of criminal careers which consisted of little more than an unending tramp from one market town to another according to a carefully worked-out programme based on the dates of annual fairs. It seems unlikely that the creation of urban police forces had much, if any, influence on this sort of activity. In the absence of statistical evidence (and the contemporary statistics are inaccurate and incomplete), it seems now impossible to establish what truth there may be in the migration theory, but the important point is that the Commission attached some weight to it: 'It is established as a conclusion to our minds, by satisfactory evidence, that in the greater proportion of these cases the migrant habits were formed long anterior to the establishment of any police in cities and towns. But it is also clearly shown in evidence that these habits of vagrancy have received a considerable impulse from the operation of the new police established in the provincial towns upon the principle of the Metropolitan Police.'

In the final paragraphs of its report this far-seeing Commission, so palpably influenced by Chadwick's inherited Utilitarianism, addressed itself to the risk that a centrally directed professional police force for England and Wales would endanger liberty. The Commission had no hesitation in declaring that it would not: 'The safe course for maintaining the freedom of the subject appears to us to be, not to render the authorities impotent, but to make them strictly responsible for the use of the power with which they may be invested for the public service. . . . The great mass of evil indicated in our Report is ascribable not to the abuse, but to the neglect and disuse of beneficial powers. The chief and proper objection, as we conceive, to the police forces abroad are, that they act on powers which are arbitrary: the force which we propose could only act on powers which are legal, and for which they would be responsible to the courts of law, and ultimately to the Parliament.' More than 100 years were to pass before the dangers of a national police force were again to be so succinctly dismissed: the Royal Commission on Police of 1960–2 employed remarkably similar language. After commenting that British liberty has never depended on the dispersal of police power, or indeed on any particular form of police organisation, it added: 'it depends on the supremacy of Parliament and on the rule of law'. It has been widely commented that this recent Royal Commission failed (with one dissentient) to pursue the logic of its findings, but it should be borne in mind that, while its recommendations were virtually all implemented by the Government within a couple of years, those of the 1839 Commission proved otiose—an illustration of the disadvantage, well appreciated by Peel in 1822, to which any inquiry lays itself open if it seeks to place itself too far ahead of contemporary opinion.

Chartism

The Commissioners signed their report at the end of March, 1839, and the spate of legislative activity which followed before the year was out must have astonished them, both because of its variety and volume, and also because it bore little relationship to their three years' task. As it transpired, the problems of the Birmingham, Manchester, and Bolton police forces (as well as those of the Metropolis and the City of London) were between them to occupy much more of Parliament's time than the few hours spent on debating rural police. The reason for this was the sudden rise of Chartism.

The demands of the Chartists, at the inception of the movement the year before, in 1838, were modest. It was, according to Trevelyan, 'A cry of rage and class-consciousness on the part of the suffering wage-earner';[17] in Carlyle's contemporary view, 'The bitter discontent grown fierce and mad, the wrong condition therefore or the wrong disposition, of the working classes of England. It is a new name for a thing which has had many names, which will yet have many . . . weighty, deep-rooted, far-extending. . . . Reform Ministry, constabulary rural police, new levy of soldiers, grants of money to Birmingham . . . all this will put down only the embodiment or "chimera" of chartism.'[18] The present concern is not with the nature of the movement, but with two of the means adopted by Russell's Government in 1839 to suppress it: the reform of the rural constabulary and, as Carlyle put it, the grants of money to Birmingham.

Chartism was quickly recognised as a direct challenge to constitutional authority, and a glance through the pages of the Home Office letter-book entitled *Disturbances*[19] for the anxious months of 1839, when the early idealism of the movement was already giving way to dangerous extremism, brings out vividly the Government's mounting concern. The idealism had an evangelical appeal which rapidly secured over a million adherents to the cause. To many, and especially to the new factory hands who lived and worked in squalor, the appeal was irresistible: 'that all shall have a good house to live in with a garden back and front, just as the occupier likes, good clothing to keep him warm and to make him look respectable, and plenty of good food and drink to make him look and feel happy'.[20] But militancy worked its way to the fore. Torchlight meetings were held secretly at night on the northern moors, and men were drilled and trained to force their demands, if necessary by bloodshed. In the face of the mounting threat, the Government had at their disposal only levies of troops scattered about the country, and the Metropolitan Police. The Home Secretary set up as a sort of general officer commanding home forces, ordering troops here and there as the threat developed in one area after another. Magistrates everywhere were told to swear in special constables to preserve the peace and to take full notes of all that passed at Chartist meetings; but if the civil force was inadequate, the Home Office advised them to apply for military assistance to the officer commanding troops in the nearest town. A Home Office circular issued in May undertook that the Department would supply arms to any 'principal inhabitants of a disturbed district' who wished to form an association to protect life and property. Where military resources were lacking, the Home Secretary himself directed troop movements. Early in April, for example, he was telling the Bath magistrates that he had decided 'to exercise the Military Force in the district of the principal manufacturing towns of Somersetshire, and have directed that an additional troop of cavalry be stationed in Frome'. The use of Metropolitan Police officers seems in general to have been confined to plain-clothes work. On April 16th the Home Office were refusing a request by the Cardigan magistrates for Metropolitan officers, advising them instead to apply to the officer commanding the troops at Brecon, but on the following day two Metropolitan men were promised to Colne at Government expense, 'for the purpose of procuring information as to the Drilling and Training and to assist the magistrates in bringing the offenders to Justice'. If, however, the magistrates wanted to keep the men for more than a fortnight they were to swear them in as special constables and meet the additional cost themselves.

The situation continued to deteriorate. A Royal Proclamation in May empowered magistrates 'to take the most prompt and effectual means for putting down and suppressing unlawful meetings'. Groups of law-abiding citizens, special constables, and Chelsea Pensioners were to be armed. The Home Office continued to move troops hither and thither. But as the summer wore on the insurrectionary spirit gained momentum throughout the country, particularly in the new, thickly populated manufacturing towns in the Midlands and North—areas largely untouched by the Municipal Corporations Act, whose only means of protection other than the military or the enrolment of special constables lay in the pitifully inadequate Improvement Act police, or bodies of night-watchmen provided by private subscription. It became increasingly evident that the Government lacked resources to deal with the situation. On July 20th Major-General Sir Charles Napier, the officer commanding the Northern District, wrote to the Home Secretary: 'My belief is that concession must be made to the people's feelings, or the establishment of a strong rural police hurried on. I would do both thinking them absolutely necessary; if the police force be not quickly increased we shall require troops from Ireland.'[21] Russell did not wait. He introduced his rural police Bill into Parliament four days later, on July 24th.

The County Police Bill, 1839

If the threat of Chartism provided the occasion for the Bill, political necessities dictated its form. Early in 1839, before the Royal Commission had reported, but aware, no doubt, of what it was about to recommend, the Home Secretary, Lord John Russell, was conducting his own canvass of the views of magistrates throughout the country as to the best means of organising a rural police force. About half supported a resolution by the Shropshire bench in favour of establishing 'a body of constables appointed by the magistrates, paid out of the county rate and disposable at any point of the shire where their services might be required'.[22] Thus the Bill which Russell introduced into the House of Commons on July 24th, 1839, was, from the magistrates' point of view, an admirable measure. Rejecting the Royal Commission's principal recommendation—there was to be no centralisation of police powers or interference with the powers of the magistrates—he explained the background to the Bill, and its limited scope, as follows:

The grounds which had made it 'incumbent on the Government not to lose any time in introducing some Bill on the subject' were 'the meetings which had lately taken place, and the riots and alarm consequent upon them', which had 'increased the demands for the military force'. These demands tended 'to break and destroy the discipline of the troops', and, moreover, the military, although competent in suppressing disorder, were useless in arresting the persons who had caused it—a task which only the police could discharge satisfactorily. As for the state of crime, he had been impressed by the evidence published by the Royal Commission, and was satisfied that the time had come to establish an efficient constabulary force in the counties, particularly in those areas already beginning to suffer from urban spread occasioned by the growth of mining and manufacturing industries, but which were not yet ready for the grant of municipal status. The local Acts which had authorised rural forces in various parts of the country were a cumbersome, costly, and ineffective way of proceeding. He therefore proposed a permissive measure by which the magistrates in quarter session should be empowered, but not required, to establish a police force, with the permission of the Home Secretary, either for the whole county or for any particular division of it. The number of constables was not to be in excess of one to every 1,000 of the population. All appointments were to be in the hands of the magistrates, and he was confident that with the advice of the Metropolitan Commissioners they would have no difficulty in selecting wisely.[23] The cost was to fall on the county, and the Bill gave the Home Secretary powers to make rules for the government and pay of the constables, and to approve the chief constable. Thus from the start the county constabularies were to be under greater Home Office authority than the borough forces. Where a county constabulary was formed the powers of improvement commissioners to employ watchmen and constables were to cease.

These cautious proposals were at once the subject of a vicious attack on party political grounds by Disraeli, who accused the Government of sinister motives in bringing in a Bill so late in the session that would effect 'a considerable civil revolution in the country'. Several Members supported the Bill, but others, taking their lead from Disraeli, insisted that the police would be regarded as nothing better than spies. Undeterred, the Home Secretary, winding up for the Government, confessed that he himself would have preferred 'one uniform system', but at present 'it was not easy to combine all the district forces under one head'. As to any suggestion that the Bill was unconstitutional or otherwise prompted by sinister motives, he pointed out that the same might easily have been said of Peel's Act of 1829, but he and several of his colleagues on the then Opposition benches had supported Peel. 'This should not be treated as a party question', he concluded, with an irony that events were shortly to demonstrate. Leave to introduce the Bill was granted. Peel duly voted with the Government, but Disraeli had the last word. Then thirty-five, he had been a Member for less than two years, and he chose to broaden his attack on the Bill into a characteristically caustic denunciation of the Government which had produced it, sparing no one, from Under-Secretaries of

State ('coarse, vulgar, and ill-bred') to the Chancellor of the Exchequer and the Government generally. ('How he became Chancellor of the Exchequer and how the Government to which he belonged became a government, it would be difficult to tell. Like flies in amber—one wondered how the devil they got there.')

In this eagerness on the part of some members of the Tory opposition to inject party political rancour into the debates on the Bill* is to be seen the reason why the Government approached the problem of reorganising the county constabularies so gingerly. It was politically out of the question to act on the Royal Commission's recommendation in favour of a centralised force. Normanby, who succeeded Russell as Home Secretary a few weeks later, confessed to a friend on October 1st, 1839: 'I think it is a serious and almost fatal error in the Bill that the new [Rural] Police is not more closely under the Government; this arises necessarily from our weakness for all legislative purposes.' The Government was in no position to engage in the bitter party controversy which would have resulted from any attempt to interfere with that bastion of the Tory aristocracy, the country magistrates. Thus the debates on police affairs during the last four weeks of the 1839 session of Parliament show beyond any shadow of doubt, and in a striking manner, that, whatever the needs of the country as a whole, the Government was able to enact strong enough laws to satisfy these needs only within the limits of practical politics.

The Birmingham Police Bill

For, as it happened, these debates were to range much more widely than the scope of Russell's rural police Bill alone would have permitted. The fear of Chartism, which had caused the Government to take precipitate action very late in the session with that measure, also led to three other police Bills being rushed through Parliament at the same time.

---

* A readiness shared by *The Times* two days later: 'With respect to Lord John Russell's "County and District new Constabulary Force" (the appellation of it is as long as a constable's staff) . . . the friends of the constitution are put into a great difficulty. If it be requisite, undoubtedly it should be granted. But whose and what counsels have rendered it requisite?' The Whig Government had created conditions in which life and property had to be protected 'by an apparatus which we have no question will be very injurious to public and general liberty and the free expression of opinion' (*The Times*, July 26th, 1839).

Earlier that same month, July, 1839, Birmingham had suffered a particularly severe outbreak of Chartist rioting and, there being no Birmingham police force,* the magistrates requested the loan of a strong contingent of Metropolitan Police officers. On this occasion the request was granted, and about 100 men arrived, who, having no jurisdiction outside London, were duly sworn in as special constables. They attempted to break up a noisy demonstration in the Bull Ring, clashed with the demonstrators, and suffered the worst of the affray, being rescued only by the intervention of the military. A second clash occurred a few days later, from which the policemen emerged victorious; and the Superintendent, thinking the worst over, ordered about half his force to return to London. The Chartists probably got wind of it. At all events, a third encounter between them and the police was not long in coming, and this time the police, only some forty strong, were driven into a yard, while the mob ran wild, burning and looting shops and warehouses. Finally, the police charged with drawn cutlasses, aided once more by the military, and again won the upper hand; but it had been an unadmirable episode, and the Birmingham magistrates were not alone in thinking that the intervention of London police had exacerbated any danger there might have been. Anxious and often heated debates took place on the following two days in both Houses of Parliament about the breakdown of law and order in the town, and the Duke of Wellington declared, with an eye to effect rather than truth, that 'he had been in many towns taken by storm, but never had such outrages occurred in them as had been committed in Birmingham'. Birmingham, it was evident, required a police force of its own; yet the Corporation was powerless to provide one.

For this, the credit belongs to the local Tories, particularly the magistracy. They had bitterly opposed the grant of a charter of incorporation to Birmingham; and when in 1838 a charter was granted notwithstanding, they viewed the newly elected Town Council

* The arrangements for policing Birmingham in 1839 were as follows. About thirty day-time street-keepers and 170 night-watchmen (who wore the usual hats and cloaks and carried lanterns and long staves) were appointed by Street Commissioners under Improvement Acts of 1769 to 1828. These men were sworn in as constables. In addition, the court leet appointed two constables who were men of some standing in the town, together with a headborough to assist them. The last official was also the prison keeper, and he was assisted by about half a dozen 'thief-takers'. He therefore seems to have been the nearest equivalent to a chief constable. To supplement these meagre resources in times of trouble, the justices enrolled special constables. (For this information I am indebted to the Chief Constable of Birmingham.)

as their natural enemies. Means had to be found to destroy it. All was at stake: the ancient privileges, local predominance, social superiority, and personal authority which the aristocracy and their forebears had exercised unchallenged for centuries. The rude, usurping middle-class councillors threatened everything, and their power to raise local rates gave a cutting edge to the authority with which they set out to govern the town and subdue its former rulers. So the Tories replied in the only way possible. They sought refuge in the law, alleging, on technical arguments, that the charter itself was invalid, and in particular that it gave no power to levy rates. Legal proceedings once launched, they were able to breathe more easily, confident in the law's delays to spin matters out; for until these proceedings were resolved the Corporation could find no money, and so were effectively prevented from exercising their newly conferred powers and duties, including the duty of a watch committee to maintain a police force. If round one had gone to the Whig Government which granted the charter a year earlier, the Tories had won round two; though the ordinary citizens of Birmingham, suffering daily outbreaks of vicious crime as well as occasional rioting, were sparing in applause.

But the Birmingham Town Council were in no mood to surrender. Alarmed by the Bull Ring riots, the Mayor applied to the Whig Home Secretary (Russell) for a loan of £10,000 to enable the town to establish a regular police force pending the outcome of litigation. The Government very properly showed their sympathy for Birmingham; and Russell accordingly moved in Parliament on July 23rd, 1839 (the day before the first debate on the County Police Bill), an urgent motion, to take precedence over the scheduled business of the House, to authorise an immediate loan for the purpose.[24] Peel, now leader of the Tory Party, assured his political opponent of support; and, thus encouraged, the Government promptly introduced a Bill which would enable the Town Council to maintain and control a police force. Round three therefore went to the Whigs.*

* The validity of the charters granted to Manchester and Bolton was similarly contested, and measures were also introduced into Parliament to enable these towns to create police forces pending the completion of legal proceedings. The struggle between the Manchester Town Council on the one hand and the Improvement Commissioners and manorial authorities on the other to maintain a police force, and a similar struggle in Bolton, are described in *Public Order in the Age of the Chartists*, by F. C. Mather (1959), pp. 119 *et seq.* A statement of the legal position was given to Parliament by the Attorney-General in the course of proceedings on the Manchester Police Bill (*Parliamentary Debates*, 3rd ser., Vol. L, August 9th, 1839, col. 140). A much simpler course would have been to promote legislation to establish

This harmless and much-needed Bill rapidly foundered in the political storm. While accepting the need for legislation, Peel had suggested that a preferable course might be a temporary measure enabling the Crown to appoint a Birmingham Police Commissioner, with equivalent status to the Metropolitan Commissioner, and having full control over a new police force, but he did not immediately press the proposal. The local Birmingham Tories, however, drew up a petition to the Queen to annul the charter, and at the same time persuaded Peel, as their national leader, to take steps in the House of Commons to thwart the Police Bill, since, if enacted in that form, the Bill would have formally recognised the Corporation as the body authorised by Parliament to maintain a police force, and thus have weakened the legal attack on the validity of the charter. Peel moved swiftly. Grasping political advantage as well, no doubt, as acting in what he conceived to be the interests of efficient policing, he contrived to persuade Russell, when the Bill entered the committee stage a week late (July 29th), to withdraw it and substitute a measure to vest control of a Birmingham police force, for a temporary period until litigation about the validity of the disputed charter had been resolved, in a Government police commissioner, thus putting the force on an exact par with the Metropolitan Police. The dominant party in Birmingham, Peel claimed, were Chartist sympathisers, and 'the country could not see with satisfaction Chartists and Political Unionists in situations where it was their duty to preserve the peace.'[25]

Probably Peel and Russell reached a private understanding: it is not without significance that Peel, in the same speech, undertook to support his opponent's County Police Bill. Russell may well have had his own misgivings at the prospect that the fiery Whig-controlled corporations of Birmingham and Manchester might operate their police forces in a manner sympathetic to the Chartists, and the idea of an impartial Government-controlled force to hold the ring until political passions subsided must have been attractive to him. At all events, he declared his support for Peel's alternative proposal and introduced the very much more radical Bill a few days later (August 2nd).

In this way the Tories, in round four, got in their knock-out blow. The alliance between political opponents was irresistible, and in the heated political atmosphere of the time the Birmingham Corporation,

---

beyond doubt the validity of the charters, and this was, in fact, adopted three years later by Peel's Tory government (The Charters (Confirmation) Act, 1842).

advanced radicals to a man, seethed with indignation that the Government they themselves supported should seemingly have entered into league with the Tories to grant the form of a charter while denying its substance, adding insult to injury by publicly branding them as unfit to control a police force. Indignant resolutions tumbled over one another, the town boiled with resentment, and the Corporation of the City of London loyally expressed sympathetic support. Birmingham, indeed, had just cause to complain; an urgent plea to the Government to grant a loan to enable them to fulfil their obligation to set up the police force the Government intended them to have, at first readily acceded to, had been converted almost overnight into a measure to impose a centralised force, for which the Birmingham ratepayer would have to find the whole cost. And the town's bitterness was replete in the knowledge that it was the leader of the Tories who had artfully persuaded their Government so to humiliate them. The Birmingham radicals leapt to what appeared to them the only possible conclusion: they were being punished for holding opinions more radical than those of the Government they supported. This view, however, was rapidly elevated into an issue of the highest constitutional importance. The Bill, declared the mover of one resolution of protest in the Town Council, 'was directly at variance with the principles of the constitution . . . ancient institutions were carried on upon the self-governing principle, and now it was proposed to impose upon them an absolute centralised despotism'; and the speaker concluded by expressing his 'abhorrence and disgust at this attempt to rob the people of their liberties'. The Town Clerk summed the feeling up in a letter to the Home Secretary: the Bill was 'insulting and despotic . . . as tending to that system of centralisation which every good Englishman must utterly abhor and abjure'.*

* *H.O.*, 40/50, letter of August 2nd, 1839. A full and fighting account of the affair, as seen through the eyes of the Birmingham Corporation, is given in Chapter X of the *History of the Corporation of Birmingham* (2 vols.), by J. T. Bunce, 1878, a work commissioned by the Town Council when Joseph Chamberlain was Mayor. Bunce proudly recalls the spirited 'political characteristics of the borough, and the antagonism between Liberal and Tory, and Nonconformist and Churchman, which had never wholly ceased since the Civil Wars, when Birmingham was mainly Puritan and anti-Royalist'. And now (writing in 1878) 'no words can express the depth of the animosity with which, according to the statements of the survivors of that period, the opposing parties regarded each other . . . private intercourse, and the exchange of the courtesies of social life, were mutually denied'.

The Police Bills of 1839 receive the Royal Assent

The ingredients of the Parliamentary debates on police during the last weeks of the 1839 session were thus well riddled with politics and inflamed by the burning issues of the time. Simultaneously, the House of Commons considered the timid proposals for rural policing and the highly contentious proposal to establish a Government-controlled force in Birmingham (and others on the same lines in Manchester and Bolton); and attention was switched daily from the one to the other, as Members once more came to grips with the great issues that had vexed the previous generation. There is little doubt that the attitude of some Members towards the County Police Bill was conditioned by what they now knew to be the Government's intentions for policing Birmingham—coupled with an uncomfortable recollection (occasionally referred to in the debates) that the much-overshadowed Royal Commission had recommended the appointment throughout the country of a police force under the authority of the Home Secretary. This, at all events, seems the only possible explanation of how one Member could bring himself to say of the County Police Bill that he was convinced that its object 'was not to preserve the peace, but to establish a tyranny'.[26]

Inevitably, the Birmingham Bill occupied very much more Parliamentary time, although the alliance between the front benches spared the Government embarrassment. The outraged Birmingham Members represented the only serious opposition, but the Government's comfortable majority was proof against their anger; and in the House of Lords the Bill received weighty support from the Duke of Wellington, as well as the Prime Minister, Melbourne. Together with the Manchester Police Bill (the Bolton Police Bill was a day behind), it received the Royal Assent on August 26th. It was a notable date; mixed as the motives on this occasion were, Parliament had provided for two more major police forces to be set up under the direct authority of the Home Secretary. The Birmingham Police Act declared that, as questions were pending as to the powers of the Town Council to levy rates, the Crown was empowered to establish a Police Office and appoint a Chief Commissioner of Police, who would be a justice of the peace. By the directions of the Secretary of State, he was to appoint a sufficient number of fit and able men as a police force, and during the continuance of the Act (three years) all the powers of the Metropolitan Police Act were to apply to Birmingham. The money

85

lent by the Treasury for police purposes was to be repaid from the rates. 'It was a document', writes Birmingham Corporation's historian, 'which, even after the lapse of nearly forty years, no Birmingham man can look back upon without a feeling of shame and indignation, and an ineradicable sense of wrong.'*

The Government's thinking about the right role for the police in the State, as a body subject ultimately to the control of the Home Secretary, had emerged clearly enough in the course of these spirited debates. Perversely, Disraeli, who had taken no part in them, reserved his fire for the less contentious County Police Bill, which he continued to condemn as dangerous and unnecessary. Crime, he declared as 'an incontestable fact', had diminished during the last twenty years, and the credit must go to 'the old system of constabulary' that there was 'as little crime in the rural districts of England as in any country in the world'.[28] Finally, when the Bill came up for its Third Reading in the House of Commons, he divided the House on it. What was to become of the celebrated national dogma that every Englishman's house was his castle if rural policemen were allowed to pry into people's homes? Shrewdly adverting for the first time to the Birmingham Bill, he summed up in a few sentences the Government's motives: 'The Birmingham Police Bill, on its introduction, was founded on a popular principle; in a very few days that was changed, and the principle of centralisation adopted. The present Bill was founded on a report which recommended centralisation. When he saw that the Government adopted that principle with avidity when they were sure of a majority to carry it, and gave it up only when they could not induce the House to agree with them, it was quite clear to him that the principle on which they were proceeding was that of centralisation and which, he believed, would be fatal to the liberties of the country.'[29]

The County Police Bill received the Royal Assent on August 27th, 1839 (the day after the Birmingham Bill), and on the same day Queen Victoria was moved to express, in her Prorogation speech, her

* Bunce, *op. cit.* p. 199. The Act was repealed in October, 1842, when control of the police was transferred to the Watch Committee. By that time Peel had formed a Government, and the story receives its final ironic twist from the fact that it was this Tory Government which both sponsored legislation to confirm the validity of the disputed charters and also promoted legislation to vest control of the police in the Corporation's Watch Committee. But the transfer of control opened up new hazards: 'Many of the constables have an idea that the police force is shortly to fall into the power of the local authorities', the Commissioner of the Manchester Police told the Home Office in 1842, 'and consequently are inclined to mix themselves with the borough politics of the day.'[27]

satisfaction with what had been achieved during the last arduous month of the session: 'I have given a cordial assent to the Bills which you have presented to me for the establishment of a more efficient constabulary force in those towns which peculiarly required it, and for effecting the important object of generally extending and invigorating the civil power throughout the country.' On August 31st Russell asked the Metropolitan Police Commissioners to draft the first constabulary rules,[30] and in the meantime he had appointed police commissioners in Birmingham, Manchester, and Bolton. In Bolton the experiment was not a success, but the Birmingham and Manchester forces, each well over 300 strong (the Manchester force, however, contained 'a very liberal proportion' of the Improvement commissioners' watchmen), were soon well established on the principles of the Metropolitan Police. On November 11th the Birmingham Commissioner, Francis Burgess, who had fought as a captain at the Battle of Waterloo, wrote a conciliatory letter to the Mayor of Birmingham expressing the hope that 'whatever may have been the difference of opinion in respect of this Act in its progress through Parliament . . . we may cordially unite in carrying into effect its objects and provisions'.[31] The skill of the police in crowd control, together with the successful efforts made by the commissioners in overcoming opposition, and even in winning over the confidence of Chartist sympathisers by their manifest impartiality, testified to the success of the experiment; and by the late autumn Burgess was reporting regularly to the Home Office on the state of order in the town and drawing from the Home Office the lessons of bitter experience elsewhere: 'With respect to the employment of spies or informers', the Home Office told him on November 22nd, 'let me assure you it is the most difficult and dangerous thing to manage, and generally ends in nothing but disappointment. If the fact of your employing a spy is known to any living being excepting to you and the spy himself success is hopeless.'[32]

These stirring but little-known events have been described at some length because they vividly illustrate the manner in which the arrangements for policing, ever the most sensitive of local government functions, were, at the time we are considering, totally subordinated to contemporary social and political currents. It is, of course, arguable that political considerations ought to be the prime influence in matters of this kind, for that is what Parliamentary democracy is about. On the other hand, it is undeniable that the merits of great public issues are frequently obscured by political overtones; and the Birmingham episode provides a notable instance of the way in which the arrangements for policing this country were determined, in the early stages, by a combination of far-sightedness and political realism that defeat any attempt to explain them in logical terms. The readiness of Parliament in 1829 to create a Metropolitan police force under the authority of the Home Secretary, and its manifest success, encouraged a Royal Commission, ten years later, to propose the same system for the counties of England and Wales. The leaders of both the political parties in the House of Commons made no secret of their sympathy with the recommendation. Nevertheless, they judged the political climate unsuitable for anything more radical than the permissive Act, setting their faces against centralisation. Birmingham, however, was a different matter, and here the expediency of politics, coupled with misgivings about the wisdom of allowing a notoriously radical town council to have control of its own police at a time of political tension, led to the opposite result. The merits of one form of policing or another, it is clear, had little chance to be heard amid the welter of acrimonious debate.

Early effects of the County Police Act

The Home Office *County Constabulary* letter-book from October, 1839, to May, 1840,[33] shows the Home Office to have been active in helping magistrates all over the country who desired to avail themselves of the County Police Act to get their new forces off to a good start. Innumerable queries were answered, and Lord Normanby (who succeeded Russell as Home Secretary at the end of August, 1839) circulated his new regulations to all who cared to ask for them. Lancashire magistrates were told that he would not sanction the employment of two illiterate recruits, as the Home Secretary considered 'the ability to read and write so essentially necessary to the proper performance of a constable's duties';[34] and several inquirers were promised the help of relatively junior Metropolitan policemen to organise their forces—although the Metropolitan Police commissioners were soon protesting to the Home Office about the effect on the force of so many successive raids on their manpower, and the Home Secretary himself was insisting that 'he ought not to lay upon the Metropolitan Police Commissioners the responsibility (as they consider it) of recommending persons' to the situation of chief constable.[35]

The principal results of the permissive Act were seen in the first two years after it was passed. Of the fifty-six* counties in England and Wales, eight adopted the Act in 1839, twelve in 1840 and four more in 1841—a total of twenty-four counties.[36] These figures, however, need to be treated with reserve, for the magistrates in four of the counties initially adopted the Act in one or more divisions only: in Cumberland, for example, the 'force', confined to the Derwent division, comprised only one superintendent and three men for many years, and in Staffordshire a force of twenty men operated in the southern part of the county only until the formation of the county constabulary proper in 1843. Limited as this early action was, however, it is clear that the impetus of the Act had been spent by the end of 1841, and from this time onwards a growing body of opinion all over the country was complaining about the cost of rural policing. As a result, during the next fifteen years, until county forces were made obligatory in 1856, only four more counties adopted the Act.†

* i.e. counting Suffolk and Sussex as two each, Yorkshire as three, Lincolnshire as one, and excluding the Liberty of Peterborough.

† The following dates of origin of county police forces have been extracted from *Returns of Police Established in Each County or Division of a County in England and Wales under the Acts 3 Vict., c. 93 and 3 & 4 Vict. c. 88, 1842, P.P.,* XXXII, from Table VII of the appendix to the report of the Select Committee on Police Superannuation Funds, 1877, *P.P.,* XV, and from the first inspection reports of the inspectors of constabulary for 1856–7. There is some disparity between these sources, and yet further disparity between them and evidence given to the Select Committee of 1853 (Qus. 7–9). The list is therefore offered tentatively. An asterisk denotes adoption of the Acts for only parts of the county at the date of origin of the forces; some of these were little more than token forces at the start. Some of the counties shown under 1856–7 had, similarly, employed a few paid policemen some years earlier.

1839   Durham, Essex, Gloucestershire, Hampshire, Lancashire, Leicestershire, Wiltshire, Worcestershire.

1840   Bedford, *Cumberland, Denbighshire, Montgomery, Norfolk, Northamptonshire, Nottinghamshire, Shropshire, *Staffordshire, Suffolk (East), Sussex (East), *Warwickshire.

1841   Glamorgan (?1840), *Herefordshire, Hertfordshire, Isle of Ely.

1844   Cardiganshire.

1849   Rutland (1 man only).

1851   Cambridgeshire, Surrey.

1856–7   Berkshire, Buckinghamshire, Cheshire, Cornwall, Derbyshire, Devonshire, Dorsetshire, Huntingdonshire, Kent, Lincoln, Northumberland, Oxfordshire, Somersetshire, Suffolk (West) (?1840), Sussex (West), Westmorland, Yorkshire (East Riding), Yorkshire (North Riding), Yorkshire (West Riding).
Anglesey, Brecknockshire, Carmarthenshire, Carnarvonshire, Flintshire, Merionethshire, Monmouthshire, Pembrokeshire, Radnorshire.

Thus, outside London two different systems of policing existed for some years side by side. In some rural areas, as in a few large boroughs, the new professional police were well entrenched, but tens of thousands of acres of rural England continued to rely on the old system of parish constables, augmented here and there by a paid watchman or two, employed under the Lighting and Watching Act, or local improvement powers.

Dealing with this period, Melville Lee, in a frequently quoted passage, has commented that 'Between 1840 and 1856 the history of rural police divides into two branches: in the counties which adopted the Permissive Act, the record is one of almost constant progress towards efficiency; in the counties which preferred to prolong the defective régime of the parish constable, the story is largely one of stagnation, unnecessary friction, and weak-kneed experiment'.[37] This is something of an over-simplification. The criticism of the un-progressive counties is valid, but the suggestion that the counties which adopted the Act of 1839 were soon efficiently policed overlooks several facts. In the first place, some counties (notably Lancashire) which had been quick off the mark to set up a police force as a means of dealing with industrial unrest, substantially reduced the size of the force when the threat of riots diminished. In the second place, several counties made only a token acceptance of the Act. Third, the new arrangements did not bring the parish constable system to an end, even in the enlightened counties, although it is true that the obligation to serve which lay at its root was increasingly disregarded.* And, finally, while the Act of 1839 automatically extinguished the pockets of local Improvement Act police in any county which adopted it, the tiny borough forces which the Municipal Corporations Act had willed on small boroughs were left intact; nor did the Act interfere with any little parish police 'forces' set up under the Lighting and Watching Act. It is indisputable, looking back, that a more satis-factory police pattern would have emerged had the counties been dealt with before, rather than after, the boroughs. As it was, the new county forces were blotched and weakened by these little urban patches in which they had no authority to exercise police powers, and where criminals could congregate with impunity.

The Government made an attempt to deal with these anomalies. Within a year of the enactment of the permissive Act, a second rural

---

* That there was still life in the old constabulary as late as 1857 is evidenced by a parish constable who arrested a drunken member of the new police in Dorset that year.

constabulary Act of 1840[38] declared that any police force constituted under the Lighting and Watching Act should be discontinued upon the chief constable of the county undertaking the charge of the district. The borough forces, even the smallest of them, were spared, but the Act optimistically provided for the consolidation of borough and county police by mutual agreement. The second rural Act also made a shrewd move to overcome the powerful opposition of the landed gentry to the formation of a county constabulary on grounds of expense, by enabling the justices (subject to the control of the Home Secretary) to form separate police districts in the county, so that people who wanted more police protection than their neighbours could provide themselves with it at their own expense by raising a separate police rate. Thus the wealthy and heavily rated landowner in the quiet rural part of a county need not bear the cost of policing the rapidly growing industrial areas, where the danger of riot and renewed Chartist activity was endemic. This principle proved popular in Lancashire, Staffordshire, and Shropshire—counties where the new manufacturing districts were fairly well separated from the rural areas. When the Staffordshire Constabulary was set up in 1843, for example (pp. 94–7) the county was divided into three districts; the pottery district (which bore the brunt of Chartist rioting the year before) paid a 5*d*. rate, the mining district 3*d*., and the rural district 1*d*.[39]

These well-intentioned afterthoughts, offered as further inducements to better policing, proved, however, of limited value. By the early 1840s only a minority of the counties had established police forces, and there was mounting scepticism about their value. Local ratepayers were up in arms about the cost,* and where it was realised that the new county force meant the end of the little bodies of watchmen and constables set up under Improvement Acts, improvement commissioners joined in the chorus of protest. 'The conduct of those

---

* A typical resolution declared: 'perfectly aware of the depressed state of agriculture, [the Magistrates] are adverse to imposing any heavy additional burden upon the Yeomanry and Industrious population of the County until they receive such information as shall clearly demonstrate the impossibility of preserving the peace and security without the introduction of the expensive agency of a Rural Police' (quoted in the *History of the Pembrokeshire Police Force*, by R. W. Jones, p. 8). A petition from the inhabitants of Kesteven in March, 1840, declared: 'A PAID police would cause a separation of the people. . . . 'It was 'a system which tends to break the link of society, and to destroy that chain of good NEIGHBOURHOOD upon which our glorious Constitution was founded, and by which it was carried into effect by King Alfred' (*Lincolnshire Constabulary, 1857–1957*).

persons who have been instrumental in bringing [the county police] into operation is highly censurable', complained the Police Commissioners of Rochdale in 1841, after the formation of the Lancashire Constabulary. 'They have thereby incurred an additional expense of several hundred pounds a year at a time when the poor ratepayers are not half fed and many of them absolutely starving from the want of the common necessaries of life.'[40]

In fostering this resistance, and in encouraging a spirit of reaction, few voices could have been more influential than that of *The Times*. 'We perceive with great satisfaction', a leader declared early in 1842, 'that a strong feeling is gaining ground in different parts of the country, and in most respectable quarters, against the continuance of the Rural Police System.' The writer recalled with satisfaction the newspaper's years of ardent opposition to the Act of 1839: 'We have assigned it a prominent place in the catalogue of those despotic and unconstitutional measures which alienated from the Whigs the affections of the middle classes of England. . . . It is now but a few weeks since an attempt was made to introduce the system into the West Riding of Yorkshire, which signally failed. Later still it was repudiated after trial by the gentlemen of Nottinghamshire.' The system was objectionable on grounds of its 'inutility and expense', but even more as an instrument capable of being used 'for the purposes of arbitrary aggression upon the liberties of the people'.[41]

New life for the old constabulary

The Government dealt with this situation by means of an Act of Parliament which has been widely criticised, yet against the flood tide of hostility to any extension of regular rural policing there was evident political sense in the option they now offered—a compromise well described by Maitland as 'a gallant effort to put new life into the old constabulary'.[42]

The Parish Constables Act of 1842[43] was an Act for all seasons, containing something for everybody involved in the police dispute. It legalised almost everything that had been tried before. The obligation of each community to police itself was once more reaffimed by a requirement that justices were to hold special sessions for the purpose of compiling lists of fit men between the ages of twenty-five and fifty-five, all to be ratepayers of good character (with privileged exceptions for peers, Members of Parliament, professional men and a few others), who were to be sworn in as parish constables. Thus the principle of universal obligation to serve was given a last brief lease of life. So also was the old practice of paying substitutes belatedly legalised. But the twilight of the old discredited ideas was recognised too, and power was given to parish vestries to appoint paid constables as an alternative to relying on amateurs. Finally, in its most important provisions, the Act made a bow towards the new professionalism by creating a novel type of stipendiary police officer to be known as a superintending constable. He was to be paid from the county rate and was to have control over the parish constables in his petty sessional division. Thus the effect of the Act was to graft a measure of optional professionalism on to the old amateur system.

This curiously contrived hybrid was popular, because on the face of it the Act offered a compromise system of rural policing which looked like being much cheaper than the creation of a full-time county constabulary under the Act of 1839. Some counties looked to it for relief from a costly experiment they now regretted. Thus in Glamorgan, only two years after the formation of a county constabulary, 3,000 ratepayers petitioned the magistrates for the abolition of the force on the grounds of their preference for the new Parish Constables Act, which was less costly.[44] The Glamorgan justices, however, were more far-seeing, and kept their force intact. Elsewhere counties which had not adopted the Act of 1839 advertised for superintending constables, and a number of police officers from the Metropolitan Police and a few other organised constabularies were taken on at salaries of from £80 to £150 a year. Some must have been astonished to find themselves placed under the authority, not only of the justices, but also of the archaic high constables of the hundred.[45] All agreed, in giving evidence to a select committee of Parliament a few years later, that the experiment was a total failure.* There is

* Select Committee on Police, 1853, *P.P.*, XXXVI, Session 1852–3: Evidence of J. Dunne, Chief Constable of Norwich, and formerly Superintending Constable in Kent, W. Hamilton, Superintending Constable of Buckinghamshire, and D. Smith, Superintending Constable of Oxfordshire, who had served for ten years in the Essex Constabulary. Smith maintained that half a dozen regular policemen from Essex 'would be equal to the 70 parish constables now under me' (Qn. 3,672). By 1853 fourteen of the counties which had not by then adopted the Act of 1839 were employing superintending constables. They included Pembrokeshire, whose resolution in opposition to a regular constabulary is quoted in the footnote on p. 91. A useful description of the system may be found in the *History of the Pembrokeshire Police Force*, together with a list of the articles of clothing and equipment with which superintending constables were provided. Appendix 4 to the *History of the Anglesey Constabulary* sets out *in extenso* the regulations for the superintending constables in that county.

little evidence that the able-bodied ratepayers contemplated by the Act were ever sworn in (though as late as 1855 forty-five men seem to have been sworn in to meet an emergency in Swansea), and the superintending constables usually found themselves left with only the old parish constables to superintend. No assertion of authority could teach illiterate parish constables to read, or persuade the cobbler or baker or farm-labourer to abandon his work and lose money by undertaking police duty for the small fees to which he was entitled. The system of fees still precluded poorer people from employing constables to capture thieves who had robbed them. The system favoured the rich, and there was even some evidence that, overall, it could actually be more expensive than a regular constabulary. Moreover, the superintending constables were usually unable, in practice, to supervise the wide areas they were expected to cover; and if, in exasperation, they were to report a parish constable to the justices as inefficient, the justices had no powers of correction. Thus the whole system, lacking any effective central control or discipline, was a failure from the start, and it was left for outside pressures to give the only further fillip to lasting reform in at least one county in 1842, just as they had done in 1839; the principal cause, as then, was Chartism.

Renewed influence of Chartism

Late in 1839 the movement had received a severe check when, plans for widespread military insurrection being then far advanced, a column of armed miners was engaged in battle by troops concealed in the Westgate Hotel, Newport. There were numerous casualties, the leaders were arrested, and the movement was forced underground. Deteriorating economic conditions during the next two years, however, exacerbated the bitterness of the working classes and led to a resurgence of Chartism. Early in 1842 more than 3 million people, over half the adult male population, are said to have signed the Chartists' petition.[46] Widespread strikes followed, and wherever police were lacking the old remedies were again called into play. One such area, still pitifully vulnerable to mob violence, was Staffordshire. The magistrates of the southern hundred of the county had adopted the County Police Act, 1839, by providing a force of twenty men; but the northern Potteries district was totally unprotected, and from the Home Office papers in the Public Record Office it is possible to trace the precise steps by which this renewed Chartist activity directly paved the way to the creation of a major county constabulary. The circumstances also illustrate the obduracy with which some county magistrates still clung to the old parochial constable system, discredited as that system was.

From all the mayors and magistrates of the pottery and mining districts a series of increasingly alarming reports poured into the Home office during July and August, 1842. Placards announcing giant demonstrations were enclosed with anxious letters reporting the swearing-in of vast numbers of special constables, and stressing again and again the people's utter dependence for protection on the troops now being moved into the district. A Potteries Police Act of 1839 had empowered the appointment of a superintendent to cover several districts, but no appointment had been made, and the few town watchmen and parish constables were wholly irrelevant to the massive threat which was developing all over the northern counties and the Midlands.[47] Indeed, evidence was mounting that the county faced armed insurrection, as news came flooding into Whitehall from Burslem, Dudley, Bilston, Stoke, Wolverhampton, and Walsall of the menacing bearing of colliers and unemployed. The magistrates' counsels were divided. The Home Secretary offered to send a contingent of the Metropolitan Police, but the offer was declined.[48] Nevertheless, on July 28th, a group of Newcastle magistrates requested that two men be sent; others, on the following day, countermanded the request. The Home Secretary, who had already sent the men, expressed his displeasure, and was told that the resistance to accept Metropolitan Police in the district stemmed from the Police Commissioners of Burslem, i.e. commissioners set up under a local Improvement Act. The Commissioners, it transpired, held police in low esteem, for on August 11th they passed a resolution (their honorary Chief Constable being in the chair) declaring that 'the present police forces of the different Townships is wholly inefficient' to deal with 'the very alarming Riots', and that any police force formed under the 'General Constabulary Act would be alike inadequate unless supported by a permanent military force'. This was the universal opinion. Copies of a privately printed Chartist newspaper, *The Commonwealthsman*, were seized and sent to the Home Office as evidence of 'the supineness and inefficiency of the police', in not being vigilant enough to notice 'papers containing scandalous and seditious matters'[49]; and no one, except the Home Office, seems to have thought the creation of a constabulary force would be of the slightest avail.

Instead, all hopes for relief centred on the strong detachments of troops which had now been stationed in the area for some weeks, and the belief gained ground that the Home Secretary would allow them to remain indefinitely. The Vice-Lieutenant of Staffordshire, the Earl of Dartmouth, took personal charge of the situation, keeping the Home Office informed (on expensive gilt-edged notepaper that contrasts starkly with the crude intercepted notes of the Chartists—or were they forgeries?) of his direction of troop movements. On August 22nd ammunition was required 'for the two two-pounder guns and for the muskets kept in Stafford County gaol', and he was seeking 'cannon shot and ball cartridges' from Government stores. More than 2,000 special constables had been sworn in, including Chelsea Pensioners. But there was a strong feeling, which found expression in town resolutions, that, willing as men were 'to act in their civil capacity . . . unless supported by a military force the weapons with which they are armed will be totally ineffective against a mob, which carries not only weapons of the same kind more effective, but Fire Arms also'.[50] The troops therefore continued to stand by.

But protests soon began to arrive from the soldiers, and now the Staffordshire magistrates were under a double pressure—from the military, who wished to withdraw the troops, and from the Home Secretary, who was insisting on the need for a proper police force to take their place. Early in September the Lord-Lieutenant was told in response to feelers that the Home Secretary could hold out no promise of stationing a permanent military force in the Potteries 'as would render unnecessary an efficient police in that district'. It was desirable that 'immediate steps should be taken to institute such a force', and attention was called both to the Rural Police Act of 1839 and to the recently enacted Parish Constables Act.[51] At about the same time the Colonel commanding the Midland district was complaining that it was 'highly objectionable and very injurious to discipline' to continue to billet troops in the area. The threat of their withdrawal caused consternation. The Newcastle-under-Lyme magistrates set about maintaining their own troops, having secured promises of contributions from local residents totalling £500 to fit up a temporary barrack. If the Home Secretary would undertake to keep a military force in the district during the winter, they wrote on September 16th, 'an extended subscription will be speedily obtained'. This proposal, with its clear indication of the lengths to which the magistrates were prepared to go to avoid creating a regular police force, brought matters to a head. 'I can give no pledge,' the Home Secretary replied,

'that any given amount of Military Force will be maintained permanently in any one particular place: but I can say that I will not allow
the Troops to remain for any length of time in Billets: and that unless
an adequate Police Force be provided in the Potteries, the military
must be withdrawn, since they cannot be allowed to supply the place
of constables.' The answer came at once: 'Thirteen Magistrates of the
County have given Notice that at the next Quarter Sessions they will
move for the adoption of the Act for the establishment of County and
District Constables in the County of Stafford.'[52] A force several
hundred strong was established a few months later.

Relapse into laissez faire

A certain nonchalant opportunism seems to have characterised the
attitude of the Home Office towards police affairs during the 1840s.
The superintending constable system introduced in 1842 was an
ingenious but backward-looking attempt to offer policing on the
cheap, and as the events that led to the establishment of the Staffordshire Constabulary show, there was a readiness to advocate the use of
police rather than troops for the suppression of riots. On the other
hand, no pressure seems to have been brought to bear on counties
still largely untroubled by industrial unrest, nor were any means
available, even if there had been the will, to coerce the smaller
boroughs into establishing efficient police forces themselves or to
consolidate with their neighbours under the Act of 1840. Public spirit
and private incentive were equally lacking, and as a result the momentum generated by the reforms of the previous decade lapsed.

One result of this state of affairs was to leave the Home Office to
act, in default of any other co-ordinating agency, as a kind of
clearing-house for much major crime, and magistrates throughout the
country looked to Whitehall for assistance. Applications for the
Government to offer substantial rewards for the apprehension of
murderers were commonly granted, and on at least one occasion the
Home Secretary publicly announced his intention of recommending a
free pardon to any accomplice who (not having himself fired the shot)
gave information that led to the arrest of a man wanted for the
murder of a policeman by shooting.[53] The extent of Home Office
involvement is illustrated by a case in 1836, in which the Home Office
received from the Admiralty a confession written on board ship from
a man named Armstrong to the effect that he had been the accomplice

in a murder in South Shields of a man subsequently hung in chains. Today such a document would be handed over to the police as a matter of course. At that time the Home Secretary sent a copy of the confession to the South Shields magistrates, kept the original, and when the ship on which Armstrong was serving reached Portsmouth requested the magistrates to send someone capable of identifying the prisoner. 'Lord John Russell', the Home Office wrote, 'will provide for the payment of the Coach hire there and back and for the personal Expenses of such person at the rate of seven shillings per day, not exceeding, eight days.' The magistrates were to report the outcome, so that 'his Lordship may be enabled to judge whether any and what further proceedings should be adopted by Government'.[54]

This day-to-day concern with individual cases, rather than with any attempt to formulate constructive policies, occupied the slender resources of the Home Office for much of the decade, and under the doctrine of *laissez faire* the police system, such as it was, grew or dwindled according to local inclination. The Home Office was content to see nothing, hear nothing, and do nothing—unless correspondence came its way, and then it did as little as possible. Lord Normanby, who succeeded Russell as Home Secretary in 1839, had made regulations under the County Police Act of that year, and these were sent out to any county magistrates who expressed interest in setting up a constabulary, great care subsequently being taken to ensure that Lord Normanby's regulations were strictly observed. The county of Surrey continued to rely on the old parochial constable system until as late as 1850, when a particularly brutal murder of a clergyman at Frimley suddenly mobilised public support for a police force. The magistrates passed a unanimous resolution to set it up, and sought the Home Secretary's approval 'with the least possible delay', but the only immediate reaction of the Home Office was to observe that the magistrates proposed to pay the inspector less than the annual £65 prescribed by the regulations. The point was referred—as most correspondence was—to the Home Secretary personally, but Sir George Grey, who then held the office, took a broader view. 'Why is it necessary to insist on £65 for an Inspector? If competent persons can be obtained for a lower salary I've no ground for compelling the county to pay a higher, especially now that the price of provisions is lower than it was.' Similar difficulties arose about the prescribed maximum age of chief constables on appointment. Lord Normanby's regulations laid it down at forty-five, but outstanding older candidates presented themselves from time to time, and the Home Secretary made

98

a number of exceptions to the rule. When in the autumn of 1851 the Cambridgeshire magistrates resolved to create a county constabulary ('the Justices are desirous of having the benefit of the Force before the winter', they told the Home Secretary on October 16th), approval was given to the appointment of a chief constable of forty-nine. As the rule had been relaxed before, the Home Secretary minuted, it might be again, adding that he did not know what the rule was. It is, indeed, characteristic of the lackadaisical attitude to administration at the time that no one thought of altering the regulations in the light of experience, and no one was troubled that the legality of the appointments might be in question, until the Home Secretary himself expressed misgivings about a candidate in West Suffolk who was fifty-one: 'I think it is important that the gentlemen unqualified according to the existing regulations for the office of chief constable should not be admitted as candidates for such appointments, and I doubt whether it was intended that the Secretary of State should exercise a discretionary power in the case of the chief constable.' The power was, however, duly exercised.[55]

But it would be unfair to blame the Home Office, and in particular Sir George Grey (who occupied the office of Home Secretary for no less than fourteen years between 1846 and 1866, in the course of which he displayed great ability, kindliness, and compassion, and secured the enactment of the County and Borough Police Act, 1856), for displaying a *laissez-faire* attitude that did no more than reflect the spirit of the age. Moreover, when energetic measures were required they were taken. It must not be forgotten that, at the very time when the Home Secretary was standing so aloof from police affairs outside London, he was in day-to-day touch with the Metropolitan Police; and when in 1848 the Chartists made what was to be their final large-scale threat, this time in London itself, Sir George Grey took personal command of the situation. It seemed desperate enough, for 1848 was the year of revolutions throughout Europe, and the Chartists, invigorated by the general excitement, planned a mass demonstration on Kennington Common designed to intimidate Parliament itself. The horrors of the Gordon Riots seemed about to be repeated. The Duke of Wellington ordered troops to London and took command of them himself (at the age of eighty); but the troops were not wanted. When the day came, April 10th, the Metropolitan Police, supported by no fewer than 200,000 special constables, preserved the peace. The Commissioner persuaded the Chartists' leader, Feargus O'Connor, that the police firmly held Westminster

Bridge, and the demonstrators quietly dispersed from the south bank.* With the disappearance of this last threat of armed insurrection the tempo of life in the Home Office was once more adjusted to the less exacting demands of administering Lord Normanby's regulations, and the cause of police reform, lacking the spur of necessity, languished for another four years.

* Superintendent Mallalieu, of 'R' Division, told the Select Committee of 1853 that he had attended every riot in London since the time of the Reform Bill riots, including the Chartist demonstration in 1848, and 'the military have never been called out since the establishment of the police force; we have never felt the slightest doubt of being able to preserve the peace' (*P.P.*, XXXVI, Session 1852–3, Qn. 2,832).

Chapter Four

Consolidation of the Nineteenth-Century Police System 1853-88

The achievement of the first half of the nineteenth century was the establishment of the prototype Metropolitan Police and the provision of means for creating similar local forces elsewhere; the achievement of the second was to consolidate a police system throughout the country by arming the Home Secretary with coercive powers to raise local standards uniformly. In this way, some thirty years after Peel established the Metropolitan Police, a nation-wide system came into being, a congeries of parts rather than a whole, which nevertheless seems to have been adequate for the needs of the time. Moreover, the principle of reconciling central supervision with local management outside London, which gave the evolving system its characteristically English form, struck a balance so nicely adjusted to the British genius that it survived with little correction until the middle of the twentieth century. In policing the country, as in many other branches of public affairs, the Victorians builded better than they knew.

Palmerston's reforming influence

The stagnant decade, arid in ideas and bankrupt of policy, came to an abrupt end when Palmerston arrived at the Home Office in December, 1852, having fallen out badly, as Foreign Secretary, with Queen Victoria. Whig by conviction and Tory by temperament (the converse of Peel), he was at the height of his power and popularity, the outstanding period at the Foreign Office just completed, the Premiership two years off. His correspondence shows that his heart was still in foreign affairs, but he told his brother-in-law that he chose the Home Office for its concern with the lives of ordinary people; and for a period of two years he was able to concentrate some part at least of his ebullient genius on the task of police reform. It would no doubt be more accurate to say that his abundant energies flowed out towards domestic reform despite himself rather than to regard Palmerston as a natural reformer. At all events he contrived, for a year or two, to galvanise the department into a show of life.*

He was not wholly unaware of what needed to be done. Living at Broadlands in Hampshire, he had headed those who presented a memorial to the Romsey Watch Committee urging the amalgamation of the police force with that of the county, only to be defeated by the efforts of local publicans and tradesmen, who feared the loss of their livelihood and even liberty at the hands of the county police.[1] This experience no doubt left its mark. And then, within three weeks of becoming Home Secretary, a Devonshire landowner drew his attention to happy-go-lucky arrangements that still survived in many of the counties. The letter,[2] with its display of enlightened self-interest, is worth quoting in full:

'*Private* 　　　　　　　　　　　　　'Castle Hill.
　　　　　　　　　　　　　　　　　　'January 17th, 1853.

'My Dear Palmerston,

'Your unvarying kindness to me, and the opinion which I have of your clear and sound views in all matters connected with your Department, encourage me to invite your attention to the miserably defective state of the rural police of England.

'You are aware that throughout the rural districts generally the only existing machinery for the detection of crime and the apprehension of criminals consists of one or more constables according to the size of the parish, selected annually by the overseers from among the resident householders and appointed and sworn in by the magistrates at petty Sessions.

'In some counties the Justices at quarter Sessions under the power given them by the Act of W. 4th have established a paid Constabulary, but they are rare exceptions to the general practice, and the stricter administration of the law in those counties, and generally in the towns (all of which now have their regular policemen) naturally have the effect of throwing the offending classes in larger numbers on more [? isolated] districts.

'True it is that even in them crimes of deep dye, especially those accompanied with violence or bloodshed, do not often escape

---

* Palmerston's biographers all seem to have ignored his contribution to police reform, although he is credited with introducing the convict ticket-of-leave system, improving London drainage, dealing with smoke-abatement, and other useful measures.

102

detection, because happily throughout England every man's hand is against the perpetrators of such acts, but that is by no means the case with respect to all kinds of petty depredations or even to sheep-stealing which not only are carried on to a great extent with impunity in the purely agricultural parts of the country, but are frequently submitted to without an attempt to discover the offenders owing to the difficulty, trouble and expense of putting legal means of detection into operation. In a great sheep district beyond Barnstaple the farmers have lately clubbed together to keep bloodhounds for the pursuit of the plunderers of their flocks. Nor are these nightly offences all we have to complain of. Numbers of sturdy beggars, particularly in summer, invade our farm houses and cottages and in the absence of the men extort money or provisions from the women whom they find at home. Indeed in this house I have for some years kept at my own expense an assistant constable in the shape of a trusty labourer to repel the above class of visitors, some of whom when they have been saucy I have committed to Bridewell where they have almost invariably been recognised as old offenders.

'Now then look at Ireland where the sympathies of the people are ever too generally at enmity with the law, scarcely any outrage passes unreported by the constabulary, and if the author escapes punishment it is far oftener by perjury of witnesses or the profligacy of juries than by the fault or failure of those employed to detect and apprehend him.

'Why then not apply a portion of the surplus revenue proposed to be given up by d'Israeli on the Malt tax, in extending to Great Britain the benefit of a force which has worked so admirably in Ireland?

'Though the application of from £700,000 to a million for that object might not at first gain for you that clap-trap popularity which formed the sole ruling principle of the late government, it will, unless I greatly mistake, very soon be acknowledged as a vast benefit to the country at large, and a special boon to the landed interest, in the increased security which it will extend to the most unprotected portion of their property, and in the exemption of the farmers from a most troublesome and disagreeable office wholly alien to their ordinary pursuits.

'If then you agree that in our present social conditions we have outgrown the rude machinery framed by our ancestors for the enforcement of the law, I hope you may not be indisposed to

103

consider of a mode of improving it which in addition to its efficacy for the attainment of that object, would have the advantage of giving you in case of need a valuable accessory to our national defences against a foreign invader.

'And if you think favourably of such a measure I feel sure that you will not be be deterred from recommending it, and that your government need not in the present temper of the public mind be prevented from carrying it by any fear of a popular outcry on the score of its cost. Let it not be forgotten that against that cost (even were the whole of it to be charged to the Consolidated Fund) is to be set the saving of private property now plundered and destroyed, the eventual diminution of criminal prosecutions, and above all, it is to be hoped, the gradual check to the training of boys in the habits of thieving of which the description given by Dickens in his novel is but too well confirmed by the evidence of official reports.

'Believe me always,
'Yours very sincerely,
'(*signed*) FORTESCUE.'

Palmerston minuted on this letter: 'What Ld. Fortescue proposes is impossible, but could any Improvement be made in the Rural Police without any additional charge on the public Revenue?' The Permanent Under-Secretary of State replied that it could. The remedy was in the hands of the magistrates, who by adopting the County Constabulary Acts 'may establish a perfectly efficient Police Force. This was not done in Surrey until the Frimley Murder frightened the Ratepayers, and I suppose that the Devonshire farmers are waiting for some similar event. The Government has no power to compel the Magistrates to adopt the provisions of these Acts but the law might easily be altered so as to give that power to the Secretary of State.' Palmerston contented himself with merely sending copies of the Acts to Lord Fortescue, but there is no doubt that he continued to brood on the problem, and every reason to suppose that the appointment three months later of a select committee of Parliament was the direct outcome of his concern. At all events this select committee provided the evidence on which, later in the year, he was able to carry matters further.

Select Committee on Police, 1853

The report of this select committee,[3] a somewhat neglected document, is not only valuable for what it accomplished—unlike several of its predecessors it paved the way for early legislation—but also for the light it throws on the state of policing in the mid-nineteenth century at a time when the reforms of the 1830s had had time to work themselves out, and their results were ripe for review. The enquiry is notable, too, for the concordance of opinion in the evidence submitted to it, and the lack of controversy about the way in which the nascent and fragmented police forces of the time should now be built up and integrated into a nation-wide service. It is also of some historical interest in that it provided Edwin Chadwick with an opportunity to put a gloss on the report he and Rowan had prepared fifteen years earlier, and to give his own assessment of what had been achieved in the interval.

The policing arrangements which the committee discovered were, as is to be expected, haphazard and confused. Some boroughs, and especially the large towns, had complied faithfully with their obligations under the Municipal Corporations Act, and the efficiency of the police forces in such places as Birmingham, Manchester, and Liverpool rivalled that of the Metropolitan Police. Elsewhere local blindness and concern for the level of the rate had quenched any enthusiasm there may have been to create effective forces, and the committee learned of towns where, when the threat of Chartism had subsided, the size of a force had been reduced.[4] And there were still, in 1853, thirteen municipal boroughs which had not set up police forces at all.

The pattern in the rural areas was equally diverse. Of the fifty-six counties in England and Wales, about half had adopted the Act of 1839, and several others had adopted it in some districts of the county only. The remainder still clung to the old system of parish constables, now in its last stages of decay, though still preserving the forms and offices of ancient times. The High Constable of the Hundred of Aveland, in Lincolnshire, appeared before the committee as one of the two high constables for the hundred whose predecessors in forgotten times had been required by the Statute of Winchester to inspect the assize of arms. Now he was paid £24 a year, mainly to collect the county rates, and only met the parish constables, all of whom had full-time occupations, such as carpenters and shoemakers, at the annual Stowe Green Fair; otherwise, 'they come to me rather in the way of a friend; they know I have no control over them. I have nothing to do with them in any sort of way, only in the management of this fair.'[5] The innovation of superintending constables authorised by the Act of 1842 was now universally condemned as a failure, except by a few magistrates who still employed it and persuaded themselves that it was economical. Moreover, the second outbreak of Chartist rioting in 1842 had shown that the time was long past when reliance could be placed on the enrolment of special constables to combat rioters—although, as one chief constable shrewdly observed, it was sometimes useful to enlist known trouble-makers on the side of law and order.[6] The total regular police strength in England and Wales (excluding the Metropolitan and City Police) amounted in 1851 to 7,381, costing some £445,000. A spokesman for the chief constables estimated that a total of about 12,300 men and 500 horses were required to meet the country's true needs, the cost of which he reckoned, with nice precision, at £773,799 5s. 2d. On this basis, the ratio of police to population would be 1:1,200 in the rural areas and 1:1,000 in the boroughs.[7]

But it was not merely a deficiency of manpower that crippled the fledgling service; its fragmented organisation, too, stood in the way of radical reform. All the evidence testified to the efficiency of each particular force where the new system was in operation, and statistics were handed in to the committee to show that crime had decreased and the detection rate was rising. Moreover, the police had generally succeeded in replacing the military in controlling disturbances. So far as it went, the picture in each of the separate areas that had adopted the new police was encouraging. But the whole was bedevilled by a total want of co-operation between the parts. Jealousy between borough and county forces was intense, not least because the borough men had jurisdiction in the counties, but the county men had no jurisdiction in the boroughs. An unhealthy rivalry and spitefulness worked only in the interests of the criminal and the disorderly. Crime tended to centre on the towns, and most witnesses thought that an efficient rural police ought to centre on them too. As Chadwick put it, 'In the towns the hand must be placed, from which fingers may be extended and withdrawn according to the need'.[8] Virtually all the other witnesses, with scarcely a dissentient, said the same, but the system was too ossified: the fingers could not reach out. Magistrates and chief constables,[9] well aware of the evil, spoke out with a striking concordance of view: the next step in developing a national police system must be to consolidate the borough forces with those in the neighbouring county. Only thus could an end be put to local jealousies, together with all the other evils already seen to be associated with small borough forces—the undesirable local connections within an organisation too narrow to allow men to be posted to distant areas,[10] the jobbery,[11] and the quarrels between watch committees and magistrates.[12]

This emerging consensus of opinion favourable to the consolidation of borough and county forces is the more surprising in that it was shared alike by borough magistrates as well as county magistrates, borough chief constables as well as county chief constables. Radical thinking ran amok. All agreed that the patchwork of rudimentary policing could no longer meet the needs of the time, rent as it was by local jealousies wherever the new county constabularies were enveloping the boroughs, and suffering huge gaps in important areas of the country, such as the West Riding of Yorkshire, where the old parish constable system limped along untouched. That rationalisation was urgently required none doubted; the only question was: How far should it go? The small borough forces should disappear, and it was essential to establish a uniform police system for England and Wales, but should it be run by the Government or by the local magistracy? Should borough forces serving populations of over 100,000 survive, thus sparing Liverpool, Manchester, and Birmingham, or should they go too? Opinions differed. Several chief constables opted for central control: the Chief Constable of Essex, whose force was much admired at the time, considered that a national constabulary would be 'the greatest blessing that could be conferred upon the country'. A Hampshire magistrate was of the same opinion. Asked whether he would approve of a national police, he replied, 'Yes. I should. Decidedly so. . . . It ought to be made under the control of the Government, and the Government ought to contribute a portion of the expense'.[13] A West Riding magistrate concurred. Some years earlier, as mentioned in the previous chapter, the county had been praised by *The Times* for refusing to adopt the rural police system. That system was still objectionable on grounds of cost, but the Government ought now to 'appoint a rural police over the whole kingdom' and meet the full cost itself.[14] Other magistrates were content with county and borough mergers, although the Rev. W. G. Townley, a far-sighted Chairman of the Quarter Sessions in the Isle of Ely, favoured a union of that county and Cambridgeshire for police purposes—a combination that was in fact to come into effect, but not for another 111 years.

Similarly, the Chief Constable of Bath sought an amalgamation with Somerset and the Chief Constable of Manchester thought it a positive 'evil' that Manchester and Salford should be separate police areas, with merely a river dividing them[15]—a river still divided separate police forces in the area in 1966.

Some voluntary mergers had already taken place, and the results were acclaimed.* Elsewhere, however, bitter opposition from sectional interests (represented in Romsey for example, as Palmerston had discovered, by a powerful alliance between the town's publicans and the managing secretary of the Watch Committee, who was a brewer) had prevented an amalgamation with the county police. In some towns reactionary councils had withdrawn from formerly combined areas, and here robust pressures were not lacking. The troubles of an upstart force of this kind are illustrated by affairs in Blackburn. The town had formerly been policed by a contingent of twenty-two county men, but had since chosen to create its own force, numbering only thirteen. Fearing trouble on the occasion of a recent election, the Town Council applied to Colonel Woodford, the Chief Constable of Lancashire (later appointed to be one of the first inspectors of constabulary) for assistance. Woodford declined to provide it, riots occurred, and the Blackburn magistrates had to call in the military, as in the old days. A member of the select committee put it to the Chief Constable that his refusal to provide help was 'by way of signifying to them your displeasure', and the Chief Constable frankly agreed. Blackburn 'would have acted more wisely to have remained under

---

* But of the sixty-four boroughs with a population of under 5,000 only thirteen had amalgamated voluntarily by 1856 (*Parl. Deb.*, 3rd Ser, Vol. CXL, col. 232). Some efforts foundered, despite goodwill on both sides. Bridgnorth sought to unite with Shropshire, the county agreed, and the agreement was signed. The borough then asked that their single constable should be appointed to the force. The county magistrates demurred, pointing out that appointments lay in the hands of the chief constable, but agreed to the appointment if the man was efficient. The chief constable reported that he could not read. 'We met the mayor of Bridgnorth', Sir Baldwin Leighton, one of the county magistrates, told the select committee, 'and there was a great discussion; the poor man wrote in our presence, and certainly very badly; the Mayor said, "He is nervous." There was a letter written by the Mayor lying on the table, and I said, "Let him read the Mayor's letter, which is very plainly written." It was handed to him, but it was evident he could not read it. The Mayor said, "I have nothing more to say, gentlemen. Will you allow us to break our engagement, and not to unite with you?" Although £20 had been paid to the county treasurer, the deal was promptly undone on account of loyalty to the constable. Six months later Bridgnorth found him another job, and the merger took place' (Qns. 2,502–3).

our charge, and perhaps it was thought desirable that they should be allowed to feel their weakness'.[16]

This recital of the defects of the police arrangements in the 1850s must not, however, be allowed to obscure the evidence of what had been achieved against all odds. The select committee was at pains to enquire whether the newly formed police forces were popular, and all witnesses agreed that they were.[17] Considering that many county forces had had as their first task the suppression of Chartism, their early popularity with the public is a notable tribute to the pioneers, and probably also to the many Metropolitan policemen who lent a hand in the early days and inculcated Metropolitan practices. They seem to have been strikingly effective in dealing with rioters. The Chief Constable of Durham described the way in which one of his superintendents had gone into 'a crowd of upwards of 1,000 men, a great number of those men being armed with picks, and some with guns, and merely from the fact of his being dressed as a policeman, and seeing that there was another force of policemen at hand, captured the ringleaders, for whose apprehension he held a warrant, and the crowd have been too terrified or astonished to offer any opposition'.[18] Police experience in handling crowds was being shared between forces in a manner that helped to overcome local jealousies, for already the practice had started which has done an immense amount to vitalise the service over the years, whereby men moved from one force to another on promotion. The Chief Constable of Norwich provides a contemporary example. He started his career with the newly formed Manchester City Police in 1840 (when the force was run by the Crown Police Commissioner), served for seven years in the Essex Constabulary, where he rose to be an inspector, two years at Bath, and a year as a Superintending Constable in Kent, the experience of which convinced him of the merits of the new system compared with the old.[19] Cross-fertilisation of ideas, it is evident, was already breaking down the formal barriers. Moreover, a start had been made in organising police forces in British territories overseas on the lines developed at home: Superintendent Mallalieu of the Metropolitan Police told the select committee that he had been sent out to the West Indies to organise a force in Barbados in consequence of the abolition of slavery in the island.[20] We find about this time, too, the first stirring of interest in the exploitation of new scientific discoveries as aids to efficient policing. Several chief constables thought it possible that the newly invented 'electric telegraph', if it could be used as a means of communication between all the police stations throughout the country, would be of value to the police, but the cost, at more than 2*d*. a mile for a short message, was prohibitive. Even so, Durham had occasionally used it.[21]

Edwin Chadwick was among the last witnesses to be called. He insisted that the Royal Commission of 1836–9 had intended that the borough forces should be absorbed by the counties, and this remained an essential condition for establishing an efficient national police system. Recent experience in Lancashire, where small borough forces were unable to cope with trouble unaided, underlined the need for wider police areas. Nevertheless, the results of the 1839 Act had been better than he had expected, considering its piecemeal application, and he had been impressed by the quality of the men appointed as chief constables. These appointments, and the manner in which they had been made, were 'highly honourable to the county magistrates'. The 'general and complete' extension of the new police to the whole country was now an urgent need which had been alarmingly underlined by the ending of transportation to the colonies as a punishment. 'We have now constantly under confinement, in the prisons of Great Britain, a force of able-bodied men, equal to an army of about 30,000, numerically greater than the British force which fought at the Battle of Waterloo. . . . Superior officers of police and very competent persons view the prospect of an unguarded change of practice with very serious alarm.' In one important respect, Chadwick said, he and Rowan (who had died a few years earlier) had modified their proposals of 1839. At that time the Metropolitan Police had offered the only source of trained men from which a constabulary might be recruited and developed, but circumstances had now changed, and he no longer regarded it as desirable to 'attempt its extension' to the whole country. On the contrary, he attached importance to 'the consultation of local feelings and conveniences' as a means of conciliating 'the support required for the efficient action of any police'.

The select committee's report on all this evidence is disappointingly brief. It sets out no arguments, but merely records eight resolutions. The evidence they had heard had been so overwhelmingly consistent that they perhaps felt it needed no embroidery. The first resolution maintained that the 1839 permissive Act had failed 'to provide such a general and uniform Constabulary force as . . . is essentially required for the prevention of crime and security of property'. The second accepted that, where the County Police Act had been adopted, its results had been 'highly advantageous'. The third and fourth praised superintending constables as individuals, but wrote off any system based on the continued use of parish constables as a failure, particularly for the poorer classes, and claimed that the cost of the superintending constable system had been far greater than was generally believed. The fifth suggested means of adjusting the level of the police rate to meet the circumstances of different areas, so as to remove an impediment against the adoption of rural police. The kernel of the committee's proposals was contained in the last three resolutions. The sixth maintained that the efficiency of all police forces had been impaired by the want of co-operation between rural and borough forces. To remedy this the smaller boroughs should be consolidated with the counties for police purposes and the larger boroughs should share a system of management and control with the adjoining county, and where practicable be under the same chief constable. The seventh resolution proposed a notable innovation; the Government should make a contribution towards the cost of 'an improved and extended system of police without, however, interfering with local management'. Finally, the eighth resolution recommended urgent legislation to make it compulsory to adopt the new police everywhere throughout the country.

Police legislation of 1854–6

It is refreshing to find, in the mass of evidence heard by the select committee, an open-minded willingness to consider any means of improving the arrangements for policing this country on their merits, however radical these means might be, and however repugnant to long-accepted traditions. In all this evidence no repetition can be discovered of the long-cherished view that a strengthening of the police system would endanger liberty. More surprisingly, on the face of it, was a similar absence of concern about the effect which the abolition of so many borough police forces might have on the strength of the municipal corporations, themselves not yet twenty years old. The explanation lies, however, in the narrowness of the range of witnesses called. Apart from the police (and Chadwick), the committee heard only magistrates and landowners, and the case of the watch committees consequently went by default. This was soon remedied.

Meanwhile, the select committee had given Palmerston the backing he needed, and the way was clear for him to introduce legislation. During the winter of 1853–4 he was considering the report,[22] and seems to have been taking an increasing interest in police affairs.

His attitude to a Devonshire landowner who complained of sheep-stealing in March, 1854, is in sharp contrast to the off-hand reply he sent to Lord Fortescue a year earlier. Asked whether he would recommend the grant of a free pardon to any accomplice who gave information, he now minuted: 'Pardon would be granted as suggested, but I would submit that the most effectual means of checking these Depredations would be the establishment of a good county police.'[23] Not long afterwards a complaint was received in the Home Office that the Warrington police were too few in numbers to give adequate protection. Palmerston requested a report from the Mayor, who replied that with a force of nine men it was impossible to afford proper protection to a population exceeding 23,000, that it was by his own efforts that he had recently persuaded the Watch Committee to raise the strength from six to nine, that more men were undoubtedly needed, and that in the meantime he must disclaim any further responsibility. 'I believe the force in the Boroughs is very generally inadequate', a Home Office official commented, with the advice that the papers should be laid by. But Palmerston refused to let the matter drop. The Mayor was to be told that he should represent to the Watch Committee that the discontinuance of the system of transportation would add to the criminal population of the towns, and that the cost of crime 'will probably in the course of a year be greater than would be the expense of maintaining a police sufficient for the purpose of duly protecting the property'. The Mayor undertook to use his influence to see that this recommendation was carried out.[24]

But to a man of Palmerston's temperament the inability to do more than advise and recommend must have been intolerably irksome, and he set about preparing a Bill which went even further than the select committee's report, a main object being to strengthen the Home Secretary's powers. That report, meanwhile, had caused consternation enough among the municipal corporations, whose outcry was gathering strength. They not unreasonably took the view that the select committee had tried them in their absence and condemned them on partial evidence.[25] They sought to have another inquiry set up containing a proportion of members from the larger boroughs; and, on learning that Palmerston was preparing to introduce a Bill, they organised a great protest meeting of mayors and Members of Parliament at Furnivals Inn on February 2nd, 1854, which passed an angry resolution condemning the select committee's proposals as an attack on the rights and privileges of municipal corporations, and expressing a determination to resist the passage of the threatened Bill by every legitimate means.[26] Palmerston, handed a copy of the resolution, minuted it airily in much the terms with which he might have dismissed the representations of a foreign ambassador, 'Put with Police Bill papers', worked away at his Bill, and introduced it into Parliament in the following June. It did not get very far.

Like his distinguished predecessors as Home Secretary, Russell and Peel, Palmerston made no secret, in introducing the Bill, of his hankering after a centrally controlled police force. 'No doubt the best police, if they simply looked to its efficiency as a preventive force, would be a police raised on the principle of the Irish, or the Metropolitan Police, acting on the orders of Government.' However, he attached great importance to 'the principle of local self-government'.[27] When details of the Bill were published, however, it was evident that the Home Secretary attached considerably less importance to that principle than did the boroughs. All counties were to be obliged to maintain police forces, and Government inspectors were to be appointed to ensure uniformity. Boroughs with fewer than 20,000 inhabitants were to lose their independent forces (this would have affected about 120 boroughs out of a total of 180 with their own forces), so that the watch committees would in effect surrender their powers to the rural justices; the five smallest counties were to be amalgamated with their neighbours for police purposes; the Home Secretary was to make rules for borough forces, as he already could for the counties; and much power was to be transferred from the watch committees that escaped the slaughter to borough chief constables, whose selection was to be subject to the Home Secretary's approval. There was to be no provision for financial aid from the Government.[28]

These radical proposals barely survived the first angry deputation from the boroughs, which attended the Home Secretary a few days later. Palmerston weakened. He still defended the merits of the Bill to the House of Commons, but 'he would not consider it rendering a good service to the country to force it upon boroughs against their own will', and he accordingly withdrew it, undertaking to introduce a less contentious measure, confined to the needs of the counties alone. This second attempt was equally ill-fated, and, like its predecessor, it failed even to gain a Second Reading. Palmerston was unrepentant. He still insisted that the right course was to amalgamate the smaller borough forces with the counties, and was 'convinced the country must come in the end' to some such system.[29] He was to be proved right, but not for almost 100 years. Like many others, he had

113

underestimated the political strength of the municipal corporations. Meanwhile, Parliament was prorogued, and six months later (in February, 1855) Palmerston became Prime Minister, so that he was denied the opportunity to carry through the reforms his initiative had done much to inspire.* As the head of the administration, however, he was in a position to encourage Sir George Grey, his successor.

Eighteen months elapsed before Grey ventured into Parliament with a third Police Bill, and in the interval the Home Office was gathering further facts about the state of the police from all parts of the country. These colourfully supplemented the evidence collected by the select committee. The city of York (whose Lord Mayor had led the protest against Palmerston's Bill) had established a police force, but the inspector ran several brothels and had introduced a profitable arrangement under which crime complaints were followed up only on payment of a fee of from 4*s.* to 5*s.* In Leominster the Superintendent had the perquisite of all fees derived from serving summonses and warrants. In Preston, a town of 70,000 inhabitants, there were only thirty-seven policemen, and many people had continued (or reverted to) the payment of voluntary subscriptions to maintain private watchmen; similar arrangements were in force in the West Riding. Portsmouth, with 80,000 inhabitants, maintained a police strength of forty-two, allowing four men to patrol by night and two by day. Conditions were much the same in Plymouth, Blackburn, Bolton, Coventry, Stockport, Warrington, Derby, and many other important towns throughout the country. In a number of boroughs there were still no police at all. Moreover, the demands of the Crimean War had now obliged the Government to withdraw the small military detachments which were stationed in several areas. Initiatives to fill the gap in the ranks of the defenders of law and order came from all quarters— most surprisingly, perhaps, from the Treasury, who caused consternation in the Home Office with the news that their Lordships had authorised the employment of fifty policemen and six horses in Hampshire to protect the vicinity of Aldershot Camp, at an annual cost to the Exchequer of £65 12*s.* 1*d.* per constable and £50 per horse. The Permanent Under-Secretary of State minuted furiously: 'This is the first time I ever heard of this. I should certainly decline to be a

* A few weeks before Palmerston left the Home Office the indefatigable Chadwick had written to him proposing terms of reference by which Palmerston should commission him to undertake yet another enquiry (*A History of English Criminal Law*, by L. Radzinowicz. Vol. 3, p. 474 (1956)). Nothing came of this initiative, which followed several earlier efforts by Chadwick to secure the revival of the 1836–9 Royal Commission.

Secretary of State upon such terms as these—unless at least the Treasury, having taken upon themselves the care of the public peace, would turn over to me the preparation of the Budget.' Acrimonious correspondence ensued, in which the Treasury compounded their error, in Home Office eyes, by claiming that their action had followed a personal intervention by the Speaker of the House of Commons.[30]

But the impulse imparted to the Home Office by Palmerston's administration survived his departure. On March 28th, 1855, the department issued a circular to thirty-eight boroughs with populations under 20,000 which had not established a police force with a ratio of at least one policeman to every 1,000 inhabitants. The circular drew attention to the state of lawlessness, and warned that the Government were to discontinue the practice of posting small detachments of troops in various parts of the country. It called for 'prompt measures to place the police force of the borough upon a more satisfactory footing'. Only fourteen of the thirty-eight recipients troubled to reply, several of whom went so far as to say that the 'suggestions were under consideration', while others were quite satisfied with the condition of their police. Honourable exceptions were Leeds and Wolverhampton.[31]

Matters could not be left thus, and Grey introduced the third Police Bill in under two years into Parliament early in the following year, 1856. He dropped the proposal to abolish the smaller police forces, but otherwise remained faithful to the select committee of 1853 and the two abortive Bills withdrawn by Palmerston. Under Grey's Bill, all counties were to be compelled to establish rural police forces; county policemen would have the same jurisdiction in the boroughs that the borough men had always had in the counties; the Crown was empowered to appoint three inspectors of constabulary to assess the state of efficiency of all forces, and their annual reports were to be laid before Parliament; an Exchequer grant amounting to one-quarter of the cost of the pay and clothing[32] of the men was to be paid in respect of forces certified by the inspector to be efficient, save that no grant would be available to forces serving populations of under 5,000; this financial incentive to the merger of small forces with the counties (in effect they were offered the choice of consolidating or paying the full cost of their force) was backed up with provisions which prevented a consolidation agreement, once entered into, from being broken without the Home Secretary's consent, and enabled an order in council to impose an agreement on a reluctant county; all police authorities were to submit statistics of crime in

115

their areas to the Home Secretary; and the Home Secretary was to have power to make regulations for the borough forces—as he had been able to do for the county forces since their inception in 1839. Only the last proposal was dropped in the course of the Bill's passage through Parliament: the remainder reached the statute book on July 21st, 1856, thus inaugurating a notable experiment in reconciling the principle of central supervision with local management in a politically acceptable form. Indeed, so successful was the experiment that the new pattern of administration established by the County and Borough Police Act, 1856, was to survive for more than 100 years.

It needed all the Home Secretary's pertinacity, however, to overcome the hostility with which this Bill was assailed. On its first introduction into Parliament, on February 5th, 1856, all was beguilingly sweet. There were suggestions that the Bill did not go far enough, and that it should abolish the smaller forces outright; and the House was reminded, just as it had been during the first debate on the County Police Bill of 1839, before the political storm burst over Lord John Russell, that policing 'was wholly removed from the sphere of party politics'. Sir George Grey joined the lengthening list of Home Secretaries who regarded a centralised police force, such as that recommended by the Royal Commission of 1839, as theoretically the best system, but felt however that it would not meet with much support in the country—'from its interfering so largely with the different local authorities'—and wound up the debate by thanking the House for the very favourable reception which it had given to the Bill.

The first waves of anger from the municipal corporations were not long in reaching Westminster. Just over a week later, on February 13th, Mr. Hadfield, the Member for Sheffield, arrived at the House armed with protests from some thirty town clerks, warned that other protests were on the way, and went on to give an intriguing glimpse of what seems to have been the birth of the infant Association of Municipal Corporations, a body destined to play a formidable role in police administration for many years: 'There has been an association formed some years ago to watch measures of this nature, but it comprised so many boroughs, that the chairman of it had not yet had time to consider the Bill, though, so far as it had been considered, the association did not approve of it at all. The great objection was, that it took away the right of self-government . . . [the result] would be little better than the Continental spy system.'[33] Mr. Muntz, the Member for Birmingham, who had been at the centre of the great controversy seventeen years earlier, went further in believing that the

116

liberties of the country depended on 'local institutions which had been in existence since the time of King Alfred'.

Encouraged by these opening shots in Parliament, the boroughs gathered strength for more sustained assaults on the Bill. A week later, on February 20th, a large gathering of mayors assembled in a hotel near Old Palace Yard. They were joined by Members of Parliament and other influential people to a total of more than 100, and the Lord Mayor of York from the chair denounced the Bill, to a chorus of 'Hear. Hear', as dangerous and unconstitutional. If the magistrates of the country allowed it to pass, 'they were certainly not the fine old English gentlemen for which he took them'. Next day the deputation waited on the Home Secretary. They were not interested in having the Bill amended, but demanded its withdrawal: 'After the examples the country had had of the perfect inability of the public departments to conduct the affairs of war, they must have only brought forward this measure to show their inability to manage the peace of the country'. That, the Home Secretary replied philosophically, 'furnished matter for argument on both sides', which was best conducted in Parliament.[34] The mayors accordingly went away to canvass all Members, and the debate was resumed in the House of Commons a month later.

To describe the buffetings which the Bill underwent during a stormy passage through the House of Commons would be tedious. The borough Members outdid one another in vituperation. Bentham, Colquhoun, and Peel might never have lived; to Chadwick, the sole survivor of the early tussles, the hysteria would have an all too familiar ring. The House was warned against tampering lightly with those municipal institutions in which English liberty was cradled; the Bill was the most un-English measure ever introduced, and seemed more fitted for Naples than for England; it was an insult to the nation; no government, however tyrannical, could have constructed such a measure; the country would soon be overrun by 20,000 armed policemen—'perhaps Irishmen or foreigners'; the Government betrayed an indecent lust for power; the boroughs should not be subject to 'the degradation of inspectorship'; the Home Secretary would become a second Fouché, with spies all over the kingdom. The Bill received the Royal Assent on July 21st, 1856. Three days later the Home Secretary addressed a circular to the magistrates in all counties which had not adopted the Act of 1839, insisting on Parliament's intention that they should now create 'a really efficient police force for the prevention and detection of crime', in which task the inspectors of constabulary who were about to be appointed would 'render every assistance by

117

information or advice'.[35] The most accurately prophetic words on the whole matter were perhaps those of Mr. Rice, who had been the Chairman of the select committee whose recommendations three years earlier had laid the Bill's foundations. The time would shortly arrive, he said, when Parliament 'would reflect with surprise and astonishment that it had been seriously debated whether they should have throughout the country a uniform system of police, subject entirely to local management; or whether they should continue the present isolated, disjointed, and absurdly anomalous system, which was useless to the country at large'.[36]

The first inspections

No time was lost in appointing the first inspectors of constabulary under the Act. Their number was statutorily limited to three, and two were appointed immediately at a salary of £700 a year. They were Major-General Cartwright, a veteran of the Peninsular War and Waterloo, who seems to have had no previous police experience,[37] and Lieut.-Colonel John Woodford, who had been the Chief Constable of Lancashire since the formation of the force in 1839. The Home Secretary admonished them 'to secure the goodwill and the co-operation of the local authorities', and expressed his reliance on their 'judgement, temper, and discretion'. He invited them to submit to him a plan 'which will divide the country into North and South',[38] and they spent the autumn of 1856 making a preliminary survey. Cartwright took the southern counties, with South Wales, and Woodford the northern areas, but it rapidly became apparent that the burden was too great to be shared between two; following their representations, a third inspector was appointed in January, 1857, the probable need for whom had been seen from the start. He was Captain Edward Willis, formerly Chief Constable of Manchester, who had earlier served under Woodford in Lancashire. Woodford retained the northern counties, Cartwright took over the Midlands and North Wales, and Willis was given the southern counties and South Wales— an arrangement that survived, with minor boundary changes, until 1907, when the number of inspectors was again reduced to two.

From the start, the inspectors established their independence of the Home Office. They lived in their own districts, conducted a stream of correspondence with Home Office officials in London, and dealt directly, not only with the chief constables in their areas (as their successors still do today), but also with the mayors of boroughs and chairmen of quarter sessions, who represented the police authorities of the time. So far as it can be said that national policies for the police began to emerge, these policies were now for the first time being formulated by the inspectors of constabulary in the light of what they discovered; and their conclusions, duly reported to the Home Secretary in their first annual reports,* at last placed the Home Office in a position to adopt its own policies—if it cared to do so. But policy-making, as it is understood today, was in its infancy in the Whitehall of the mid-nineteenth century. The immediate task was to appraise the state of the efficiency of 237 separate forces in England and Wales, and to pay the limited Exchequer grant to those certified by the inspectors as efficient in point of numbers and discipline. Belying the hostility with which the idea of Government inspection had been greeted by Parliament, the inspectors were generally warmly welcomed, and most local authorities co-operated with them cordially.

Most of the counties emerged creditably from this first test: all but seven of the fifty-nine county constabularies which existed at the end of the first inspection year (October 1st, 1857) qualified for grant and six of the defaulters qualified in the succeeding year, leaving only Rutlandshire, which was not certified efficient until 1861–2. Woodford reported that the counties which had until then still relied on the old parochial system had all not only reorganised their forces, but the new chief constables were 'displaying great activity'. To him fell the task, oddly as it would now seem, of inspecting and reporting on the Lancashire Constabulary, of which, until a few months earlier, he had been Chief Constable for nearly seventeen years. It would ill become him, he said modestly, to dilate upon its merits; but 'he cannot, however, deny himself the gratification of recording his deliberate conviction that, in all the essential qualities of a good police force, whether in the zeal and ability of the officers, or the demeanour, intelligence, and steady obedience of the sergeants and constables, it will stand in favourable comparison with any similar establishment in the kingdom'.

Not that everything was well with the county forces: strong pressure was brought to bear on some to increase their strength. In

* Each inspector made a separate report, but all three were laid before Parliament in a single volume. Because the inspectors were appointed in the autumn of 1856, they made their first annual reports a year later in September, 1857. The inconvenience of this inspection year, running from September to September, was tolerated until 1959.

one case (Durham) the magistrates had the ingenious idea that the saving from payment of a Government grant would enable them to reduce the size of the force;[39] and in another (East Riding of Yorkshire) grant was only paid, after initial refusal, in consequence of lengthy correspondence with the Home Office, a deputation to the Home Secretary, and further reference to the inspector, Woodford.[40] Often the station houses and lock-ups which were taken over from the parish authorities were severely criticised by the inspectors. Some in Northumberland were found to be so isolated and accessible from all sides that, it was reported, prisoners had been put in sober and taken out drunk; a lock-up in Kirkby, in Westmorland, was discovered to be the cellar of an abandoned workhouse accessible only by a narrow stair, and not without the aid of a lighted candle. At Longtown, in Cumberland, the lock-up was also a deserted cellar without any arrangement for heating. The floor was of earth strewn with loose straw, and small holes in the door were the only means by which air and light filtered through. Complaints were made that, where no lock-ups were available, prisoners were being chained—a long-standing practice that had caused the Home Secretary to tell the Chief Constable of Norfolk, in 1841, that 'the Superintendent ought not to have chained his prisoner and left him chained to a manger in a stable, nor was the constable justified in chaining a prisoner to a bed-post'.[41]

The first inspections of many of the borough forces produced disquieting reports—hardly surprisingly in view of the evidence which had come to the notice of the select committee a few years earlier. No fewer than 208 boroughs had police powers in 1856, made up as follows: fifty-seven large boroughs, with a population exceedin₃ 20,000; eighty-six medium boroughs, with a population between 5,000 and 20,000; and sixty-five small boroughs with a population under 5,000.[42] Not all the boroughs with police powers were, however, exercising them, since a number had voluntarily amalgamated with the county for police purposes.*

* It is not easy to establish how many boroughs had amalgamated with the county for police purposes by 1856. Many were unable to do so even if they had been inclined, since many county forces were not created until 1856–7. By deducting the number of actual police forces outside London in 1856–7 (237) from the total number of counties and boroughs with police powers (267), it appears that some thirty boroughs had consolidated by this time. (Only Major-General Cartwright's report deals specifically with the subject: in his district—No. 1, comprising the eastern counties, Midlands and N. Wales—seventeen boroughs had already been consolidated.)

Most of the large boroughs were found to be efficiently policed, and Woodford was as generous in praise of Liverpool as he had been of his own county force, Lancashire. The proportion of police to population in Liverpool was unequalled and in 'general efficiency and discipline' the force was unsurpassed by any similar establishment. Such towns as Birmingham, Manchester, and Bristol also seem to have had no difficulty in securing the grant, although there were a few sizeable and growing boroughs (of which Stockport was an outstanding example) which failed for many years to come up to standard. Of interest among this group is Warrington, with a population of 23,000. Palmerston, it will be recalled, had urged the Mayor four years earlier to see that the size of the force was increased beyond nine men, and the Mayor had undertaken to use his influence with the Watch Committee. Inspection disclosed that he had failed. The strength still remained at one superintendent and eight constables, and the towns-people had reverted to the old practice of paying voluntary contributions towards the cost of maintaining night-watchmen. Woodford took the matter up with the Mayor himself, but it was not until 1865 that the borough force could be certified as efficient, and even then the certificate was granted only with misgivings. Three large boroughs, Gateshead, Sunderland, and Southampton, carried their hostility to the principle of government inspection to the point of refusing to participate in the Government grant even if found efficient. This gesture did not save them from inspection, and the inspector even reported that he had been cordially received by the Mayor and members of the Watch Committee in both Gateshead and Sunderland. Gateshead proved to be below standard, but Sunderland and Southampton each received favourable reports their contempt for which, however, the corporations expressed by refusing the grant which was subsequently offered to them.[43]

Among the medium-sized boroughs (5,000–20,000 population) the proportion of forces reported to be inefficient on the first inspection in 1856–7 was predictably higher than among the larger boroughs: more than half of the eighty-six in this group failed on the first inspection to qualify for grant, although by 1870 the number had fallen to nineteen, most of which were then concentrated in two areas—the north-west and south-west of England. Below these, in the group of small boroughs (under 5,000 population) the test of efficiency had no significance, for they were not entitled, under the Act of 1856, to receive any Government grant, whether efficient or not. Of interest was the discovery that thirteen boroughs had successfully contrived for over twenty years to evade their obligation under the Municipal Corporations Act, 1835, to set up a police force, and many of the 'forces' which had been set up were farcical. 'The men in the force are generally old', Major-General Cartwright reported, 'and unfit for their work from physical infirmity, and represent more the old style of watchman than police officers of the present day'; and Captain Willis commented that, 'in many of the smaller forces no police office is established or books kept'. A few extracts from the first inspection reports illustrate the point. In Southwold 'The Superintendent has no force to superintend'. In Stratford-upon-Avon there was one day constable and three night, 'with permission to earn what they can'. Bewdley employed 'two under-paid constables, one of whom is 66 years of age; the other is over 60, and is allowed to work at his trade'. The one constable in Bradwinch, in Devonshire, was not 'provided with any clothing or furnished with books, and he performs his duty in such manner as he deems desirable, and without supervision'. Totnes was 'totally unprotected' except for two elderly sergeants-at-mace aged sixty-five and seventy-four, who, however, 'take no regular police duty'. In Sandwich the single constable who nominally constituted the force still followed his trade as a hairdresser, while at Tenterden the Superintendent, with two constables under him, was a shopkeeper.

No threat to withhold the Government grant was available to cure these shortcomings. The inspectors could only stress the advantages, to the small boroughs, of consolidation with county forces; and from the start they embarked on a vigorous campaign to promote consolidations. Many small boroughs seem to have needed little or no persuasion; the advantages of economy and enhanced efficiency were self-evident. By 1856–7 some thirty borough forces had been consolidated, and by 1869–70 the number had risen to fifty-eight. A provision of the Act of 1856 prevented a consolidation agreement from being broken without the consent of the Secretary of State, but this was of questionable advantage for it evidently discouraged some boroughs[44] from taking the plunge. On the other hand, it ensured that most agreements made after 1856 tended to be more permanent than those entered into between 1840 and 1856.[45] Even so, there were many local interests working against consolidation, not least those of the brewers and publicans of a small town (such as Romsey), who could still effectually control the negligible police force they themselves provided, or the local shopkeepers, who had no wish to see the inspection of their weights and measures conducted by an impartial county man—a duty commonly assigned to the police, both as a contribution towards finding them sufficient employment to justify their cost, and also as a means of establishing them as friends of the poor.

In assessing the efficiency of a force, the inspectors were required by the Act of 1856 to form an opinion whether it had been 'maintained in a state of efficiency in point of numbers and discipline'. In carrying out this duty, they seem to have applied four main tests: the absolute strength of the force; the ratio of police to population; the degree of co-operation extended to neighbouring forces; and the quality of supervision exercised over the men. Enough has already been said on the first point. As to the second—the ratio of police to population— the range varied widely. The limitation imposed by the County Police Act, 1839, of not more than one constable per 1,000 of population, had not been lifted by the Act of 1856, but the Home Office considered that the ratio should be more favourable in the larger and more densely populated boroughs.[46] In practice it ranged, for example, from 1:6,500 in St. Ives (where one constable served the whole town) and 1:11,491 in Rutland (where one chief constable aided by one constable served the county) to 1:646 in Birmingham, 1:540 in Manchester, and 1:393 in Liverpool. (The last figure is remarkable when compared with the then ratio of 1:450 or 500 in London, and the 1966 ratio in Liverpool of 1:325.) The other two assessments which run continually through these early inspection reports—of the co-operation extended to neighbouring forces and the quality of supervision—need little comment. Inevitably it was the small borough forces which failed on both tests. Co-operation between the county and larger borough forces was growing, and the discipline, though as yet unregulated by a uniform code, was widely regarded as satisfactory: generations of policemen, down to the present day, would endorse the comment in Major-General Cartwright's first report in 1856–7 that 'there is no rank more valuable to the well-working of a force than that of a sergeant'.

The state of the police in 1860

The early reports of the newly appointed inspectors of constabulary dispose of any idea that this country possessed a uniform police system in the years immediately following the enactment of the County and Borough Police Act, 1856. It possessed 226 separate police forces, ranging in size from the Metropolitan Police to one man in no fewer than thirteen of the small boroughs. These forces were infinitely varied in their outlook, efficiency, status, and popularity with the public, in their standards of discipline, and even in their rates of pay. There was no uniformity, even, about the uniform itself—the Lancashire police patrolled in rifle green frock-coats. Some forces had established pension schemes, but many had not. The Metropolitan Police remained an entity within itself. The inspectors of constabulary had no authority to inspect it (nor have their successors today) and the movement of police officers seems to have been entirely outward from London: few, if any, returned with fresh ideas gathered from the provinces. Forces were beginning to learn the need for co-operation, but as late as 1897 the Head Constable of Reading could order his men to simulate a breaking at the house of the Chief Constable of Berkshire 'to frighten the old man'.[47] There were vital differences between the arrangements for controlling and administering the county and borough forces, and the constitution of each was different again from those of the Metropolitan and City of London Police; and there were still, in 1870, five forces maintained under local Acts.[48] Lord Normanby's regulations of 1840 still governed the county forces, and the appointment of the chief constable was subject to the Home Secretary's approval, but once in post the county chief constable was an autocrat over whom the justices had no power other than the ultimate sanction of dismissal. In his hands lay the appointment of the constables (subject to the approval of two justices of the peace), and he could at pleasure promote, punish (by a fine of up to one week's pay or reduction in rank), suspend, or dismiss them. Thus he fulfilled many of the duties which in the borough were assigned to the watch committee—a situation which remained substantially unaltered until 1964.

For in the boroughs the term 'police authority' had a literal meaning. The control of the watch committee was absolute. In its hands lay the sole power to appoint, promote, and punish men of all ranks (by a fine of up to one week's pay, or reduction in rank) and it (or two justices of the borough) had powers of suspension and dismissal. The watch committee prescribed the regulations for the force and, subject to the approval of the town council, determined the rates of pay. Until the appointment of the inspectors of constabulary, their authority was supreme, and they suffered no guidance from the Home Office. In the large cities, where responsible, public-spirited men controlled the council, this was of no account, but in small towns malpractices were rife. Where the interests of publicans and brewers predominated, a watch committee would insist that no proceedings be taken against a licensee without their express authority. The Chief Constable of Norwich was dismissed for defying such a ruling, and in Devonport the arrangement survived for many years. It suited the purposes of many small boroughs in such circumstances to appoint as chief constable a local man of quiet and tractable disposition; and, as the appointment was not subject to the approval of the Home Secretary, no one could prevent a mischievous town council from exercising improper pressure on its police. It could use them to support groups of local tradespeople, sectional interests or political parties, and where the population was under 5,000 (and hence no Exchequer grant was payable) no threat to withhold a grant was available to bring redemptive influences to bear. The 'chief constable', in any case, held no exceptional position comparable with that of the county man: he was simply the constable who held the highest rank in the force, and his status depended on the numbers under him. Sometimes they were very small. The chief officers of most borough forces were known as head constables, but in an appreciable number they were styled by their rank, often that of superintendent.*

All these anomalies, irregularities, and deficiencies were, of course, well known to the inspectors of constabulary, and they were energetic in framing recommendations to the Home Secretary suggesting a variety of means by which the standards of the worst forces might be raised up to those of the best: rates of pay should be increased and made uniform; pension funds should be made mandatory; discipline should be uniformly administered; the Home Secretary should make rules for borough forces; men in the liquor trade should not sit on watch committees; above all, the small forces should be abolished. But powerful vested interests were involved in all these matters, and it

---

* The titles 'superintendent', 'head officer of the police', 'head constable' and 'chief constable' can all be found in relation to borough forces in early Police Superannuation Acts (11 & 12 Vic., *c.* 14, s. 2; 19 & 20 Vic., c. 69, s. 9; 22 & 23 Vic., c. 32, s. 10; and 28 & 29 Vic., c. 35, s. 4). From time to time representations were made to the Home Secretary that the borough men should be given a single statutory title, to distinguish them from the chief constables in the counties, (see, e.g. the printed memorandum by the Chief Constable of Norfolk dated October 27th, 1858, in *H.O.*, 19,774, and Cartwright's report for 1858–9.) but the Home Office insisted that as they were generally known as head constables, little confusion arose in practice—see, e.g., *H.O.* 45, O.S. 6,646 (1858). The term 'chief constable' was not formally applied to all chief officers until regulations were made under the Police Act, 1919.

was not until well into the twentieth century that anything resembling a uniform police system began to take shape under the influence of pressures unknown in 1860: the mounting discontent of the men with their pay and conditions of service; the growth towards professional status of chief constables, accompanied by a developing sense of common purpose; and the recognition by the Home Office that it had a part to play in police administration outside London. In 1860 all these trends lay in the remote future, and the only spur to reform was provided by the reports of the inspectors of constabulary. 'After the hopeful note of their first reports', Mrs. Hart has observed, 'the inspectors constantly comment on the slackness and apathy of the smaller boroughs who seemed to desire to evade for as long as possible the performance of their duties under the Municipal Corporations Act, 1835. This no doubt reacted unfavourably on the inspectors, who became disheartened and less energetic. As time went on they did less and less work. . . . '[49] Nevertheless, their constructive proposals in the early days entitle them to an honourable place in any history of the police as pioneers in the century-long process of rationalising the pattern of separate local police forces into the coherent national system we know today.

Later structural and administrative changes

These proposals were reiterated with a cogency that impressed the Home Office. Acts of Parliament in three successive years, 1857, 1858, and 1859, modified, but only in minor respects, the new structure laid down by the Act of 1856;[50] but during the next decade the momentum of reform again lapsed—probably no bad thing while the new organisation settled down. Then, some eighteen years after the act of 1856 reached the Statute Book, there came a fresh round of reforms, starting in 1874 and culminating with the police provisions of the Local Government Act, 1888, which established the final pattern of the nineteenth-century police service, a pattern that endured well into the twentieth century.*

* During the 1870s (as in the 1770s) the spirit of radicalism was rampant. In Trevelyan's picturesque language, 'Democracy, bureaucracy, collectivism are all advancing like a silent tide making in by a hundred creeks and inlets.' It was an age of intellectual aristocrats: Mill, Darwin, Huxley, Matthew Arnold, Browning, and many others, with Disraeli and Gladstone sparring for the leadership. But it is typical of the gingerly attitude always adopted towards police reform that it alone should languish until the reform of local government was undertaken in the next decade.

The starting-point of this final cycle of reforms was the decision in 1874 to increase the Exchequer grant towards the cost of all forces from one-quarter to one-half of the cost of pay and clothing.[51] The Home Office was determined to have value for money, and extracts from a submission made to the Home Secretary (Sir Richard Cross) at this time are worth quoting for the light they throw on current thinking about police organisation: 'The very considerable addition about to be made to the contribution from Imperial funds in aid of local police expenditure, affords the government an opportunity, of which it may be well to take advantage, of endeavouring to secure for the Secretary of State a greater amount of supervision and control over the police forces of Great Britain than he now possesses'. The memorandum goes on to comment on the very limited authority possessed by the Home Secretary over the county forces, and as regards the borough police 'he has no power whatever beyond that of withholding a certificate of efficiency; and it is therefore clear that the supervision exercised by him, in counties as well as in boroughs, is very limited both in character and amount. As now constituted, the police force is a fragmentary body, acting within, and subject to the control of, separate jurisdictions and having no general cohesion. The time has not perhaps arrived for making an attempt to place it entirely under a central authority, however desirable that might be as regards its efficiency and utility: but the conferring of additional powers of supervision upon the Secretary of State would be a step in that direction, and entirely warranted, if not absolutely called for, by the appropriation of so large a sum of public money towards its maintenance.'[52]

The inspectors of constabulary were quick to take advantage of a climate of opinion in the Home Office so favourably inclined to reform, and they accompanied with their report of October 1st, 1874, a summary of proposals which had long been maturing. This time they found a ready ally in Sir Henry Ibbetson, then Parliamentary Under-Secretary of State at the Home Office, and soon to be Chairman of a select committee of Parliament set up to consider police superannuation.

'If a Bill of this kind is necessary', Sir Henry advised the Home Secretary in January, 1875,[53] 'and I imagine it will be if the present grant to Counties and Boroughs is to be altered in accordance with the promise of last year, I feel very strongly that there are several points in the administration of the force which could not be omitted without rendering the Bill open to grave attack. I entirely agree with the reports which have been long in the office from the Chief Inspectors of Constabulary, that one most important point which should be made a condition of any further Imperial Grant is that the appointment and disposal of Chief Constables in Counties and Head Constables in Boroughs should be made subject to the approval of the Secretary of State, as the appointments of Chief Constables in Counties now are under the 2 & 3 Vic., c. 93, s. 4. And I think the Sec. of State should also have power to make Rules for the government of Borough Forces similar to those he now possesses in Sec. 3 of the same Act with regard to Counties.

'In my opinion, one of the cardinal points however of police Reform, and which if possible should also form part of any fresh legislation, is subject to grave political considerations, but which I do not think outweigh the value of the change. It is that the grant for a separate force should not be given to any Borough having a separate police force under 10,000 population instead of 5,000 as now. The Chief Constables go further and would suggest 15,000. ... I am aware of the opposition which some towns might make but after all the number affected are only thirty. And it is in these small Boroughs, where the forces and especially the staff are ridiculously out of proportion to the want, and when great advantage might be secured both in economy and efficiency, by their being merged in the Counties for police purposes, that real practical reform is wanted.

'I think the power suggested also by the Chief Constables, that the police should be empowered to act in any jurisdiction when their services may become necessary on the requisition of the Authority of the jurisdiction would be a valuable amendment. But no Bill should I think omit dealing with the question of superannuation. At present there is no doubt the Superannuation funds, generally, are either at present or on the verge of being, insolvent, they are supplied now by certain fines payable to the fund and by contributions from the forces, but natural objection is made by the men who feel they are contributing to funds which from their condition are hardly ever likely to be of benefit to them. On these funds becoming insolvent pensions must fall upon the rates, as unless some system of pension is adoped in the present state of the question of labour, you will fail to keep a force together at all. . . . '

This brave new thinking came to nothing—at least for some time. It illustrated a welcome change to a positive attitude on the part of the Home Office towards police affairs, but no one was disposed to underrate the difficulties in the way of radical reform. A Bill was prepared, but not introduced. Instead, reforms proceeded piecemeal, most of which took years to accomplish. A select committee on police superannuation was set up in 1875, and then, two years later, the Municipal Corporations (New Charters) Act, 1877, imposed the first compulsory check on the formation of new police forces, by providing that no scheme for the incorporation of a borough might allow the formation of a separate police force unless the population exceeded 20,000.

Police history moved slowly: 20,000 was the identical figure which Palmerston had written into his abortive Bill more than twenty years earlier, but his far-reaching proposals would have swept away all police forces serving populations below this figure. The Act of 1877 spared those that already existed. Yet many had done little, in the intervening years, to justify this second reprieve. On the credit side it could be said that several of the thirteen small boroughs which, on the first inspections in 1856–7, were discovered never even to have complied with their obligations under the Municipal Corporations Act, 1835, to maintain a police force, had now done so, seemingly on account of concern about outbreaks of public disorder rather than crime. It was also true that consolidation of some of the smaller boroughs with the counties had made good progress—eighty of the 245 boroughs with police powers had entered into consolidation agreements by 1876.[54] On the other hand, there were still six 'forces' consisting of only one man in the mid-1870s, and as late as 1881 some thirty forces had fewer than six men.

The continuance of these small pockets of parish-constable-style policing would have made little difference to the standard of policing in the country generally had inefficiency been confined to them, but it was not. Fifteen years after the enactment of the County and Borough Police Act, 1856, the inspectors of constabulary were still reporting no fewer than forty-four borough forces as inefficient, including large and rapidly growing towns like Oldham, whose population had risen from 27,000 in 1861 to 82,000 in 1871, and Stockport, with a population of 53,000. In one case, Ashton-under-Lyme (population 32,000), the inspector reported flatly that 'he was informed by the head constable that he had been directed by Alderman Mason, the chairman of the watch committee, not to parade the force for inspection'. A common cause of inefficiency in the expanding industrial towns was failure to accept that more money had to be spent on more police simply to keep pace with the growth of population—Sheffield forfeited its grant on this account in 1862–3.

It is against this background that the significance of the Municipal Corporations (New Charters) Act of 1877 is to be seen. Britain's rapid industrial expansion had led to the incorporation of a large number of new boroughs, each of which possessed, and most exercised, police powers. Thus in 1876, the year before the limit of 20,000 population was imposed on this entitlement, five new forces came into existence in Lancashire alone. Mr. Parris makes a valuable point (though perhaps he rather overstates the position) in commenting that, 'It was the grant of police powers to newly incorporated boroughs that created the twentieth-century problem of small borough forces, rather than the survival of ancient independent corporations'.[55]

The Act of 1877, while checking the formation of new forces, left existing small forces untouched—perhaps because the Government hoped that the financial squeeze on those with a population under 5,000, who were disqualified from receiving an Exchequer grant, would eventually persuade them all to consolidate—and the Home Office was soon displaying a marked tenderness towards the town halls. Sir Mathew Ridley, who succeeded Sir Henry Ibbetson as the Parliamentary Under-Secretary of State at the Home Office in the following year, 1878, ordered that anything which went out to police authorities should be absolutely free from any taint of dictation or direction: 'The Inspectors may approach the local authorities, and lead them in the right direction—but it must be done with discretion.'[56] This delicate reserve was carried to its limit by Sir William Harcourt, the autocratic Home Secretary of 1880–5, who delighted to pour scorn on any suggestion that Whitehall knew best: 'I cannot consent to accept the Procrustean rules of the Inspectors who are quite ignorant of the needs of the localities . . . against the local authorities, who know their own affairs much better.' As for the suggestion that the appropriate test of police efficiency was so many men for 1,000 inhabitants, 'Nothing can be more ridiculous. . . . It is time that a little practical common sense should be brought to bear on these matters. To make these people keep more police than they want is like the old story of compelling the Brahmins to develop butchers' shops because beef is thought to be good for them.'[57]

This policy, admirable from the point of view of the local authorities, must have disheartened the inspectors of constabulary. They succeeded in persuading the Home Secretary to correct some of the worst abuses and deficiencies by threatening to withhold the police grant, a threat used on an average at least once a year during the last sixteen years of the century, according to Mrs. Hart's perusal of Home Office files. But the Home Office stood aloof when the inadequate state of the law governing the borough police forces led to inevitable clashes between watch committees, who regarded their chief constables as their servants to carry out orders, and chief constables, who, taking their cue from colleagues in the county, insisted on their independence in matters concerning the enforcement of the law. Where goodwill existed differences were readily resolved, but in its absence a conflict of principles could check or even ruin a man's career.

A clash which occurred in 1880 between the Chief Constable of Birmingham and the Watch Committee, over the extent of police discretion to prosecute, brings out clearly the difficulties inherent in a relationship which the law had never satisfactorily defined—and incidentally throws light on the roles played by the local justices and the Home Secretary in police administration in the boroughs at this time. Before 1880 it had been the practice of the Birmingham police not to interfere with drunks who were able to make their own way home, so long as they were not also disorderly. The Chief Constable decided to alter this, and ordered that all persons found drunk were to be brought before the magistrates. The justices, as well as members of the public, criticised the new policy, and it was abandoned; but in the following year the Chief Constable again overstepped the mark, this time attracting the censure of the Watch Committee. He instituted a prosecution against the manager of a music-hall, alleging improper performance, and for performing stage plays without a licence. The case broke down, and the Chief Constable, summoned to report to the Watch Committee, claimed an independent right to institute prosecutions as 'the guardian of public morality and order'. The Committee promptly passed a resolution that he should not take special proceedings 'likely to affect a number of ratepayers, or to provoke public comment' without previously reporting to them his intention of doing so. The Chief Constable refused to give any such undertaking unless so directed by the Home Secretary and the magistrates. The Home Secretary refused to intervene, but made his view plain by referring the Chief Constable to a section of the Municipal Corporations Act which empowered the Watch Committee to make regulations 'for preventing neglect or abuse, and for rendering constables efficient in the discharge of their duties' with provision for the Committee to dismiss any constable 'whom they

131

shall think negligent in the discharge of his duty, or otherwise unfit for the same'—words doubly memorable in that they were lifted almost verbatim out of the Middlesex Justices Act, 1792, and were to be applied, seventy years hence, in the dismissal, in 1958, of the then Chief Constable of Brighton. The justices were similarly reserved. They replied that, while they could not divest themselves of authority and control over the police, they had no desire to interfere with arrangements made between the Watch Committee and the Chief Constable in the interests of public order. The upshot of this exchange was that, under the threat of a Council resolution that it was undesirable to retain the services of a chief officer of police who was 'not subordinate to or not in harmony with' the Watch Committee, coupled with the threat of a requirement to resign, the Chief Constable gave way.[58]*

It is understandable that the Home Secretary should have preferred to regard an incident of this kind as a local matter: governments were not then, as now, inquisitive about every aspect of local affairs, and a town of the size and importance of Birmingham could safely be left to regulate its own police. But it became increasingly clear, in the face of the annual criticisms made by the inspectors of constabulary, that the continuance of small borough forces could not indefinitely be regarded as a local matter. The fresh thinking in the Home Office that had produced the memoranda of 1874 had no doubt spent itself as the years went by and opportunities for radical reform petered out with every parliamentary session. But the goal of abolishing small forces had remained an object of policy which survived every change of Home Office ministers and high civil servants, until at last, in 1888, the decision to promote comprehensive legislation to

* An even more confused and serious situation arose in Margate in 1902, when the Mayor and an ex-Mayor, acting as *ex-officio* magistrates, granted an extension of licence to local publicans to celebrate the Boer War peace night. The borough justices regarded this as a usurpation of their authority, and maintained that extensions could only be granted in open court. They accordingly ordered the Chief Constable to take proceedings against any publicans who kept open. The Watch Committee refused to allow summonses to be issued, and the borough justices, announcing that the Chief Constable would be suspended, summoned him to appear before them for neglect of duty in not carrying out their instructions. The proceedings were adjourned, and three weeks later the Town Clerk applied for the reinstatement of the Chief Constable. The matter was eventually settled by the withdrawal of the suspension and a decision not to prosecute the publicans. But the intolerable position in which the Chief Constable was put made it impossible for him to continue as a pawn in the local game, and he tendered his resignation.[59]

132

reform local government in the counties by establishing county councils (analogous to the town councils set up by the Municipal Corporations Act, 1835) offered the long-awaited chance. A provision in the Local Government Act, 1888, abolished police forces in towns with a population under 10,000, and Parliament accepted the change without a murmur of protest; the only amendment suggested was that the Bill should go further by setting the population limit at 20,000. The effect was to reduce the number of separate police forces by forty-eight—from 231 in 1888 to 183 in 1889.*

Creation of Standing Joint Committees

The debates[60] on the other police provisions in the Local Government Bill, 1888 were, however, a very different matter, for they were riddled with fresh confusion and misunderstanding about the role of the police in relation to local and central government. Several ingredients went to the making of this confusion, but the wide gulf in ideas and ways of life between nineteenth-century urban and rural England probably lay at the bottom of it. Members spoke freely of the 'control' of the police in different senses, according to their local experience of county or borough policing; and there was, naturally, no common ground about the part played by the Home Office. The debates rarely echoed the temper of the great police debates earlier in the century, when the main principles of the new police structure had been hammered out, although one undercurrent in both Houses was again a familiar and unmistakable one—namely, the tug-of-war for control of the police between the new democracy and the old guard representing the country gentry. As it entered the House of Commons, the Bill gave a nod in the direction of hereditary privilege—the balance

* The number of forces rose again to 197 in 1900 as additional boroughs were incorporated. In 1910 it had fallen to 190, by 1920 it was 191, and in 1939 it had been reduced again to 183. The counties of 1888 were not pleased with their inheritance. At a luncheon held on April 1st, 1889, which led to the foundation of the County Councils Association, the President of the Local Government Board, who had steered the Bill through the House of Commons, recalled: 'We were approached by a borough whose police had to be handed over to the county. The county would not take over the police. (*Laughter.*) Then arose the question of whether they could superannuate the police force in the county, but we asked: What is the strength of your force, and what do you think was the answer? One man, over 70 years old and under 5 ft. 7 in. (*Loud laughter.*)' (*County Councils Gazette*, October, 1963.)

of power in the control of the police was to be in the hands of the county magistrates, with increased powers for the Home Secretary. The Commons evened out the balance by equating the powers of the newly created county councils and the magistrates, and they struck out the additional power proposed for the Home Secretary. Finally, the Lords made a gallant but empty gesture towards redressing the balance once more in favour of the magistrates, by inserting a clause which established beyond doubt that the police were to obey the lawful orders of the justices.

Moving the First Reading of the Bill, the President of the Local Government Board, Mr. Ritchie, succinctly stated the main issue: 'As the House is aware, the county police is at present entirely under the control of quarter sessions, and the question arises whether the control of the police should be considered a judicial or an administrative matter.' The Government's conclusion represented a compromise: 'the management of the police should be considered as partaking partly of the judicial and partly of the administrative character'. The 'raising and management' of the force should be in the hands of a joint committee of the county council and of quarter sessions, but the appointment of the chief constable should continue to be the responsibility of the justices alone, since, as the Attorney-General later put it, 'the judicial duties were not to be transferred to the new councils, and it would be unwise at once to take away from the county magistrates the control over the police'. The special police grant for county forces was to be merged in more general grant arrangements, and the standing joint committees (unlike the watch committees) were to be financially independent of the parent councils. To ensure that county constabularies maintained a high standard of efficiency, the Home Secretary was to have a new power to give directions, enforceable by *mandamus*, to ensure the maintenance of proper standards of discipline, efficiency, and also of the number of policemen employed. The proposal to establish combined committees of county councils and magistrates (standing joint committees) was justified, in the Government's view, by the argument that it would not be right to enable the new councils to manage the police (as the borough councils had done for years through their watch committees) because 'the inhabitants of the borough have been for many years accustomed to municipal government, and they have become educated in the science of government to a degree which it will take the new councils some years to attain'.[61]

Few Members cared for these compromise proposals. They were

at once attacked on the grounds that divided responsibility for the police would create friction and lead to irresolution in operating them in times of trouble. Most wished to see a single body responsible for the police, but views were evenly divided whether that body should be the new county council or the justices. Consequently, the idea of a standing joint committee, comprising representatives of each, was not dislodged. Those who favoured the county councils had the advantage in debate, for they were able constantly to return to the real weakness in the Government's compromise: if it was true that the boroughs had only been given police powers when they were sufficiently 'educated in the science of government' to be entrusted with them, what had the Municipal Corporations Act been all about? True, the lesson of Birmingham in 1839, when the new Town Council had been judged insufficiently educated to be entrusted with police, might have been cited in support of the Government's case. But nobody seems to have thought of that; and the city's champion fifty years later, Joseph Chamberlain, spoke for many when he claimed that the borough councils had administered the police with 'signal efficiency', and he could not understand 'why we cannot safely entrust to bodies which would be so dignified and so important as the new county councils, the power which has been entrusted to the boroughs for more than fifty years without a single complaint being raised with regard to it'. As another Member put it, the boroughs were 'self-educated'; why could not the counties similarly educate themselves to undertake the work of democracy? To this question the Government from first to last gave no answer, for there was none to give.

The debate took a further turn into confusion on the question who controlled or ought to control the police? Reference was constantly made to questions on which 'political and popular public feeling' might be very strong, and it was suggested that those who controlled the police ought to be persons free from any sort of popular pressure.[62] This argument again overlooked the fact that watch committees had successfully managed the police in the boroughs for fifty years, but there was a revealing hint in it that county chief constables had always accepted operational orders from the justices in times of threatened riot, in much the same way that the military had been under the authority of the magistracy during the Chartist riots earlier in the century.*

* There were also interesting suggestions that the justices, and not the watch committees, took command of the police in times of threatened

135

The Committee stage of the Bill was even more prolonged and confusing. The Government were able to adhere to their main bastion of creating standing joint committees because hostility to them, though universal, was still evenly divided among those who supported giving police powers to county councils and those who wished to see them retained by the justices. However, a concession was made to democracy by amending the Bill to provide that the appointment of the chief constable should be in the hands of the standing joint committee and not of the magistrates only—a point that was to alarm the House of Lords in the later stages. The Government sought to justify their original proposal by arguing that 'the Quarter Sessions of magistrates in counties were responsible for the peace of the county,' and it therefore followed that they should have 'responsibility of the appointment of the executive officer over the police'.[63] This, replied the local authority lobby, showed that the Government were going from bad to worse: the idea of control by a joint committee was evidently a mere pretence; the Bill was a reactionary measure designed to keep the control of the police in the hands of the magistrates, and hence 'all the evils of the absence of popular control over the police force' were to be perpetuated. The Government eventually gave way after prolonged debate. They were also attacked[64] on the proposal to give the Home Secretary a new power of direction as to the numbers of policemen. It was argued that the *mandamus* procedure was likely to be unworkable, and that it was objectionable that the Home Secretary should attempt to lay down the numbers of police required in any area. Harcourt recalled that when he had been Home Secretary he had 'absolutely prohibited any interference on the part of the Home Office with the municipalities or the local councils in these matters. If these councils knew anything at all, they knew much better than any central authority about such matters as local police. The inspectors of constabulary, to his mind, were absolutely useless for the purposes for which they at present existed'[65]—to which he later added for good measure that the whole staff of the Home Office 'was most imperfect and the duties were not satisfactorily performed'. Other Members

---

riot in the towns—see, e.g., the speech of Mr. Henry Fowler, the Member for Wolverhampton, who described how on one occasion of threatened disorder the magistrates sat up for the greater part of a night since 'the town council or the watch committee had nothing to do with the preservation of the peace. At that critical moment the whole control of the police and of the chief constable was in the hands of the mayor and magistrates' (*Parl. Deb.*, Vol. CCCXXVII, col. 540).

claimed that the Home Office was too prone to press a local authority against its better judgement to employ more police. . . . 'In the counties of Lancashire and Cheshire,' said one, 'he could find dozens of men who were far better fitted to decide this question than any permanent officials at the Home Office.' The Home Secretary, Mr. Matthews, protested that he himself had exercised his powers 'almost universally in the direction of retrenchment', but it was the local people who always wanted to increase the size of their forces. Among these mutual recriminations, the proposal to give the Home Secretary power to direct the number of men in a force was quietly dropped.

Surprisingly, two voices were raised in the House of Commons in favour of putting all the police under Home Office control (the Members for West Ham and Oswestry), a heresy with which Mr. Ritchie said delicately 'he was very far indeed from saying that there was not a good deal to be urged in favour'. But when the Bill reached the House of Lords the cause of centralisation received very much more powerful support, this time from Lord Carnarvon and the Prime Minister himself, Lord Salisbury, who 'believed that we were slowly developing from the Dogberry and Verges position into that of a highly perfected system of organised police, which prevailed in every country but our own. He believed that we should ultimately get it. He should be glad if we were able to shorten the journey.'[66] The Prime Minister recalled that, in the form in which the Government had introduced it into the House of Commons, the Bill would have given the justices the power to appoint and control the chief constable. The Government, he said, must disclaim responsibility for the emasculation of the powers of the justices by the House of Commons, and the somewhat revealing question in his mind was, 'Who was to have the command of the police for the purpose of repressing disorder?' The boroughs had been 'educated in this duty by a long course of history', and the county councils might reach that point in time, but they had not reached it yet. Swayed by these anxieties and moved, no doubt, by instinctive sympathies, the Lords accordingly inserted a new clause in the Bill to provide that nothing in it affected the powers and duties of the justices as conservators of the peace, and that the county constabulary were to obey the lawful orders of justices—a provision that can have meant little in practice, since this was already the common law position. However, it satisfied the honour of the country gentry, who embarked on their new role as members of standing joint committees, administering the county forces in partnership with the newly elected county councils. This partnership, despite the almost universal hostility with which its birth was attended, was to survive much longer than seems to have been expected at the time, and it worked in a fashion that was to be warmly praised by the Royal Commission on the Police some seventy years later.

This was the last of the great police debates of the nineteenth century, and the issues were not to be joined again until modern times. Already the role of the justices was in eclipse, and that of the local authorities in the ascendant. But who now controlled the chief constables? 'It would be intolerable', the Home Secretary was saying in 1888, at the time when the Local Government Bill was before Parliament, 'that in any large town the Commander of the police force . . . should hold irresponsible authority.'[67] But the law on the matter was as inadequate as ever, and the Royal Commission on the Police, reporting in 1962, was probably right in concluding that a situation was gradually coming about, 'unregulated and probably unrecognised by Parliament, in which chief constables, able and intelligent men, growing in professional stature and public esteem', were assuming authority and powers which their predecessors would formerly have sought from justices.[68] For as the justices dropped out of the picture the contenders for power were chief constables and local police authorities; and the county men, with their generally greater social acceptability, wider powers of command over the force and looser subordination to the standing joint committee, slipped easily into a dominating position to which their borough colleagues could scarcely aspire without colliding with the watch committee.

But the tensions and troubles implicit in this situation were for the future, and must count for little in relation to what the Victorians had achieved. That achievement was marked, and deserves for ever to be commemorated, by the preamble to a somewhat obscure statute enacted in 1872. Thirty years after the Parish Constables Act, 1842, had tried for the last time to put new life into the old constabulary, 35 & 36 Vict., c. 92 declared that 'whereas the establishment of an efficient police force in the counties of England and Wales has rendered the general appointment of parish constables unnecessary', no more were to be appointed in future unless the justices in quarter sessions so ordained. The old order was dead, or seemed to be, and Maitland was able to comment a dozen years later that the Act of 1842 'seems as obsolete as the laws of Ethelbert. We have been living very fast.'[69] He should have known better. Nothing which touches police affairs moves fast. The liability of every able-bodied man, not specially exempted, to service as a parish constable or to find a substitute, was not finally brought to an end until 1964, and it seems to have been exercised in a few areas for limited purposes as late as the 1950s.[70] Thus the last remnants of the old system long lived side by side, at least in the pages of the Statute Book, with the new.

Chapter Five

Life, Work, and Welfare of the Victorian Policeman 1856-1908

The previous two chapters have described the main steps which led to the formation of regular paid police forces throughout England and Wales. The process has necessarily been observed from the centre in an attempt to show, from contemporary Parliamentary and Home Office papers, the currents and cross-currents of thinking that produced so disjointed a system. An attempt must now be made to penetrate the administrative structure in order to see something of the kind of men who joined the new police forces, the sort of lives they led and the work they did. For this purpose, the point of view shifts from a central to a local one, and the stuff of local force histories usefully supplements national public records. The period selected is a long one: the half-century that began with the implementation of the County and Borough Police Act in 1856, and ended with the Edwardian sunset; and it is impossible, within the limits of a single chapter, to attempt to do more than catch a whiff of it all. In a sense, this may not matter because, for reasons which will be apparent, conditions in the police forces of England and Wales changed very slowly and very little over this long period, despite the pace of change outside. For good or ill, the police were from the start the 'stable element in society' which a Royal Commission recognised 100 years later.[1]

Recruitment: chief officers

From early times the new police authorities, watch committees in the towns and the justices in the counties, were seeking different kinds of men to command their forces. Only the largest and most prosperous towns could afford to offer the kind of salaries that would attract first-class candidates. Liverpool, the biggest force outside London

140

(with an establishment of 956 men in 1857) offered, at £650 per annum, the highest salary of any provincial force, county or borough; Manchester (554 strong) came next, at £550; while Birmingham (350 strong) offered £450—a salary rather higher than that offered by most counties at the time—and Bristol (301 strong) £350. The great majority of the boroughs set their sights much lower, the range varying from £40 to £200. Some looked to the Metropolitan Police for their first chief constables, and commonly attracted officers of the rank of inspector; bringing with them the experience and traditions of the Metropolitan force, they undoubtedly helped to set and develop common standards everywhere. Many small boroughs, however, were reluctant to spend their ratepayers' money on a qualified outsider, and chose the simpler course of appointing one of the earlier generation of watchmen to be the head constable, whose pay would be only marginally higher than that of the handful of men under him. Rock bottom was reached in such places as Romsey, whose Head Constable (there was only one other) was paid a weekly wage of 19s., and Bewdley, where the senior man received 5s. 10d. and his only subordinate 3s. 10d.

The counties present a very different picture. To the justices, previous police experience mattered less than social acceptability. Most spurned the experience of the Metropolitan Police, preferring good family connections—if possible, local ones—and above all the cachet of military service. The permissible salary range was laid down in Lord Normanby's rules as £250 to £500 per annum, and several counties—Lancashire (with a police establishment of 657 in 1857), the West Riding (487 strong), and, surprisingly, Gloucestershire (only 254 strong)—offered the maximum. A more common salary was £400 or £450, but a few counties, particularly the Welsh ones, offered the minimum of £250. A few examples of the county chief constables appointed to the forces newly created in 1856–7 illustrate the kind of men the justices were seeking. The first Chief Constable of Dorset was Lieut.-Colonel Samuel Symes Cox, 'late of the 56th Regiment, aged 39 years', and he was followed eleven years later by Captain Amyatt Brown, 'late of the 5th Lancers, aged 37 years'. Herefordshire secured Captain James Drummond Telmer, aged thirty-two, formerly an artillery officer, who was succeeded thirty-eight years later by Captain the Hon. Evelyn Theodore Scudamore Stanhope, who served until 1923. Oxfordshire similarly progressed up the social scale. The county's first Chief Constable was Charles Mostyn Owen, aged thirty-eight, who had previously raised and organised a Kaffir police force; on

141

his retirement in 1888, Lieut.-Colonel the Hon. E. A. Holmes à Court, the fifth son of the second Lord Heytesbury, was appointed. Occasionally 'a local man of good family' who had attained only modest military rank would be preferred to more senior candidates.

Many of these men were appointed in their thirties, or even twenties, and went on to serve in the same force for long periods, for no age of retirement was laid down. As a result, there are some remarkable instances of long continuity of command. Thus Gerald de Courcy Hamilton, appointed to be first Chief Constable of Devonshire in 1856 at the age of twenty-nine, remained in post for thirty-five years, retiring in 1891. Major Harper, the first Chief Constable of Monmouthshire, was thirty-three on his appointment in 1857. He retired in 1893 after commanding the force for thirty-six years, and his successor held the post for the next forty-two years, retiring at the age of seventy-three in 1936. Thus for almost the first eighty years of its life this force was led by only two men—a record shared with Surrey, whose first Chief Constable retired in 1899 at the age of eighty-six, after serving for forty-eight years; his successor was in the post until 1930. Chester City force had only four chief constables during the whole 113 years of its existence—from 1836 until 1949. The first began his service as a superintendent of the watch in 1824, gave evidence before the Royal Commission of 1836–9, and retired as first Chief Constable of the force in 1864, having commanded it for twenty-eight years. The second served for thirty-four years (1864–98); the third for twenty-two years (1898–1920); and the fourth and last for twenty-nine years—from 1920 until the amalgamation of the force with the county in 1949. Long continuity in command helps to explain why traditions in the police service have survived with little change from one generation to the next. It would be unthinkable today to leave a man in command of a force for so long; the force, as well as the man, grows stale and stagnates. Nevertheless, there can be no doubt that the traditions established by many of the early chief constables, particularly the county men, were of the greatest value, and it is probable that their longevity in office was no bad thing during the formative years of a force. Ex-Superintendent George Ford, formerly of the Kent Constabulary, recalled as recently as 1957, on the centenary of the birth of the force, the memory of the first Chief Constable, Captain Ruxton, who attested him shortly before Ruxton's retirement in 1894. He had then served for thirty-seven years as Chief Constable, and Ford remembered him as 'a beloved and kindly old gentleman whose portly form, prominent beard and inevitable

142

umbrella were a feature of the parade ground, as was the four-wheeler in which he used to drive around'. He was not so much a disciplinarian as 'a typical English country gentleman in cap and tweeds, building a police force in an English tradition of fair-play and no nonsense'.[2]

Mrs. Hart has pointed out that the arguments for and against appointing the 'thorough gentleman' or the policeman with administrative experience to the post of chief constable were going strong as early as 1855–6;[3] but for many years the counties ran true to form, and even as late as 1908 only 12 per cent of county chief constables had risen from the ranks, in contrast to 93 per cent in the boroughs.[4] The towns preferred police experience to family background; and an attitude which is probably not unrepresentative comes out pleasingly in remarks attributed by Sir William Nott-Bower, when he appeared as a young candidate before a selection board in Leeds in 1878, to a town councillor who was a fruit-dealer by trade and auctioned figs in the Leeds Market on Saturday nights. The councillor, who afterwards became Mayor, moved an amendment in the Town Council to reduce the salary offered to the Chief Constable on the grounds that, 'The office of Chief Constable isn't worth the figure. We'd 'ave lots of applicants if we put it up at 'alf the wages. We don't want one of these 'ere Gentlemen, who can play lawn tennis and go a-fishing, or make a nice bow in the Mayor's drawing-room, or say 'ow-d'ye-do without dropping his H's. What we want is a man as can catch a thief when a chap's 'ouse is broken into.'[5]

This attitude brings out the important contrast between the status of borough and county chief constables which has already been stressed in the last chapter: the county man, once appointed, was supreme commander of his force and acknowledged little higher authority; the status of the borough man, on the other hand, was probably accurately described by the Chief Constable of Norfolk in a memorandum to the Home Secretary in 1858 as 'merely the superintending and executive officer of the watch committee'.[6] In other words, the counterpart of the county chief constable was the watch committee itself, not the head constable of the borough.*

---

* That this point was fully understood and accepted by the Home Office for many years is shown by a memorandum dated May 1st, 1876, in *Home Office Printed Papers*, Vol. III, which states: 'The head constable of a borough police force holds an inferior position as compared with the chief constable of a county force. In fact, in a borough, the watch committee, subject to the council, discharges several of the functions which with respect to a county police force belong to the chief constable or Secretary of State.'

Reference has already been made to the practice, already common during the early, formative years of police forces, of men transferring from one force to another on promotion. This practice continued and probably increased during the later decades of the century, and there is evidence that movements of this kind came to be regarded as an essential condition of success for the ambitious man. Local police histories are full of examples. Between 1836 and 1847 the small borough of Congleton had twelve chief constables, five of whom left on transfer to other forces. Swansea appointed a superintendent to command the force in 1851 who had formerly served as a chief inspector in the Bath Police, following early experience as a Metropolitan Police officer; he was succeeded six years later by an officer who had served for fifteen years with the Colchester Police, and when the latter transferred on promotion to Preston, the newly appointed Head Constable of Swansea was a man who had served as a superintendent at Carmarthen and subsequently in the Metropolitan Police. These examples might be multiplied by hundreds. To some extent, no doubt, the cross-fertilisation of ideas brought about by these interchanges was a valuable counter to the tenacity with which some chief constables of the larger forces clung to their jobs for several decades.

It is tempting to form some generalised picture, a sort of identikit, of the chief constables of the period. From contemporary descriptions and old photographs, it is easy enough to form an impression of the county man. Typically, he is a portly, heavily bearded person, the expression stern or sometimes patriarchal, the real man tending to be lost behind a luxuriant growth of whiskers. The uniform, with its accompanying sword, braid and plumed hat, is invariably magnificent. His colleague in the borough is a more elusive figure, and no general picture emerges. The few top men in the large cities seem generally to have been of a common stock with the county men, and in the medium-sized boroughs the head constable was, typically, the able, intelligent and ambitious young man in his thirties, who had early made good in the Metropolitan Police or one of the larger county or city forces. In the small boroughs, where self-interest and economy led to the promotion of a local man who could be relied on to obey orders and not ask questions, the head man would either be described as a superintendent or head constable. So far as it is possible to form a general impression of these minor officials, an identikit picture emerges of big, burly, grim men with big beards and ample moustaches, huge tunics buttoned up to bulging necks—men to strike terror into their constable(s), a single glance from whom would seem likely to have cured many youngsters of delinquency for life.

Recruitment: constables

The average age of the men who enrolled as policemen 100 and more years ago was 26 years.[7] Most came from the labouring classes, the great army of unskilled who otherwise would look to the field or factory or colliery for a life-time's drudgery, and whose fathers, haunted by memories of the hungry forties, would pull every string in the parish to get their sons into secure employment. Moreover, a job in the police offered not only security; it offered respectability, warm clothes and the opportunity for self-improvement, eagerly exploited by men who were to fill the rank of the sergeants, inspectors and superintendents in years to come; and, most attractive of all probably, it offered the allure of a tiny pension in old age. In exchange for this, a recruit enrolled in a para-military organisation which demanded little less of its adherents than did the Order of the Franciscans, with its vows of poverty, chastity, and obedience. He was attested in the terms of an oath that differed scarcely at all from that sworn by the parish constable of the Middle Ages, and was then issued with a top-hat, frock-coat, baton, and cutlass, so that he could start duty next day.

Four successive waves of recruitment built up the regular police force during the thirty years that followed the passing of the Metropolitan Police Act, 1829. First came the intake which formed the Metropolitan Police itself, a body some 3,300 strong, who were mostly drawn from outside the old system of parish constables and watchmen. Second came the demands of the boroughs in 1835–6, all but the largest of which were less fastidious, and re-employed some of the old watchmen under a different authority; this intake was of the order of 4,000 men, a small proportion of whom came from London.*

* There is some uncertainty about the extent to which the Metropolitan Police helped in the formation of the new borough forces. According to Charles Reith (*British Police and the Democratic Ideal*, 1945), the following Metropolitan Police officers had been lent or permanently transferred by January 31st, 1838: four superintendents, twenty-two inspectors, forty-six sergeants, and ninety-five constables; and these had gone to 111 centres in the provinces. The Metropolitan Police Commissioners themselves, however, in List 'B' with the Commissioner's letter of November 14th, 1838, in *H.O.*, 61/21, set out a total of 136 places 'where a police has been established with the aid of the Metropolitan Police to November 1st, 1838', involving a total of 221 men of all ranks. Mrs. Hart has pointed out (article on 'Reform

The counties which adopted the permissive Act of 1839 came next. Their demands were also of the same order (between 3,000 and 4,000) and they commonly milked the Metropolitan and larger borough forces. Finally came the intake following the Act of 1856, when the remaining counties were obliged to set up constabularies, a demand which resulted in a further enrolment of upwards of 3,000 men. The progress of the build-up outside London was accordingly somewhat as follows:

	*By 1851**	*September 30th, 1856†*	*September 30th, 1857†*
Counties	3,006	3,936	7,200
Boroughs	4,375	4,831	5,448
Totals	7,381	8,767	12,648

Lord Normanby's rules prevented the counties from lowering their standards to the extent that some of the smaller boroughs had done, for many of the old parish constables and watchmen were automatically disqualified. Under the rules the upper age limit was forty and the minimum height without shoes 5 ft. 7 in. A candidate had to be 'able to read and write, intelligent and active and certified to be free

of the Borough Police, 1835–56', *op. cit.*) that only thirty-four of these places were municipal corporations, the others being mainly rural areas, and she comments, 'the impression of more extensive help may have been derived from confusing the loan of policemen to help set up a force with their loan for a temporary crisis, such as races, fairs, elections, disturbances or particularly serious crimes', temporary loans for which purposes were made on a large scale. This cannot, however, be reconciled with the fact that List 'A' attached to the Commissioner's letter gives a separate total of 3,010 men 'sent to the country for a temporary purpose from June, 1830, to November 1st, 1838'. The inference is that List 'B' relates to permanent transfers; if this is correct, the question must be asked: What kind of forces did these men help to create in the rural areas? And the answer may well lie in the strengthening of Improvement Act police, or police set up under the Lighting and Watching Act.

* Estimated. The total, 7,381, was given in evidence to the Select Committee of 1853 by the Chief Constable of Hampshire; the allocation to the county forces can be deduced from the strength of the borough forces, estimated by Mrs. Hart at 4,375 in 1853 (see 'Reform of the Borough Police, 1835–1856', *op. cit.*).

† Extracted from the reports of H.M. Inspectors of Constabulary for 1856–7. In addition, London had about 6,600 policemen in 1857.

from bodily complaint and of a strong constitution; and recommended as of irreproachable character and connections'. During the latter part of 1856 advertisements for the new men were appearing all over England, of which that of the newly appointed Chief Constable of Dorset in the *Dorset County Chronicle* on November 17th, 1856, is typical: 'I am prepared to receive applications from all persons wishing to join. Except under special circumstances, such as previous service in the police, no person will be appointed who is under twenty-two or over thirty-five years of age, or under 5 ft. 8 in. in height, or who has more than two children dependent upon him for support. No candidate will be admitted who cannot write and read writing.' Preference was, naturally, given to applicants with former police experience elsewhere, and there was a great deal of cross-movement about this time from the by now well-established county and larger borough forces, as well as the Metropolitan Police, to form the backbone of the new county constabularies. Second preference tended to go to ex-soldiers, and to men employed under local Improvement Acts or professional parish constables who were not wholly unfit and illiterate. Beyond these categories the justices took what they could. According to the historian of the Kent Constabulary, practically any hefty and healthy-looking young man of known honesty was accepted and put in uniform. But many were very soon wearing civilian clothes again. Of 214 constables appointed to form the new Cheshire Constabulary in 1850, for example, 112 had been discharged within three years, sixty-five of them in the first twelve months.[8] By far the most frequent cause of dismissal in all forces was drunkenness.

Little or no formal training apart from drill could be given in the new forces. The first General Order issued in Dorset called on the new constables 'by individual zeal and discretion and intelligence' to 'make every effort to supply the unavoidable deficiency of general instruction'. But before long the well-established forces were making great efforts to inspire in new recruits a sense of loyalty to the service and to teach them the rudiments of the job. Particular care was taken, as it had been when the Metropolitan Police was formed, to remind men of their obligation to the public and of the constant need to cultivate good relations with the public, and most general orders were modelled on those issued by Rowan and Mayne to the Metropolitan Police in 1829. The text survives of *An address by the Head Constable to Young Men on joining the Liverpool Police*,[9] written in 1852 and revised in 1879. It is of interest not only as an example of an enlightened attitude towards the induction of new recruits into the force, but also for its period flavour, and the way in which it brings out the paternal attitude of the chief constable towards the rank and file. It is a long address, and here there is room only to give brief extracts from it:

'As I am about to speak to you at great length I wish you to stand in as easy a position as possible, changing your position as often as you choose; and in return for the pain I take (not *trouble*, for I dislike that word), I want you to lend me your eyes and your ears, and give me your best attention. . . . In addressing you I will use very simple words, earnestly telling you what you may expect from me, and what I expect from you.

'Not one of you has entered the Force by any letter from rich Merchant, Magistrate, or Town Councillor, or from any friend of my own. You have been selected from my own opinion as to your health, strength, intelligence and respectability . . . of two men, however, now before me, one may rise rapidly to a superior rank, because of superior ability and superior conduct, while another must serve the usual time. . . .

'The Watch Committee allow you very excellent uniform, and a Constable who does not take the trouble to keep it and himself clean is a discredit to the Force. It is very simple and becoming; it is easily kept bright and clean, with its belt-plate, buttons and helmet. . . .

'I am very glad when my men are rewarded—it shows you have rendered someone a service. . . . The English are a very generous people, and quick to reward . . . rewards are entered into the Conduct Book, and weigh much in promotion. In this book is also entered any punishment incurred. I will not blot that book for a trifling fault. . . .

'Those of you who live in a Section House have many comforts and conveniences: mess-room, smoking-room, reading-room, etc., books and papers, hot meat for dinner every day; and on the very lowest rate of pay you can each save somewhere about 12*s.* a week. . . . If you marry (and I hope you all will, if she is a good washer, and can mend and darn) it is a nice thing to have plenty to begin house with. It is a good thing to save 12*s.* a week, for you will be able to send to the "old folks at home" a guinea at Christmas, and I wouldn't wait until Christmas; do it every now and then—they were kind to you "all the year round".

'You are not sent naked into the streets: for the first three or four weeks you are of no use to me: but that is not your fault. You cannot perform your duty until instructed. You are formed into a Probationary Class and taken to the Police Court, where you will see the Constables in the position that you will be in bye and bye. Observe how differently one Constable gives his evidence from another. One speaks low and thick, tells a long story, which is so rambling that when he has finished you hardly know what he has been talking about. Another stands erect, fills his chest, speaks distinctly, with voice sharp and clear, telling his case in a very few words, and when he has done you know all he heard, all he saw and all that happened. When you come out of Court, ask yourself the one question, "Have I learned anything?" Great pains are taken to instruct you whilst in the Probationary Class, and you will be sent out from six to nine in the evening, along with an intelligent Constable, to whom you must put all manner of questions, turning your thoughts into the groove of your new duties. Ask what kind of people live in this or that neighbourhood; what big building that is; where are the nearest railway stations, etc., etc., and especially where the nearest fire station is. In order to make you acquainted with the whole town, you will be in one neighbourhood today, in another tomorrow. Last of all, ask yourself the question, Do I know the name of the very street in which I have been walking for the last three hours, or the name of that church "whose lofty spire points to heaven?" If you thus make your duties the subject of your conversation and thoughts, you will get to be intelligent, and intelligence with good conduct leads to promotion. . . . While in this class, an opportunity will be taken of teaching you drill. . . . Drill opens out the chest, the great seat of life; drill will make you a healthier and, what may be of consequence to some of you, a handsomer man. . . .'

The Chief Constable then turned to his hobby horses, kite-flying and public relations. 'Kite-flying in the streets is a very dangerous practice; and if the string breaks and the kite flaps in the face of a horse, it will frighten it: the horse may injure himself, kill his rider, and, seeing how crowded the crossings of our public thoroughfares are, cause great danger to many. The kite is almost always in the hands of a very little boy or girl, bought probably with a penny given by a next-door neighbour. To bring such a little creature before the magistrates would never do, although it is an offence against the bye-laws. To put a stop to flying kites, one constable, of rough disposition, snatches the kite, snaps it in two, at which every person passing by will say something like "What a horrid fellow that is; the police are not at all a good sort of men." Another constable, seeing the same thing, will call out in a pleasant voice, "My little lad (or lass), go to the fields and fly your kite there, it may cost a man his life flying it in the street;" thus showing the public that, whilst a constable has his duty to do, he has some regard for what people will think of him. The opinion of the public is often formed by the single act of a single individual, whether rough or smooth.'

Instructions on fire-fighting, diligence in the discharge of duty, the control of licensed premises, and good temper followed, but 'I give no lessons as to the use of the baton, except that the human skull in some persons is as thin as a worn-out sixpence. . . . ' Punctuality, neatness, the overriding importance of always telling the truth, disreputable houses, returned convicts, church attendance—all were faithfully dealt with; and finally—'If you don't like the police duty, don't quarrel with me. A new coat, a new shoe, does not fit well at first, neither will your new duties. Give them a fair trial, and if they do not suit you, leave the Force with the same good character you brought into it.'

The early policeman's lot

Gilbert did not overstate the truth about the contemporary policeman (*The Pirates of Penzance* was first staged in 1880) in the much-quoted refrain, 'A policeman's lot is not a happy one'. Once enrolled, the policeman embarked on a way of life that demanded almost unremitting hard work performed under conditions of severe discipline, in exchange for a weekly wage that left him, particularly the married man with a family, near the breadline. No Police Federation existed to protect and promote his interests, and, apart from a provision in Lord Normanby's rules which laid down rates of pay in the counties, the whole of his conditions of service (including in the boroughs the rates of pay) were left to local discretion. Nevertheless, the wage for constables in all but the very smallest borough forces soon settled down to a fairly uniform level. The county constabulary rules laid it down at not less than 15*s.* and not more than 21*s.* a week, and this range was generally observed by the borough forces as well—the Bewdleys were rare exceptions. Up to three classes of constable were found in the largest forces, and men were able to move from one class to another on promotion, with an increase of pay within the range laid down.

In return for wages at the level of unskilled agricultural labourers, a man worked a seven-day week. The average day's duty was ten or twelve hours, usually performed in two shifts, the longer—up to seven hours—at night. Sometimes, particularly in the middle years of the century, it was much longer: thus the Swansea Police petitioned in 1843, following a reduction in their weekly wage from 18s. to 16s., against so low a wage for men 'employed on duty from 14 to 17 hours of every 24'.[10] All patrolling was done on foot, so that men would tramp upwards of twenty miles a day for continuous weeks at a stretch. No boot allowance was paid before 1873. Uniform was to be worn at all times, and it was the practice to charge a deposit for the uniform; alternatively, 5s. were deducted from a man's wages when he left the force, in order to pay the cost of altering his uniform to fit the next recruit. Other regulations governed a policeman's private life. 'All men of the force who shall associate, drink, or eat with any civilians, without immediately reporting that same to the Superintendent, will be dismissed the force', declared an early order of the Pembrokeshire Constabulary. Police were not allowed to vote in Parliamentary elections until 1887. Attendance at church on Sundays, generally in uniform, was compulsory, and strict orders governed a man's personal appearance. In the Maidstone borough force, for example, whiskers were compulsory until 1873; in Monmouthshire beards were to be not more than 2 in. long. Policemen, however, took care of their looks. 'Where's the pelisse?' Mrs. Gamp complained. 'If they greased their whiskers less and minded the duties which they're paid so heavy for a little more, no one needn't be drove mad by scrouding so.'

The uniform worn by the early policeman outside London generally consisted of a swallow-tail coat of dark blue cloth, a well-glazed 'stove-pipe' top-hat, with white duck trousers in summer and blue serge in winter. He was issued with oilskin cape, staff, handcuffs, rattle, and button brush, and he carried with him an instruction book on the lines of that given to the Metropolitan Police. Higher rank was signified by finer uniform rather than distinctive badges: thus the Kentish constable's complete uniform cost £4 6s. 3d., with an extra 1s. for mohair lace on a sergeant's collar, or £6 5s. for the superintendent's superior frock-coat with braided collar. Cutlasses were issued for night patrol, and men were trained to drill with them. During the 1850s and 1860s the top-hat and white trousers were on the way out, and helmets were coming in. Whistles replaced rattles in the 1880s.

151

Rest days were rare in the 1860s and 1870s. A man was lucky to have one day off in the course of four or six weeks, and his pay was liable to be stopped or reduced if he were absent from duty on account of ill-health. In this respect, however, the Metropolitan policeman was temporarily better off than his provincial colleague. In 1868 the force was augmented by 1,120 men so as to enable one day's leave in seven to be granted, but the concession was short-lived. Two years later it was withdrawn on the grounds that the day off duty 'detracts from instead of increasing' the man's efficiency, and the 'constable becomes unhinged and unsettled by constant interruption to duty, and not infrequently unfitted by one day's leave for duty on the next'.[11] Instead, the Metropolitan Police had to be content with two days every month, one of which was to be a Sunday. In 1882 this arrangement provoked a memorial by the Lord's Day Observance Society, of which the signatories included the Archbishop of Canterbury and the Bishop of London, asking that the men should be given more leave, particularly on Sundays to enable them to attend divine service. This was rejected, and the matter was allowed to smoulder for another twenty years when, following considerable agitation in Parliament, the Government decided to set up a select committee on the question of a weekly rest-day for the police.

It was a common practice in all forces to allow an annual week's holiday, but this was generally without pay. These seven days must have been rarely prized: the strict routine left little time or opportunity for other relaxation from one year to the next. Policemen were even discouraged from entering the public houses and beer-houses which formed the centres of much of Victorian working-class life. Nor, perhaps, was the policeman on his annual holiday able to relax entirely: one of the duties of the Ramsgate and Margate police in the 1870s was to 'watch the bathing'.

Discipline was strict and punishments were imposed arbitrarily. In the counties the chief constable was the sole disciplinary authority, with power to fine a man, reduce him in class or rank, or dismiss him. In the boroughs the watch committees were the disciplinary authorities, but they shared the power of dismissal with the justices. In neither case was there any right of appeal. We read of men being 'ordered to pay the expenses of medical attention caused by using more violence than was necessary in self-defence'; 'fined for neglect of proper performance of duty by keeping company with singers on 24th and 25th December'; and 'fined for allowing prisoner to escape and to pay expenses involved in the recapture'.[12]

It is not surprising to find that the turnover in manpower was very high. In the early years of the Metropolitan Police it amounted to about $33\frac{1}{3}$ per cent a year. Out of 100,000[13] men entering the service, no fewer than 40,000 (or in the boroughs 45,000) would leave before they had served for twelve months. Of the same 100,000, only some 28,000 would remain for as long as five years (22,000 in the boroughs) and the number still serving after twenty-five years would have shrunk to a mere 1,600 in the Metropolitan Police (where a pension was available on medical grounds after fifteen years' service), and to 6,000 to 7,000 elsewhere. About one-half of the 100,000 would resign without pension, and nearly one-third would be dismissed. Of the remainder, some 4,000 would die in service, leaving a residue of pensioners and men discharged with a gratuity varying from 17,000 in the Metropolitan Police and 13,000 in the county forces to 9,000 in the borough forces. Not all the men dismissed for misconduct, however, were lost to the service: the inspectors of constabulary frequently complained that, while such men were statutorily barred from enlisting in a county force, many of them were recruited into borough forces without any inquiry having been made as to their character.

If the turnover in manpower is a fair index of the state of morale in an occupation, as it is commonly regarded to be today, it is impossible to maintain that all was well with the police forces of the period. Discontent was undoubtedly rife, and it was to boil up in minor police strikes later in the century. Yet it is a matter of common experience that shared endurance of adversity welds, tempers, and strengthens a disciplined body, and it requires little imagination to believe that in the early testing-times the true and lasting quality of the police service was forged in a manner that would have been quite impossible today. Many quitted, but the stoics who stuck it out, while no doubt enjoying a show of grumbling their working hours away, must surely have found the way of adversity sweet. At all events, these tough men brought to the service qualities of patience and endurance that have been some of its finest characteristics ever since. They also brought, or developed, other endearing and enduring characteristics, such as police jargon—the policeman of 100 years ago was 'proceeding on his beat' when he 'accosted' a suspect whom he 'had reason to believe' might wish to come to the station 'to help with inquiries in hand'. They also founded the many police families, in which son followed father in the same force for generations down to our own times, numerous examples of which can be found in local police force histories. Some had been founded even before the creation of the 'new police'. Chief Inspector Frankish, who was serving in the Birmingham force during the Second World War, was the great-grandson of Joshua Frankish, an Improvement Act watchman who transferred to the new borough force in 1839. A Mr. Jennings, formerly Deputy Chief Constable of Surrey, who died in 1951, was the great-grandson of a Bow Street Runner.

Promotion to intermediate rank

For a small proportion of men the hardships of police life were alleviated by the prospect of promotion. Lord Normanby's rules for county forces embodied the well-established principle in the Metropolitan Police that, 'when vacancies occur in the office of superintendent, inspector or sergeant, it is desirable that encouragement should be given to meritorious men serving in the subordinate station by their promotion to the higher stations, when they are qualified'. Opportunities for advancement varied according to the size of the force. Generally, promotion went by seniority as much as by merit. The inspectors of constabulary constantly urged that the interests of efficiency should be the only valid test, and it is refreshing to find as early as 1859 a chief constable declaring that 'over-zeal in getting convictions will effectually retard promotion—it will be accorded to those who strictly obey the printed regulations and the orders of their superiors and who perform the duties assigned to them in a conscientious and impartial manner'.[14] There is little evidence that the system of promotion in the counties, where the chief constable had complete discretion, gave rise to dissatisfaction. The abuses, where they occurred, were in the boroughs, for the Act of 1856 contained nothing to prevent the kind of irregularities which had been reported to the select committee of 1853. The inspectors of constabulary refused to be drawn into the merits of individual cases, and there was therefore no way of preventing unscrupulous members of watch committees from seeking favours of the police in exchange for early promotion.

By Lord Normanby's rules, the qualifications for appointment as sergeant were the same as those for enrolment as constable—that is, a sergeant had to be able to read and write, he had to be intelligent and active, of strong constitution, and recommended as of irreproachable character and connections; and an appreciable number of sergeants

154

and inspectors for the forces newly formed in 1856–7 were recruited ready-made from former superintending constables. A description of the sergeant's duties in 1889[15] shows that they have not changed in essence from that time to this, although the status of the rank has grown: in the middle of the last century the sergeant was paid only 4*s*. a week more than the constable, and might spend much of his time on ordinary beat patrolling. More often, however, he commanded a group of from six to eight constables (known then, as now, as a 'section'), took charge of the police station, read out to his men their instructions on the morning parade, and kept them under close supervision throughout his period of day or night duty, visiting them on their beats at prearranged points. He was responsible for seeing that the men kept their clothing and accoutrements in good order, that they were clean, and that their whiskers conformed to the force regulations. To qualify for promotion to the rank of sergeant, a man had to be able to drill his constables and to ride a horse.

According to a Home Office memorandum of 1878, it took a man from four to five years to be promoted to the rank of sergeant and a further eight to ten years to be promoted to the rank of inspector. The inspector, according to the same author of 1889, was 'looked upon as a guide, guardian and referee by those whose unpleasant business causes them to seek police aid. In contrast with bygone days an inspector must be a man of education and capable judgement; the public must feel a firm reliance in him as such.' He took charge of a sub-division containing several sergeants (as many inspectors still do today) and spent much of his time in court. Inspectors were commonly appointed as inspectors of weights and measures and assistant relieving officers for vagrants. They supervised common lodging-houses and reported on the highways and bridges, and on any outbreak of cattle diseases.

The indiscriminate use of the title 'superintendent' in Victorian times is apt to be confusing. The rank (like that of sergeant and inspector) was first established in the Metropolitan Police, and the jurisdiction of a superintendent was defined in the County Police Act of 1839 as a petty sessional division. By the Act of 1840 it might be any area which the justices determined. Lord Normanby's rules laid down that the superintendent 'must be a man of general intelligence, able to read and write well, and to keep accounts', and he was to be paid between £75 and £150 a year. From the start the post was recognised as a key one, and by 1889 the writer on the police already quoted regarded it as 'the one great binding link in the police system'. A superintendent had 'a pretty firm hold on his appointment and he may occasionally rise to the post of chief constable', although as a rule superintendents did not apply for these 'prizes of the service', being content 'with the comforts and respectability of the position they had attained. . . . Their love for the service, matured through many years, usually induces them to hold on to the verge of their physical disability.'[16] Here, incidentally, we have a further illustration of the longevity in office that must also have contributed to the ossification of a force. The same writer paints the following picture of a superintendent of earlier days: 'a well to do man who kept horses, cows and pigs, and on market days he was always found trading. He was a little over fifty years of age, rotund, and when standing at attention he could not see his feet, and had not done so for years. He had a short thick neck, bullet head, low brow, fox terrier eyes, rubicund nose, ruddy complexion, and light brown mop-like hair.' But in the 1880s, we are told, there was a marked improvement in the standard of education of superintendents, a claim borne out by experience in Monmouthshire, where a young man named Bosanquet was appointed as Superintendent in the force at the early age of twenty-four, after serving for only seventeen months in Hertfordshire. He was appointed Chief Constable for the county six years later.

Zeal and ability were (or ought to have been) the principal qualifications for promotion, and by the 1860s county chief constables were introducing formal promotion examinations. An example drawn from 1867 is that of the newly appointed Chief Constable of Dorset, who had shown early initiative in obtaining Mayne's permission to qualify himself by studying the duties of the Metropolitan Police. He now drew up a syllabus for examination in the following subjects, a suitable pass mark being the necessary qualification for promotion to superintendent:

'1st. Multiplication and division of money. Rule of Three, Tables of Weights and Measures used by Inspectors.

'2nd. Making out a Superintendent's Journal, Pay, Charge and Summons Sheet.

'3rd. Classification of Offences.

'4th. Answering written Questions as to the duties of a Superintendent and as to the general knowledge of the County, with the names of the principal towns and means of communication by railway and Telegraph.

'5th.   Such a knowledge of drill as to be able to put a squad
through the simplest movements of a company drill.'*

Police work in Victorian times†

In principle, the task of the policeman 100 years ago did not differ
from that of his successor today. He was appointed to keep the
Sovereign's peace and to apprehend the disorderly and criminal; and
his powers, from time to time amplified by Parliament, were rooted in
the common law of England. Many of the methods he still employs
had their origins then. In the 1850s men were paraded before going
out to patrol their beats, when the sergeant would read over the instructions for the day or night for the benefit of any who were unable
to read themselves. Men took notebooks with them and occasionally
carried lists of known criminals. As the Police Postwar Committee
reported in 1947, 'the present principles [of the beat system] differ
little from those first instituted when police forces were established
something like 100 years ago'.

'Constables will proceed to their respective "meets" or "places of
conference" by the nearest Turnpike Road', an early force instruction

* *Dorset Constabulary, 1856–1956.* The requirements for promotion
from the rank of constable to sergeant or inspector were:
'1st   Reading.
'2nd   Writing neatly and correctly from dictation out of the Instruction
Book.
'3rd   The first four rules of arithmetic with addition and subtraction of
money.
'4th   Making out a Sergeant's Report.
'5th   Answering written Questions as to a Sergeant's general duties.'
† In the last century the police were given many extraneous duties, which
generally included appointments as inspectors of nuisances, inspectors of
weights and measures, and inspectors under the Diseases of Animals Acts;
they commonly undertook the inspection of dairies and shops, contagious
diseases and petroleum and explosives. They would carry on the old-time
practice of the night-watchmen in calling early risers, and sometimes they
were responsible for switching on street lighting. The local ambulance was
frequently under police control, and for many years—in some cases until the
formation of the National Fire Service during the Second World War—the
borough forces ran the fire brigade, so that policemen took turns on fire
duty, often receiving a supplementary allowance. The reason for assigning
extraneous duties to the police was, of course, to justify their cost, as an
order issued to the Lincolnshire Constabulary in 1858 made clear. Constables were to be required to whitewash lock-ups, 'and they are to be
informed that this, or any other similar service, is to be cheerfully rendered
by them'.

said, 'or if there be none by the nearest highway, but not diverge through lanes or fields. They will wait at the "meet" half an hour, and state in their diaries the time of arrival of the other Constables, the duration of the conference and the subject on which conferred.' It was a common practice, as a means of ensuring that men worked their beats properly, to insist that some token of a man's attendance in a particular place should be recorded. The same force instructions go on: 'Sergeants and Constables will each day leave tickets at the house of some respectable person residing at the most distant point of that day's patrol, and also at the residence of any Magistrate or Clergyman or Gentleman by which they may pass. They will state in their diaries the names of the persons on whom tickets have been left. Should the parties called on have retired for the night the ticket must be inserted under the front door.' Innovations were introduced in very early days, for which originality has been claimed in modern times. Thus Cartwright, reporting for the inspection year 1859–60, foreshadowed the system of mobile-team policing introduced in Aberdeen eighty years later: 'In Essex I find a system of dropping night patrols in practice, which appears worthy of imitation, that is to say, the superior officer taking a patrol constable in his cart to a certain part, and dropping his men and taking up others from time to time and place to place, as they may be required during the night.'

No meal breaks were allowed in the early days of policing, and a man's ingenuity was constantly taxed by the need to find privacy where he could eat a snack to sustain himself over the six or seven hours of each shift on duty. The Leeds Watch Committee resolved as early as 1845 to supply each policeman going on night duty during the winter with a 'tin bottle containing a pint of ready-made coffee'. In another force men were granted the 'privilege' of eating a snack in public conveniences, but the more athletic would shin up gas-lights in the street to warm a can of tea on the gas jet.[17] A former police surgeon told the Select Committee on the Police Forces Weekly Rest Day in 1908 that every policeman carried a spirit lamp and had 'a little arrangement for cooking his food up an entry'.[18] Readers of *Punch*, however, were led to suppose that Victorian policemen spent much of their time in kitchen basements eating rabbit pie, and indulging a weakness for plump cooks and pretty parlourmaids.

From the contents of early personal diaries or journals which have been examined, and other sources, it is possible to form an impression of the kind of duties that occupied the bulk of the rural constable's time.[19] Most of the days consisted simply of many hours of patrolling the long, unmade country roads, hot and dusty in summer, muddy and wet in winter, on the chance that some such incident as petty larceny, sheep-stealing, drunkenness, or (a common offence) 'riding without reins' might enliven the day's work. The everyday offences were poaching, vagrancy, sheep-stealing and drunkenness, and the supervision of public houses (which were then open all day) constituted a great part of the daily work; and attention had often to be given to cock-fighting or prize-fights. Vagrancy continued well into the century to present much the kind of problem that the Royal Commission of 1836–9 had described. A vast army of tramps, thugs, poachers, and swindlers begged or pedalled or thieved their way from one market town to another, following the progress of the fairs. Primitive records of known vagrants were registered locally, and the police were able to acquire useful information about suspicious characters from workhouses or common lodging-houses. Probably over most parts of the country, as R. L. Stevenson put it in his *Essays of Travel* ('An Autumn Effect'), written in 1875: 'The crime and the law were in admirable keeping; rustic constable was well met with rustic offender.'

Long hours of toil and tedium, aching feet, boredom and blisters, coarse jokes over a mug of tea, countless brawls in streets and pubs, more foot-slogging by moonlight or starlight with a lantern searching down a dark alleyway, a sergeant breathing down a man's neck on morning parade, the stink of police cells when tramps are unlocked on a fine summer's morning, wearing in a new pair of boots, issue of a whistle in place of a rattle, the chase after a youth when a man finds himself out of breath at forty and begins to see the end, the longed-for day of release on a small pension if luck or ill-health earn it after all: it is surely possible for a policeman of today (even, with a stretch of imagination, for the war-time soldier) to catch a faint breath of the daily routine of the policeman in Queen Victoria's time. But what is to be said of his heroism? How can justice be done in a summary account to the men in a couple of hundred forces in a period of half a century who were maimed or killed in the course of duty, setting the early traditions of selfless devotion that even the brave men of today can scarcely surpass? Local force histories tell of the ingenuity and skill and courage of Victorian policemen in tackling major crimes, often squalid and brutal and sickening, the excitement of action and the battle honours that have been handed down to create the traditions that inspire their successors today. Here there is space only for a respectful tribute.

Detective work

Heroism is one thing, professional skill quite another. As early as 1859 Cartwright stated in his inspection report that 'in almost every force of average number one or two trustworthy officers' had been selected for detective duty, but there is little evidence that these honest men had much success outside the field of ordinary local crime committed by known criminals. Team-work was in its infancy. Co-operation between detectives in neighbouring forces barely existed, and virtually no scientific aids were available except photography and plaster of Paris for taking footprints. Many people were led by Conan Doyle to regard even Scotland Yard's men as ignorant bunglers, and in the early days there was foundation for the belief. A few detectives seem to have exploited qualities of native skill and cunning that matched the brains of major criminals, but at least until 1878, when the Metropolitan C.I.D. was formed, most English detectives were very far from being in the same class as, say, the French. Detective work, during much of the nineteenth century, was the Cinderella of the police service.

To discover the reason for this it is necessary once more to look back to the circumstances in which the 'new police' were created. Their primary function, as Peel had insisted, was to *prevent* crime, and their main method was to patrol the streets in uniform. The special craft of thief-catching had always had something of a mystique about it since the time of the Bow Street Runners, and Peel's guinea-a-week policemen were not recruited primarily for their intelligence. It was a gain to a poor man that a policeman would try to catch the thief who had robbed him without charging a fee, as the parish constable would have done, but it did not follow that the prospects of success would invariably be higher. Moreover, the Popay incident in 1833 (p. 55) served as a reminder of the extreme sensitivity of public opinion towards anything that savoured of 'Continental' methods in using police for espionage purposes or to trap people, and this no doubt discouraged the formation of a detective department at Scotland Yard. Nevertheless, a nucleus of detectives, comprising two inspectors and six sergeants, was set up in 1842. Dickens, in *Household Words* (1850), compared it favourably with the 'vast amount of humbug' that attended the Bow Street Runners, but it was slow to develop; and at the time of the Fenian outrages, in the 1860s, the Prime Minister, Lord Derby, told Queen Victoria that the Metropolitan Police was 'especially deficient as a detective force'. *Punch* good-humouredly dismissed it as the Defective Department. Part of the trouble was that detectives had been forbidden to hobnob with criminals, and there remained a strong prejudice against allowing them to work in plain clothes. The information that came their way must have been scanty. Efforts were made in 1869 to improve matters, but in his report for that year the Commissioner complained that the difficulties were great: a detective system was 'viewed with the greatest suspicion and jealousy by the majority of Englishmen and is, in fact, entirely foreign to the habits and feelings of the nation'.

But if the general climate of opinion in which the Metropolitan C.I.D. came into being was hostile, the circumstances which finally led to its formation could hardly have been more discreditable to the force. In 1877 three out of the four chief inspectors in the detective branch (as it was called) were found guilty at the Old Bailey on charges of corruption. Later that year the Home Office set up an inquiry into the state of the branch, from which it appeared that several members (they included one of the convicted chief inspectors, who possessed the un-English name of Druscovitch and spoke with a foreign accent) had been direct entrants brought in to raise the educational standards of the branch, and improve its linguistic capabilities. An enterprising young lawyer named Howard Vincent went to Paris to study the French system, reported on it to the inquiry, and successfully applied for the newly created post of Director (later Assistant Commissioner) in charge of the new Criminal Investigation Department. He started with about 250 men, which within six years he had expanded to a force of 800.*

Even so it does not seem to have been very efficient. Sherlock Holmes made his first supercilious appearance in print in 1887, and London was stunned by the Jack the Ripper murders in the following year. Criticism of the C.I.D., some of it perhaps unjustified, was widespread. The Whitechapel murders, as they were alternatively known, stirred up a wave of public panic comparable with that which had followed the East End murders of 1811. The bodies of five women were discovered, disembowelled and savagely mutilated, and the technique pointed to a single murderer. C.I.D. inquiries got nowhere, and a complaint even arrived from Windsor: 'The Queen fears that the detective department is not so efficient as it might be.' Bickering between the high-handed Commissioner, Sir Charles Warren, and the Home

* Vincent formed a Special Irish Branch of the C.I.D. in 1884 to counter Irish terrorists. Later, when its activities broadened, it simply became known by its present title, the Special Branch.

Secretary did not aid matters. The Commissioner sought support for any action, 'however illegal', he might take, and the Home Secretary declined to give it. He asked for authority to offer a reward for information leading to an arrest, but again was refused. In the event, the identity of the murderer was never discovered. Warren resigned in dudgeon, partly over this incident, partly through pique occasioned by quarrels with the Home Secretary about his methods in dealing with rioting in Trafalgar Square a year earlier (the incident is described below), but mainly because he refused to submit to the authority of the Home Office. (He later fought in the Boer War and helped Baden Powell to form the Scout movement in 1908.) In such circumstances it was not difficult for Sherlock Homes to establish a decisive superiority over the Metropolitan C.I.D.

Many (but by no means all) provincial forces had set up separate detective departments by the end of the nineteenth century, and by 1892 the Home Office had evidently interested itself in detection methods, for in that year the department issued a circular explaining how the cast of a footprint could be taken with the aid of a copper-bottomed kettle, resin and wax, a proprietary method, the full rights of which had been bought by the Government, and which was said to be much superior to the use of plaster of Paris. In the same year Francis Galton published a work on fingerprints which contributed to the appointment by the Home Secretary, Asquith, in 1893, of a committee 'to inquire into the best means available for identifying habitual criminals'. The Committee heard evidence from Galton, and as a result the system he propounded (based on the pioneer work of a Frenchman named Bertillon) was introduced at Scotland Yard. It was soon replaced, however, by a more efficient system, which has remained in use ever since. The antecedents of this apparently derive from China and other east Asian countries, where fingerprints have for thousands of years been used for purposes of identification. The system was brought to Scotland Yard by Sir Edward Henry, a former inspector-general of police in Bengal (he was subsequently appointed Commissioner of Police in London, and was made the scapegoat for the police strike of 1918), who perfected an earlier system developed by an Indian civil servant, Sir William Herschel. Hence, in the early years of this century, Scotland Yard was perfecting means of tracing the criminal antecedents of convicted persons and the identification of criminals from prints left at the scene of a crime. But it was not until the years between the wars that the rudiments of a nation-wide system of detection techniques were laid down.

Public order

Crime was one challenge to the police; the other was public order—the forgotten industrial and political disputes that made up the news headlines long ago. Local and Parliamentary elections were a constant source of trouble. Passions ran high and mob violence was not uncommon. Magistrates frequently swore in additional special constables on the eve of an election, and it was not unusual for the day to culminate in a pitched battle between opposing factions in which the roughs for miles around joined in. The disorders of Chartism became a thing of the past as the century progressed, but, as Carlyle had foreseen, its spirit lived on as working-class consciousness grew. To the police fell the unenviable task of appearing to oppress the working people from whom most had come, and the tension of these encounters was the tension of a whole society in the grip of sociological forces beyond men's comprehension. Caught up in the wider issues, the police could only carry out their traditional duty of maintaining law and order, regardless of personal involvement. They stood (as they sometimes do today) at the storm centre of the conflict between two naturally antagonistic and mutually uncomprehending systems of virtue—radicalism and authority. And to aggravate matters, the public demonstrations which offer the greatest challenge to the police frequently attract some of the most intelligent and enlightened people of the day, as well as the scum of the Metropolis, ready to seize and exploit any opportunity for mischief-making. Such a combination of circumstances demands from the police qualities of tact, discretion, and firmness of the highest order, and these qualities have to be exercised on the instant without time for reflection. All the earliest police force orders followed the lead of the Metropolitan Police in emphasising the importance of cultivating good relations with the public. As the century progressed and conflict between police and public, particularly in London, increased, the wisdom of these orders was constantly borne out.

A notable example of conflict between police and public occurred in the autumn of 1887, when riots of a severity unknown for many years —probably not since the high-tide of Chartism—continued intermittently for several weeks, culminating, on November 13th, in a pitched battle in Trafalgar Square. William Morris, the early socialist, writer, and artist, took part in these events; and it is of interest to compare his view of police activity with that of Sir Charles Warren, the Commissioner.

'A strange sensation came over me', Morris made the visionary say in *News from Nowhere*, which he published three years later. 'I shut my eyes to keep out the sight of the sun glittering on this fair abode of gardens, and for a moment there passed before them a phantasmagoria of another day. A great space surrounded by tall ugly houses, with an ugly church at the corner and a nondescript ugly cupolaed building at my back; the roadway thronged with a sweltering and excited crowd . . . a paved be-fountained square, populated only by a few men dressed in blue . . . guarded up to the edge of the roadway by a four-fold line of big men clad in blue, and across the southern roadway the helmets of a band of horse-soldiers, dead white in the greyness of the chilly November afternoon.'

The Commissioner reported to the Home Secretary:[20] 'The police were drawn up round Trafalgar Square proper in the manner I showed you on plan on the 12th November, viz. a solid row, four deep all round the south end, and about two deep round the other sides, making in all about 1,700. About noon all was quiet. Information was received that a number of socialist and extreme Radical Clubs intended to march on Trafalgar Square at 2.30 p.m. At 1 p.m. all was quiet, but crowds were commencing to assemble about Trafalgar Square. The General Officer Commanding was requested to move four squadrons of cavalry at 3 o'clock. . . . ' 'Some people', recalled the old man in William Morris's idyll (for the old man had read a history "of a fight which took place in Trafalgar Square in or about the year 1887") 'were going to hold a ward-mote here, or some such thing, and the government of London, or the Council, or the Commission, or what not other barbarous half-hatched body of fools, fell upon these citizens (as they were then called) with the armed hand . . . unarmed and peaceable people attacked by ruffians armed with bludgeons.'

The Commissioner reported: '4 p.m. Simultaneous attacks were made by the various bodies and mobs upon the police . . . at the various points [approaching Trafalgar Square] the police were but a handful amid thousands of the mob . . . in order to relieve the enormous pressure upon the police I called for two squadrons of cavalry. . . . 4.30 p.m. For half an hour the riot raged furiously in all directions, and I sent a squadron of Life Guards to Waterloo Place, where the police were nearly overpowered, and called on the 400 Foot Guards at St. George's Barracks to line the north side of Trafalgar

Square. It was a most critical half-hour. . . . At 5.15 p.m. a second attack was made on police. . . . At 6.20 p.m. quietness began to reign, and the cavalry were withdrawn.'

'I opened my eyes to the sunlight again and looked round me, and cried out among the whispering trees and odorous blossoms, "Trafalgar Square." "Yes," said Dick, who had drawn rein again. "So it is. I don't wonder at your finding the name ridiculous: but after all, it was nobody's business to alter it, since the name of a dead folly doesn't bite. Yet sometimes I think we might have given it a name which would have commemorated the great battle which was fought on the spot itself." '21

William Morris not only took part in the incident; he was already well known to the police, and had appeared in court two years earlier on a charge of striking a policeman, which, however, was dismissed. Ten days before 'Bloody Sunday' the Commissioner reported to the Home Secretary: 'November 3rd. A meeting held in the square. A few speeches delivered, and Morris was cautioned as to his language by Superintendent Sheppard.' But Morris was fair with his report of the fighting on November 13th. The Commissioner enclosed 'a letter in *Commonweal* from Mr. Morris, the Socialist, in which he clearly allows that if the disposition had not been so successfully made and the various points round Trafalgar Square so successfully held by the police, nothing but bullets and cold steel would have prevented the mob getting into the Square—in other words that the arrangements made by the police prevented riots and bloodshed of the most serious description.' The story might thus end with as satisfactory an exchange of courtesies as could reasonably be wished for, although the most apt comment on the whole situation is perhaps that recorded by a contemporary writer by no means unsympathetic to the police: 'The temper of the constables, overstrained by long hours of duty, was beginning to give way, and there was a good deal of significance in the observation of one policeman as he bound up his bruised fist in a handkerchief, after a hard bout, "This is what we have been waiting for. We are not going to do double duty for nothing!" '22

Later improvements in conditions of service

As the century advanced to its turn, the life of the Victorian policeman became slightly easier, although two widely separated police strikes served to remind the authorities that all was far from well.

165

Lord Normanby's regulations of 1840 survived until 1866, when they were replaced by others on similar lines, which raised the constable's maximum weekly rate of pay from 21*s.* to 23*s.* 4*d.* The rate remained unchanged when fresh regulations were made in 1873, but 1886 brought a further rise to 29*s.* 2*d.*, to attain which, however, a man had to serve for eight years.* These scales remained in force until 1919, although local improvements were commonly granted without reference to the Home Office. The pay of the higher ranks was correspondingly bettered, and the 1886 regulations introduced a new principle for chief constables by which their salaries were to be settled in relation to the strength of the force, subject to the approval of the Home Secretary.

Other improvements in conditions of service came gradually. In 1887 policemen were allowed, for the first time, to vote in Parliamentary elections; and six years later, in 1893, a similar concession was made to enable them to vote in municipal elections.[23] These were important signs of the times, showing how far the police had advanced in public esteem. The allowance of annual leave was increased in many forces to ten or fourteen days, and in a few instances the rate was even more generous.[24] It was about this time, too, during the last decade of the century, that many police athletic and sports clubs sprang into being, giving an outward and visible shape to earlier informal developments of the kind. The importance of these recreational activities can hardly be exaggerated. They fostered *esprit de corps*, brought the policeman's wife and family into closer touch with police life, and, by introducing the policeman into the community off duty as well as on duty, helped to establish the image of the policeman of the 1890s as a clean, smart, athletic young fellow, who was a distinct cut above the average working man. When half the force turned out for the annual sports and the police band played waltzes at the summer fête or carnival even the older generation, brought up in the 1830s and 1840s, would realise that the modern policeman represented a complete break from the watchman and parish constable of their boyhood.

However, it would be misleading to paint a rosy picture of police life towards the end of Queen Victoria's reign. A realistic note is struck by the evidence given on behalf of the police to a select committee of Parliament ten years later about the waste of time at bands and sports 'as privileges of the few at the cost of the many'.[25] If time off could be arranged for some to play while the rest worked, it was

---

* It will be recalled that the regulations applied only to the county forces, although many boroughs also chose to observe them.

argued, it would be fairer to give a weekly rest-day to all. Much had certainly improved since the early, formative years, but grievances enough remained to keep the barrack-room lawyers happy, and on two occasions—in 1872 and 1890—these grievances led to minor strikes in the Metropolitan Police. Though separated by eighteen years in time, the demands that lay behind each were much the same— namely, the 'right to confer' (i.e. to form an authorised trade union), higher wages, a pension as of right, and, in the background, the longing for a weekly rest-day.

A series of clandestine meetings and demonstrations calling for a pay rise precipitated the trouble in 1872. In the course of these the language of militant trade unionism was heard for the first time in the police, and men were demanding the right to combine in order to bring pressure to bear. The Commissioner conceded an increase of pay but the meetings continued. Their organiser was victimised by dismissal on a trumped-up charge of insubordination, and about 180 men refused duty. The four ring-leaders were brought before the magistrates, and three received sentences of imprisonment. Meanwhile, more than 100 strikers had been dismissed; afterwards, having expressed contrition, they were reinstated with reduced pay. The strike was thus not about wages, but about the 'right to confer'.

The second Metropolitan Police strike, in 1890, occurred when a Police Pensions Bill, the successor of several abortive measures, was actually before Parliament. Thirty-nine men were dismissed on this occasion, and none was reinstated. By that time the demand for a pension as of right had virtually been conceded—it had never, in any case, had much substance in it for the Metropolitan policeman, who had always been more generously treated in this respect than his colleague in the county and borough forces—but the men were exasperated by the delay in passing the Bill and, as presented to Parliament, it could actually worsen their benefits in some ways. The claim for a weekly rest-day and the 'right to confer' also remained unredressed, and dissatisfaction with pay added to the general grievance. Exciting scenes occurred outside Bow Street when the men went on strike, and troops of the Life Guards were called in to restore order. To this chapter belongs an account of the painful steps by which the police, eventually aided in each case by the backing of a select committee of Parliament, tardily secured their pensions charter in 1890, and a weekly rest-day ten years later. The struggle for 'the right to confer', which precipitated the final and much more serious police strikes of 1918–19, is described in the next chapter.

The right to a pension

For sixty years, from 1829 until 1890, members of the new police force enjoyed no absolute entitlement to a pension. Probably most recruits hoped eventually to qualify for one, but only a small proportion outside London succeeded in doing so. Even when a man had served long enough and had reached the minimum pensionable age of sixty, the justices in counties, or the watch committees in boroughs (who had to obtain the approval of the town council), still retained complete discretion whether or not to grant a pension, and also to determine its amount, subject to a fixed maximum. Many authorities paid scant regard to the need to obtain actuarial assessments, and when the first generation of policemen was due for retirement local superannuation funds were commonly discovered to be insolvent. The early reports of the inspectors of constabulary constantly drew attention to the need for placing these funds on a sound financial basis and for conferring an absolute right to a pension, but many years passed before effective action was taken. In London, on the other hand, the Metropolitan Police had from early times enjoyed a firm expectation (though not a right) to a generous pension; and much effort during the second half of the nineteenth century was directed to placing the provincial police in a similarly favourable position. Here there is room only to give the briefest outline of the successive steps by which the unequivocal right to a generous pension was finally granted to policemen everywhere.[26]

In the Metropolitan Police Act of 1829 power was given to grant pensions, but no absolute right was conferred, no scale was prescribed, and no provision was made for a superannuation fund. The latter deficiency was remedied in the 1839 Act, which provided for the fund to be supplied from a variety of sources, including deductions from pay, fines for misconduct, and fines imposed by the courts for drunkenness and assaults on the police; and the Act authorised the dividends from the fund to be paid out in pensions for not less than fifteen years' service. The pensions were not to exceed half-pay if for less than twenty years' service, and not in any case to exceed two-thirds pay. No pension was payable under the age of sixty except on medical grounds. From the beginning, on account of what the Permanent Under-Secretary of State of the Home Office described fifty years later as 'a ruinous mistake', the superannuation fund was quite unable to bear the demands made on it. The scale of pensions awarded was too

168

generous; it enabled a man to retire, for example, on a two-thirds pension after only twenty-four years' service. By 1856 the capital of the fund was exhausted, and Parliament authorised the deficiency to be made good from the Metropolitan Police Fund in the following year. The Government then called in the superintendent of the statistical division of the General Register Officer, a Dr. William Farr, to advise how matters could best be put right. Farr was a joint architect of the civil servants' pension scheme and from time to time, over a period of some thirty years, he devoted much time and skill to promoting fair and workable arrangements for the police. The first result of his efforts was to put the Metropolitan scheme on a sound basis. The early, over-generous arrangements were replaced in 1862 by others under which policemen qualified for a two-thirds pension after twenty-eight years, two-fifths after twenty years, or three-tenths after fifteen years.

The position in the counties was even less satisfactory. The Act of 1840[27] had obliged the justices to maintain a superannuation fund to be supplied from similar sources to that of the Metropolitan Police, i.e. from deductions of pay (which amounted to about 6*d.* a week), fines, etc., and the statutory limitations on pensions were also modelled on the earlier arrangements in London. However, the justices, lacking sound administrative and financial advice, were erratic in the exercise of their discretion whether to grant a pension. Generally they acted on the recommendation of the chief constable. In some forces no provision at all was made for the man who retired normally on the expiration of his service, an award of a small pension or gratuity being granted exceptionally to a policeman who was found to be medically unfit after substantial service.[28] Elsewhere the police authority would vote on whether a sergeant with twenty-two years' service should receive a pension of 14*s.* or 18*s.* a week.[29] In 1866 and again in 1877, Dr. Farr was reporting that in the aggregate the county police superannuation funds were insolvent, their failure being only a question of time. The deficiency was generally made good out of police rates.

The boroughs presented the worst picture of all. The Municipal Corporations Act, 1835, authorised the borough treasurer to pay pensions, but made no provision for a superannuation fund; and an Act of 1848[30] enabled, but did not compel, town councils to form such a fund. Most boroughs chose not to do so. A further Act of 1859[31] made the establishment of a superannuation fund obligatory and required its solvency to be guaranteed by the borough rate fund.

Still, however, the watch committees retained complete discretion whether or not to award a pension. These arrangements did not work in the interests of borough policemen: the watch committees exercised greater economy and reserve in granting pensions than did the county justices, as a result of which the borough funds, unlike those in the counties, were on the whole not insolvent. It was the policemen, not the ratepayers, who suffered. The inspectors of constabulary reported instances where no superannuation funds existed, and others where contributions which ought to have gone to the superannuation fund found their way into the borough rate fund instead. Where the force received no Government grant (either because it was inefficient or too small to qualify for one), the Home Office could do nothing but draw the attention of the mayor to the failure of the watch committee to observe the law.[32] Bizarre arrangements occasionally came to light. The report of the inspectors of constabulary for 1869 disclosed that at Cardiff a substantial part of the Chief Constable's salary was taken out of the superannuation fund. Arrangements of this kind must have fomented much indignation among men from whose meagre wages compulsory deductions were made to support the funds from which they could barely dare hope to be lucky enough eventually to draw a small pension themselves.

Following much agitation, a select committee of the House of Commons,[33] set up in 1875, spent two sessions hearing evidence about the state of these superannuation funds, and they must have been impressed by the colossal rate of premature wastage which the introduction of a firm pension entitlement could do much to check. They recommended, in their final report in 1877, that pensions should be awarded as a matter of right after twenty-five years' service, that the standard of pensions payable in the provincial forces should be brought up to the level of those available in the Metropolitan Police, and that pensions should be a direct charge on the rates. The last point was solidly opposed by the advocates of rating relief, who argued that the Exchequer itself should bear the cost of police pensions, and when a Bill was introduced into Parliament five years later, in 1882, it foundered on this issue. The same Bill was reintroduced in several successive years, but still made no progress. Eventually, after no less than fifteen years' abortive effort, the recommendations of the select committee set up in 1875 were largely embodied in the Police Act of 1890. Every policeman gained a legal right to a pension after twenty-five years' service or, on medical grounds, after fifteen years. Police authorities were free to settle the amount of pension within a prescribed maximum and minimum, and to impose a minimum qualifying age, but the ordinary expectation (and in the Metropolitan Police the rule) was that a man could retire after twenty-five years' service with a pension amounting to three-fifths of his pay, whatever his age.* Special pensions were provided for officers injured in the course of duty and for the widows and children of officers who died during their service, and an Exchequer contribution was authorised in aid of local superannuation funds.

A weekly rest-day

The police secured their pension right despite the lack of any federation or union to act as their advocate; it was gained for them largely by men of goodwill, in and out of Parliament, who realised their worth and spared no effort to procure their desserts. The absence of formal means of making representations about their conditions of service was to hamper them for many years yet; but in 1892 an enterprising man named John Kempster founded a journal entitled the *Police Review*. He told a select committee of Parliament sixteen years later why he had done so: 'It was started by me because, in communication with some Metropolitan constables, I discovered that they had many difficulties, but that no individual constable dared to make any complaint. I saw that they needed a paper that would ventilate their troubles, advocate their interests, and assist their better education.'[34] To Kempster must go much of the credit for the fact that during 1906 and 1907 the Order Paper of the House of Commons contained repeated questions urging the need for policemen to be allowed one day's leave in seven, a campaign which eventually led to the appointment of a select committee on the matter in 1908, and the passing of the Police Forces (Weekly Rest-day) Act two years later.

The importance to the police of this select committee, as a milestone in marking the progression towards conditions of service which today are taken for granted, needs no emphasis. The committee's report is also of great value to the historian for the light it sheds on the police service at the turn of the century, for most of the police witnesses spoke from experience of the 1880s and 1890s. But the document is

* A return was presented to Parliament after the Act had been in operation for a year, which sets out the scales adopted in all forces. Most adopted the maximum and few imposed a qualifying age, though some forces prescribed a minimum age of fifty-two or fifty-five, and sixty for the higher ranks.

something more, again, than the mere lens of a camera, focusing vignettes of the last of the long line of Victorian policemen. If there is something about it of an afterglow of the sunset of the old century, there are anxieties enough about the dawn of the new. The debate was ostensibly about men's need for more rest and relaxation, but there are constant refrains of deeper issues: the police service the Edwardians had inherited was leaderless and lacked inspiration; the men were groping for a sense of unity and means of corporate expression; the nature of police work, more demanding than ever before, called for higher qualities.

In the perspective of history, these underlying problems dwarf the narrow issue the committee was to settle. On this, the arguments were simple enough. Hostility to the grant of a weekly rest-day stemmed, naturally, from those responsible for the public purse: the ratepayer could not afford the augmentation of strength which would be required. Kempster, the Editor of the *Police Review*, ably argued the men's case, and a succession of policemen of all ranks testified to the mounting strain of police life, underlining the disadvantage to a policeman and his family if they were unable to enjoy leisure at the same time. Police doctors conceded that more time for relaxation was needed, but offered conflicting views about when it should be taken. One thought the men stood to gain more from an additional seven days' summer holiday (which, however, it was generally accepted that they would be unable to afford to spend at the seaside), while another attached more importance to relieving the constant strain by awarding one regular day off in seven. A police doctor's wife probably spoke with more practical common sense than any of the men. One day off in seven would often avoid long illnesses: 'After having got a chill, having been out day after day in rain, fog, etc., clothes scarcely dry before they have to go out on duty again. After recovering from an illness, hardly knowing how to keep up till they go off duty (especially with those heavy overcoats). After days or nights of broken rest owing to the illness of wife or children, as soon as they come off duty, they have to turn to and help in the house, or look after a sick child while the wife goes out to do her shopping . . . a man is practically deprived of going anywhere with his wife and children. When the leave comes round, he is constantly obliged to spend it in mending boots, or doing things in the home which he has had no time to do on ordinary days. . . . By the time the man has had his breakfast, it is time for the children to be put to bed, and there is no chance of turning out the room properly. It is often a great strain on the wife trying to keep the

172

children quiet all day long during the night-duty month, and one day a week would be of the greatest benefit in relieving the strain, in enabling the wife to clean the rooms, and making it possible for the children to see something of their father at least once a week.'[35]

These issues were straightforward enough, and it is good that Parliament arrived at the humane conclusion. But the larger questions, which they were not called upon to answer, continued to hang in the air long after the committee reported in 1908.

The first—the lack of leadership in the police service—emerged early in the inquiry.[36] In what must have been the most uncomfortable ten minutes of his official life, the senior Home Office witness was obliged to admit that the Home Office had no view on the question of a rest-day, and that the department had made no attempt to find out the views of the police service. 'Have the Home Office no desire to consider the well-being of the men socially?' a member of the committee demanded, and was told, reasonably enough, that they had every desire to do so, but that they were also concerned on behalf of the London ratepayer. The Home Office, it was clear, could not or would not express the corporate view of the police service, and its representative was shown up, no doubt unfairly, as somewhat insensitive and aloof. Perhaps somebody else could speak for the men?

Here the second unsolved issue emerged. Were there any facilities for the men to hold meetings and discuss grievances, the committee asked a former member of the Liverpool City Police. It was possible, he replied. 'They have to apply to the Superintendent first, and then he sends the application through to the Head Constable.' But, according to an ex-Metropolitan Police sergeant, 'men are very careful not to speak too freely, even to their comrades, lest it may be talked about, and cause them to be marked as discontented men'.[37]

A weekly rest-day could do something for a man's health, but it could do nothing to supply the want of leadership or to remedy the frustration of an inarticulate rank and file. Probably these things would not have mattered if the Victorian way of life had continued to pursue its tranquil way, but the pace of civilisation was yearly imposing new strains on the police and making demands no Victorian policeman had had to meet. An inspector of the Sheffield City Police told the select committee, as though it was a matter of course, that three men had recently been seriously injured—one with a bullet in his neck, the second with an eye cut out in a drunken brawl and the third—representing the new hazard—run over by a motor-car.[38] For these were the years that saw the beginning of the road-traffic problem. They also brought the suffragettes. 'I believe in most of the cases where a policeman loses his temper [with a suffragette], it is because a man has not had proper rest for his nervous system every week', a police doctor testified shrewdly.[39] Moreover, the spate of legislation was increasing—between 1900 and 1908 eighteen Acts of Parliament affected the duties of the police.[40] And the strain of law-enforcement did not diminish. The Sheffield Inspector touched a contemporary note when he declared that 'the merciless cross-examination of an unfeeling barrister or solicitor . . . is an experience a policeman never forgets, and upon which he looks back with dread.'[41] The Chief Constable of Manchester probably summed the matter up fairly when he commented that police duty in 1908 bore little resemblance to that of twenty or thirty years earlier. Then the policeman dealt largely with the criminal; now he was rendering a public service to all classes, and this demanded higher standards of intelligence and of personal conduct than ever before.[42] The policeman as a social worker was a new phenomenon, introducing a concept of policing in which the policeman's wife also had a part to play. 'In future where a constable applies to me for permission to marry', the Chief Constable of Surrey had ordered in 1899, 'his application must be accompanied by a recommendation or testimonial from a clergyman, or some responsible person, who can guarantee the respectability of the woman whom the constable intends to make his wife.'[43]

It was not only the chief constables who were aware of the spirit of change that was converting a job into a vocation. The men, too, saw it and welcomed it. 'When I joined the force', said a man who enrolled in the Liverpool police in 1882 and retired as a sergeant in 1908, 'it was the exception to find one man who did not drink on duty. Today it is the exception to find one man who does.' It was essential that policemen should have a high moral character, for 'there never was the opportunity that they have now of doing good'.[44]

These were the hidden tensions that underlay a series of major events, occurring ten years later, which were to transform the Victorian system of police forces into something like the police service we know today. The absence of central leadership was gradually remedied by the assertion of authority by the Home Office. The Police Federation gave the men the sense of unity and moral purpose (as well as the negotiating strength) without which 180 separate police forces could never have grown into the dedicated service which won the affection and esteem of the public in the 1930s to an extent that persuades men still serving to look back on the period as a golden age. And although the strain and complexity of police work continued to grow, there is evidence that the quality of new recruits matched the new challenges. The mid-Victorian policeman, for all his stolid, drunken worth, had receded as far back into history in 1908 as the watchman and parish constable had long ago receded from him.

Chapter Six

Towards a Police Service 1908–39

The police institution on the eve of the First World War was still a collection of Victorian bric-à-brac. There remained fifty forces with a strength of fewer than fifty men. Little co-operation existed, and there were no common standards of pay and other conditions of service. Foot-patrolling was the basis of all good police work, though bicycles were appearing in the 1890s and senior officers toured their area by horse and trap. The Home Secretary's rules of 1886 still governed the county forces, but left the watch committees in the cities and boroughs to follow local wishes. There was no direction from the centre, no special police department existed in the Home Office, and, as though to emphasise its lack of concern about standards of local policing, the department in 1907 reduced the number of inspectors of constabulary from three to two. Apart from the stereotyped reports these inspectors sent in annually, little information was available about what was happening outside London. Policing was still a local function, as it had been for hundreds of years, and no one wanted things different. Upper- and middle-class England would welcome the sound of known feet in times of trouble; otherwise they were still able to relax over the comical figure of the rural constable of stage and fiction, with the uneducated jargon he brought from the Victorian working classes, for to the favoured minority the policeman was still far from being a figure of authority—until they bought motor-cars.

Police, motorists, and public

The first petrol-driven motor-cars appeared on English roads in the 1890s. Probably owing to their scarcity, it seems that the police did not at first prosecute drivers who disobeyed an early law requiring steam-propelled vehicles to be preceded by a man on foot, limiting their speed on the open road to four miles per hour. By the turn of the century, however, it was clear that the regulation of motor-cars would need its own legislation. The permissible speed limit was gradually raised to twelve, then to fourteen, and in 1903, to twenty miles per hour. Each limit seemed to the police to be realistic enough to be enforceable. To the motorist, in that period of swift invention, each was irksome enough to be disregarded. Conflict was inevitable, and nowhere, perhaps, was it more bitter than in the county of Surrey, from the first the Mecca of many London motorists. As early as 1901 the *Daily Mail* carried the headline, 'Surrey police make war on automobiles'. The Chief Constable was reported to have declared, 'I will stop them at any cost,' and motorists complained that the police were not playing the game in a sportsmanlike way.[1] They played it in the way they were told to play it, often by chief constables who had been in post for upwards of thirty years and who, being ex-military men, were loyal to the horse (though the Chief Constable of Surrey at that time was a very young man who simply disliked motor-cars). Under such guidance, policemen showed much devotion to duty in crouching behind hedges or in ditches with stop-watches.

In 1905 the A.A. was started to protect motorists, with the result that the police were soon prosecuting the A.A. patrols who dared to warn them of speed-traps, thus 'obstructing the police in the execution of their duties'. Guerrilla warfare intensified, and the A.A. adopted the new tactic of making failure by a patrol to salute a member a sign that the motorist would be well advised to stop. He could thus be quietly warned of police activity in the area. Then slowly, with the growth in the number of motorists, particularly among the wealthy and influential, and the rapid expansion of the membership of the A.A., the conflict diminished. In 1910, when the first police motor-boats replaced rowing boats in the Thames Division of the Metropolitan Police, a number of chief constables were exchanging horse-drawn vehicles for motor-cars for their own use. Three years later the Home Secretary advised the police that speed-traps could only be recommended where high speeds were really dangerous, so that motorists at last had a taste of victory. The taste has long since vanished.

Relations between the police and motorists are, of course, only one part of the wider complex of relations between the police and the public generally. Before the First World War these came under critical review by that most authoritative form of Government inquiry, the Royal Commission.

The Commission was appointed in 1906, following sensational reports that Metropolitan Police officers had taken bribes from prostitutes and street bookmakers, and allegations of brutality and other unsavoury scandals. Its terms of reference related only to the Metropolitan Police, but it also heard evidence from provincial forces. (It seems to have been only the second Royal Commission to have been appointed to inquire into police activities. The first was in 1855, following outbreaks of disorder in Hyde Park, and this reported a certain amount of misconduct, 'a result more to be regretted on account of the high character' of the Metropolitan Police.) The Commission reported in December, 1908, and its report is a mine of information about the organisation and practices of the Metropolitan Police at that time. It is also an illuminating commentary on West End night life in Edwardian days. The Commission encouraged anyone with a serious complaint against the police to state his case, and it conducted its inquiries openly. The report sets out its findings at great length and in convincing detail, in a manner that recalls the methods of some celebrated inquiries of modern times. It all has a very familiar ring. The system for dealing with complaints is described in detail; and the Commission noted with surprise the 'somewhat rare combination of mental and physical powers' required of the constable, and how much more difficult and demanding his work is than that of the 'private soldier or the artisan'. Statistics of complaints are produced to show how few they are in relation to the strength of the force, and evidence is adduced to show how the most versatile and tolerant of all public servants could go out of his way to be kind to the prostitutes and sinners who walked the London streets of sixty years ago. Finally, the Commissioners conclude robustly that they have no hesitation in declaring that the Metropolitan Police discharged their duties with honesty, discretion, and efficiency, and 'the fact that upon the materials before us we must also find that occasionally constables have been guilty of misconduct of various kinds, and of various degrees of seriousness, is one that every person conversant with the difficulty of governing men, and who has had experience of life, would naturally expect. No reasonable man would, in approaching the question of the efficiency of so large a body as the Metropolitan Police, expect that every one of them should on all occasions act with sufficient intelligence and be invariably courteous and good-tempered in the discharge of very difficult duties.'[2]

This, an article in *The Times* declared, should put an end once and for all to attempts 'shamelessly and falsely' to attack the police, and there should be no further danger of misunderstanding between the police and the public for many years to come. Nevertheless, the newspaper acknowledged, within a year or two public opinion would be quite ready again to 'devour with gusto and credulity another "shocking police scandal" and demand "reform".' No sooner did someone stir up mud against the police 'than every one of us pricks up his ears, and is ready to take seriously the most absurd lies . . . the public cannot expect to be served as it would wish by men who know that, whether they do well or ill, at the first breath of calumny the very people to whom they give their best are ready to believe almost anything . . . '.[3] These words are unfortunately as true today as they were sixty years ago.

The Tonypandy Riots

The few years that followed the Royal Commission's report saw one of the most sustained periods of civil unrest this country had known for years, and the temper of the police, when dealing with strikers and suffragettes, was time and time again strained to the limit.

Occasionally, when serious rioting threatened, one force would come to the aid of another, but co-operation of this kind was exceptional. The Police Act, 1890, authorised standing agreements to be made between forces providing for mutual aid, but by 1908 fewer than sixty forces out of a total of nearly 200 had entered into such agreements.* In that year a select committee of Parliament on 'The Employment of Military in Cases of Disturbance'[4] reported that troops had been called out to aid the police on twenty-four occasions during the previous thirty-nine years, on two of which the order to fire had been given. The committee deplored the use of soldiers, and recommended that the Home Secretary should have power to requisition up to 10 per cent of any county force and direct them to any area threatened by riot. This recommendation was not adopted, but two years later a newly appointed Home Secretary, Winston Churchill, gave a singular demonstration of the way in which the old principle of local responsibility for law enforcement could be subordinated overnight, by the action of a forceful Home Secretary, to the overriding authority of the Crown. This martial episode, reminiscent of the attempts made seventy years earlier to suppress Chartism with the

* Mutual-aid agreements did not become general until 1925, following a recommendation of the Desborough Committee.

aid of soldiers, may perhaps fitly ring down the curtain on the arrangements for policing the country before the First World War.*

Serious rioting broke out among miners in the Tonypandy area
of the Rhondda Valley on November 7th and 8th, 1910. Churchill
had read Press reports of trouble a few days previously, on November
2nd, and that morning he despatched a telegram to the Chief Constable of Glamorganshire requesting a report.[5] On the same day the
local magistrates applied to the War Office for troops. Police and
military dispositions were made, but early on November 8th, the
Chief Constable reported a serious clash: 'Many casualties on both
sides. Am expecting two companies of infantry and 200 cavalry
today. . . . Position grave.' Churchill at once called a conference with
Haldane, the Secretary of State for War, A strong man was needed
to take over from the Chief Constable. Their choice fell on Major-
General Macready, son of the famous Victorian actor, William
Macready, who was a man of parts after Churchill's own heart,
urbane, cultured (he had known Dickens and the Brownings in his
youth), and a romantic imperialist. Churchill replied:

'Your request for military. Infantry should not be used till all
other means have failed. Following arrangements have therefore
been made. Seventy mounted constables [in fact, 100 were sent] and
two hundred foot constables of Metropolitan police will come to
Pontypridd by special train leaving Paddington 4.55 p.m., arriving
about 8.0 p.m. They will carry out your directions under their own
officers. The County will bear the cost. Expect these forces will be
sufficient, but as further precautionary measure 200 cavalry will
be moved into the district tonight and remain there pending
cessation of trouble. Infantry meanwhile will be at Swindon.
General Macready will command the military and will act in conjunction with the civil authorities as circumstances may require.
The military will not, however, be available unless it is clear that the
police reinforcements are unable to cope with the situation.

* It was not the last occasion when soldiers were called in to aid the
police. August 13th, 1911, was Liverpool's 'Bloody Sunday', when, following industrial unrest on Merseyside, Tom Mann and other trade union
leaders held mass meetings near St. George's Hall. Rioting broke out, in
which the Superintendent in charge of a contingent of the Birmingham
Police was seriously hurt and many police and civilians were injured. About
100 men of the Royal Warwickshire Regiment helped to restore order. The
Home Secretary, Winston Churchill, afterwards gave an account of the
affray to the House of Commons. Soldiers were used in Liverpool again in
1919, on the occasion of the second police strike.

Telegraph news Home Office and say whether these arrangements are sufficient.—CHURCHILL.'

An hour later, at 2.40 p.m. the Home Secretary sent a message to the strikers undertaking that, 'confiding in the good sense of the Cambrian Combine workmen', the soldiers would be held back for the present, and only the police employed. His optimism proved to be unfounded. The Chief Constable telephoned during the afternoon to say that the situation was deteriorating. At 8.0 that evening Churchill authorised the cavalry to move in. A second contingent of 200 Metropolitan Police was despatched at 3.0 a.m., and a third, consisting of a further 300 men, the following afternoon, in all providing the Chief Constable with a force of 1,400 men, of whom 120 were mounted, together with about 500 soldiers under General Macready. Little seems to have been left to chance. Thereafter Churchill directed operations from hour to hour from his desk in the Home Office. He advised against the use of troops. General Macready should 'act as you think best for the preservation of order and the prevention of bloodshed . . . vigorous baton charges may be the best means of preventing recourse to fire-arms', and the Chief Constable was to use 'the whole of the third contingent of 300 Metropolitan Police in Tonypandy tonight and establish a decisive superiority once and for all'. Thus the 'battle' proceeded; by November 15th Macready reported, 'A football match between the strikers and the soldiers was played at Tonypandy in which the soldiers were victorious', and Churchill replied with further detailed instructions: 'Pray consult me on any points which cause you embarrassment.' The Metropolitan Police remained in the area until the situation was quiet, but Churchill continued to maintain the closest control over their employment, having sent his own personal emissary, a young Home Office official named John Moylan (later Sir John Moylan, Receiver for the Metropolitan Police District) to send him confidential reports. 'I have again reminded the police of your instructions to me', the Chief Constable reported on November 18th, 'to act with firmness in dealing with a hostile crowd, especially now, when the police are in such force'; to which Churchill returned the characteristic admonition: 'You are quite right to act vigorously with your police force against serious riot. A certain amount of minor friction is, however, inseparable from present situation. Both sides are unreasonable in many ways and I should recommend you to go gently in small matters.'

181

Influence of the First World War on the police service

Police history would almost certainly have taken a different course had Churchill remained at the Home Office to direct the police, and not the Navy, after 1914. He would probably have succeeded (his successor tried, but failed) in persuading Macready to accept appointment as Commissioner in London that year, and Macready possessed the qualities, as he showed in 1918–19, that could have averted the Metropolitan Police strike. Thus Desborough would have fallen and all that followed. But Churchill left the Home Office in 1911, and the 'ifs' of history remain to tease. He had interested himself in contingency preparations during 1910—a chief constable who had been responsible for the 'egregious nonsense' of giving publicity to plans for requisitioning horses and vehicles was to have 'a sharp rebuke', and no other such publicity was to be allowed until a chief constable 'sees the gleam of the German bayonets'.[6] Apart from his concern with the Tonypandy incident, however, Churchill's most notable involvement in police affairs was in piloting the Police Forces Weekly Rest-day Bill through the House of Commons in 1910, and in attending outside a house in Sidney Street, in the East End of London, on a cold January morning in 1911, when armed policemen and soldiers fought out a battle with two Russian anarchists, whose gang had already murdered three policemen and maimed two others.

When war broke out, the police assumed many new duties under emergency measures. They were required to arrest enemy aliens, guard vulnerable points, enforce lighting restrictions, and deal with the consequences of air-raids—responsibilities shouldered a second time in the Second World War, and more fully dealt with in the next chapter. These emergency duties came to an end in 1918, and they had no lasting influence except to accustom the police to receiving instructions from the Home Office. In the meantime, however, events were stirring whose significance was not long in doubt. The hidden strains that weakened the police institution during the first decade of the twentieth century were described briefly at the end of the previous chapter: the lack of leadership from the Home Office, the absence of a sense of unity and direction among the rank and file, and the increasing demands made on the individual policeman. Conditions created by the war were largely responsible for the way in which, in the immediate postwar years, the first two of these difficulties were overcome in a manner that led to the transformation of the Victorian police system into something very much like the national institution we know today.

One catalyst in this process was the need, suddenly and for the first time apparent under the stress of war, for the Home Office to co-ordinate the war-time operations of chief constables, and to supply a measure of leadership; from the recognition of this need sprang an organisation of district conferences of chief constables, and a central conference of delegates from each district, which met for the first time in the Home Office in 1918. The consequences of these meetings of chief constables were far-reaching. For the first time in police history the county and borough men had regular opportunities for exchanging experiences, and people in the Home Office were at last in direct touch with them all, and not only with the county men. Within the short space of three years, the inspectors of constabulary were attributing to these conferences the fact that forces were co-operating much more closely than ever before, and that it was 'quite evident to an inspector that old diversities of procedure and custom are disappearing'. Nor were the conferences limited to promoting inter-force co-operation. They also paved the way for the Home Office to act, as Sir Frank Newsam, a former Permanent Under-Secretary of State has put it, 'as a general clearing-house for the exchange of ideas and experience, and to make its contribution to fostering the well-being and sense of common purpose that invests the whole police service'.[7] From the time of the First World War must be dated an ever-expanding administrative effort on the part of the Home Office, manifested in countless departmental circulars, conferences, committees, and working parties, which in course of time have effected virtually every aspect of police administration, and gradually replaced the total want of system that characterised the disparate police forces of the nineteenth century by a federal structure of local forces, each of which forms part of a greater whole and employs recognisably similar techniques and policies in serving national as well as local interests. All these consequences were not, of course, intended by those who inaugurated the district and central conferences of chief constables during the war; they simply flowed out from the conferences, as a tide of administrative activity tends to flow, according to needs that are still sometimes only partially recognised.

The other change effected by war conditions was complementary to the first: it was equally fundamental, and it completed the mutation of the Victorian police system. Its accomplishment, however, by the

Desborough Committee of 1919 and the Police Act of the same year, was preceded by two police strikes, which must first be described.

The police strikes

Two grievances soured many policemen during the war years. One, the absence of any 'right to confer', as the catch-phrase went, was mentioned in the previous chapter. By the outbreak of war it was a long-standing and festering grievance, focused and publicised by the activities of a man named Syme. As a young Inspector in the Metropolitan Police, Syme had shown great promise, but in 1909 he fell out with his superiors, accusing them of oppression and injustice. Syme, as an inquiry many years later showed, had right on his side, but he lacked discretion. He inspired an agitation in the Press and in Parliament against the senior officers of the force. Disciplinary action was taken against him, and he was dismissed. An uncompromising bigot, he embarked on a vendetta against the Commissioner, Sir Edward Henry, a patriarchal ex-Indian civil servant who administered the force on pro-consular lines. He published libellous pamphlets about Henry and associated himself with Kempster, the founder of the *Police Review;* then, in 1913, Syme started a clandestine union, the Metropolitan Police Union, afterwards styled the National Union of Police and Prison Officers. Syme's later career was sad and inglorious. He was in and out of prison many times for criminal libel and for trying to cause disaffection among the police in war-time. He frequently went on hunger strike, received a rough deal from a judicial inquiry in 1924, and was admitted to Broadmoor. The Government awarded him substantial compensation in 1931, but by then his mind was unhinged, and he ended his days, a pitiful creature, throwing bricks through the windows of the Home Office. He died in 1955.

Long before this, however, the Police Union had rid itself of so embarrassing a member. It had troubles enough without him, for men joined at the risk of dismissal. As the war advanced, many, in the provinces as well as in London, were prepared to incur this risk, as a new grievance embittered them. This was the failure of police pay to rise with the cost of living, which doubled during the war years. Policemen, contrasting their meagre weekly wage, augmented by an inadequate war bonus, with that of munitions workers, were an easy prey for the malcontents with mutinous talk. By 1918 many policemen and their families had sunk so low in poverty that they were actually under-nourished, and the temptations held out by bribes of food and money must at times have been irresistible. The Home Secretary convened a conference of police authorities in the Home Counties early in 1918 to consider the men's pay, and there was a movement among several of the larger authorities to co-ordinate (though not necessarily to standardise) their rates. By then, however, the clandestine Police Union seems to have made up its mind that, without collective-bargaining strength, the police would never have a fair deal. Nor did the Union lack powerful political support. Ramsay MacDonald in 1907 and Philip Snowdon in 1914 had both represented its case in Parliament, and by 1917 it had a substantial backing among Socialist Members. The police, indeed, had a fair and legitimate case, but the Government was not prepared to listen to it, at all events during the stress of war. And Sir Edward Henry, now nearing seventy, was unable to understand either what was wrong, or why the men wanted a union to represent them.

The inevitable happened. Early in the week beginning Sunday, August 25th, 1918, when a somewhat tardy review of the pay and pensions of the Metropolitan Police was already in hand, a policeman was dismissed for Union activities. On Tuesday, August 27th, the Police Union, provoked by Press reports (subsequently denied) that a pay rise was imminent, addressed letters to the Prime Minister and the Home Secretary making three peremptory demands: a substantial increase in pay, reinstatement of the dismissed policeman, and complete recognition of the Police Union. These demands were to be complied with by midnight on the following day, August 28th, under threat of strike action.

The stage was thus set for the most dramatic episode in the history of the English police—an episode that was to end a year later in tragedy. The main actors were well cast: the Commissioner, Sir Edward Henry, elderly, upright, and aloof, who was thrown out of office at the end of the week; Sir Nevil Macready, Churchill's flamboyant hero of Tonypandy, who supplied troops to guard London for forty-eight critical hours and then succeeded Henry; Lloyd George; Smuts; a somewhat obscure Home Secretary, Sir George Cave, who seems to have known little of what was going on; and a few militant policemen well indoctrinated by the trade-union movement, and determined to fight to the end, their plans now well laid. All was at odds. It was a collision of generations, outlooks, ideals, and personalities that left no room for a meeting of minds. Besides, the situation had grown too tense for talking round a table, even if all the actors had been there to talk. They were not, for late August was (and is) Whitehall's close season: the Home Secretary was on holiday in Somerset, the Permanent Under-Secretary of State, Sir Edward Troup, refused for twelve critical hours to return from Berkshire, and the Commissioner was in Ireland. Thus the Whitehall machine was scarcely strong enough to avert the threatened strike even if it had wanted to, and there is evidence that it did not. The deputies who were left in charge wholly underestimated the strength of the Union's position, and seem to have been in a mood to bluff things out.

By midday on Friday, August 30th, some 6,000 of the Metropolitan Police were out on strike, and Londoners were astonished to see them marching in columns of four, determined, but in good humour, with a solitary piper at their head. According to *The Times*, traffic continued to flow freely, but Guardsmen armed with rifles were posted outside Government offices in Whitehall.[8] The War Cabinet met and appointed General Smuts, as a Home Secretary extraordinary, to act as an intermediary to confer with the superintendents. Smuts invited two men from each division to meet him at the Home Office. Instead, a deputation from the Police Union arrived. Smuts refused to deal with them, and they went away threatening to bring out the City Police, which they did. The real Home Secretary arrived back from Somerset that evening, followed a few hours later by Sir Edward Troup. By then the strike was virtually total. Apart from a few hundred soldiers, London was as defenceless as at the time of the Gordon Riots. The Prime Minister, Lloyd George, called in the Home Secretary and Smuts, together with a Mr. Charles Duncan, who, as well as being a Member of Parliament, was President of the Police Union and General Secretary of the Workers' Union, with which the Police Union was affiliated. Duncan was asked to get in touch with the strikers with a view to a settlement on the basis of a liberal increase of pay but with no recognition for the Union, for the Government were fearful that any recognition of a Police Union in wartime would lead to demands for an Army Union. The war was at a critical stage, and the horrors of the Bolshevist uprising in Russia, only ten months earlier, persuaded them that any false step could precipitate revolution in England. Fanciful as such fears seem fifty years later, they were real enough at the time to dominate events.

Duncan arranged to bring the men's representatives to see the Prime Minister at noon on the following day, Saturday, August 31st. Hundreds of policemen, distinctive even in plain clothes, converged on Whitehall, and it was clear that they had public opinion on their side.

Even *The Times* came out with a sympathetic leader. Sir Edward Henry returned from Ireland that morning and joined the Prime Minister, Smuts, and the Home Secretary at 10 Downing Street. The strikers' leaders were then admitted. It was a confused meeting. No agreed record was made of what had been decided, and to this day there remains a difference of opinion about the significance of the Prime Minister's meeting with the Union. Did it imply recognition? The strike was bought off with a substantial pay rise for the Metropolitan Police and the dismissed man was promised reinstatement, but the Prime Minister seems to have been adamant that a Police Union could not be recognised in wartime, although some sort of representative machinery would be permitted at Scotland Yard. Was there an inference that the Union would be recognised at the end of the war—then less than three months distant?

Sir Edward Henry was made the culprit and he went the same day. Macready's appointment was announced that evening. Henry was, however, spared the agony of what was to come. The Union claimed that they were promised recognition after the war, but the Home Secretary denied it. Thus the seeds of further contention were sown. The representative board for the Metropolitan Police was a failure. It was to represent all inspectors, sergeants, and constables, and a quorum was to have the right of access to the Commissioner. Membership of the Police Union was permitted, and the extremists from the Union obtained control of the board. It was not long before they clashed with Macready, who had been persuaded, against his inclination, to vacate the post of Adjutant-General in order to restore firm discipline in the Metropolitan Police. He was soon at loggerheads with both the Union and the representative board. He regarded them as disloyal and subversive; they regarded him as an autocratic tyrant. Relations were virtually severed. Macready tightened up discipline as the prospect of another strike loomed up. The ingredients in the new situation were complex, but basically it seems to have been a struggle between organised labour to secure control over the police in a way that would encourage their sympathy in industrial disputes, and the determination of the Government to preserve their neutrality. Russell it will be recalled, had dealt with a somewhat similar situation in 1839 by promoting legislation to prevent the police of Birmingham, Manchester, and Bolton from falling into the hands of Chartist-dominated town councils. The Union again requested formal recognition. The Home Secretary refused it. By May, 1919, protest marches were being conducted, and policemen openly displayed

187

banners denouncing 'militarism' in the Metropolitan Police and demanding, 'Macready, make ready to go'. A particularly distasteful feature of the situation was that Special Branch men were set to report on the activities of some of their comrades.

Meanwhile, on March 1st, the Government had appointed a committee under Lord Desborough to review the pay and conditions of service of the police. It was a race against time. The committee worked rapidly, and by the middle of May it told the Home Secretary what its main recommendations were likely to be: much higher pay, standardised for all forces, and machinery for the police and police authorities to make representations to the Home Secretary. On May 26th the Home Secretary obtained authority to bring in urgent legislation to prevent policemen from belonging to a trade union, and to set up alternative representative machinery. A few days later he announced these proposals to the House and declared that any policeman who went on strike would be dismissed without hope of reinstatement. At the same time the Home Secretary undertook to accept the Desborough Committee's recommendation to raise the constable's weekly starting pay from £1 10*s*. to £3 10*s*.

These firm and conciliatory measures dampened (as they were intended to do) the enthusiasm of a mass meeting held by the Police Union in Hyde Park on June 1st. But the leaders bided their time. On July 8th the Police Bill was introduced into the House of Commons. It provided for the establishment of a Police Federation, and created a Police Council as a consultative body. But the Bill carried out the threatened ban on policemen belonging to a trade union, and the hot-heads were determined to strike a second time before it became law. They felt that they had been let down by the two leading trade unionists who had served on the Desborough Committee. They appealed once more to Lloyd George, but the Prime Minister, preoccupied in Versailles, no longer had any sympathy with them. The Bill completed its passage through the House of Commons on August 1st, and received the Royal Assent on August 17th. In the meantime, on July 31st, while it was still before Parliament, the Police Union, *in extremis*, called its second strike. This time it was a strike for the survival of the union, not pay. Thousands of policemen were dismayed, and many tore up their Union cards. The pay rise and the promised Police Federation had consolidated their loyalty to the police service and the Government. Nevertheless, a total of 2,364 men responded from seven forces: Metropolitan, 1,056; City of London, 57; Liverpool, 954; Birmingham, 119; Birkenhead, 114; Bootle, 63;

and Wallasey, 1. Severe rioting broke out in Liverpool, and steel-helmeted troops, and even tanks, were sent to Merseyside, where there were bayonet charges and bloodshed.[9]

The strike lost momentum after the first twenty-four hours, and it rapidly collapsed. Promises of support from other unions came to nothing. All the strikers were dismissed, and none was ever reinstated, despite a long series of representations on their behalf which continued until as recently as 1950. The police service was thus weakened by the loss of a very large number of men, the majority of whom were probably foolish, misguidedly loyal, and hopelessly misled. They paid a tragic penalty for the irresponsibility of the few extremists in London. It is a sombre reflection that Syme's high principles and unbending rectitude should have created, in the Police Union, a Frankenstein whose death-throes were to destroy so many careers in a manner that cruelly matched its founder's own heroic martyrdom. These were the agonising circumstances in which the police Federation was born. Lord Tenby (formerly Mr. Gwilym Lloyd George, Home Secretary from 1954 until 1956), has very kindly given me one personal recollection:

'My father, David Lloyd George, was at that time Prime Minister. Looking out of the window of 10 Downing Street, I saw a crowd of men outside, some wearing police uniform and others in civilian clothes. They seemed to appoint a small deputation and a few men came up and knocked at our door. The Prime Minister was told what was happening and was asked whether he would receive a deputation from the Police Union. He refused point-blank to do so, as he did not recognise such a union. At the same time he expressed his willingness to receive a deputation of policemen. The strikers went and there were anxious talks among the crowd outside in Downing Street. Eventually the original deputation returned and the Prime Minister saw them and listened to what they had to say.'

Lord Tenby adds:

'Years later, one of my early tasks as Home Secretary was to receive, in my room at the Home Office, a deputation from the Police Federation. As we talked I was conscious of the startling contrast between these mature leaders of 70,000 police officers in England and Wales, discussing problems of common concern with the Home Secretary of the day, and the anxious, angry men who had come to see my father in Downing Street over 30 years earlier.'

189

The Desborough Committee and the Police Act, 1919

The circumstances in which the Desborough Committee was set up in March, 1919, during a period of tension unparalleled in the history of the police, have already been described. Lord Desborough and his colleagues rose nobly to an occasion that demanded tact, sympathy, and understanding if the suspicions and resentment of the past months were to be overcome. The police forces of 1919 were in a sickly state. It was the achievement of the Desborough Committee not only to put them into new heart, but to pave the way to twenty years of contentment, during which the police service of modern times was born—a service so rapidly restored to health that by the time of the General Strike in 1926 policemen everywhere won the most enthusiastic praise for their bearing, impartiality, and good humour. The Committee also wrought profound changes in the structure of the police system. In Sir Arthur Dixon's words, it offered 'what amounted to a new conception of the police as a service, an integrated system, rather than a collection of separate forces each concerned with its merely local requirements and personnel'.[10]

The Committee's terms of reference were: 'To consider and report whether any and what changes should be made in the method of recruiting for, the conditions of service of, and the rates of pay, pensions, and allowances of the police forces of England, Wales and Scotland.' It heard a great deal of evidence from the Home Office, the local authority associations, the inspectors of constabulary and all ranks of the police. Alternative versions of the origins of the police strikes were offered by some of the men, and also by Sir Edward Henry and his successor, Sir Nevil Macready. It was abundantly clear that the war had imposed unprecedented strains on the police. The inspectors of constabulary insisted that police work in 1919 was very much more demanding than ever before, and that it demanded higher qualifications. Yet many policemen were living near the bread line: the Committee published specimen budgets of police families, which showed no margin for anything beyond the elementary necessities of life. A representative of the men, Sergeant George Miles, expressed their point of view picturesquely: 'In the past a policeman has been paid no more than an ordinary labourer; consequently, he has been respected and valued accordingly. He has been looked upon as one who, for a tip or free drink, could be made to neglect his duty. Unfortunately, his continual fight against poverty has only too often made him susceptible to bribes and tips. There is no doubt we are now suffering from our lowly origin. There is no comparison between what is expected from the policeman of today and the policeman of old. Our predecessors were invariably big, illiterate men, from whom little was expected.' Nowadays a policeman 'must be as brave as a lion, as patient as Job, as wise as Solomon, as cunning as a fox, have the manners of a Chesterfield, the optimism of Mark Tapley, must be learned in criminal law and local by-laws, must be of strong moral character, able to resist all temptations, be prepared to act as a doctor, be a support to the weak and infirm, a terror to evil-doers, a friend and counsellor to all classes of the community, and a walking encyclopedia.'[11] This estimate of the constable's responsibilities, or something like it, seems to have been accepted by the Committee (as it had been accepted by the Royal Commission of 1906–8), who reported: 'We are satisfied that a policeman has responsibilities and obligations which are peculiar to his calling and distinguish him from other public servants and municipal employees . . . the burden of individual discretion and responsibility placed upon a constable is much greater than that of any other public servant of subordinate rank.'[12]

Accepting the logic of this, the Committee recommended that the pay and conditions of service of all police forces should be improved, standardised, and placed under the control of the Home Secretary. It considered whether nationalisation of the police might be the best means of securing this, but nationalisation had long been out of fashion and the Committee received little evidence in favour of so drastic a step. The Assistant Commissioner in charge of the Metropolitan C.I.D. favoured a national detective force, but the Home Office witness modestly observed that, 'when you get a big organisation under an office in Whitehall the result is rather apt to be that it gets into a sort of groove'; and he doubted whether a Government office could manage the police as well as some of the big boroughs.[13] The Committee abstained from comment on so delicate an issue, preferring to rely on more lofty grounds in rejecting the case for nationalisation, which would be 'foreign to the constitutional principle . . . by which the preservation of law and order in this country is primarily the function of the proper local authorities'—a 'constitutional principle' which the Royal Commission as long ago as 1839 had declared even then to be derelict. In any case, the Committee argued, nationalisation would prejudice the intimate relations between the police and the localities where they served, thus doing disservice to relations between the police and the public.

However, the Committee recognised that the advantages of greater economy, efficiency and uniformity could only be gained by a greater measure of centralisation. The Home Office evidence[14] showed clearly enough that the department's position was still 'very much the same as it was at the beginning' and that, at all events until recently, the various police forces in the country 'had been treated as entirely independent of each other'. The first signs of co-ordination had come through 'chief constables putting their heads together', but in the meantime the Committee decided that the wide variations in such matters as pay, housing, allowances, leave, hours of duty, and other conditions of service had 'very materially contributed to the unrest and dissatisfaction' of recent times.[15] In addition to uniform and improved scales of pay, it recommended the provision of rent-free accommodation (or the payment of a rent allowance in lieu) and the assimilation of many other conditions of service. The pay of the constable at the maximum was to be increased to £4 10s. a week, with two additional long-service increments as inducements to men to remain in the service. Thus for the first time in the history of the police, the pay of a policeman would cease to be related to that of the agricultural labourer or unskilled worker. In future the constable was to be a semi-professional man.

It followed from the Committee's view that rates of pay and conditions of service should be standardised, that representatives of police authorities and all ranks of the service should be given an opportunity to offer their collective advice before changes were made. From this sprang two pieces of machinery of great importance. One was the idea of a Police Council, as a central advisory body to the Home Secretary, comprising representatives of police authorities and all ranks of the service sitting under the chairmanship of the Home Secretary or one of his senior officials. The other consisted of means by which the police themselves would be able to submit their views on any matters affecting the service as a whole. This—the long-desired 'right to confer'—was to be provided by the establishment of what was afterwards called the Police Federation, the joker with which the Government trumped the Police Union. Finally, the Committee recommended that, in view of the substantially increased cost which would fall on public funds as a result of the improved pay and pension arrangements, half the total cost of the police (and not, as formerly, only half the cost of the men's pay and clothing) should be borne by the Exchequer—an arrangement which has continued to the present day.* As a result the cost of the police rose from about £7 millions in 1914 to about £18 million in 1920.

The Desborough Committee presented its first report on July 1st, 1919, and its second on January 1st, 1920.[16] In this it recommended, *inter alia*, the creation of a Police Department in the Home Office to enable it to cope with its new responsibilities, an increase in the number of inspectors of constabulary from two to the original three (three were appointed from 1927 to 1929, and again after 1938), the development of co-operative arrangements between police forces, such as 'clearing houses' for information about crime and criminals, improved and more systematic arrangements for training, the abolition of police forces in non-county boroughs with a population under 50,000, a uniform discipline code, the transfer of power of appointment, promotion, and discipline in borough forces from the watch committee to the chief constable, a new right of appeal against disciplinary awards, standard arrangements for annual leave, and various changes in the pension arrangements.† Some of the more

---

* It seems that this arrangement would have been introduced in 1914 but for the outbreak of war. The subsequent history of the police-grant arrangements is complex, and it was not until 1951 that the grant was put on a statutory basis (the Police Grant Order, made under Section 3 of the Miscellaneous Finance Provisions Act, 1950). Its payment was made subject to the conditions that the area was efficiently policed; that adequate co-operation was afforded to other police forces; and that the force was efficiently and properly maintained, equipped, and administered, and that the rates of pay and allowances were as laid down by the Home Secretary. These conditions enabled the Home Secretary, by threatening to withhold the whole or some part of the grant, to require a police authority to increase the strength of its force, provide better accommodation, or appoint as its chief constable someone other than the authority's first choice—because, for example, broader experience was required. These conditions still govern the payment of the grant, and are an important means by which the Home Secretary is able to influence local police administration. The threat to withhold the grant has probably been used, on average, less than once a year during the past thirty years.

Sidney Webb, in a thesis published in 1911 (*Grants in Aid: A Criticism and a Proposal*), singled out the police grant as an example of a particularly successful grant. It is significant that, during the period following the Second World War, when most grants to local authorities were being merged into the general grant, a separate police grant was retained. (A special contribution of £500,000 a year is paid to the Metropolitan Police Fund towards expenses incurred on services of an imperial or national character.)

† The principle of the Police Act, 1890, was undisturbed, but, following the recommendations of the Desborough Committee, the Police Pensions Act, 1921, laid down the rate of pension at half, instead of three-fifths of

193

important of these recommendations are discussed later in this and other chapters.

The Police Act, 1919, was the instrument which gave effect to Desborough's central recommendations. It killed the Police Union and introduced the new concept of a centrally guided and largely uniform system of local police forces. The Act not only prohibited policemen from joining a trade union, but made it a criminal offence to induce a policeman to strike. The Police Federation was established as the representative body for all police officers up to the rank of chief inspector, and its neutrality, too, was guaranteed by a prohibition against associating with any body or person outside the police service (such as a trade union) on the grounds that, as the Home Office later put it, 'the responsibilities of the police to the community require that they shall at all times be manifestly free from any partisan bias or sectional interest'.[17] Power was given to the Home Secretary to regulate police pay and conditions of service, and a Police Council was established as a central consultative and advisory body before which regulations were to be laid.

The Police Federation and other representative bodies

The Police Federation came into existence in the autumn of 1919.

The Act defined its purpose as that of 'enabling members of the police forces in England and Wales to consider and to bring to the notice of police authorities and the Secretary of State, all matters affecting their welfare and efficiency other than questions of discipline and promotion affecting individuals'. A schedule prescribed the Federation's constitution. In each force a branch board was established for each of the three ranks of constable, sergeant, and inspector, and these were permitted to combine into joint branch boards. Central committees for each rank were elected at central conferences attended annually by delegates from all forces. The three central committees were able to sit as a single joint central committee, and they were empowered to submit representations direct to the Home Secretary. From the start, the Home Secretary of the day has made it an almost invariable practice to address the Annual Conference of the Federa-

---

pay after twenty-five years' service, and two-thirds after thirty, instead of twenty-six years' service. These arrangements remain in force at the present time. The 1921 Act also improved the arrangements for widows' pensions.

tion. All members of police forces in England and Wales below the rank of superintendent automatically become members by virtue of their office. The whole cost was borne by public funds,* and the Secretary of the joint central committee was authorised to spend his whole time on the Federation's work. In 1924, when the Desborough Committee was re-convened to have a fresh look at police pay in the light of the change in the cost of living, Sir Arthur Dixon testified to the 'broadmindedness and public spirit' shown by the leaders of the infant Federation, and added that he had no fear for its future. His confidence was amply justified, and much of the success in the early years was due to the outstanding quality of the Federation's first Secretary, Mr. J. M. Branthwaite, and the close co-operation of the Home Office in overcoming teething troubles.

The chief constables, in the meantime, had developed their own representative machinery. The district conferences of county and borough chief constables which the Home Office instituted in 1918 for the purpose of discussing war measures were continued in peacetime; and the central conference, to which each district sent delegates, and which sat under the chairmanship of the Home Secretary (or more often one of his officials), was seen to have continuing value. At its fourth meeting, held in the Home Office in December, 1920, the Central Conference of Chief Constables, as it has been known ever since, was established permanently as the recognised channel through which collective representations might be made by chief officers. At first it handled questions of pay and conditions of service, but with the growth of the Association of Chief Police Officers of England and Wales† (which also looks after the interests of assistant chief constables) and the establishment of negotiating machinery (pp. 260–1) the Central Conference has been free to concentrate, as an entirely professional body, on operational matters. It meets two or three times

---

* Since 1955 the Police Federation has been authorised to bear the cost of limited additional activities from the voluntary subscriptions of its members. It has also in recent times employed a paid consultant; the first holder of the office was Mr. (now the Rt. Hon.) James Callaghan, M.P., afterwards Chancellor of the Exchequer.

† A Chief Constables Association was founded in 1896 for the chief constables of cities and boroughs; it later accepted county chief constables as members. A County Chief Constables Conference was set up in 1920. The present-day association was formed in 1948 by the fusion of these two bodies. Its members include all county and borough chief constables and assistant chief constables, the Commissioner and ranks down to deputy commander in the Metropolitan Police, and the Commissioner and Assistant Commissioner of Police for the City of London.

195

a year, and provides a permanent link between the Home Office and police forces, and also a means of bringing other Government departments into touch with the police. The district conferences have similarly grown in importance, and now meet at least quarterly to discuss common problems and to promote common action. The offspring of these central and district conferences today are very numerous, comprising sub-committees (some of them *ad hoc* and others permanent) which deal with such matters as detection, traffic, policewomen, the administration of district training centres, crime clearing houses, crime squads, and much else.

Thus the seminal period 1919–20 saw the establishment of a Police Federation to represent the ranks up to chief inspector and a system of central and district conferences through which the voices of chief officers could be heard. It remained to provide representative machinery for the superintendents, and this, too, came into existence in 1920. A system of four district conferences and a central conference was set up, mainly to elect members of the rank to the newly formed Police Council; these arrangements paved the way to the formation of the representative body now known as the Superintendents' Association.

The Police Council and police regulations

When the Police Council met for the first time in a room in the Home Office, on July 6th, 1920, 'for the consideration of general questions affecting the police' it created history. It was the first occasion on which representatives of all concerned with the police system—Home Office, local authorities, Commissioners, and policemen of all ranks—had ever assembled together. The Home Secretary, Mr. Edward Shortt, took the chair, and referred to the historical significance of the meeting. Few of those present had met before. Having taken one another's measure, they then embarked on a joint enterprise whose novelty called for the greatest tact and forbearance. To some, the idea of sitting down as equals alongside representatives of the men in a disciplined service would seem doubtfully proper; to the representatives of the new Police Federation it was an opportunity to show statesman-like qualities. They seized it. From its inception, when the radical changes recommended by the Desborough Committee were being put into effect, the Council was, in Sir Arthur Dixon's words, 'an invaluable medium, not only for getting things settled relatively smoothly and expeditiously, but also for giving the Police Federation a chance to find their feet as a consultative body and for easing both them and the police authorities into a co-operative attitude of mind'.[18]

The Police Council was an advisory, not an executive body; and its first main task* was to consider a draft of some hurriedly prepared police regulations. They occupied the Council for four consecutive days, and the regulations came into effect on October 1st, 1920. For the first time they established universal standards for most of the conditions of service, and a common pattern for at least the elements of organisation for all forces. Some idea of the novelty and magnitude of the exercise can only be grasped if the rich diversity of the nineteenth-century police forces, some hint of which was given in Chapter Five, is borne in mind; for they were still essentially those same Victorian forces which had now to be re-modelled and brought into line. The problems ranged widely. Should *head* constables of boroughs be formally recognised as *chief* constables, and their appointment be made subject to the approval of the Home Secretary? What ranks should comprise a force? What qualifications should recruits possess? What height, and education? What annual leave should the police have, and what hours of duty should they work? What rules should govern promotion? A standard code of discipline had to be worked out, and a procedure laid down for hearing disciplinary charges (a right of appeal was not available until 1927). Limited restrictions on a policeman's private life and liberty had to be agreed, and, to maintain standards of efficiency, the authorised strength of a force was made subject to the approval of the Home Secretary. It is a remarkable tribute to those from the Home Office, the local authorities and all ranks of the police service who assembled to form this first Police Council in 1920, that the early regulations on all these and many other matters remained substantially unaltered for more than forty years. The four days in July, 1920, were well spent.

Meanwhile, history was repeating itself. The cities and boroughs mobilised their strength in opposition to the Desborough Committee's move towards centralisation, with its encroachment on their right to maintain their own local police forces in their own way. (It will be recalled that the boroughs, unlike the counties, had never before been subject to the Home Secretary's regulations.) The committee's proposal to abolish the smaller borough police forces

---

* The first business of all concerned an attempt by the Police Federation to ensure that the standard of pay awarded by Desborough should not be allowed to fall.

and to transfer the duties of appointment, promotion, and discipline from watch committees to chief constables added to their dismay. Protest meetings were called, as they had been when Palmerston had dared to challenge the strength of the municipalities in 1854, and in October, 1920, Mr. Neville Chamberlain led a deputation to the Home Secretary. Predictable assertions were made that the new arrangements were making for 'a more militarised and centralised system', which was liable to be 'regarded as a reflection on the capacity, the integrity and the loyalty' of local authorities.[19] Perhaps the protests had some effect. It was not until 1946 that the smaller borough forces were abolished, and the powers of watch committees for appointment, promotion, and discipline survived until 1964.

But in the early 1920s those involved in the administration of the police had more urgent things to think about. The new regulations had to be made effective in nearly 200 separate police forces, and members of watch committees and standing joint committees, chief constables and policemen of all ranks had to get used to the idea that they all formed part of a single police service, with the Home Secretary, a new Police Council, and a new Police Division in the Home Office at its apex. A whole pattern of changed relationships had to be sorted out, and spheres of influence established that would guide the police service for twenty years. The Home Office, in particular, had to try to weld the hitherto separate components into some kind of a whole, taking account of local pride and custom and eccentricity, in a manner that would conciliate the local authorities and yet inspire the confidence of chief constables, and encourage them to look beyond their local boundaries to a concerted lead from Whitehall. Anyone familiar with the working and interrelations of local and central government in Britain will realise the difficulty of the task; to those unfamiliar with these matters, explanations would be idle.

The General Strike and the Royal Commission of 1929

It is not possible to attempt to follow the fluctuations in public regard for the police during the tensions of 1919, and the period of industrial unrest and social and economic readjustment that followed the First World War. Mention must, however, be made of the General Strike, which for several days in May, 1926, paralysed much of the country's activities and brought organised labour as near as it ever came to achieving a revolution. For the police, this strike gave an impressive

198

demonstration of the way in which Desborough had healed the wounds of a few years earlier, and it also provided experience in adapting the system to meet a major emergency that was to be of great value when war broke out thirteen years afterwards.

The strike started as a stoppage of work in the coalfields, which by May 1st was complete. During the next two days other workers, including railwaymen, came out in support of the miners. Civil Commissioners were appointed in eleven districts in England and Wales to help local authorities to maintain essential supplies and preserve public order, particularly if communications with London were interrupted. Emergency regulations followed up a recommendation of the Desborough Committee that the Home Secretary should have power to require any police force to send men to the aid of another force up to 10 per cent of its strength. (Desborough had recommended 15 per cent; the select committee of 1908 on the 'Employment of Military in Cases of Disturbance' had suggested 10.) The power as such was not used, although some hundreds of men were sent by agreement, under arrangements made by the Home Office, from counties that were not badly affected by the strike into Derbyshire, Nottinghamshire, and the West Riding. All these activities helped to consolidate the unity of the police in operational matters at a time of crisis. They also underlined the extent to which, in the course of less than ten years, the Home Office had emerged as their natural co-ordinator, and to some extent their leader.

When the General Strike was over *The Times* launched a fund as a means of expressing the nation's gratitude 'for the large measure of peace and safety' it had enjoyed during the strike, and 'in recognition of the fidelity with which the men of the [police] force discharged their duties'. Many people had cause to be thankful (though few would realise it) for the firm stand Lloyd George had taken in 1918–19 in rejecting a Police Union which would have been affiliated to other trade unions, and a relieved public subscribed about a quarter of a million pounds. The resulting fund, known as the National Police Fund, has been administered ever since by a body of trustees, all of whom are Ministers or ex-Ministers, with the Home Secretary as Chairman. It is used for welfare, compassionate, and recreational purposes among the police and their families. Thus the country's means of maintaining public order had demonstrably moved a very long way since the time of the Chartists, when large sections of the wealthy and middle classes felt that there was no hope in looking for protection beyond the military. Times had also moved on from

Tonypandy. Sympathy between the public and the police during the General Strike seems to have been deep and spontaneous, and it was characteristic of Britain that, just as the soldiers had done in the Rhondda Valley, so now the police played football with the strikers. They emerged from it all with greatly enhanced status, not only as protectors of the public, but almost as their guardians, so agreeable was their good humour and so implicit was the nation's trust in their impartiality and forbearance at a time of national danger.*

The police, for their part, must have been startled by the flood of praise they now received. They were at last able to take a well-deserved pride in the extent to which they had won the confidence of the public. There had been no occasion to call out the military, and there seem to have been no complaints about the way the police handled demonstrations. The Police Federation, in their annual report for 1925–6, generously attributed much of the success to 'the wise reforms' that had followed the Desborough report. The police had striven to prove worthy of the improvements they had been given, and now they were resolved that the prestige and reputation of the service would progressively increase: 'The Service itself has never been so free from grievances. We are sure this is more than a coincidence, and vindicates the policy which has sought the fair and decent conditions which in turn have produced contentment.' The words, and the occasion for them, are worth pondering over.

The cosy relationship with the public was not, however, to endure. Within two years the Press and public opinion had once again decided, as they are apt to do from time to time, that the police were corrupt and oppressive; and matters came to a head with the appointment of another Royal Commission, in 1929, which this time followed an incident in which a girl named Irene Savidge and a well-known writer on financial matters named Sir Leo Chiozza Money were arrested after dark in Hyde Park. A case brought by the police was dismissed. A statement was then taken from Miss Savidge with a view to further proceedings, but allegations were made in the House of Commons that the girl had been subjected to unfair treatment

---

* In addition to the ordinary special constabulary, many members of the public, estimated at 140,000, enrolled in a special whole-time and paid extension of it, known as the Civil Constabulary Reserve. This body came under the control of the police, but was organised and recruited by the War Office. So great was the demand for truncheons that Scotland Yard had to send to High Wycombe for a lorry-load of chair-legs, which were fitted up with lengths of rope and issued to those who were not lucky enough to have conventional truncheons.

while in police hands, where, so it was said, she had been bullied for five hours. A tribunal of inquiry was set up, but it failed to agree. A majority of two members exonerated the police, but the third, who was a Labour Member of Parliament, did not. The Commission's terms of reference covered the administration of the Judges' Rules, a code to regulate the conduct of the police, first formulated in 1912 and since modified and amplified by administrative directions from the Home Office made with the approval of the Lord Chief Justice.

This Commission produced few recommendations of permanent value—though its remarks about the employment of policewomen, mentioned later in this chapter, were a useful contribution to the debate on the subject. It did, however, make some sensible if unoriginal remarks about relations between the police and the public: 'The police, in exercising their functions, are, to a peculiar degree, dependent upon the goodwill of the general public and the utmost discretion must be exercised by them to avoid overstepping the limited powers which they possess. A proper and mutual understanding between the police and public is essential for the maintenance of law and order. . . . Many complaints which have reached us have proved, on investigation, to be in effect directed not against the police themselves, but against the laws which the police are called upon to enforce. . . . In our view, the attempt to enforce obsolete laws, or laws manifestly out of harmony with public opinion, will always be liable to expose the police to temptations and to react upon their morale and efficiency.'[20] It also laid down a doctrine of more questionable value: 'The police of this country have never been recognised, either in law or by tradition, as a force distinct from the general body of citizens . . . the principle remains that a policeman, in the view of the common law, is only "a person paid to perform, as a matter of duty, acts which if he were so minded he might have done voluntarily".'* It seems doubtful whether Peel and the other founders of the English police system would have subscribed to this view. If the Commission merely intended to stress the civilian character of a policeman, the passage is harmless enough, but if it was intended to be taken literally as a constitutional or legal maxim it is open to the obvious rejoinder that the whole point of the new police was to provide

---

*The Royal Commission seem to invest the quotation with the authority of a pronouncement of the courts. It is, however, taken (and slightly misquoted) from a general description of the nature of the constable's office contained in Stephen's *A History of the Criminal Law of England* (1883), Vol. 1, Ch. XIV, page 494.

a force 'distinct from the general body of citizens', since the arrangements under which citizens policed themselves had broken down with the collapse of the voluntary system in the eighteenth century, and the myth received its death-blow with the coming of the motor-car. When *Punch* depicts the celebrity stopped for exceeding the speed limit demanding, 'Don't you know who I am?' and the constable replies, 'No, and I'll want your address as well,' a clear line is drawn between 'police' and 'public' which no amount of sophistry or sentiment ought to be allowed to blur.

The police and the motorist between the wars

The police themselves were becoming motorists in the early 1920s, at about the time when Scotland Yard was reorganising the Mounted Branch it had inherited from the Bow Street Runners. Judging from not-so-old photographs, some divisional superintendents in rural areas seem to have shared this reluctance (though with less good reason) to part with equestrian transport. The first acute clash between police and motorists was over, and the second period of prolonged estrangement, of more recent times, lay in the future. During the inter-war years it seems that, on the whole, relations between the police and the motoring public were cordial. But a substantial problem was building up. In the ten years from 1920 to 1930 the number of registered motor-cars rose from under 200,000 to more than 1 million. In that year, 1930, the general speed limit of twenty miles per hour was abolished (the thirty miles per hour limit came four years later), and Parliament was promised that the police would make a special effort to deal with careless or dangerous driving by an attempt to promote the greater understanding between police and motorists which, from early times, was seen to be a prerequisite to any successful traffic law enforcement policy. One consequence of this was the so-called 'courtesy cops' scheme.

The scheme owed as much, however, to local concern, particularly among the smaller counties, about the cost of maintaining police patrols on main roads which they were unlucky enough to have running through their territory. For years they had been urged by the Ministry of Transport to put more patrols on the roads, and by 1936 the Minister, Mr. Hore-Belisha, had ideas of instituting his own Ministry enforcement officers. The idea of a corps of special police road patrols, paid from the national Road Fund, emerged as (in the

Home Office view) a preferable alternative. The main object was to secure a higher standard of road sense and behaviour by educating road-users, and giving them verbal warnings, rather than by taking them to court: hence the popular name, 'courtesy cops'. The Exchequer bore the whole cost of 800 men, who were additional to police patrols already employed. About 500 of them operated in Lancashire and the adjacent counties, and the others in London and Essex. A Metropolitan Police driving school which was opened at Hendon in 1934 (it is still there) trained instructors.

This scheme lapsed on the outbreak of war, so that it only operated for three years. It gave the police useful experience in developing new methods of dealing with motorists, and provided a start from which most forces in the postwar years were able to develop their own traffic policies and methods of law enforcement. But the Exchequer subsidy, which first put the scheme on its feet, came to an end with the scheme itself, and it is doubtful whether there has ever again, at all events until very recent times, been as full a recognition by the Government of the vast scale on which police manpower has had to be diverted from dealing with crime to promoting the flow of road traffic—a point well made by the small girl depicted in *Punch* during August, 1937, who, glancing at the policeman holding up the traffic for her to cross the road, asks: 'Mother, what *did* policemen do when there weren't any motors?'[21]

Finding the leaders: the Hendon Police College

It seems improbable that the motor-car had driven a wedge between the police and the public by the beginning of the 1930s. The speed limit was temporarily lifted, and when a new one was reimposed courtesy cops appeared on the roads to soften the blow. Yet something was wrong, and the Royal Commission of 1929, though it recognised the importance of establishing a warm relationship, was unable (as who would be?) to show how it was to be achieved. Public opinion, fickle as ever, alternately praised and condemned the police, and by 1931 morale in the Metropolitan Police had sunk dangerously low. The Government decided, as they had done in 1918 when Macready was appointed Commissioner after the first police strike, that a strong man was needed. This time they turned to Lord Trenchard. He became Commissioner in that year after making his memorable contribution towards the foundation of the Royal Air

203

Force, and it did not take him long to decide that one of the main troubles was a lack of effective leadership. The police were paying the penalty for keeping faith, for 100 years, with Peel's principle that vacancies in the higher ranks should be filled from below.* The urgent need, in Trenchard's view, was for 'officer material', and the result was the establishment, in 1934, of the Hendon Metropolitan Police College—a five-year experiment still viewed by the Police Federation with implacable hostility.

The problem Trenchard set out to solve was no new one. For years it had been apparent that not enough men qualified to reach high rank were being recruited. Nor was this situation likely to improve so long as recruits faced the tedium of a long period of beat-patrolling before they became eligible for consideration for promotion. Able, ambitious, and well-educated young men looked elsewhere for employment, and the paucity of talent at the top was to some extent met by the practice of appointing chief constables from outside the ranks of the service.

The Desborough Committee had approached the problem gingerly and offered a compromise: no one without previous police experience should be appointed as chief constable unless he had exceptional qualifications or experience. This recommendation was embodied in the first police regulations made under the Act of 1919. Nevertheless, of a total of 240 appointments to the post of chief constable made during the period 1918–39, no fewer than sixty-five were filled by candidates drawn from outside the police forces of England and Wales—some of whom, however, had had police experience in other countries.[22] By the late 1920s the trend of informed opinion was running strongly against Peel's principle, and the Royal Commission of 1929 rejected it, declaring that it would 'regard as inimical to the public interest any system which limited appointments to the higher posts to those who had entered the police as constables . . . such posts should be filled by the best men available, irrespective of the source whence they are drawn'.[23] The existing arrangements, in fact, satisfied no one. The knowledge that outsiders were monopolising many of the most attractive county posts acted as a constant irritant to the Police Federation. The value of a police career was diminished, and it was debatable how far other qualifications could ever make up

* A few direct appointments to the Metropolitan Police into a post known as chief constable were made during the latter part of the nineteenth century. The posts were converted into that of commander and deputy commander in recent times.

in the higher command for the lack of police experience. The object, it was evident, should be to enable the police service to produce its own cadre of leaders. But how was it to do so?

By the end of the 1920s the Home Office had drawn up a plan known as the Dixon Scheme, after its author. This proposed the establishment of a national police college. A two-year course in general and police subjects was to be offered to policemen who had already served for five years, provided they had passed the examination for promotion to sergeant, and were (normally) under thirty-five years old. In this way it was hoped to bring out latent ability, and at the same time to attract more men into the service with higher education. The modest nature of the plan owed everything to a desire to conciliate the Police Federation; there was to be no question of offering privileges to a favoured few. Its democratic appeal, however, was not allowed to smother the ambitions of its author, who saw the college growing into a centre for police research—a first step, perhaps, towards the formulation of Colquhoun's 'science of policing'. It was also contemplated that, in due course, successful attendance at the college was to be a prerequisite for appointment in the higher ranks. Thus the scheme went a long way towards anticipating the Police College of today. Nevertheless, it was untimely and still-born, for it coincided with the economic crisis of 1930-1. The Police Council endorsed the plan in principle, but the local authority associations rejected it on grounds of expense; and at the same time the Police Federation, after flirting with the idea, finally decided that it 'would cause serious discontent which would far outweigh any benefits'. Faced with this general hostility, the scheme was accordingly abandoned, and the problem of finding the future leaders of the police service remained as apparently insoluble as ever.

This was the bleak situation that challenged Lord Trenchard's impetuosity when he arrived at Scotland Yard a year later—an old man in a hurry, as he described himself. He looked in vain for 'officer material', as he put it, and was determined to do something about the large number of policemen who, having missed promotion, had little incentive to do more than stroll about in uniform. His answer to this was a novel short-service scheme, by which up to 5,000 constables were to be recruited on ten-year engagements—short enough, Trenchard thought, to retain their keenness, and not too long to have them all merely plodding their beats and keeping out of trouble. This scheme, with its obvious defects, had to be abandoned early in 1939. Trenchard's measures to produce 'officer material' survived it by a few months, and indelibly associate his name with the pre-war Hendon Police College.

Sir Arthur Dixon, who, as Head of the Police Department of the Home Office, was intimately associated with the project, has recorded the following recollection of its origins. He had lunched with Trenchard at Brooks's Club, and the subject of the ill-fated police college plans of 1929 came up afterwards in the smoking-room. Sir Arthur, 'after assuring Lord Trenchard that he saw no chance of the original police college plan being revived in the foreseeable future, remarked that, though the county and borough forces must be out of it, might not there be a college for the Metropolitan Police? The force was surely large enough. Thereupon Lord Trenchard shot out of the low chair in which he was lounging, and started pacing up and down, as he often did when he was "worked up". He said little then, but a college for Metropolitan Police appeared as one of his proposals for reform in the Force.'[24]

The background to these proposals was expressed in characteristically blunt terms in Trenchard's famous second annual report, for the year 1932.[25] In it he said publicly what many people in the Home Office and elsewhere had been saying privately for some years, but he went a good deal further. 'On coming to Scotland Yard I was surprised to find that the very great improvements in the status and pay of the police after the Desborough Committee's report had not led to much change in the type of men entering the service.' The number of recruits from universities and public schools was 'altogether negligible', educational standards had improved little over pre-war years, and between 80 and 90 per cent of the Metropolitan recruits had not progressed beyond an elementary education. The last two years had shown some improvement, no doubt attributable to economic conditions, and the attractions of a police career ought to be presented imaginatively to school-leavers. But much more drastic steps were needed if the Metropolitan Police was to fill its higher posts in future years. The survival for 104 years of Peel's principle of finding the senior officers from among men 'from whom little more was demanded at the start than that they should have a good character and a satisfactory physique' struck him as 'very remarkable'. It was now 'no longer possible to shirk the problem of how to secure a steady supply of the best brains from every available source', for the criminal himself had become 'more skilful, more mobile and more scientific'. It was essential to devise a scheme 'which both opens up a clear avenue of fairly rapid promotion for outstanding men who join as constables, and also provide for the direct recruitment into the officer posts of men who have acquired good educational qualifications'.

Trenchard's report was published on May 3rd, 1933. A White Paper setting out the proposals for a Metropolitan Police College, as part of a comprehensive plan of reforms which included the short-service scheme and other important proposals, followed a week later, on May 11th.[26] Planning proceeded rapidly, and the Metropolitan Police College was opened at Hendon on May 31st, 1934, by the Prince of Wales. The buildings had been designed for a country club, and were later used as a factory. The first course comprised thirty-two students carrying the new rank of junior station inspector, of whom twenty were drawn from within the force; among them were two men who in 1966 were to fill the highest posts in the service—those of H.M. Chief Inspector of Constabulary and Commissioner of Police of the Metropolis. The remaining twelve students were direct entrants from outside. Entry was by selection from men aged twenty to twenty-six from the force or from outside who passed a competitive examination at about the level of the School Certificate, or who possessed higher educational qualifications, together with a number of candidates from within the force (for whom the upper age limit was extended) who, though academically disqualified, were thought to be particularly promising. The course was of fifteen months' duration (it was later extended to two years), and the syllabus was devised on the lines proposed in the abortive Home Office scheme of 1929. The principal difference, indeed, was the controversial element in Trenchard's scheme to recruit 'officer material' from outside. From the start, the Home Office had little enthusiasm for this part of the plan, fearing that it would lead to the division of the Metropolitan Police into officers and 'other ranks'; nor was the department happy about another controversial feature of the scheme, whereby posts higher than that of inspector were in future to be filled only by college-trained men.

Home Office misgivings, however, were nothing to the hostility with which the foundation of the College was viewed by the Police Federation. They lost no opportunity to attack its aims and methods, contemptuously deriding 'Trenchard's young men', and the direct entry of an 'officer class' from outside embittered them. This hostility has continued until the present day, and helps to explain the delicacy with which those concerned with the establishment of a national police college after the war (dealt with in Chapter Eight) approached their task. Beyond an occasional jibe at the picture of policemen dining in dinner jackets or studying Horace while on traffic duty, the Press seems, on the whole, to have accepted the case for a police college, though with reservations about the wisdom of taking direct entrants from outside. Several Labour Members of Parliament from the first denounced Trenchard's reforms as 'class measures' and 'militarism'.

The College had a short life. It lapsed on the outbreak of war and was never revived. By 1937 Trenchard had gone from Scotland Yard, leaving his name as a legend to be worked up in canteen gossip, and a legacy of lasting reforms ranging from improved section houses, and a re-vitalised building programme, to the provision of fine new amenities for sports. His successor, Sir Philip Game, introduced important changes in the College which, however, were largely frustrated by the war. Game attached more importance to the value of practical police work in training future leaders than Trenchard had done, and he modified the conditions of entry to the College in favour of policemen, restricting the number of direct entrants to about six a year, who were to carry out duties as constables for at least twelve months beforehand. The rank of junior station inspector was abolished, and the College was opened to men from county and borough forces.

Particulars are available of the subsequent careers of the total of 197 students who attended courses at the College, and from these it is possible to support almost any point of view as to the success or otherwise of Trenchard's plans. That it produced some excellent officers is beyond doubt, but some of the best of them were already serving as policemen before the College opened, and would presumably have risen to the top in spite of it. The lasting criticism of the experiment must be the suspicion, hostility, and resentment it aroused in the hearts of many thousands of ordinary, loyal policemen everywhere. As a memorandum submitted by the Home Office to the Oaksey Committee in 1948 put it: 'The police service of this country depends for its reputation and efficiency upon the character and ability of the ordinary constables who walk the beat. No matter how brilliantly qualified a cadre of officers produced by a Police College might be, this would be no compensation for any falling off in the quality of the constable and it is, therefore, fundamentally important that any scheme of higher training, designed to pick the best qualified men for the senior posts, should be recognised by the rank and file as fair, and as not involving any suggestion of favouritism based on social qualifications or even academic attainments.'[27] This, by and large, has remained the guiding principle ever since.

Detection, scientific aids, and common services

The machinery of the Police Council, and the opportunity it had given for regular intercourse and mutual understanding between the constituent parts of the police service, paved the way to technical developments of the first importance which were to lift the standards of efficiency of the police right out of the nineteenth century. When the barriers between police forces, police authorities, and the Home Office were breaking down, co-operation in promoting professional excellence was seen to be not only desirable, but possible.

Little systematic attention seems to have been paid to the development of detection techniques in police forces generally until the late 1920s. Methods varied widely, and although there was a movement to promote co-operation between forces there seems to have been little attempt to pool experience and information. Scotland Yard had set up a criminal record office by statute as early as 1871, and this contained particulars of convicted persons which were collected from, and made available to, police forces throughout the country. Scotland Yard also circulated *The Police Gazette*, containing particulars of missing and wanted persons, stolen property, and so on*—'the modern way of raising a hue and cry after a criminal', as Sir John Moylan puts it. The West Riding Police circulated their own *Police Gazette* in the North of England, and in 1913, in co-operation with several neighbouring forces, they set up a crime clearing-house and developed a *modus operandi* system of classifying crimes according to the idiosyncrasies of the criminal and the particular characteristics of the crime. The value of these arrangements was, however, limited.

* The original *Gazette* (or *The Public Hue and Cry*) had been started by John Fielding. A later offspring, *The Hue and Cry and Police Gazette*, was being issued from Bow Street early in the nineteenth century, and in 1828 it was issued weekly as *The Police Gazette*. In 1882 Scotland Yard was complaining to the Home Secretary that the *Gazette* (still edited by the Chief Clerk of Bow Street) had changed little since its inception, was defective in form and contents, was not read by the police, and was of little value. The upshot was that the editing and management of the *Gazette* was transferred to Scotland Yard in the following year, 1883, and in 1922 the printing and distribution of the paper was also transferred to Scotland Yard. Originally issued weekly, two issues a week came out in 1914 and three in 1920; daily issues started in 1927.

The two systems of classifying information were incompatible, and the slowness of communications prevented their full potential from being realised. And few forces at this period were aware of the vast potentialities which lay in the application of scientific aids to detective work.

In 1933 the Home Secretary set up a committee to inquire into the whole field of detective work. It spent five years on its task, and a five-volume, 500-page report of the greatest value scrapped most of what had gone before, and laid the foundations of all that has come since. Visits were paid to Canada and the United States of America, and the collective experience of all police forces in Great Britain was reviewed in the light of recent scientific discoveries. The committee concluded that England lagged behind other countries in the use of scientific aids in the detection of crime, and the outcome of its work was the introduction of systematic training courses for detectives; the establishment of regional crime clearing-houses to assist in identifying convicted persons, particularly mobile criminals; the issue by the Home Office of instructions on scientific aids, drawing detectives' attention to the ways in which laboratory work could help them; the consolidation of a system of forensic science laboratories; and the provision of rapid, reliable, and systematic means of collecting and communicating information about criminals between all police forces in the country.* The committee emphasised, for the first time, that in modern conditions it was impossible for a police force to be self-contained. In criminal investigation work, interdependence was the key to success.

Collectively, all these achievements must rank in importance with those of the Desborough Committee, for in the course of the next ten years they rationalised the whole complex field of criminal detection. They did away with much of the inter-force rivalry and insularity that still survived from Victorian times, and opened up entirely new vistas in the application of scientific aids to the detection of crime. Thus

* Sometimes between countries. Interpol came into existence during the period covered by this chapter. It started with an International Police Congress in Monaco in 1914; a second was held in Vienna in 1923, when an International Police Commission was instituted, with headquarters in Vienna. In 1946 the headquarters were transferred to Paris, and ten years later the title was changed to the International Criminal Police Organisation. Its aims are to promote mutual help between police in the spirit of the declaration of human rights, and to develop activities likely to contribute to the prevention and suppression of crime. In 1966 the Organisation had eighty-five member countries, and it offered a rapid means of communication between the police forces of all of them.

they imposed a national pattern on detective work and procedure comparable with the national pattern of pay and conditions of service established by Desborough. The vision and drive that secured the agreement of the inspectors of constabulary, chief constables, and police authorities to these far-reaching reforms, and then carried them through, were the outstanding qualities of the Chairman of the Detective Committee, Sir Arthur Dixon, who as a relatively junior civil servant had been the Secretary of the Desborough Committee (and the author of its report) some twenty years earlier, and who had taken charge of the newly created Police Department in the Home Office in 1919.

At the time when this committee reported, in 1938, it had formed a clear idea of the way in which wireless communications should be developed for police purposes, but unsolved technical problems still stood in the way of any comprehensive planning. The first operational police wireless scheme in this country was started by the Metropolitan Police in 1923, using telegraphy and morse code. (Experiments were being conducted by the Detroit police as early as 1921, but progress seems to have been slow in the United States also.) This pioneer scheme offered two-way communications with a van used for C.I.D. purposes, but by 1925 the Assistant Commissioner in charge of the C.I.D. expressed the view that there had been very few occasions when the use of wireless had proved of value. Meanwhile, experiments were being carried out in other forces. Lancashire discovered the value of a wireless-equipped van during the General Strike, and Captain Popkess, the Chief Constable of Nottingham, pioneered several mobile two-way radio units for crime prevention and detection. The West Riding and Manchester were also experimenting, and Brighton even developed a pocket set which could be carried by a policeman on his beat. The chief technical obstacle to progress was the limitation imposed by medium-frequency transmissions (high and ultra frequencies were not then available), which restricted a wireless system to purely local communication with policemen in motor-cars, on motor-cycles, or on foot. Wide coverage with two-way radio was not feasible. Some of the country's best brains, including the B.B.C.'s chief engineer and Mr. Watson-Watt, the inventor of radar, were asked to help, but little progress could be made towards establishing the nation-wide network of police wireless communications that from an early time had been recognised, at least by the Home Office, as the ultimate object. Even so, the use of wireless was gradually increasing, and when the Metropolitan Police instituted their first Information

Room, in 1934, it linked the entire communication resources of the force, including some fifty wireless patrol cars operating by day and thirty by night. Nottingham also seems to have kept up its early lead in developing the potentialities of wirelss.

By the time the Detective Committee reported, in 1938, the threat of war had begun to influence matters, for it was realised that wireless communication would be of vital importance if the normal land-line communications were interrupted. Emergency schemes were operated to serve the needs of the fire service as well as the police; and then, during the early years of the war, a comprehensive regional network, on lines recommended by the committee, became possible with the introduction of high-frequency techniques. Ten Home Office wireless depots were established to provide a wireless network which served all police forces in England and Wales, and these have been maintained ever since, under a Communications Branch in the Home Office. They install the main transmitting equipment used by the police, and equip police cars and other vehicles with wireless. Nowadays they provide and maintain a wide variety of highly sophisticated equipment, including radar meters and personal radios.*

In the meantime important progress had been made in harnessing scientific effort to other aspects of police work. By about 1930 reports were appearing about laboratory work being done in other countries in aid of the investigation of crime. This was no new idea in England, for the police had long been accustomed to call in scientific experts in cases of homicide, poisoning, and sex offences. Poisoning, in particular, had excited scientific investigation as early as the first century B.C., and its heinousness has always marked it out as calling for the most ruthless inquiries (and punishments: Henry VIII ordered poisoners to be boiled to death). Taylor's *Handbook of Poisons*, in 1848, established toxicology on a scientific basis, and for many years experts in pathology, chemistry, and forensic medicine, some of them household names, regularly appeared for the Crown in serious criminal cases (not only where poisoning was alleged) where scientific evidence was of value. But the idea that science could aid the identification of minute traces in connection with the more ordinary crimes of burglary and housebreaking was slow to develop.

Among the pioneers in establishing primitive forensic science

* The Home Office wireless depots also provide and maintain equipment for the Fire and Civil Defence Services. The Metropolitan, Birmingham, and Lancashire police maintain their own schemes, and the City of London is comprised in the Metropolitan Police scheme.

laboratories was Captain Popkess, the Chief Constable of Nottingham, who had also interested himself in the development of police wireless. In association with Nottingham University College, he attached a laboratory to the C.I.D., and at about the same time, or soon afterwards, similar laboratories were established in Sheffield and Cardiff. The scale of these efforts, however, was necessarily too small to make them of more than limited value, for police work demands a combination of first-rate scientists and expensive laboratory apparatus at a cost that no single police force outside London could at that time have justified. To the Home Office it seemed evident from the start that a system of forensic science laboratories would have to be planned regionally, but it was far from clear how police authorities were to be persuaded to meet the heavy cost that would be involved; nor was there any experience at that time of co-operative agencies that served the needs of several police forces.

It was at this point that, by great good fortune, the former Government Chemist in Ceylon, a Mr. C. T. Symons, retired from his position and returned to this country. He had had great experience in the application of laboratory work to the investigation of crime, and had made a special study of such work being done on the Continent, particularly at Paris, Lyons, and Lausanne. In 1934 he made himself available as an adviser to the Home Office to assist in planning further laboratories. The administrative drive of Dixon, combined with Symons's mastery of the subject, rapidly infected chief constables, who soon realised the value of the new facilities the laboratories offered. The eventual upshot was the establishment, on lines expounded by the Detective Committee, of seven forensic science laboratories to serve all the forces in their areas. A Metropolitan Police laboratory was also opened in 1934 at Hendon, adjacent to the Police College; it later moved into central London. Police officers were seconded to the laboratories to act in liaison with the scientists, and arrangements were made for detectives to attend courses at them, so as to gain a first-hand knowledge of the kind of traces or specimens they ought to look for at the scene of a crime, and an understanding of the importance of even the most minute clues which might lend themselves to the scientist's skill.

From these early beginnings the forensic laboratory system has grown until today it is an integral part of the police service, employing pathologists, chemists, biologists, experts in hand-writing, and many others. Nowhere else, perhaps, is the quiet drama of police work so vividly presented to the layman as in these quiet laboratories, where the examination of blood-stained sheets, the comparison of hairs and bits of skin, the analysis of human organs pickled in jars, and the microscopic examination of stains, specimens and minute tell-tale traces of all kinds from the scenes of innumerable crimes make up the daily work. These laboratories are not places for the squeamish.

The rationalisation of detective work throughout the country in a coherent system, and the increasing use made of scientific aids, underlined the importance of yet another innovation which resulted from the work of the Detective Committee. This was the introduction of systematic training for detectives. The Desborough Committee had taken the view that most detectives could be adequately trained by experience and practical work alongside others. They also thought that more use might be made of training facilities already being provided by the Metropolitan Police, and that a second centre for detective training should be set up in the North. Following the Detective Committee's recommendations, a standard syllabus of instruction was drawn up, and the first eight-week courses for detective constables started at Hendon and Wakefield in 1936. Later that year the Home Secretary asked the head of the C.I.D. at Scotland Yard, Sir Norman Kendal, together with several experts (who included Mr. Symons, the adviser on forensic science laboratories), to plan the extension of detective training, and in 1937 more advanced courses were instituted for sergeants and higher ranks. Two more detective training schools were opened at Birmingham and in Lancashire, but these promising developments were interrupted by the war.

The establishment of Home Office wireless depots and forensic science laboratories during the 1930s led to the idea of what are now known as 'common police services'. These are services provided by the pooling of resources which it would be impracticable or uneconomic for each police force to provide on its own. A central fund (the 'common police services fund') was established in 1939, under the authority of the Home Office, to finance wireless depots, laboratories, and crime clearing houses, together with a token provision for the training of police dogs. It operated on the principle that half the cost would be borne by the Exchequer and half by the police authorities who used the service, each authority contributing in proportion to the establishment of its force. A body known as the Common Police Services Committee, comprising representatives of the Home Office and the local authority associations, was set up to advise the Home Secretary on the financing of the services. In 1939 they cost some £40,000; their cost in 1966, following an expansion in recent years in the scope and variety of services provided under these central arrangements, is nearly £3 million.*

Policewomen

It remains to deal with one other development in policing during the two world wars, but this time the story is a depressing one of apathy and prejudice. In 1919 there were about 150 policewomen; ten years later the number had shrunk slightly, and twenty years afterwards, in 1939, it had risen to only about 230. During the twenty-year period three committees of inquiry reviewed the employment of policewomen, and each, with varying degrees of emphasis, testified to their value. Most police authorities, however, regarded them as an unnecessarily extravagant luxury. Many who conceded that women were better qualified than men to undertake social and moral welfare work among women and young people, nevertheless preferred to see them enrolled in voluntary organisations rather than in police forces, an attitude reinforced by concern for economy. Few chief constables saw much value in policewomen, some suspected them of feminism, the Police Federation were openly hostile towards them, and the Home Office abstained from encouraging their employment, in spite of constant pressure from women's organisations. General recognition of the value of policewomen, and their ultimate incorporation as an integral part of every police force, only came with the Second World War.

Rival voluntary organisations during the First World War provided the pioneers. One, the National Union of Women Workers (which afterwards became the National Council of Women) established Voluntary Women Patrols who did preventive work among women and girls in the vicinity of military camps, in munition factories, and in parks. Between 4,000 and 5,000 women were trained for this work, and as the war progressed many exchanged their voluntary status for paid full-time employment under a chief constable or, in London, the Commissioner. These women formed the nucleus from which a body of 100 officially recognised policewomen

---

* The Metropolitan Police had no need to co-operate in these early arrangements, since the force was big enough to maintain its own wireless organisation, laboratory, and training schools. The Metropolitan Police Fund now contributes in respect of the cost of the Police College, the negotiating machinery, and promotion examinations.

215

was recruited by General Macready, the Metropolitan Police Commissioner, in the autumn of 1918. The rival organisation was started by a group of well-to-do Chelsea ladies led by Miss Damer-Dawson and continued, after her death in 1920, under Miss Mary Allen. This originated out of concern for the plight of Belgian refugees who were arriving in London in 1914. Both these private-enterprise organisations were welcomed by the authorities during the war, but by 1919 Miss Damer-Dawson's Women's Police Service, as it was called, although it had done valuable work in training hundreds of women in preventive work in munitions factories, was being viewed with disfavour by the authorities. It was blemished by a degree of militarism which alienated many people, and it was further handicapped by the fact that several of its leaders had earlier been active as suffragettes. Its continuance after 1919 as a purely private venture which paid women to patrol the London streets in uniform resembling that of a police officer's,* however well-intentioned, harmed the growth of the idea of regular policewomen as members of police forces along with men; and Mrs. Hart is no doubt correct in observing that 'it has taken policewomen many years to live down their reputation as eccentrics and feminists'.[28]

In 1920 the Baird Committee (its Chairman, John Baird, was then Parliamentary Under-Secretary of State at the Home Office) reviewed the whole question of the employment of policewomen in peacetime, and concluded that the experience of the war had proved their value in undertaking police duties which hitherto had been discharged exclusively by men.[29] There was an urgent need for substituting policewomen for men in thickly populated areas for some duties, but discretion whether or not to employ them should be left to local police authorities. At that time most policewomen were not attested as constables, but the committee recommended that they should be (many, however, were still not attested in 1939), that they should be highly trained, and that they should form an integral part of a police force. A woman assistant inspector of constabulary should be specially appointed to inspect policewomen and promote their welfare and efficiency. These forward-looking proposals had little effect. No woman assistant inspector was appointed (the first woman

---

* The leaders of the organisation were successfully prosecuted in 1919 under a section of the Police Act which made it an offence to wear uniform resembling that of a police officer. The uniform was subsequently modified, and the name of the organisation was changed from 'Women's Police' to 'Auxiliary Women's Police'. It gradually faded out.

to hold such a post, as staff officer to the inspectors of constabulary, was Miss B. M. Denis de Vitré, who was appointed in 1945), and the combined prejudice of police authorities, chief constables, and the Police Federation ensured that very few women were recruited, despite constant pleading by the inspectors of constabulary. The scene further darkened as a result of economy measures in 1922, when the number of women employed by the Metropolitan Police was cut from 112 to twenty-four—they would have been abolished entirely but for a spirited campaign in Parliament led by Lady Astor—and many forces outside London dispensed with their policewomen entirely.

A second inquiry, the Bridgeman Committee, came two years later, in 1924, and once again the value of policewomen was timorously recognised.[30] By this time their total strength was a mere 110, distributed among the Metropolitan Police, six county, and twenty-seven borough forces. The chief constables of several large forces, Lancashire, Gloucestershire, Birmingham, and Bristol, spoke highly of their value in detective work and in dealing with women and children, but elsewhere there remained a strong feeling that the work they were doing could better be done by voluntary organisations. The Police Federation, jealous of the introduction of women into a traditionally male occupation, expressed continued hostility towards them. This second inquiry reached much the same conclusions as the Baird Committee had done. They tepidly recommended the employment of policewomen wherever a police authority wanted them, but now thought that the numbers were too small to justify the appointment of a special woman assistant inspector of constabulary. Not surprisingly, the cause remained in the doldrums.

The third inquiry to consider the employment of policewomen was the Royal Commission on Police Powers and Procedure of 1929, which stretched its terms of reference somewhat in concluding that 'the time is ripe for a substantial increase in their numbers, more particularly in cities for patrol work in uniform'.[31] It was, they thought, particularly important to have policewomen available to take statements from young girls and children in sexual cases. However, they recognised that it was useless to try to force the employment of policewomen on those who were not convinced of their value and, like the two previous inquiries, they concluded that the matter would have to be left to local discretion. The Commission urged that all police authorities and chief constables should have their attention drawn to the success with which women had been employed in various parts of the country. In the following year, 1930, the Home Office raised the whole matter with the Police Council. The Council reflected the general apathy, but the Home Secretary nevertheless made some police regulations for women. These standardised their pay and conditions of service and laid down that their main duties were to include patrolling, duties in connection with women and children reported missing, found ill, destitute or homeless, or in immoral surroundings, taking statements from women and children, and dealing with female prisoners. By 1939, however, only forty-five police forces out of a total of 183 were employing policewomen, and in London their number had only risen to about the total it had been in 1921.

Throughout most of these two decades the pioneer policewomen had much to put up with. Miss Lilian Wyles has written sensitively of the ordeal of the original twenty-five when first they appeared in the London streets early in 1919, and of how she 'shuddered, and for the first time regretted my choice of career' when she saw herself in the mirror clad in an appalling uniform supplied and fitted by Harrods.[32] This first batch, drawn from all walks of life—shop-girls, a laundress, a tram conductress, typists, nurses, schoolmistresses and a few with university degrees—faced, at times, the 'downright malice and vindictive spirit' of some of the men. They were required to patrol in pairs, followed at a distance of from 6 to 10 yards by two tough uniformed policemen, who were given strict orders not to let the women out of their sight, and to go to their aid at once if they were in trouble. Later, however, at all events in the C.I.D., it seems that their male colleagues recognised that policewomen were much better qualified to deal with cases involving women and girls than they were, a view strongly held by the inspectors of constabulary from the beginning. The difficulty in the early days was to steer an ill-defined course between legitimate police activity and moral welfare work. As Sir Leonard Dunning put it in his inspection report for the year 1921 (striking, incidentally, a modern note): 'Principally owing to the decay of parental influence, the girl of today does not attach so much value to chastity, while modern knowledge has deprived the fear of natural consequences of its value as a protection; . . . a woman by advice and personal influence can do more than a man to protect a girl from the temptations of her own nature; . . . there is a definite place for women in the police force of any place where those temptations are many.'

The achievement 1919–39

The unifying influences described in this chapter had by no means exhausted themselves by 1939, when they were overtaken by further structural changes made necessary by war. They continued to operate in the postwar period in ways described in later chapters. Nevertheless, it is useful to pause on the eve of the Second World War and attempt to assess the extent to which, during the formative inter-war years, these influences had altered the police institution in its essentials. Were they paving the way towards a national police service?

The importance of the Desborough Committee, in introducing a new era for the police service, can hardly be exaggerated. The current of change ran deep, and its course was permanent. Standard conditions of service, uniform rates of pay, national representative bodies for all ranks, regular central and district conferences of chief constables—cumulatively, these changes tended to invest the police with the characteristics of a national rather than a local service. By 1939, too, the Home Office had built up a position of quite remarkable influence in police affairs, when it is remembered how detached the department had been before the First World War, and how the absence of central leadership and lack of concern had reflected on the well-being of the men. Latterly, the prolific 'advice' and 'guidance' contained in Home Office circulars on all manner of subjects became a euphemism for 'direction'; and chief constables, resentful of any attempt at interference from outside, would look to an informal exchange with the Home Office to settle almost any problem. Thus, for good or ill, the department had worked itself into a position of exercising great power without formal responsibility: for, apart from the important changes introduced by the Police Act, 1919, the control and administration of the police was still governed by the nineteenth-century laws which, as earlier chapters have shown, gave the Home Secretary very few powers, and so called for scarcely any accountability by him to Parliament. This situation was criticised in evidence given to the Royal Commission of 1960–2.* It seems, how-

* The Police Act, 1919, barely affected matters. It did not even require the police regulations made under it to be approved by Parliament. The Inns of Court Conservative and Unionist Society complained that 'the present fiction that because he [the Home Secretary] does not control them [the provincial police] he should not be answerable for them, seems to us to result in us having the worst of both worlds, in that control is in fact exercised by anonymous Home Office officials whose conduct cannot be

ever, that the Home Office should be praised rather than blamed for trying to fashion an antiquated police service, based on out-of-date laws, into an instrument that served the needs of the nation, and not only those of the parish.

The other important changes during the period pointed in the same direction. The rationalisation of detection techniques and the growth of such common services as wireless depots, forensic science laboratories, and crime clearing houses encouraged men to think of criminal detection as an aspect of police work whose success depended on the pooling of knowledge, the systematisation of techniques, and co-operation between forces. The increased spread of communications, made possible by the substitution of motor vehicles for horse-drawn transport or bicycles, and above all the development of wireless techniques, facilitated these changes and opened up new horizons. Operationally, the police were yearly becoming more efficient.

These were powerful influences working towards the integration of the police service; and there can be little doubt that they were further strengthened by the attitude of the public, particularly that of the motoring public. To many non-Londoners before the First World War the policeman was still recognisably the local officer that he had always been, and police forces, particularly borough forces, 'belonged' to their own communities in a meaningful way. The local tradesmen and shopkeepers who composed the watch committee still disciplined and promoted their constables, and took a pride in turning out for the annual ceremonial inspection by the inspector of constabulary. Probably most criminals were local men, and travellers on foot or horse or bicycle would have little or no contact with the police in the towns and villages they passed through. Parish-pump policing served the spirit and needs of the age. But with the advent of the motor-car criminals became increasingly mobile, the proportion of local crime diminished, and strangers were seen in every locality. And now, to a growing number of citizens for whom any dealings with the police would have been exceptional, the policeman of every village and town became a man to be reckoned with. What had been a rather endearing figure of fun turned out, after all, to be a figure of authority. The comical rural policeman of stage and fiction ceased to be credible

---

examined or questioned' (*Royal Commission on the Police, Minutes of Evidence*, 11–12, p. 691). (The Home Secretary's accountability for the Metropolitan Police has, of course, always been much greater, because of the terms of Peel's Act of 1829.)

by the 1930s, and the town policeman was showing more interest in catching speeding motorists than in his traditional weaknesses for rabbit pie, plump cooks in basement kitchens, and pretty parlourmaids. Less was heard of 'coppers' or 'bobbies' as the romantic upper- and middle-class idea of the police faded. The classless motoring public were obliged to strike complex new attitudes, blending truculence and ingratiation in a manner that expressed itself in the fashion of addressing every policeman as 'officer'. So the instability of relations between the police and the public was aggravated, and it mattered nothing to the motorist that a constable might belong to one particular force or another. In his eyes policemen everywhere were much the same (after 1934, following the recommendations of a Home Office committee, they wore similar uniform, though the helmets differed), and if they were not—if Surrey men behaved more oppressively than men of Kent—he demanded to know why. In this way the many other influences working towards integration were strengthened by pressure for uniform policies of law enforcement.

However, it is easy to exaggerate the effect of these unifying influences. All that can be said with safety is that they probably gave some policemen a growing sense of belonging to a national service as well as to their own local forces, and that ordinary citizens recognised in the police the characteristics of a national rather than a local body. For just as many of the public were becoming, for the first time, and by personal contact, aware of the police as an institution, as individuals, and as presenting problems which concerned them, so the institution itself, and its men and problems, would be seen, and discussed by the newspapers and in Parliament, as primarily national, and not local matters.

The contradictions in the situation are manifest. Much of the law had not been changed since Victorian times, and countering all the unifying influences was the right of 183 separate local police authorities to run their own local forces largely in their own way, together with the isolation of the Metropolitan Police, comprising nearly one-quarter of the whole, where Trenchard's experiments had probably had a disruptive rather than a unifying effect. Moreover, strong ties of local loyalty bound most policemen to their own town or city or county forces to a degree that would have made talk of a 'national' police service meaningless to them. By the outbreak of war local authorities had accepted the case for common police services, but each was still jealous to guard the separate identity of its own force. The achievements of the inter-war years were very great, but many barriers remained to be broken down before the process of integration had run its course. It is doubtful whether it has done so yet. The old tug-of-war between central and local government, with its attempt to reconcile operational efficiency with local democratic control over many separate police forces, had plenty of fighting spirit left in 1939. No one at that time, however, wanted any radical change, for the police had now gained many of the advantages of an integrated, nation-wide system, without sacrificing the local ties that to most people were an essential condition of its success.

Chapter Seven

War Interlude 1939–45

At the height of the Second World War, in February, 1942, when it seemed that the worst of the air attacks on Britain was over, Winston Churchill broadcast a tribute to the civil defence services who had 'helped our people through this formidable ordeal, the like of which no civilised community has ever been called on to undergo'. The Prime Minister went on: 'If I mention only one of them tonight— namely, the police—it is because many tributes have been paid already to the others. But the police have been in it everywhere all the time. And, as a working woman wrote to me in a letter, "What gentlemen they are".'[1]

Under the stress of war the police gave a striking demonstration of service to the community in its most exalted form. The accompanying structural changes in the service (which are described first in this short chapter) are also of interest, in showing how a system that still comprised 183 separate local forces was adapted to serve the national purposes—not by radical innovations, but by exploiting the authority already acquired by the Home Office in the manner described in the previous chapter, and backing it with formal powers under the Defence Regulations. In the working out of these changes there are possibly lessons for those who advocate a unified police service today.

Composition of the wartime police service

To enable the police to enforce the innumerable restrictions imposed on civilians during total war, and to help the civil defence services in coping with the effects of air raids, the police service was expanded by about 50 per cent. This expansion, and the subsequent contraction as pressure on the police relaxed, was controlled from beginning to end by the Government. Although the Home Office was not formally constituted as a Ministry of Police, there are times when it acted like one. Once the war had been well launched police authorities and chief constables had a reduced voice in the scale of policing their areas.

On the outbreak of war immediate heavy air attacks were expected, with the prospect of extensive fires, broken communications, looting, and panic—situations that would require ample resources of trained policemen if the initial attacks were to be withstood without a disastrous breakdown in civilian morale. The call-up of nearly 3,000 policemen with reservist obligations to the armed forces was deferred, and about 6,000 policemen under twenty-five, who were liable to conscription, were retained. Thus the total of some 60,000 regular policemen available at the onset of the war was kept temporarily intact. These, however, were merely expedients to deal with what it was assumed would be the early critical weeks. Long-term plans involved the recruitment of auxiliaries from four distinct sources. One was the First Police Reserve, which consisted of ex-policemen (there were also a few men with no former police experience), who volunteered to come back to full-time service when called upon, in return for which they were paid a retaining fee. Each police force maintained its own reserve, and at the end of 1938 the total number of reservists was over 10,000, a total which compared with only 4,000 who had been available in 1914. When war came, however, the number available soon fell to half this figure, and it rapidly dwindled as the pensioners became unfit to stand up to the strenuous life of a policeman in wartime. A second source was the special constabulary, which comprised, on the eve of the war, more than 130,000 men. A substantial number of these continued to serve throughout as whole-time paid special constables. The third source was derived from the formation, in 1938–9, of a new Police War Reserve, consisting of men recruited for war service only.[2] Recruitment was from men over thirty, who wore uniform similar to that of the regular police and whose full range of duties they eventually carried out. Women provided the fourth source of wartime recruitment. The National Council of Women (whose initiative in the First World War had provided the women police patrols from whom some of the earliest policewomen were recruited) complained early in 1939 that the Government's recently published National Service Handbook had no plans for enrolling women as special constables, a fact that reflected the indifference of the Home Office and most chief constables to the value of policewomen. A Women's Auxiliary Police Corps, instituted in August, 1939, for women between the ages of eighteen and fifty-five was the result. In the early part of the war the women were allowed to carry out only a restricted range of police duties, which typically included the driving and maintenance of motor transport, and clerical, telephone, radio, and canteen work, but many were later attested as constables, so that their duties extended over the whole range of law enforcement. They wore uniforms rather similar to those of auxiliary firewomen.

During the frenzied pre-war months there was no way in which these plans to augment the police could be forced on reluctant police authorities. The more far-sighted were anxious enough to expand their forces beyond the narrow requirements of local policing, but others earned the censure of the inspectors of constabulary, who commented in their report for the year 1938–9: 'Almost up to the outbreak of war there was a lamentable failure on the part of some police authorities to appreciate the extent of the police burden and the need to make adequate provision for it. The view was expressed by prominent members of some police authorities either that they did not believe in war, or that war could not or would not come to them. They had in some instances the sole idea of avoiding added costs to the local rates.'

There is no need to trace in detail the subsequent expansion and contraction of the police service.[3] The agreement that policemen with reservist obligations to the armed forces should be retained lapsed at the end of three months. The expected air attacks had not materialised, and the War Office needed all available ex-Servicemen to train Army conscripts; some policemen were also wanted as military police. To offset the loss to the police service (and a similar loss to the Fire Service), the Police and Firemen (War Service) Act, 1939, suspended the right to retire on pension without a medical certificate, except with the consent of the chief officer of police (or, in the case of a chief constable, that of the police authority), and auxiliary policemen were prevented from resigning by the Defence Regulations. To the corps of 60,000 regular policemen (or 57,000 when the reservists had gone to the armed forces) were then added the auxiliaries, the total of which was settled at about 35,000 additional full-time men, made up as follows: First Police Reserve, 7,000; paid special constables, 3,500; Police War Reserve, 24,600. Thus the total strength of the police in the early part of the war was increased to nearly 90,000, to which were to be added policewomen, the members of the Women's Auxiliary Police Corps, and the large number of part-time special constables, who, as one inspector of constabulary with a nice sense of police history put it, 'find it easier to strengthen the watch by night

225

rather than to carry out the ward by day'. In 1941 the total police strength reached 92,000. Never before had the country had so many policemen.

As the war progressed the shortage of manpower to supply the competing demands of the police, the armed forces, and industry required constant attention by the War Cabinet, and early priorities were adjusted. By November, 1942, over 4,000 of the younger policemen had been released for other forms of service, and yet a further source of recruits to the police had been opened up by the National Service Act, 1941, which enabled men to be conscripted to the Police War Reserve. All had expressed preference for police service, and were allocated by the Home Office to areas where they were most needed. In total, nearly 5,000 men were recruited in this way in 1941 and 1942, the first to suffer a measure of compulsory enrolment for police duties since the abandonment of the parish constable system in the nineteenth century. Their quality naturally varied, but the inspectors of constabulary said in their report at the end of the war that the arrangement had proved more successful than might have been expected.

The changing fortunes of war, in the later stages, placed even greater demands on the armed services, and the inflated police forces were regarded by the War Cabinet as a milch cow. Recruitment of men for the regular police was stopped towards the end of 1942, and all forces were classified according to their geographical situation and the hazards of war. One group was allowed up to 20 per cent addition to their pre-war establishment, a second was allowed up to 10 per cent, and a third was to revert to their former strength. Thus the police service gradually dwindled, a process interrupted, however, by the flying-bomb attacks in 1944. By this time the aggregate strength of the police was once again approaching its pre-war figure, of around 60,000, although its distribution continued to reflect the needs of war: forces in the militarily sensitive areas in the South of England continued at something like 20 per cent above their pre-war strength, while other forces had been run down to about 5 per cent below it.

The Women's Auxiliary Police Corps, in the meantime, had expanded to take over some of the duties relinquished by the men. But its growth was slow, and the women's organisations enlisted the support of the Archbishop of Canterbury in pressing their case to the Home Secretary. This intervention seems to have done something to overcome prejudice, for by March, 1942, the 226 regular policewomen employed on the outbreak of war had risen to 2,800 regular and auxiliaries. Later, as the country's shortage of manpower became increasingly acute and the Ministry of Labour's controls extended to the employment of women, a substantial number of women were directed into the police, where they proved highly successful, particularly in keeping order in the vicinity of the camps in which American and British troops were concentrated before the Normandy landings. By the end of the war the strength of the Women's Auxiliary Police Corps had risen to 3,700, and in addition there were over 400 regular policewomen.

The following table shows the varying composition of the police service during the war years:

POLICE PERSONNEL*

Year	Regular police	Police War Reserve and full-time special constables	First Police Reserve	Police-women	Total
1940	57,012	25,220†	5,725	282	88,239
1941	55,868	29,719	6,782	325	92,694
1942	49,735	27,706	5,374	340	83,155
1943	44,430	25,350	4,655	346	74,781
1944	43,026	17,527	2,568	385	63,506
1945	46,623	12,951	1,646	418‡	61,638

* Extracted from *The Report of H.M. Inspectors of Constabulary for 1940–5*.

† In June, 1940, 2,611 of these were full-time special constables, all but 242 of them in London; their number fell sharply as the war progressed.

‡ In addition, there were in September, 1945, over 3,000 whole-time unattested members of the Women's Auxiliary Police Corps, together with 342 attested members.

Wartime structural and administrative changes

Plans were drawn up before the war to orientate the structure of the police service towards national rather than local purposes. The extreme course was rejected at the outset: the police, unlike the Fire Service, was not nationalised.* Instead, the advantages of nationalisa-

* That there was a case for nationalisation is undeniable, but the Government no doubt considered that its objects could be better secured by the measures they took under the Defence Regulations to increase the powers of the Home Secretary. They were probably fortified in this view by the

tion were secured by three specific means, which in practice amounted to little more than a formal recognition, for the duration of the war, of arrangements that had already served the needs of peace: the Defence Regulations gave the Home Secretary a degree of control over provincial chief constables; a regional organisation was established; and arrangements were made under which policemen could be moved from one area to another, if necessary by the Home Secretary's direction. A further structural change must also be noted here, which, because of its greater affinity with postwar rather than wartime developments, is dealt with in the next chapter: this was the temporary amalgamation of several borough and county police forces in militarily sensitive areas in the south of England. All these changes left substantially intact the functions of local police authorities and the independence of the police in law enforcement. They did, however, make significant inroads into the peacetime arrangements.

By Defence Regulation 39 the Home Secretary was empowered to give to any police authority or chief constable 'such general or special instructions as appear to him necessary or expedient in the interests of the public safety, the Defence of the Realm, the maintenance of public order or the efficient prosecution of the war'. The effect of this was, for the first time in the history of the police, to put the provincial chief constables under the formal (as opposed to the informal) authority of the Home Secretary, though still not to the extent that the Metropolitan Police had always been. The Home Secretary was also given power to require the retirement of a chief constable if he considered him to be unfit to perform his duties in the conditions which prevailed, or which might be expected to prevail, in his area. These powers do not seem to have been extensively used, but their mere existence was enough to consolidate pre-existing patterns of influence.

The second structural change effected on the police service by the war had as its aim to build up the strength and efficiency of each

---

successful experience of inter-force co-operation between the wars, particularly during the General Strike. Commenting on a demand by some local authorities that the Exchequer should bear the cost of bringing their police forces into a state of wartime efficiency, the inspectors of constabulary said tartly: 'it is curious that those who argue that the Government should take over the whole responsibility for the cost of any measures which are necessary in the national interest would be the first to resist stoutly anything in the nature of nationalisation or any increase in the measure of central control'.

separate force, while at the same time superimposing on the pattern of local forces a form of regional organisation derived from experience gained in 1926 during the General Strike, when eleven civil commissioners had been appointed. If communications with the central Government had broken down, the new wartime commissioner, one of whom was appointed to each of the eleven regions into which England and Wales were divided for civil purposes, was to assume the full executive powers of central Government in his area; short of this, he was to co-ordinate the work of Government departments with that of local authorities. He was operationally responsible for the civil defence services.

To each of these regional headquarters outside London was appointed a small police unit, consisting of an assistant inspector of constabulary and a staff officer.* They acted as liaison officers between the regional commissioner and the chief constables in their area, kept in touch with the inspectors of constabulary, and served as a channel of communication with the Home Office. In time the scope of their duties widened, and they helped with civil defence and military exercises, planned arrangements for reinforcing the police where necessary, and worked out police plans for troop movements and convoys.

Relations between regional commissioners and chief constables were delicate. The Government made it clear that if an invasion came the commissioners would be expected to give operational orders to chief constables, which they would have a duty to obey. In areas where fighting took place, the police were also to consider themselves under the authority of the military. These encroachments on their peacetime status were viewed with misgivings by some chief constables, particularly when it came to their notice that the regional commissioners had asked whether they could suspend or dismiss a chief constable in whom they lacked confidence. Inherent in the situation was a conflict between the obvious need for unified control of all the services in a threatened area, and the immunity for so long enjoyed by provincial chief constables (particularly in the counties) from external control or direction by anyone other than the Home Office. They were naturally jealous of their privileged position of apparent independence, little as it owed (as this history will have shown) to any deliberate intent of government or Act of Parliament.

* At the beginning of the war, staff officers only were appointed, but the threat of invasion made it desirable to strengthen the police unit at each regional headquarters by the addition of an assistant inspector.

229

In the event no clash of authority occurred; and for this much credit is probably due to the regional police units for their success in helping the civilian, military, and police authorities to understand the problems of each other. As the war progressed chief constables looked for guidance from the regional headquarters, and in areas subjected to heavy attack they accepted directions for the reinforcement of one police area by another as a matter of course.

The General Strike had not only provided experience of working a regional organisation; it had also given an opportunity to try out arrangements for reinforcing one police force by another. By a wartime regional reinforcement scheme, these arrangements were further developed. Every force with an establishment over fifty men had a quota fixed by the Home Office, ranging upwards from 10 per cent of the establishment, which was available for reinforcing any other area as the need arose. The total number of men reserved in this way was about 7,600. The scheme worked in three stages: one third of the men could be moved under local arrangements; the remainder could be called upon by the regional commissioner to reinforce any force in his region; and the Home Office reserved the right to call on any force for inter-regional reinforcement.[4] These arrangements proved their value when the test came. By the end of 1942, when the worst of the air raids was over, some twenty-two cities and towns had been sent police reinforcements. Liverpool gained most, with 1,225 men despatched from seventeen other forces; Coventry received 941 men from thirteen forces, and Bristol and Exeter each received 315 men. In all, 5,500 men were moved in reinforcements at one time or another, involving 103 forces.

Significance of wartime changes

It is instructive to compare the nature of the changes caused in the administration of the police service by the stresses of the two world wars. Those caused by the First World War, described in Chapter Six, may be summarised briefly. First, war conditions forged, for the first time, a direct link between the Home Office and chief constables. Second, the inauguration of district conferences between chief constables paved the way for the co-operative enterprises between police forces that constituted such an important development of the service in the inter-war years. Third, the rise in the cost of living during the war was not matched by corresponding increases in police pay, with the result that the Desborough Committee was appointed, with all the momentous consequences that flowed from its report.

Similar pressures in the Second World War produced similar effects, which this time, however, went further in some ways and less far in others. The link between the Home Office and chief constables, so tentatively established a quarter of a century earlier, and since grown so strong, was formally recognised by the Defence Regulations; a type of regional organisation was set up to promote co-operation between police forces and the civil defence services, and the success of the reinforcement scheme aided the process of replacing the old concept of separate police forces by that of a single police service; and once again the police emerged from a major war to find the purchasing power of their pay reduced comparatively with that of many other workers (despite a war bonus added to their salaries), a situation which led, within three years of the cessation of hostilities, to the appointment of a further independent inquiry (the Oaksey Committee) into police pay and conditions of service.

That the stresses of the two wars to some extent moulded the shape of the police service and influenced its future development in the immediate post-war years is evident. Yet it does not follow that either war was uniquely responsible for stimulating the kind of reforms which otherwise might have been delayed for many years, or never have come about at all. The police are always at war in fighting crime, and their duties did not change in essence in 1939, any more than they changed in 1914, although the scope of these duties was broadened in ways about to be described, and they became more hazardous. It was, in fact, the exigencies of peacetime policing rather than the exceptional and temporary demands of war that determined the way in which the service evolved after 1945. The point is well illustrated by the history of the main organisational changes introduced as temporary measures during the Second World War. One, the statutory link between the Home Office and chief constables, was severed when the Defence Regulations were revoked in 1945; it was re-established (in a weaker form) by the Police Act, 1964; the second, a rather loose type of regional organisation set up in 1939, was abandoned in 1945: something on these lines, too, was re-established in 1963–4 as a result of recommendations by the recent Royal Commission on the Police; the third, the reinforcement scheme, has its rough analogue in the recent development of regional crime squads; and the fourth, the temporary amalgamation of police forces, proved to be only a first instalment of other, and more drastic, amalgamations undertaken to

231

serve the needs of peace. Thus all the structural and administrative changes made to meet the demands of war had not only been fostered during the inter-war period; they were also seen, in the postwar years, to be equally desirable in the interests of efficient policing in time of peace.

Police duties in war

The outbreak of war brought no sudden or dramatic change in the duties of the police. As in peacetime their primary duty remained the prevention and detection of crime and the maintenance of public order. Crime was, in general, effectively combated. A welcome relief came from the conscription of many regular criminals into the armed forces, offset to some extent, however, by a rise in juvenile delinquency occasioned by the closing of some schools, and difficulties of adjustment to life in evacuation areas. Traffic became a less serious problem with the introduction of petrol rationing, but there was a notable increase in accidents in the blackened streets. A severe drain on police strength was caused by the activities of the I.R.A.[5] Thus the effect of the war was to shift the balance of police duties and diversify them rather than to change their essence. But the war also added to these duties in four principal ways: the police were required to enforce new laws restrictive of personal liberty; they had to mount guard at numerous points vulnerable to sabotage; they performed various quasi-military functions; and, in co-operation with the civil defence services, they dealt with the effects of air raids. In addition, the regular police forces undertook at the outbreak of war the substantial new task of training the many auxiliaries.

All police officers had to familiarise themselves with the far-ranging code of new offences and restrictions embodied in the Defence Regulations. The general purpose of these was to protect the security of the State; their particular purposes extended from restrictions on flying carrier pigeons to a prohibition on carrying a camera in restricted areas, enforcement of the 'blackout' regulations, and many others. It became an offence to attempt to cause disaffection among members of the forces, or to influence public opinion 'in a manner likely to be prejudicial to the defence of the realm or the efficient prosecution of the war'. The Aliens Order gave power to detain, or impose restrictions on, any person with a view to preventing acts prejudicial to the public safety or the defence of the realm: acting under it, the police took into custody enemy aliens and others destined for internment, and supervised the application of restrictions on some people's places of residence, movements, and possession of prohibited articles, such as cameras, cars, field-glasses, maps, and radios. The police were asked to report to regional headquarters any supposed case of improper disclosure of secret information, and they acted throughout the war as a kind of intelligence service, reporting (to regional headquarters), for the information of the Government, on the state of public order and civilian morale, the extent to which refugees were evacuating heavily bombed towns, the conduct of the public during air raids, the effect of enemy propaganda, and signs of industrial unrest. Mingling with the ordinary population, they were uniquely placed to report on matters of this kind, and their training secured a valuable degree of objectivity.

The second of the new wartime tasks the police shouldered, that of guarding vulnerable points, imposed a heavy burden in terms of manpower. 'Vulnerable points' is a convenient short-hand term for places of such importance to the national effort in time of war (or civil emergency) that special protection is required to secure them against malicious damage. Examples are oil installations, public utility undertakings, armament factories, and important railway junctions or bridges. There was a tendency, on the outbreak of war, to over-insure against the risk of sabotage by diverting large numbers of policemen for guard duties, and in the early part of the war some 10,000 regular policemen were thus employed, in addition to large numbers of special constables. As the war progressed, however, the Home Guard relieved the police of much of this unrewarding duty— which incidentally provides one of the comparatively rare instances when policemen regularly carried arms.

Other quasi-military tasks given to the police during the war constitute an oddly assorted miscellany, and space permits of a few examples only. With the aid of the military, they helped to find billets for troops and to earmark accommodation in 'evacuation areas'; air raids brought the problem of controlling the movement of refugees and keeping the roads clear for military convoys; large areas of the country, where secret defensive or offensive installations were placed, had to be guarded against public access; a system of advance air raid warnings was operated by the police; Local Defence Volunteers (later to become the Home Guard) were enrolled at police stations, and after an appeal by the Government the police collected an astonishing assortment of arms from the public with which to equip the volunteers. At a later stage of the war selected police officers were seconded as liaison officers with the higher American formations in this country, and a special task fell on police forces in the south of England when vast numbers of troops were encamped before the Normandy landings.

It remains to describe the nature of police duties during air raids—a task which cannot be adequately performed in the space available. From the start it was evident that they would have a vital part to play, for the long tradition that the policeman was everybody's friend was bound to be fully exploited. The calm and authoritative way of a good-natured Bobby (it seems appropriate to revert, for the last time, to the anachronistic title) could, as experience during the General Strike had demonstrated, do more to dispel panic than any amount of official propaganda. Means had therefore to be found of integrating the police with the newly formed civil defence services.

It was decided in 1939 that an A.R.P. controller should be appointed by every local authority, and rather more than one-quarter of the first appointments to this post consisted of the chief constable for the area.[6] The controller had charge of the air raid warden's service, and this service, in turn, worked closely with the police. Often a policeman would be the first to arrive at the scene of an 'incident', and he would undertake the immediate tasks of rescue work, the searching of bomb-damaged premises for survivors, dealing with unexploded bombs, or tackling small fires, before the other services—wardens, rescue, first aid, ambulance, fire—arrived on the scene. As experience was gained, the vital role of the police in co-ordinating these other services was increasingly recognised, and chief constables selected officers known as 'incident officers', who were specially trained in this work. Never, surely, had the courage and initiative of the police been so severely tested, and never had they displayed greater heroism. Nor were their qualities confined to the regular and full-time officers: 'Under actual enemy attack', the inspectors of constabulary later reported, 'special constables have performed their duties with a devotion to duty worthy of the highest tradition of the police service.' The great air attacks on London started early in September, 1940, and continued until the following May. Coventry was 'blitzed' in mid-November, 1940, and then came the turn of Birmingham, Southampton, Bristol, Sheffield, Liverpool, Manchester, Hull and Plymouth. The loss of life and destruction of property surpassed anything the world had hitherto known. A single example must suffice to recall its magnitude: the city of Hull suffered seventy-three attacks, in which over 1,000 persons were killed and 100,000 rendered homeless. Here, and everywhere, the police behaved superbly. Their staunch defiance of danger and unfailing good humour steadied, stiffened, and finally rallied public morale during these critical months in a manner that won the praise of the Prime Minister in 1942, in the words quoted at the beginning of this chapter.

But the ordeal was not yet over. Later that year came air attacks on cathedral cities (the so-called 'Baedeker' raids). In 1943 London was once again the main target of the bombers. And then, in the middle of the following year, 1944, the flying-bombs started, and the Metropolitan Police, unshaken after five years of war, once more responded magnificently to meet the new menace. Children were evacuated from London again and over 1 million others left independently. The police remained. More than 2,300 flying-bombs fell in the Metropolitan Police district, killing over 5,000 people and seriously injuring another 15,000. Finally, in September, 1944, came Hitler's last secret weapon—the V2 rockets. More than 500 fell on London, killing a further 2,600 people and seriously injuring 5,000 more. Police reported that Londoners were more upset and frightened by flying-bombs and rockets than ever during the great raids of the early war years,[7] for the new weapons inspired awe. Rockets arrived with no warning, but the course of a flying-bomb was watched with dread, and the sinister cut-out of its engine meant that death and destruction were at hand.

Fragmented into separate local forces as it remained throughout the war, it is nevertheless true that the police service acted as though it were a single national force under the ultimate guidance of the Home Office. The regional organisation contributed to this sense of unity. The reinforcement scheme, under which drafts of police officers moved freely from one police area to another, gave it further substance. And if any additional reminder were needed that local police boundaries are irrelevant in the context of modern war, the Home Office announced, in March, 1941, a scheme by which policemen in need of rest after enduring months of air attack in the heavily bombed areas could be replaced by volunteers from elsewhere. Many volunteered, but few sought relief; and not one policeman moved out of London. On the other hand, the many offers from policemen in the quieter parts to provide accommodation for the wives and children of their colleagues in danger areas were cordially welcomed, and further developed the spirit of unity, always so real a thing in the police service, that grows so readily in the hearts of men engaged on a common and dangerous enterprise.

235

'The public appreciation of the police has never been greater', the inspectors of constabulary reported at the end of the war, 'the confidence that is placed in the police has never been higher, and the relationship between the public and police service was never better. For this state of affairs all ranks of the police service—men and women, regulars and auxiliaries, part-time and whole-time alike—can take credit.'[8] The Home Secretary (Mr. Herbert Morrison) paid tribute to the fine manner in which the police had carried out duties 'that were sometimes unspectacular, often dangerous, and always of the greatest importance to the Home Front'. He recalled the history of 'five and a half eventful years . . . air-raids, flying-bombs, and rockets, with their toll of suffering, death and destruction', praising the way in which the police had sustained civilian morale, saved lives and property, and assisted the military machine while carrying on their normal work of preserving law and order and bringing offenders to justice. 'It is no exaggeration to say', the Home Secretary declared, 'that the reputation of the British police for service to the community stands higher than ever before.'[9]

The cost of devotion to duty had been heavy: 278 members of the police service were killed as a result of enemy action while on duty with their own forces, and 1,275 police officers serving with H.M. Forces were killed or died from other causes.

Chapter Eight

Reform on an Ebb Tide 1945–59

For the police, as for many others, the years which followed the war were jaundiced by disappointed hopes. At the end of the war police morale stood high. Relations with the public had probably never been closer, but that intimacy was in any case bound to cloy. A crescendo of high endeavour had to fall away in the humdrum of peace. Other factors besides these were working to undermine morale. Policemen's families were poor again at the end of the war, as they had not been since 1919, and on top of their domestic worries the police faced fresh challenges which, for the first time in their history, were to give them a taste of defeat. An early hint of them came in the first post-war report by the inspectors of constabulary: 'During the past year, and especially during the last few months, crimes of serious character, both of violence against persons as well as against property, have increased'; and there was a prospect of an 'enormous increase' in road traffic as peacetime conditions returned. These warnings were, if anything, pitched too low. As year succeeded year in the postwar period the problems of crime and traffic were building up. Outbreaks of lawlessness and hooliganism added to the police task. In the late 1950s political demonstrators against nuclear weapons provoked clashes with them. Motorists, thwarted by traffic congestion, blamed them. At times it seemed that they had few friends, for the wartime legacy of goodwill and public co-operation rapidly ebbed away to a point at which, early in 1960, the Police Federation declared unequivocally: 'His [the constable's] status in the community is declining and respect for his office is lower than it was before the 1939–45 War.'[1]

Faced with these mounting problems and uncertain of their support from the public, the police were further depressed, during these difficult years, by what they regarded as the inadequacy of their rates of pay and the reluctance of the authorities to restore to them the purchasing power of the Desborough Committee's scale of 1919. A chronic deficiency of manpower, mounting crime, long working hours, indifferent relations with the public, sinking morale: the problems were multiplying and their consequences, unless they were urgently tackled, could only benefit the criminal. Yet there was no one, at this period, with a clear responsibility to tackle problems of this kind, much less to comprehend the totality of a problem which had no precedent between the wars. Piecemeal answers could be found for specific questions. But the wider issues straddled the frontiers of the Home Office, the police authorities, their representatives in the local authority associations, the chief constables and the representatives of the superintendents and men; and it was not easy to establish what was a national problem to be tackled centrally, and what was a local problem to be tackled locally. Shared responsibility inevitably led to a degree of irresponsibility,* and matters were not improved when the already involved administrative superstructure of the police was further complicated by the addition of a second Police Council, which undermined the authority of the first. By the end of the period the level of police pay had fallen to a point at which it can be seen to have dominated almost every other aspect of the police problem: inadequate manpower, impaired efficiency, reduced morale, and deteriorating public relations.

It is against this somewhat gloomy background that the period nevertheless saw many notable and lasting reforms as the police service re-shaped itself to cope with the problems the war left behind, and the strains of the fast-changing social groupings of the 1950s. They were reforms which the Royal Commission on the Police, sitting in the next decade, praised as developments, under the guidance of the central departments, which had achieved much that was of the highest quality. Their range was wide. A national Police College was established, recruit-training centres were set up in each police district, negotiating machinery was introduced into the service for the first time (it admittedly made a contribution, but did not give an acceptable answer, to the problem of pay), central promotion examinations were instituted, the forensic science laboratories and wireless depots were developed, the first crime and traffic squads were started, and notable progress was made towards the abolition of the smaller police forces in the interests of greater efficiency.

---

* Commenting on the inadequacy of police pay in 1959, the Royal Commission on the Police remarked in their final report: 'A system of control which allowed the situation to deteriorate to the extent revealed by our earlier report must itself be called in question'—(Cmnd. 1,728 (May, 1962), paragraph 132).

Postwar Reconstruction Committee

The first stimulus to reform came from the war itself. Already in 1944 there was a readiness, hitherto rare in the police service, to challenge the accepted order of things; and in that year the Home Secretary set up a committee consisting of representatives of the Home Office and chief constables to consider both immediate postwar problems and also questions of long-term policy. The committee's terms of reference ranged widely, from the employment of policewomen to the need for a national Police College. It was asked to have a fresh look at the way in which police forces were organised, the distribution of senior ranks in a force, the arrangements for training recruits and promoting men to supervisory rank, communications systems, police buildings, and much else.

Four useful reports came in due course from this somewhat overburdened committee. The first had, perhaps, the most enduring effect, for its subject was the higher training of the police, and its principal recommendation was the establishment of a Police College. The Home Office lost little time in putting this recommendation into effect. The second report dealt with the organisation of the service, but prefaced fifty-three pages with the disarming statement that the committee had 'no sweeping reforms or radical alterations in the present organisation to suggest'. It did, however, emphasise the increasing difficulty of the police task, and it carried out an interesting survey of the traditional beat system. In this report, too, the committee encouraged the employment of policewomen on a wide range of duties, and it proposed the lines on which the training of subordinate ranks should be conducted. A third report dealt with police buildings and the welfare of the men; and finally, in 1947, came a fourth report on the responsibilities of the higher ranks and the organisation, work, and conditions of service of the special constabulary.

Amalgamation of police forces

Wide as its review was, the Postwar Committee was not asked to deal with the most controversial aspect of the new pattern of the police service—namely, the future of the smaller police forces. No doubt it would have been thought inappropriate for a body composed

239

exclusively of officials and senior police officers to advise on a matter of such close interest to local government. Nor is it likely that the Home Secretary needed any further advice about it, for the abolition of small borough police forces had been an object of Home Office policy since well before the first step was taken in 1888, when the Local Government Act of that year abolished forces in towns with a population under 10,000. Palmerston, it will be recalled, had had designs on even bigger forces as early as 1854. So the Home Office cannot be accused of precipitate action in returning to the charge after the Second World War. The policy was well-matured, even though it had faded from public view for nearly sixty years.

Moreover, the policy now had the backing of the influential Desborough Committee, who recommended the abolition of all non-county borough police forces. Ideally, they held, a town of less than 100,000 should not have a separate force, and no new force should be established without the consent of the Home Secretary. These advanced views naturally outraged the small municipalities, who found a fighting leader in the Town Clerk of Luton; and for more than twenty years the strength of local government proved more than a match for the Home Office's repeated efforts to abolish the small forces. The first of these was exerted in 1922, when a Bill was prepared empowering the Home Secretary, in defined circumstances, to compel mergers of police forces in the interests of economy.[2] This Bill, like Palmerston's nearly three-quarters of a century earlier, was abandoned. In the following year the Home Office pressed on a Royal Commission on Local Government the view that a reasonable aim should be forces of at least 250 strength in the counties and 300 in the boroughs. By applying this standard, at least half the existing forces would disappear. But the Royal Commission cautiously decided that the Government should be left to make up their own minds with the help of the Desborough Committee's views without any recommendation from them.

There the matter rested until 1932, when a select committee of the House of Commons recommended, again, it seems, on grounds of economy, that all the non-county borough forces with a population of under 30,000 should be abolished, with the exception of Windsor, where 'very special conditions obtain by reason of the fact that it contains a royal residence'.[3] The Home Office had urged the committee to go much further: in their view the police forces of all boroughs with a population under 75,000 should be merged with those of the county. But the committee declared its sympathy with the claims of boroughs which had 'enjoyed the dignity of being counties of cities since the Middle Ages'. In the event nothing at all happened, with the result that at the outbreak of war in 1939 there remained a total of 183 police forces in England and Wales, thirty-one of which had a strength of under fifty men. During the 1920s and 1930s only eight of the small borough forces had agreed voluntarily to be policed by the surrounding counties.

The Government did not regard the threat of invasion in 1940 as a sufficient reason for taking emergency powers to amalgamate police forces. It was not until nearly three years after the outbreak of war that the Home Secretary (Mr. Herbert Morrison, who was a police-man's son) laid regulations[4] before Parliament made under the Emergency Powers (Defence) Act, to enable him by order to provide for the amalgamation of any two or more areas if he was satisfied that the amalgamation was necessary for facilitating naval, military, or air operations. The regulations were strongly criticised, and the Home Secretary gave an undertaking that they would not be used to provide a short-cut to nationalising or regionalising the police. He also promised Parliament that they would be revoked at the end of the war. The immediate need, he said, was to rationalise the pattern of policing in militarily important areas, particularly those parts of the country which were liable to invasion, or which were important in relation to offensive military operations. Continuance or extension of the temporary amalgamations would be a matter for Parliament to consider in the context of permanent postwar legislation.[5]

Seven amalgamation schemes were made under these regulations, reducing the number of separate forces by twenty-one. The first, a merger of the Guildford and Reigate forces with Surrey, came into force on February 1st, 1943, followed by the other five on April 1st, 1943.* The principal sacrifice from all these changes naturally fell on the chief constables of the small borough forces which disappeared, all of whom were offered re-employment as superintendents. Some of them subsequently rose to high rank again, and testified, despite the check to their careers, to the gains in efficiency and economy which the amalgamations had brought.

* These comprised mergers of the following constabularies: Penzance and Cornwall; East Sussex, West Sussex, Brighton, Hove, Hastings, and Eastbourne; Salisbury and Wiltshire; nine borough forces with Kent; and the Isle of Wight and Winchester with Hampshire. On the same date Tiverton amalgamated voluntarily with Devon.

Postwar amalgamations: the Police Act, 1946

The watch committees of the amalgamated boroughs sat uneasily under these enforced mergers,* and as early as December, 1944, before the war was over, they passed a resolution calling for the revocation of all the amalgamation schemes from March 31st, 1945. But the Home Secretary had other views. He felt that the impetus of wartime amalgamations should not be lost. He consulted the chief constables of the amalgamated forces, and they were unanimous in agreeing that the arrangements had been successful in leading to greater efficiency, economy, and improved deployment of manpower. Emboldened by these views, the Home Secretary surveyed the pattern of policing over the whole country as it had emerged from the war. It was clear that something would have to be done. Merely to allow the amalgamated forces to re-establish their separate identities would have been reactionary, yet to discriminate against them by promoting legislation to preserve their abolition would have been unfair and anomalous; there were many other small forces in parts of the country geographically remote from the militarily sensitive areas whose survival could no longer be justified. In short, the police map was an anachronism. In 1945 there remained forty-seven non-county borough police forces, and a substantial number of them had already been merged under wartime powers. Eight county boroughs, on the other hand, had agreed voluntarily, at varying dates before the war, to be policed by the surrounding counties, and a further three were policed by the Metropolitan Police. The size of the borough forces varied from 2,000 to fifteen, and that of the county forces from 2,500 to ten. Nor did the law, as it then stood, enable a more rational pattern to be established. The Home Secretary had no peacetime powers to compel the merger of police forces. A borough could merge with the surrounding county force, but a county force could not merge with another county force, nor a borough force with another borough force.

Faced with these anomalies, the Home Secretary invited the local authority associations to agree that he should promote legislation to enable him to make compulsory amalgamations, preceded by public local inquiries at which the views of all interested parties would be heard. He would use the powers only where their use seemed to him

* The watch committees continued to exist. *Ad hoc* joint authorities were set up, but they delegated some functions to the original police authorities.

242

to be in the interests of efficiency. Meanwhile, he suggested, the war-time amalgamations should continue until such time as any new legislation had been enacted. Provision would also be made to facilitate voluntary amalgamations by putting an end to the anomalies in the law.

The Association of Municipal Corporations must have yawned, as they thumbed through their nineteenth-century files, at the monotony with which history was repeating itself. But this time history moved on. Following the General Election of 1945, Mr. Chuter Ede replaced Mr. Herbert Morrison as Home Secretary, and he carried his predecessor's proposals much further. Within a few months of taking office he had introduced a Bill into Parliament to abolish all non-county borough police forces (with the exception of Cambridge and Peterborough, where the borough had a population larger than that of the county), seeking, at the same time, powers to compel the amalgamation of any other force where it seemed to him to be in the interests of efficiency. Any amalgamation would be preceded by a local inquiry, and the Order making the scheme would be subject to Parliament's approval. Other provisions of the Bill removed the obstacles in the way of two county forces or two county borough forces merging.

This Bill became the Police Act, 1946. Its passage was, naturally, controversial. The Home Secretary was accused of seeking powers that would enable him, in effect, to set up regional police forces by joining many of the remaining separate forces together. From there it would be a short step to nationalising the police. Thus were awakened echoes of speeches long buried in the archives of *Hansard*. The Home Secretary naturally denied any sinister intentions, and accepted an amendment which inserted a limit of 100,000 population for a county or county borough, beyond which no area could be compulsorily amalgamated with an area of equal or greater size. The Bill became law on April 15th, 1946, and forty-five non-county borough forces were abolished on April 1st, 1947. On the same date three voluntary amalgamation schemes came into force. Thus disappeared some splendid old police forces which had outlived their usefulness and, in many cases, the Victorian buildings that still housed them. But they were still alive enough with old tradition, and many recent brave memories of war and peace, to cause real pangs at the parting.

An important change in the arrangements for merging police forces was introduced by the Police Act, 1946. Hitherto, a borough which agreed to be policed by the county force could either agree to set up a joint committee to administer a combined police force or they could enter into what was known as a 'consolidation' agreement. Under the latter, which was the normal form of the agreements made in the nineteenth century, the borough contributed to the expenses of the county force, but the watch committee was not represented on the police committee (the standing joint committee) of the county. The Act of 1946 preserved the existing agreements, but repealed the power to make any more. Any future arrangements between counties and county boroughs were to take the form of 'amalgamation' schemes. Under these a combined police force was set up, and the separate police authorities continued to exist, each appointing members to serve on a combined police authority. The proportionate representation (usually related to the relative populations in the combining areas) and the financial apportionment were laid down in the scheme of amalgamation. But the forty-five non-county borough forces which were abolished on April 1st, 1947 disappeared entirely. They did not form part of combined forces. Their members were simply transferred to the enveloping county constabulary, but they were given a guarantee that they would not be transferred to duties which would entail their moving house without their consent. The police functions of the watch committees affected were, similarly, taken away, although the committees continued in existence for a number of years in order to discharge certain minor functions given to them long ago by the municipal Corporations Act, 1835.*

Beyond the abolition on April 1st, 1947, of forty-five non-county borough police forces, the results of the Police Act, 1946, were modest. Seven voluntary amalgamation schemes were made,† and these were accompanied by the first compulsory scheme to be made by the Home Secretary. This, a scheme to combine Chester with Cheshire, came into force in 1949 after bitter opposition from the county borough, and it was followed by three further compulsory

* They included street lighting and house-to-house collections. The rump watch committees in these non-county boroughs were finally abolished by the Police Act, 1964.

† Four schemes were made in 1947, as follows: Cornwall and the Isles of Scilly; Kent and Canterbury; The Soke and City of Peterborough; and Hampshire and the Isle of Wight. A scheme covering Durham, Darlington, and West Hartlepool was made in 1948, followed by Gwynedd (Anglesey, Caernarvon, and Merioneth) in 1950 and Warwickshire and Solihull in 1964. The effect was to reduce the total of 183 forces in 1939 (159 in 1943) to 131 in 1947, 129 in 1949, and 125 in 1960.

schemes.* The total of eleven schemes made under the Act had the effect of reducing the number of separate police forces by thirteen, although one of these was re-created when, in 1948, Bournemouth decided to withdraw from a scheme combining the county borough with Hampshire and the Isle of Wight. In 1960, therefore, when the first wave of amalgamations was completed, there remained 125 separate police forces in England and Wales, and it required a Royal Commission and a further Act of Parliament before the century-long process of abolishing the smaller police forces could be tackled afresh.

Training of lower ranks: police training centres

Recruitment to the police was suspended during the war, and in order to train the abnormally high intake of recruits in the immediate postwar period a temporary training centre was set up in each of the eight districts covered by the district conferences of chief constables (p. 183), and the old-established Metropolitan Police training school at Peel House was supplemented by a parallel establishment at Hendon. The Postwar Committee recommended that these arrangements should be made permanent.

This was an advance on earlier attitudes towards the systematic training of the police. Prewar arrangements were haphazard. The Desborough Committee recommended the appointment of a training officer to every police force, but many of the smaller forces were unable to spare a policeman solely for this duty, and co-operative arrangements were common. Immediately before the war about forty forces maintained training schools, the size of which varied from force to force, and most recruits attended one of these schools for about three months. The Metropolitan Police School at Peel House commonly had about 200 recruits under instruction. Other schools for from seventy-five to 150 recruits were maintained by some six of the largest forces, but most of the schools were small, with a single class of about twenty. Few were residential, and the method and quality of training varied widely. In addition, as noted in Chapter Six, four detective-training schools were established before the war; they reopened soon afterwards.

Hence the establishment after the war of eight district training

* These schemes were: Mid-Wales (comprising the counties of Radnor, Brecon, and Montgomery) in 1948; Leicestershire and Rutland in 1951; and Carmarthenshire and Cardiganshire in 1958.

centres* amounted to a fresh start. They were provided by the Home Office under common service arrangements (p. 214), and each was managed by a committee representing the police authorities in the catchment area. A committee of chief constables recommended the appointment of the commandant and other senior officers, and approved the syllabus of instruction. These arrangements have continued until the present time. A general oversight of all the arrangements is maintained by the Central Conference of Chief Constables. Recruits attend an initial course of thirteen weeks, which is intended to give them all-round instruction in the duties of a police officer. Their training continues in the home force, and it is completed by a return to the training centre—for four weeks shortly before the expiry of the probationary period of two years. Refresher training is given in a man's own force or at a school run by a neighbouring force. Specialist training (for example in criminal investigation or driving) is given by schools maintained by a few of the larger forces.[6]

Higher police training: the national Police College

The genesis of what is now the national Police College was the first report of the Postwar Committee. They had to tread warily in the wake of the controversy over Trenchard's Metropolitan College ten years earlier, but they declared emphatically that further provision of some kind was needed for the higher and specialist training of police, and they recommended the establishment of a police college which should open its doors to all forces. Men destined for high rank required opportunities for study and experience wider than their ordinary daily work allowed, a need underlined by the fact that much police work is carried on alone, and opportunities for exercising the skills of supervision and command are consequently restricted. The higher posts ought to be filled by promotion from below, yet without college training the prospects of finding enough leaders from within the service were bleak. There would be nothing 'to counteract, in the newly appointed inspector, the influence of long service in a subordinate capacity which may actually hamper the growth of the broad

* In 1971 the centres were situated at Bruche, near Warrington, Pannel Ash, near Harrogate, Newby Wisk, Yorkshire, Ryton-on-Dunsmore, Warwickshire, Sandgate, Kent, Chantmarle, Dorset, Bridgend, Glamorgan, and Eynsham Hall, Oxfordshire. Recruits were also being trained at Dishforth in Yorkshire.

outlook, the quality of leadership, and the independent habits of mind which are essential if a senior police officer is to command the confidence of his men and the respect of all classes of the community'.

However, means had now to be found of overcoming the prejudice that Trenchard had left behind, and in particular there had to be no suggestion that an 'officer class' was to be created. These circumstances explain the cautious nature of the committee's proposals. They rejected the advice of those (among them the former Commandant of the Hendon Police College) who regarded the primary purpose of a college as to attract able young men and train them to fill higher posts before they were too old to have lost their drive. The committee insisted that any scheme for a police college should be regarded as fair by all members of the service, and commented that it would be unfortunate if the impression got abroad that the object of the college was to secure promotion for a privileged class. The aim should be to 'broaden the outlook, improve the professional knowledge, and stimulate the energies of men who have reached or are reaching the middle and higher ranks of the service'.

The Government announced their acceptance of the committee's principal recommendations[7] and the first truly national Police College was opened in June, 1948, at Ryton-on-Dunsmore in Warwickshire. It moved to its permanent home at Bramshill House, Hartley Wintney —a fine Jacobean mansion standing in a park of 269 acres—in 1960. The College is managed by a Board of Governors consisting as to half of representatives nominated by the Home Secretary—officials of the Home Office, one of the inspectors of constabulary, and members of the various police associations—and as to half of representatives nominated by the local authority associations. From the start, the idea of the College was to broaden the outlook of the students; but for the first five years, although the activities relating to instruction and discussion about senior police duties developed steadily, those relating to wider activities, such as the machinery of government, public affairs, social history, and humanistic studies, were not so satisfactory. This part of the syllabus consisted of lectures to large numbers (usually the whole College) by visiting lecturers of distinction; but there was insufficient follow-up and tutorial work to ensure that students could take a personal and constructive part in it.

From 1953 onwards academic lecturers were brought into the College. The more general subjects were developed through small classes and tutorials on a scheme of studies worked out to complement the police studies, with studies in history, English literature, the development of our social institutions, local and central government, and so on. Thus the College was able to combine the functions of a university and a senior staff college, and the instructional staff now consists of graduates from British universities and seconded police officers. At first two main residential courses were offered: a junior course of six months, to fit sergeants for promotion to the rank of inspector; and a senior course of three months, to prepare inspectors and chief inspectors to be superintendents. Short courses were also available for selected superintendents. These arrangements continued for ten years, during which the College consolidated a reputation both within the British police service and also among police services throughout the Commonwealth, candidates from which were admitted to many of the courses. Students not only gained a deeper insight into their own work, but by exchanging experience with others helped to establish a common approach to problems that had been regarded parochially; and in the course of a few years the College probably did as much to develop the idea of a single police service, transcending the many local forces, as the Police Federation or any other of Desborough's valuable reforms had done twenty years earlier.

Nevertheless, the early arrangements were open to obvious criticisms. The average age of the sergeants who attended the courses, thirty-seven years, was in many cases too high to enable full advantage to be taken of facilities designed primarily to train men for higher command. There was a suspicion that many men arrived at the College for no better reason than that it was 'Buggin's turn', nor did it follow that a man would be promoted when he returned to his force. However, it had always been the intention that the scope of the College should be kept under review; and in 1961, soon after the College moved to Bramshill House, the Home Secretary announced important changes in the arrangements. These are described in Chapter Ten.

The Oaksey Committee and its aftermath

It is necessary to discuss the level of police pay* during this period in some detail, because it was the biggest single factor in limiting the

* In considering the level of police pay at any time, it is necessary to bear in mind that a policeman is provided with a number of subsidiary emoluments. They are described in Chapter VI of the Interim Report of the Royal

availability of sufficient manpower to conduct a successful fight against crime, and these conditions stimulated the search for new methods of policing.

The Desborough Committee, in raising the pay of the police well above the level of most of the unskilled trades, had paved the way for twenty years of near stability in police pay—years that policemen of a later generation have looked back on as a golden age.* During most of this period of the inter-war years the maximum of the constable's pay scale, at £4 15s., was of the order of 55 per cent higher than the earnings of the average adult male worker in industry;[8] and over and above this direct financial advantage, the policeman enjoyed the by no means common benefits of paid holidays, a good pension, and immunity from the risk of unemployment—itself a much-prized asset in the 1930s. It was not therefore to be wondered at that, during this period, 'the police service acquired a prestige and attracted recruits in numbers and of a quality that have been unparalleled at any time before or since'.[9]

The policeman's decline from this peak of relative affluence started during the war, and had its parallel in other public services. Rising industrial wages and increases in the cost of living outstripped the value of supplementary war bonuses granted to the police, to such an extent that by the end of the war the average employee in industry had caught up with the constable. The 55 per cent lead vanished. There was considerable discontent in the police service, and new pay scales were introduced in April, 1945. But their effect was short-lived, and they did little to solve a growing problem of recruitment. In 1939 the strength of the police was about 60,000, all of them regular officers. In 1946 it was some 61,000, but over 14,000 of them were still temporary auxiliaries—either police war reservists or pensioners. The strength of the Metropolitan Police had shrunk from 18,600 in 1939

Commission on the Police (Cmd. 1,222). Included among them are the valuable pension entitlement, free accommodation or a rent allowance in lieu, and several minor allowances connected with police duty. Their value for a married constable on his maximum rate of pay was estimated by the Home Office in 1960 to be about £300.

* The gilt was tarnished from time to time, however, when successive economic crises in 1922 and 1931 compelled the Government to erode the Desborough scales. In 1922 pay was reduced by 2½ per cent, a reduction which in 1926 was converted into a contribution towards pensions. The 1931 cuts, part of the country's general economy measures, were from 5 to 10 per cent, with a reduction of pay for new entrants; the former lasted until 1935; the latter until 1945. Even so, police pay remained throughout the whole inter-war period high in relation to average incomes and the cost of living.

to 14,200 in 1946, many of whom also were auxiliaries. Even in 1901 London had had 16,000 policemen. It was estimated at the end of the war that the police would have to embark on a recruitment programme which would swell the number of regular policemen by about 16,000 in the course of the next two years.

Confronted by this situation, the Government, in 1946, awarded a further increase of pay, which it was agreed should remain unchanged until January 1st, 1950, on the understanding that the whole range of conditions of service would be referred to an independent review before the end of 1949. The increase raised the maximum of the constable's pay to some 17 per cent above average industrial earnings, but within two years the tide of inflation had again brought the industrial worker's wage up to the level of the constable's. The Police Federation sought to reopen the bargain by pressing for an earlier independent review than had been agreed. The Government demurred, but, faced with mounting discontent in the police service, criticism in Parliament, and a serious problem of inadequate recruitment at a time when crime was yearly increasing, they finally undertook to advance by a year the appointment of this review; and in May, 1948, a committee was set up under the chairmanship of Lord Oaksey 'to consider in the light of the need for the recruitment and retention of an adequate number of suitable men and women for the police forces in England, Wales, and Scotland, and to report on pay, emoluments, allowances, pensions, promotion, methods of representation and negotiation, and other conditions of service'.

The Oaksey Committee presented two reports, in April and November, 1949.[10] The first dealt with police pay, pensions, and numerous other conditions of service; the second was concerned with a further wide range of matters, including the appointment, training and promotion* of police officers, their discipline, housing, and amenities, and the establishment of the negotiating machinery described later in this chapter. Many improvements in the police-

---

* The regulations made under the Police Act, 1919, required that a member of a police force must pass a qualifying examination before becoming eligible for promotion from constable to sergeant and from sergeant to inspector. Examinations were locally conducted, and their standard varied widely. Both the Desborough Committee and the police Postwar Committee had recommended the introduction of a centralised promotion system, and the Oaksey Committee concurred; but it was not until 1958 that a start was made by arranging for the examination to be conducted by the Civil Service Commission on behalf of a Police Promotions Examination Board composed of representatives of the service associations, the police authorities, and educational experts.

man's conditions of service resulted from their recommendations, but pay could hardly be said to be one of them.

The Police Federation had hoped to secure from the committee a second major overhaul comparable with that carried out by the Desborough Committee thirty years earlier, and they sought increases in pay ranging from 33⅓ to 54 per cent. Their hopes were shattered. The committee recommended an increase of some 15 per cent for the constable on his maximum. It followed the Desborough Committee in paying tribute to the outstanding qualities required in the policeman and noted the increasing demands made on him, the serious undermanning in the service, and the improvements in wages being granted in many other occupations at the time. But it also had regard to the Government's recently published White Paper on Personal Incomes, Costs, and Prices,[11] with its injunction that 'each claim for an increase in wages or salaries must be considered on its national merits'.

The Oaksey Committee expressed the hope that its recommendations would give rise to a reasonably long period of stability. The hope was forlorn. The new scales came into force in July, 1949, and as early as 1950 the Commissioner of the Metropolitan Police lamented that they had been ineffective either in attracting sufficient suitable candidates or in arresting wastage; he had actually lost almost 200 men from his already depleted resources during the first three months of 1951. In September of that year, during which the number of criminal offences rose to its highest yet, London (including the City) still had 1,000 fewer policemen than in 1901. The old economic forces were still doing their corrosive work, and within two years of the Oaksey Committee's report a second independent review[12] gave a further boost of some 20 per cent over and above the Oaksey rates, and also above police pay's seemingly tireless competitor—average industrial earnings. Even so, the cycle was soon repeated. Two years later, in 1954, resumed negotiations were conducted by a newly created negotiating body, the Police Council for Great Britain, which had been set up on the recommendation of the Oaksey Committee. The resulting agreement, for a 9 per cent increase, was the last of its kind, for on no less than three further occasions between 1954 and 1960, when the Royal Commission on the Police was set up, the two sides of the Police Council found their positions so wide apart as to preclude any possibility of agreement being reached, and recourse was had to arbitration. Meanwhile, money was spent on advertising for recruits and on providing more and better police houses as an incentive to men to come forward, and many forces lowered their prescribed height limit.

During this difficult period for the police the official side of the new negotiating body discovered an unexpected ally. A Parliamentary Select Committee on Estimates for the session 1957–8 expressed concern, not about the paucity of police strength, but about the growth and cost of police establishments, observed that more use should be made of mechanical aids and the employment of civilians, and thought that the police should claim a smaller share of the national manpower than hitherto.[13] It is undeniable that the fewer non-productive workers a country needs, such as policemen and civil servants, the better for everybody; but much turns on an assessment of need. The Home Office drew the committee's remarks, which can now be seen to have coincided with the most rapid acceleration in the crime rate ever recorded in this country, to the attention of police authorities and chief constables. But the department pointed out to Parliament that more generous leave scales introduced for policemen since the war, coupled with a shorter working week, were equivalent to a reduction of some thousands in strength. Moreover, there were now some 18 per cent more houses to be protected than before the war, suburbs and housing estates were spreading over wider areas, crime had increased by nearly 100 per cent, criminals were more mobile and therefore harder to trace, and road traffic had doubled. It might have been added that London was now policed by 2,000 fewer policemen than in 1911.

The eventual outcome of this unhappy chapter in the history of police pay and strength can be simply stated. By early 1960, at the time of the Royal Commission's appointment, the maximum pay of the constable had fallen to 5 per cent and the minimum to no less than 30 per cent below average earnings in industry.[14] Much, it seemed, was wrong not only with the level of pay, but also with the arrangements for settling it. And much had by now gone wrong, in consequence, with police strengths, recruitment, and even, it seemed at times, morale. The war against crime was not being won.

*The war against crime**

For the first twenty years of the century the incidence of crime had shown little variation from year to year: the annual average of indict-

* It should be borne in mind, in considering criminal statistics, that the

able crimes known to the police actually fell slightly from 91,694 in the decade 1900–9 to 91,270 in the decade 1910–19. But the next ten years saw a steady increase, and in the immediate pre-war decade, 1930–9, the curve was rising still more steeply: in this period the average number of indictable crimes known to the police was 231,000, and by 1939 it had passed 300,000. In 1947 it was close on half a million, and the inspectors of constabulary spoke of statistics which 'have touched the conscience of the nation and aroused the deepest concern'. They reported bleakly that it had not been possible to keep beat and patrolling strengths at a level sufficient to afford adequate protection to property and deter thieves. Criminals had greater opportunities than ever before.

They exploited them. Indictable offences rose above half a million in 1948, fell temporarily in 1949—fortunately enough, since this was the worst year for police recruiting since the war—then rose steadily until they were again at a peak of over half a million in 1951. Once more the inspectors of constabulary expressed their concern. They acknowledged that the build-up of police strength since the war had been slow, and referred to the increasing demands being made on the police by road-traffic and other duties. Responsible police officers, they reported, shared the public unease, and regarded the situation as a challenge to our police system and its organisation. In London the strength of the Metropolitan Police was some 300 less at the end of 1951 than at the beginning.

But the challenge to the police was not immediately pressed. In the following year, 1952, crime fell slightly, and in 1953 the number of known indictable offences again dropped below half a million. The inspectors of constabulary hopefully attributed the reduction in part to the gradual build-up of the uniformed branches of many forces, but in London the position was, if anything, deteriorating: in 1932, 87·6 per cent of the men required for beat and patrol duty were available, but now the percentage had fallen to 44·6. New housing developments had spread the population over a much wider area, and over 1,000 extra miles of road had to be patrolled. In the outer suburbs people were complaining that they never saw a policeman. Nevertheless, the downward trend in crime continued into 1954 and the police might have claimed a modest victory. Wisely, they did not.

---

standards by which they are compiled have not remained constant from 1900 to the present day. The figures quoted can therefore only be taken as a rough indication of trends, and of the order of magnitude of the crime problem that faced the police at any given time.

In their report for 1955, written with knowledge of the encouraging 1954 criminal statistics, the inspectors of constabulary were nevertheless obliged to state the lamentable fact that a year that can now be seen to have been a critical one in the war against crime ended with fewer police on duty than when it began.

For 1954 saw the end of the temporary recession in crime, and it was to increase year by year for more than a decade. In 1955 there were 438,000 indictable offences known to the police; in 1956 the figure was 479,000; in 1957 it soared by 13 per cent to 545,000, and the inspectors of constabulary drew attention to the need for 'searching questions and examination of the efficiency, mobility, numbers, employment, and other resources of our police forces'. The warning was timely. Crime rose by a further 15 per cent in 1958 to 626,000 known indictable offences. In London the increase was 20 per cent, and the Metropolitan Police were now tackling a very much greater volume of crime than before the war with a force actually some 2,000 below its pre-war strength. A further rise of 8 per cent in 1959 brought the total of offences to 675,000, and the inspectors, now deploring the 'growth of dishonesty and moral delinquency in the present age', openly feared that the belief was gaining hold that crime paid.

But if crime paid, or seemed to pay, no one could fairly blame the police. Never in their history had they, and in particular the members of the C.I.D., been so hard pressed. In 1938 the percentage of crimes cleared up was 50·1. Twenty years later, when the volume of crime had almost trebled, it was still as high as 45·6*. The figure is all the more creditable when it is remembered that in 1938 the country had just under 60,000 policemen. In 1958, confronted with three times the volume of crime, it had only about 9,000 more; and to this body of men fell not only the task of combating a crime wave unparalleled in modern times, but also the solution of unprecedented traffic problems —and, incidentally, nearly 300 volunteers were released to form a United Kingdom police unit in Cyprus. With these slender resources, it was necessary to devote more and more effort to modernising police forces so as to raise their efficiency to the highest possible degree.

* The percentage of crime cleared up in London is always lower than in the remainder of the country, on account of the peculiar difficulties of detection in large urban areas with their density of housing and shifting populations.

The quest for efficiency

All the main reforms mentioned so far—new training arrangements, a national Police College, and the abolition of small police forces— must have helped the police to meet the postwar challenge. These particular improvements were all initiated by the Home Office in the 1940s, but there was not (and rarely is) a monopoly of reforming influence in Whitehall. Some changes came about as a result of local initiatives, and experience gained in this way was made available to the whole police service through the agency of the inspectors of constabulary, and by means of Home Office circulars.

Without doubt, the greatest single incentive to research and experiment in the field was the chronic shortage of policemen, and the Home Office encouraged all police authorities and chief constables to explore ways of concentrating limited resources of manpower on duties which policemen are uniquely qualified to perform. An early result was a substained drive to replace police officers by civilians with clerical or tradesmen's qualifications on indoor duties where police training and experience, or the authority of a constable, were not required. This policy sometimes met with resistance from chief constables anxious to keep a few comfortable office posts open for policemen who were nearing their retirement, or who might be recuperating after illness or injury, but its general success can be seen from the fact that the number of civilians employed by the police increased in the ten years 1949–59 from 3,881 to 8,082. (By 1966 it had risen to 16,000.) Many policemen were released for patrol duties in consequence.

A second result of the drive for economy in the use of manpower was to encourage fresh interest among chief constables in the recruitment of policewomen. As early as 1947 the inspectors of constabulary were reporting that chief constables were taking a wider view of their role and usefulness than they had done formerly. They were frequently employed in preventive patrol work in company with plain-clothes officers, and their value was impressively demonstrated on the occasion of the East Coast floods in 1953, when elderly women and children were the main victims. The establishment of policewomen in the service doubled in the ten years 1949–59.* For this, the credit belongs very largely to the first woman to occupy the post of staff

* It continued to increase in the next decade, when a system of national and district conferences of policewomen was instituted to further the exchange of ideas, pool experience, and study new projects.

officer to the inspectors of constabulary: Miss B. M. Denis de Vitré, (who died at the early age of fifty-four) brought outstanding qualities to the task of building up the policewomen's service, and her ability and enthusiasm effected a rapid and widespread change in the prewar attitude towards their employment.

The replacement of policemen by civilians and the recruitment of more policewomen were important steps towards the conservation and more economic use of manpower. They were supplemented in other ways, the most important of which was a greatly extended use of motorised transport. Many more police vehicles were needed to deal with the vast increase in road traffic and the higher mobility of the modern criminal. The complex nature of some criminal investigations demanded both more skill and more mobility, and there was a growing tendency on the part of the public to judge the efficiency of a force by its ability to respond promptly to emergency '999' calls. The result was a rapid increase in the number of police cars equipped with radio, and the conversion of many traditional foot beats into mechanised beats controlled by policemen in motor-cars or on motor-cycles. In 1948 the total complement of motor vehicles, outside London, was 5,500: this had risen to 8,650 in 1959, an increase of 67 per cent. About 40 per cent of these were motor-cycles, and by the end of 1959 some 4,000 motor vehicles were equipped with two-way wireless, including 800 motor-cycles. Police drivers, meantime, were trained to ever higher standards of road safety, and all police forces which had not already done so created special traffic departments at their force headquarters very soon after the war.

The utility of police motor-cars was increasingly recognised and exploited, and as experience of the operational advantages was gained steps were taken to organise police vehicles and their drivers on more sophisticated lines. In 1955 the Metropolitan Police Commissioner set up a traffic squad consisting of 100 policemen under a superintendent. This squad was the first of its kind. Most of the men were mounted on motor-cycles, some of which were equipped with wireless. Their duty was to patrol the main roads in central London so as to promote the smooth flow of traffic and to deal with accidents and other emergencies.[15] A few years later the opening of the country's first motorway, M1, provided an opportunity for the county constabularies concerned to undertake pioneer experiments in what was then an entirely new kind of policing. The chief constables agreed to co-operate in arrangements for enforcing the law, and similar moves were made elsewhere as motorways were developed in other parts of the country.[16]

Traffic squads were only one of a number of types of co-operative agencies between forces which were now being tried out experimentally. A development on somewhat similar lines was the inception of crime squads, the first of which was started by the Metropolitan Police in 1954. Their progenitors were partly the detective conferences which for many years had been held in each police district under the auspices of the District Conference of Chief Constables, and partly the Metropolitan Police Murder Squad and the Metropolitan and City Police Company Fraud Department, which was established in 1945. The Fraud Squad, as it is commonly known, was the first joint venture of this kind by two independent police forces. It carried out inquiries on behalf of Government departments, the Stock Exchange, business associations, and members of the public, as well as of police forces in many parts of the world. A Metropolitan and provincial police crime branch was set up five years later, in 1954, to deal with crimes committed on the outskirts of London, and in the provinces by criminals operating from London itself. The squad became a branch of the C.I.D. and it was staffed by C.I.D. officers from the Metropolitan and Home Counties police forces. Confined at first to the Home Counties, its activities were later extended to more distant parts of the country. The success of this experiment persuaded other chief constables to establish area crime squads, first in Birmingham to cover the West Midlands, and later on in Tyneside and in the area of Bristol. They could be directed by radio to the scene of serious accidents as well as crime, and their value in rural areas, particularly at night, when police resources were depleted and detached beat constables were no longer able effectively to bear a twenty-four-hour responsibility, was rapidly recognised. Information could be quickly exchanged, police boundaries disappeared, and local knowledge and resources were pooled.

This development of mobile crime and traffic squads heralded a new approach to the problem of deploying scarce police manpower which was of far-reaching significance. Under the old mutual-aid arrangements between police forces men were freely borrowed, and the scale of these arrangements had been enlarged by the wartime regional reinforcement scheme, which was abandoned in 1945. But mutual aid was never meant to offer more than a temporary relief in times of emergency. Crime and traffic squads introduced a different principle. Men were no longer lent by one force to another; they were

257

seconded to a detached unit permanently operating beyond the boundaries of their home force. This principle, and the experience gained from its application, was of great value when a pattern of national crime squads came to be established some ten years later.

The list of co-operative enterprises on which the police service embarked during the 1950s has not yet, however, been exhausted. These years also saw the development of regional criminal record offices as crime clearing-houses for criminal records and fingerprints. The larger forces had maintained these for many years, and the West Riding Constabulary's clearing-house at Wakefield and its police reports already had a long tradition of service which went back to 1913. Additional criminal record offices were now set up at Birmingham, Manchester, Liverpool, Preston, Cardiff, Bristol, Durham, and, some years later, Hampshire.* Their value in collecting and disseminating information about known criminals needs no emphasis. Further progress was also made in the development of forensic science laboratories and wireless schemes, the foundations of which had been laid before the war.

Police dogs

It was not only on scientific aids that the police relied in their efforts to achieve higher efficiency.

For many years it had been the practice in a few forces for police officers to take dogs with them on patrol duty, and some chief constables encouraged this. The dogs were used mainly for companionship, although their sense of smell aided the man's powers of observation. They did not normally undergo any special training, and dogs of any suitable breed were used. During the early part of the century several chief constables were experimenting with the use of bloodhounds, mastiffs, Labradors, and Airedales, and it was known that the Paris police were employing them in tracking work and in dealing with thugs. Even so, the English police were slow to realise their value. In 1934 the Detection Committee (pp. 210–1) considered a report by a Metropolitan Police officer on the use of police dogs by some Continental forces which he had visited, and the decision was taken to carry out experiments in breeding and training dogs, with the aim of developing a suitable breed for tracking and general protective

* As late as 1962 two county forces stood out from the whole of the remainder of the police service in their refusal to co-operate in these arrangements (reports of H.M. Inspectors of Constabulary for 1956–64).

purposes. An expert gun-dog breeder and trainer was paid an annual subsidy of £500 to conduct them, but the arrangement came to an end on the outbreak of war. Then, after the war, experiments were resumed by several chief constables interested in the use of dogs. These gave encouraging results, and the number of forces which used dogs gradually increased; by 1954 twenty-eight of the 126 police forces were using a total of 266 dogs, the majority of them Alsatians. There were also some Dobermann Pinschers, Labradors, and Boxers.

The time had come to review the arrangements for co-ordinating the breeding, supply and training of dogs, and in that year, 1954, a working party was set up. They paid visits to Germany, where dogs had been extensively employed on police work for over fifty years, and discovered that the physical and working standards of German dogs were much superior to those in this country. They also learned that German experience confirmed the value of dogs in dealing with hooligans and in searching for missing persons and stolen property. One dog could often do the work of many policemen, and in tracking duties dogs were supreme. Up to that time most police dogs in England had been given or sold to police forces by members of the public, but the working party returned home with the conviction that a more regular source of supply was needed. As a start there was no alternative but to import a substantial number of additional dogs from Germany, and a standing advisory committee was set up to obtain them, allocate them among police forces, organise their training and that of their handlers, and plan arrangements for breeding dogs in this country. Fifteen years later the names of over 1,000 dogs were on a central register maintained by the Lancashire Constabulary. National police dog trials had (since 1959) become an annual event, an experienced police dog-trainer from Germany had launched a pilot course for instructors in this country, and the Home Office had issued a comprehensive manual on the training and care of police dogs. As aids to the police, they are now of much more general utility than horses. A recent development in their use has been the introduction of radio-equipped vans, in which dogs and their handlers are rapidly transported to the scene of a crime while clues and scents are fresh.

A new Police Council

The Desborough Committee had seen no need for negotiating machinery in the police service, but had assumed that the Police

Council would sit on 'round table' lines in advising the Home Secretary on questions of police pay. The Police Act, 1919, accordingly required that a draft of any police regulations had to be submitted to the Council. In effect, therefore, proposals to alter pay, or any other conditions of service, were discussed (and sometimes challenged) by any of the constituent parties—representatives of police authorities, chief officers, superintendents, and the Police Federation, sitting under the chairmanship of the Home Secretary or one of his senior officials. The council was not a negotiating body. It was not composed of sides, and the alignment of interests varied according to the subject under discussion. Thus in considering questions of discipline police authorities and chief officers might find themselves in opposition to the Police Federation, while on questions of pay or allowances the police authorities might be ranged on one side with the chief officers and the Federation on the other. The working rule was that the function of the Council was to enable the Home Secretary to advise himself as to the views of the parties represented.[17]

At the time when the Oaksey Committee was appointed in 1948, the Police Council had been in existence for nearly thirty years, and it had proved its worth in many ways, not least as a means of keeping all those concerned in the increasingly complex task of police administration in regular touch with one another. In particular, it gave the Home Office a useful opportunity to take many of the initiatives described in Chapter Six, and through its agency the Police Federation obtained many improvements in the conditions of service of their members. But since 1939 the Federation had grown increasingly dissatisfied with the Council. The more conscious they became of the fall in the value of their pay, the less acceptable it seemed that the Home Secretary, with his responsibility for keeping the cost of the police within reasonable bounds, should be the final arbiter. It did not need the suspicious mind of a policeman to suppose that his sympathies might sometimes lie on the side of the police authorities in effecting economies. During the war the Federation requested the Home Secretary to allow recourse to arbitration. This was denied, but the question of providing negotiating machinery was referred to the Oaksey Committee; and it was on that committee's recommendation that a Police Council for Great Britain was set up in 1953 as a negotiating body. The committee thought that the police should be insulated from the ordinary processes of industrial negotiation, but proposed machinery to give them the same rights they would have had if they were given access to some such tribunal as the Industrial Court.

This machinery (which covered Scotland as well as England and Wales) consisted of a Council comprising three separate panels—for chief officers, superintendents, and federated ranks respectively. Each panel was composed of a staff side and an official side, with provision for the whole Council to sit to consider general questions, and for reference of certain disputed matters to a panel of three arbitrators appointed by the Prime Minister. The Council and its panels were to sit under an independent chairman, and the official side was to comprise representatives of all the police authorities, including the Home Office.*

Welcome as this negotiating machinery was, it was not an unmixed blessing for the efficient development of a police service still in the transitional stage described in Chapter Six. The unifying influences received a fillip during the war, but the whole needed a continuing firm hand at the centre if the initiatives of the 1930s were to be carried forward with the determination and sense of urgency required by the much greater challenges of the postwar years. The Police Council for Great Britain largely eclipsed the old Police Council set up in 1919. It suited the interests of the local authorities, as well as those of the Police Federation, to make the fullest use of the new machinery, with its independent chairman, where their influence stood high. The Home Office consequently found itself edged out of things where formerly it would have taken a lead. A useful forum for free-ranging discussion was thus lost, and initiative faltered. The factors which underlie any changing pattern of administration are complex, and those at work in the present situation cannot be fully analysed here. Among them was undoubtedly the increased professionalisation of the local authority associations, and their reluctance to acquiesce in the discussion direct between the Home Office and chief constables of various matters which before the war were concluded without the local authorities being brought in at all. Divisive tendencies, nevertheless, persisted in a habit of conducting private discussions between separate components of the police system (for example, Home Office/chief constables or Home Office/local authority associations) rather than open discussion between all; and it is significant that during this period a number of important new co-operative agencies, such as criminal record offices, were set up without any central discussion or regard for comprehensive planning.

* The Council, constituted on these lines, continued as a non-statutory body from 1953 until 1964, when it was reconstituted by the Police Act, 1964. Its constitution does not now provide for an independent chairman.

Police and public

Unsettling as they were to many aspects of the nation's life, the postwar years saw no widespread threat to law and order on the scale of the General Strike, the Suffragette movement, or the riots of the nineteenth century. Nevertheless, resistance to authority was rife, particularly among many discharged from the armed forces. Radicalism and free-thinking found expression in a growing tendency among young people to defy established conventions. It was an age of beatniks and teddy-boys; 'mods and rockers' came later. Strikes in the docks and railways in the early 1950s placed their usual strain on police resources, and in 1956 public controversy over the Government's handling of the Suez Canal situation led to excited demonstrations in Trafalgar Square, in the course of which the police made a large number of arrests. In the following year came angry protests against the Government's Rent Bill, with the usual pattern of meetings in Trafalgar Square, a march down Whitehall, and attempts to gain access to Downing Street; and that year also saw the first serious threat to public order from those who objected to Britain possessing nuclear weapons.

About this time the Metropolitan Police were facing other threats to the good order of London's streets. Outbursts of hooliganism occurred among gangs of youths patrolling after dark, and in an attempt to disperse one such gang a policeman was viciously murdered by a youth who stabbed him in the back. Hooliganism is infectious, and a series of incidents broke out involving the coloured population of Notting Hill. Similar troubles occurred in Nottingham. Many members of the public found themselves, or chose to find themselves, involved, and there were ugly scenes. Firm measures by the police and the courts fortunately checked these outbreaks. By 1959, too, the Commissioner was able to report that another unseemly aspect of London's street life had been largely obliterated by the Street Offences Act of that year, which virtually put an end to street prostitution.

In the meantime much thought was being given to crime-prevention. Experiments had been conducted in new methods of 'team policing', a system first started in Aberdeen, whereby a number of constables under a sergeant in a wireless patrol car are collectively responsible for the supervision of a particular area. But it was apparent that a heavy responsibility also lay on the public to protect their own property. A national crime-prevention campaign was organised in

1950, and the Central Office of Information gave their help in preparing publicity material. A start was made in some forces in selecting officers designated as crime-prevention officers, and these men were given a full-time duty to help and advise the public. Pamphlets containing advice on improving the security of premises were issued to business houses, banks, and shops, and these would be followed by personal visits by the crime-prevention officer. These early steps in developing a crime-prevention service were subsequently reviewed by the Central Conference of Chief Constables, and before long all police forces were embarking on work of this kind.

The public, meanwhile, were being offered a new brand-image of the modern policeman with an insistence, in a million homes throughout the country, that perhaps created almost as many illusions as it dispelled. P.C. Dixon made his first appearance in a film, *The Blue Lamp*, in 1950. This, like the successful television series that followed it, owed something to the co-operation of Scotland Yard, but much more to the genius of its author, Lord (Ted) Willis, and principal star, Mr. Jack Warner. Young people who grew up in the decade that saw the introduction of parking meters, street-crossing patrols, 'Noddy' bicycles, and the towing-away of badly parked cars were able to relate police activities to the intensely human policemen whom they (among them the Lord Chancellor, as the late Lord Kilmuir once told the House of Lords) met every Saturday evening at Dock Green Police Station. These friendly programmes must have taken something of the sting out of relations between police and public at a time when many people were ready to support police action to regulate any driving standards but their own.

Conscious of the dangers of the widening gap between the police and the public, the police were always seeking new ways of winning public confidence. The problem in London probably differed from that in the rest of the country, for the aura about Scotland Yard could invoke respect, and even occasionally affection, in spite of the bureaucratic nature of so large an organisation. But people do not (and ought not to) love bureaucracies, however worthy, and Metropolitan policemen went out of their way, as they have always done, to woo the people. Police officers of all ranks devoted their spare time to helping with boys' clubs, thus encouraging good citizenship by voluntary work. Efforts were made to reach the public in these and other ways, and in 1954 the Commissioner reported that an increasing number of telephone calls were being received from people who saw or heard something suspicious, and were public-spirited enough to

263

do something about it. In 1957 a new Information Room was opened at Scotland Yard where emergency calls could be handled much more rapidly; and most provincial forces had by then established information and control-rooms at their force headquarters to receive incoming calls, and to co-ordinate the operation of wireless cars, establish links with beat constables and detective or mobile patrols. It may well be that a closer rapport was established with the public by such signs of increased professional efficiency as these than by Dixon of Dock Green himself. Policemen, alas, like Victorian fathers, are there to be respected rather than loved, lovable though some are.

The police service in 1959

An attempt must be made to take stock of the state of the police service on the eve of the appointment of the Royal Commission in January, 1960.

There is much to put on the credit side. The postwar institutions developed by the Home Office, notably the Police College and the district training centres, had settled down to their work, and had already established fine traditions of service. Their value as a unifying influence was increasingly apparent, as interchanges of staff and ideas spread common standards—or, equally valuable, provoked a stimulus to challenge practices hitherto uncritically accepted. Useful progress had been made in setting up regional criminal record offices and crime squads. The valuable work of policewomen had at last been recognised. Many of the conditions of service of the police had been improved. They worked shorter hours than before the war, and enjoyed more generous leave scales. They also benefited (since 1958) from a centralised promotion system, conducted by the Civil Service Commission, which went some way towards ironing out disparities in career prospects between forces, and opened up the possibility of more rational arrangements for selecting men for the Police College. Even the police uniform had been modernised: open-necked jackets were issued to constables and sergeants, and in summer they were allowed to wear lightweight jackets and trousers. Individual acts of gallantry by police officers were frequently reported by the Press. Recruitment had resulted in the county and borough police forces having on their strength 10,000 more police than they had ten years before, and during this period the service had expanded to a greater extent than in any previous decade.[18] The total police strength in 1959 was 70,000, or one police officer for every 598 persons.

So much for the gains. On the other side it has to be recorded that relations between the police and the public had markedly cooled since the war, due in large measure to a growing tendency to flout restrictive legislation, particularly traffic laws, and blame the police for attempting to enforce it. The police, for their part, were dissatisfied with their lot, for reasons which have already been discussed, and the inspectors of constabulary were expressing growing concern at the inability of the police to check crime: 'Whatever the cause, or causes, of this upsurge in crime, it is imperative that it should be checked before it gets completely out of hand. The belief is gaining hold in some quarters that crime pays, and the criminal statistics of the past few years lend strength to this belief. It is a state of affairs which we are not alone in viewing with grave concern.' The Commissioner of the Metropolitan Police was equally anxious, and with perhaps more reason, for his recruitment problem was the worst in the country, and the strength of his force was still lower than it had been before the war: 'The infinitely greater problems of today have to be met by a numerically weaker force, the increased technical efficiency of which does little more than offset the growing ingenuity of the criminal classes and the complex nature of the modern way of life.'[19] A vigorous lead from the Home Office might have done something for morale, but for reasons which have been explained its influence was probably weaker during this period than it had been at any time since the end of the First World War.

Early in February, 1959, the Home Secretary, Mr. R. A. Butler, presented to Parliament a white paper, *Penal Practice in a Changing Society*,[20] expressing his own concern and that of the Government about the state of crime, and proposing ways in which the problem could be tackled to the extent that it lay within the reach of Government action. One of these ways, and perhaps the most important, lay in strengthening the police forces. The danger, as the inspectors of constabulary and the Commissioner had stressed, was that the growth of the forces of crime was outpacing that of the forces of law and order. A gain of 10,000 in police strength during ten years seemed, on the face of it, satisfactory. But alongside this was the fact that nearly 40,000 constables had been newly appointed as probationers during that period. Admittedly, the country had more policemen than ever before in peacetime, but it also had a very much higher proportion of untrained or partly trained and inexperienced policemen. In 1959 alone some 2,000 policemen left the service, 93 per cent of them during their first ten years. They quitted without waiting to qualify for a pension. Half of them were probationers, but the other half, totalling about 1,000 men, were fully trained policemen. A loss on this scale in only twelve months of trained men, to be replaced in turn by novices who themselves were as likely as not to move on elsewhere after a brief taste of a policeman's life, was imposing, in the view of the Royal Commission a year later, a 'crippling handicap' on a service already some 14 per cent under strength. Indeed, it was not necessary to look very far to discover one of the reasons, and perhaps the most important reason, for the inability of the police to check crime in 1959. But policemen are expensive, particularly if they are paid well enough not only to attract them into the service, but also to keep them in it; and there were many other competing demands on the country's overstrained resources in 1959.

Chapter Nine

Return to First Principles 1959–62

The early 1960s were years of uncertainty for the police service and for the organs of central and local government which administered it: for the first time since the New Police were created, a Royal Commission was appointed with terms of reference sufficiently wide-ranging to require it to examine afresh the fundamental principles on which the service had always relied.* At the same time the Commission was asked to review the principles which should govern police pay. It was also to inquire into relations between the police and the public and the manner in which complaints were dealt with. Thus the Commission was given a formidable task of reappraisal at a time when, following repeated criticism in the Press, the morale of the police was low, crime was mounting, and there was a seemingly chronic deficiency of manpower.

One underlying cause of the appointment of the Royal Commission—namely, a swift rise in the volume of crime and in road traffic which far outpaced the tardy strengthening of police forces since the war—has been discussed in the previous chapter. The problem thus baldly stated was serious, but not insoluble. More policemen could no doubt have been recruited and retained if their conditions of service had been made more attractive. But the economic situation of the country argued against this course, and experience since the war had shown that no government cared on its own unsupported initiative to grant substantial increases of pay to public servants: if any further review of police pay were to be undertaken, an independent inquiry would have to be set up on the lines of the

---

* It seems to have been the fifth Royal Commission in the whole history of police, and the terms of reference of two (those of 1855 and 1906) confined them to dealing with complaints against the Metropolitan Police. The other two were the Rowan/Chadwick Royal Commission of 1839 (Chapter Three) and the Royal Commission on Police Powers and Procedure in 1929 (Chapter six). The Desborough Committee was much more important, judged by achievement, than any of these.

Desborough and Oaksey Committees. Nevertheless, it seems un-likely that a Royal Commission would have been appointed at this time, and for this purpose, had not other factors also been at work.

These factors were as follows: first, there was growing concern, fanned by the newspapers, about the state of relations between the police and the public. Second, there came a series of isolated incidents involving the good name of the police, each of which attracted wide-spread publicity and gave further colour to the view that the police were out of touch with the public. These incidents also cast doubt on the adequacy of the means of bringing the police to account, and on the validity of some long-held assumptions about the relations between chief constables and police authorities. The third factor in the situation arose to some extent from the other two—namely, a growing sense of frustration among Members of Parliament at their inability to raise on the floor of the House matters concerning pro-vincial police forces.

The Home Secretary's answerability to Parliament

It will be recalled that the Metropolitan Police Act, 1829, placed the Commissioner of Police under the authority of the Home Secretary, and required any orders about the general government of the force to be subject to his approval. The effect of this was to make the Home Secretary answerable to Parliament for the activities of the Metro-politan Police to an extent which has never been authoritatively defined. A frequently quoted statement of the position is that made by Mr. Henry Matthews, who was Home Secretary in 1888 at the time of Sir Charles Warren's resignation as Commissioner: 'It was quite plain that it was the intention of the legislature to put the police force under the authority of the Secretary of State and to hold him fully responsible, not for every detail of the management of the force, but in regard to the general policy of the police in the discharge of their duty.'[1] In practice Members of Parliament had had no difficulty in tabling questions, not only about the general policies of the force, but also about particular incidents involving its members. Thus it was common for questions to be asked about alleged ill-treatment at the hands of the police in the course of political demonstrations or during interrogation.

But the provincial police forces were in quite a different position, for they had never been under the control of the Home Secretary to anything like the degree to which the Metropolitan force was placed under his authority. Until 1919 the county forces had been largely, and the borough forces wholly, independent local entities, except to the extent that they chose to be influenced by the administration of the Exchequer grant. Consequently, Members of Parliament who sought to raise questions concerning them found themselves checked by a ruling in Erskine May that questions 'should relate to the public affairs with which the Ministers are officially connected . . . or to matters of administration for which they are responsible', and among the list of inadmissible questions were those 'raising matters under the control of local authorities, e.g. provincial police'.[2]

Despite this ruling, attempts had been made by Members for many years to seek means of raising in Parliament matters relating to the local police forces in their constituencies. Thus the point was tested in 1905, when it was established that the action of the Manchester City Police was primarily the responsibility of the Manchester Watch Committee, and not that of the Home Secretary.[3] Again in 1917 the Speaker disallowed a Parliamentary question about rioting in Gillingham with the ruling that 'the Hon. Member should ask the Watch Committee';[4] and still in 1936, after the reforms of 1919 had fully worked themselves out, the Home Secretary, then Sir John Simon, told the House of Commons, following allegations that the police had shown partiality in handling political riots in Oxford and elsewhere: 'The Oxford police are subject to the ratepayers of Oxford and to the people who elect the City Council out of which the Watch Committee is formed.'[5] On this occasion the Chair, consistently with earlier rulings, observed that the Secretary of State had no powers to give orders to the provincial police, and added that the police authority had absolute control over the force. A more recent ruling on the same lines was given in 1958.[6] Members of Parliament found these rulings irksome. Many thought that a Member ought to be able to raise in Parliament any question affecting the liberty of the subject, insisting that experience in many fields of public administration had shown that it was on individual cases that principles of the greatest importance were often founded.* This dissatisfaction was naturally

---

* Ingenious Members had occasionally succeeded in raising such cases, following allegations of a general breakdown of, or threat to, law and order, on the argument that the Home Secretary had an ultimate responsibility. Thus in July, 1957, questions were admitted about the alleged use of violence and unlawful methods in connection with a provincial 'bus strike; but the Members asking these questions were prepared to allege, and did allege, that a general breakdown of law and order was threatened.

heightened by the ease with which Members representing Metropolitan constituencies were able to ventilate their constituents' grievances. Then, with the occurrence in fairly rapid succession of a series of *causes célèbres*, frustration in Parliament came to a head.

Incidents preceding the appointment of the Royal Commission

The first of these incidents occurred in 1956, when disciplinary action was taken against the Chief Constable of Cardiganshire following allegations that his force was not being properly administered. The upshot was the amalgamation of the Cardigan and Carmarthen police forces. In the following year criminal proceedings were taken against the Chief Constable of Brighton and senior members of his force. Two of the latter were found guilty on charges of corruption and sentenced to imprisonment. The Chief Constable was acquitted, but his conduct was censured by the trial judge, and he was dismissed from the force, although his appeal against dismissal was subsequently upheld by the House of Lords on the grounds that natural justice had not been done. Soon afterwards the then Chief Constable of Worcester was convicted of fraud and sentenced to imprisonment. Then, in 1957, persistent allegations were made in Parliament (the questions were addressed to the Lord Advocate so as to engage his ministerial responsibility for prosecutions in Scotland) that a boy in the Scottish town of Thurso had been beaten by a policeman, and that the complaint had neither been properly investigated nor effectively remedied. A tribunal of inquiry subsequently established that the boy had been provocative, but that he had suffered an unjustifiable minor assault.[7] Within three months of this report came yet another incident, which raised constitutional issues of the first importance. This was the suspension of their Chief Constable by the Watch Committee of Nottingham. The Chief Constable was the same Captain Athelstan Popkess who, in the 1930s, had pioneered the way in developing forensic science laboratories and police radio.

The circumstances were as follows. The Chief Constable had reason to think that members of the City Council (and another person) had acted corruptly. He consulted the Director of Public Prosecutions, who advised him to institute inquiries. These were undertaken by the Metropolitan Police, and on receiving their report the Director decided to take no further action. The Watch Committee promptly instructed the Chief Constable to report to them on these inquiries. This Captain Popkess refused to do, on the ground that the duty of enforcing the criminal law belonged to him and not to the committee. The committee accordingly exercised nineteenth-century powers still available to them and suspended the Chief Constable on the ground that he was unfit for his office. When the Home Secretary learned of this action from the Press,[8] it seemed to him that the Watch Committee had been guilty of a deliberate attempt to interfere with law enforcement, and he received a deputation consisting of the whole of the committee and the local Members of Parliament. The question at issue, first posed by the inadequacy of the Municipal Corporations Act, 1835, and unexplored for many years, was the degree of control exercisable by a watch committee over its chief constable.

The position in common law had been established to some extent by several judicial pronouncements, the most frequently quoted of which were *Fisher* v. *Oldham Corporation* (1930) and *The Attorney-General for New South Wales* v. *Perpetual Trustee Company* (1955).[9] The circumstances in the Oldham case were as follows. The Oldham police issued a warrant for the arrest of a suspect wanted for obtaining £150 by false pretences from a tradesman in the town. A man named Fisher was arrested and detained for some hours before the police realised that they had the wrong man. Fisher brought an action against Oldham Corporation for damages for false imprisonment, but the Court held that the police officers had not acted as servants of the borough; no liability accordingly attached to the Corporation, and the plaintiff, Fisher, lost his case. In giving judgment, the judge cited with approval the following passage from an earlier (1906) judgment: 'Now, the powers of a constable, *qua* police officer, whether conferred by common law or statute law, are exercised by him by virtue of his office, and cannot be exercised on the responsibility of any person but himself. . . . A constable, therefore, when acting as a peace officer, is not exercising a delegated authority, but an original authority.'[10] The judge held that the Watch Committee had no power to control the constable's execution of the duties of his office, since the relation between master and servant did not exist between it and the police. The second case, that of the Perpetual Trustee Company, was the subject of a judgment by the Judicial Committee of the Privy Council. The issue here was whether a police officer was technically a servant of the Crown in such a way that an action could be founded on the loss of his services. In the course of his judgment, Viscount Simonds approved the observations made in

Fisher's case as a correct statement of the law as to the relation of a constable to the watch committee. The constable was an officer whose authority 'is original, not delegated, and is exercised at his own direction by virtue of his office: he is a ministerial officer exercising statutory rights independently of contract'.

It was on these two judgments about the common law position of the constable that the Home Secretary relied in denying the right of the Nottingham Watch Committee to interfere with their Chief Constable in carrying out his duty to enforce the criminal law. Acting in this capacity, he was an officer independent of local or central control, and as such immune from external influence. But the Watch Committee was able to advance cogent arguments to counter this view of the law, or at all events its application to the particular case. The Municipal Corporations Act empowered them to suspend or dismiss a constable if they were satisfied that he was negligent or otherwise unfit for his duty, and they claimed that they had *prima facie* evidence that the Chief Constable was in fact unfit for his duty, since (in their view) he had shown bias in instituting inquiries into the activities of members of the City Corporation. It was therefore their duty to inquire into his conduct, and they were entitled to suspend him in the meantime. The views expressed in the House of Commons about the totality of a watch committee's control over a borough police force strengthened their case. It was arguable (and the Association of Municipal Corporations was to press this argument on the Royal Commission on the Police) that a watch committee had power to do whatever seemed to it necessary to police its area efficiently, so far as statute, regulation, or common law did not derogate from that power. Thus there was no reason why they should not give directions to their chief constable, for the watch committee had a duty to intervene if the chief constable ceased to enjoy their confidence.

There seems to be no difference in principle (the merits are another matter) between this argument and that relied upon by the Birmingham Watch Committee in its successful dispute with the Chief Constable in 1880 (p. 131). But if the law had not changed, times had, and the Home Office was now taking a great deal more interest in local squabbles. The argument was brought to a conclusion when the Home Secretary told the Nottingham Watch Committee that, with his general responsibility for the maintenance of law and order, he could not accept that their action was proper. The Watch Committee reinstated the Chief Constable and he retired at the end of the year, but the incident had focused public attention on the inadequacy of the law governing the functions of police authorities and chief constables and the relations between them, and the argument about principles continued elsewhere.[11] That such a clash had not occurred for very many years* could be taken as evidence that in general the system worked well, relying on goodwill and co-operation by those who understood it. On the other hand, the fact that such a clash could occur served as a reminder of how very out of date the nineteenth-century statutes which still governed the police system had by then grown.

That year, 1959, was a mixed year for the police. They, and in particular the Chief Constable, emerged creditably from the Nottingham incident. But towards the end of the year came two debates in the House of Commons censuring the conduct of the Home Secretary, Mr. R. A. Butler, in his conduct of police affairs, and the first of these was the immediate cause of the appointment of the Royal Commission. The occasion for it was an incident which, because it raised in acute form many of the issues which had already been troubling Parliament—the evident lack of public accountability of the police, their constitutional position in the State, and the adequacy of the means of dealing with complaints—attracted publicity out of proportion to its merits. This was the case of *Garratt* v. *Eastmond*.

One morning in December, 1958, Mr. Brian Rix, actor-manager of the Whitehall Theatre, motored across Putney Heath. P.C. Eastmond followed in a police car. He stopped Mr. Rix and told him that he was exceeding the speed limit. Mr. Garratt, a civil servant, was driving behind the police car. He also pulled up and spoke to Mr. Rix. An argument developed, followed by mutual allegations of assault. Mr. Garratt was taken to the police station to be charged with an offence, but the station officer refused to accept the charge and Mr. Garratt was released. He instituted civil proceedings against P.C. Eastmond, claiming damages for assault and battery and for false imprisonment. The facts were never established, because the Metropolitan Police Commissioner paid £300 into Court without admission of liability, and the plaintiff took the sum in settlement of the claim. It was then announced that no disciplinary proceedings would be taken against P.C. Eastmond.

* An incident which occurred in St. Helens in 1927 attracted much notice, but this owed more to personal antagonism, and mutual lack of respect and confidence, between the Chief Constable and the Watch Committee than to any major issue of principle. It culminated in the appointment of a tribunal under the Tribunals of Inquiry (Evidence) Act, 1921, which vindicated the actions of the Chief Constable.

The main point that troubled Parliament during the ensuing debate[12] in November, 1959, was why £300 of public money had been paid out unless P.C. Eastmond had done wrong, and if he had done wrong why he had not been disciplined. The Home Secretary explained that the payment into Court did not imply any admission of liability, and that the question of disciplinary proceedings was a matter entirely within the discretion of the Commissioner: the evidence, especially after the time that had elapsed, was not thought sufficient to justify a charge, particularly when account was taken of the different standards of proof required in disciplinary and civil cases. The Home Secretary went on: 'The case, though starting from a small incident, does have underlying it a number of questions of great importance, both to the public and to the police, in which there is evidence of widespread interest and about which there is evidence of considerable anxiety.' He referred to the questions at issue: the inability of Parliament to discuss a provincial police force, the relationship of the central government to the police authorities, and to the police themselves; the relationship of the police authority to the chief constable and of the Secretary of State to the Commissioner; the relationship of the chief officer to his force. 'Above all,' the Home Secretary said, 'there is the relationship mentioned by the right hon. gentleman, between the police service generally and the public. I do not believe that in modern conditions the police can carry out their heavy responsibilities without adequate public co-operation and the fullest measure of public confidence.' All these issues, and he included among them recruitment, training, discipline, and organisation, were complex, and underlying them were constitutional and legal principles of great difficulty and supreme importance. 'The time has come,' he concluded, 'to have them examined with the authority and impartiality of an independent inquiry.'

The direct origin of this Royal Commission, which was appointed in January, 1960, was not therefore concern about the efficiency of the police, or about the state of crime, or the adequacy of police strength. It had nothing to do, as had the Desborough and Oaksey Committees, with questions of pay or recruitment or conditions of service; nor, like the Royal Commission of 1929, with matters of police powers and procedures. Its genesis was, basically, concern about the means of controlling the police and bringing them to account when things went wrong: in short, it was the need for a redefinition, acceptable to Parliament, of the constitutional position of the police in the State. Ironically enough, it was an incident involving the Metropolitan Police, where the Home Secretary's accountability to Parliament was at its maximum, that thus finally precipitated an inquiry which was to concern itself almost exclusively with arrangements outside London.

Advantage was taken of the proposal to appoint a Royal Commission to include in its terms of reference a review of police pay. These were: 'to review the constitutional position of the police throughout Great Britain, the arrangements for their control and administration and, in particular, to consider:

'(1) the constitution and functions of local police authorities;
'(2) the status and accountability of members of police forces, including chief officers of police;
'(3) the relationship of the police with the public and the means of ensuring that complaints by the public against the police are effectively dealt with; and
'(4) the broad principles which should govern the remuneration of the constable, having regard to the nature and extent of police duties and responsibilities and the need to attract and retain an adequate number of recruits with the proper qualifications.'

Sir Henry Willink, Q.C., Master of Magdalen College, Cambridge, and a Minister in Churchill's wartime Government, was appointed Chairman of the Commission.

Interim Report of the Royal Commission

Strongly pressed by the police associations to give first priority to the fourth of its terms of reference, the Commission presented an interim report, on police pay, in November, 1960, some ten months after its appointment.[13] The report gave great satisfaction to the police service, but it displeased the local authorities and the Government, for the Commission went beyond its terms of reference. It had been asked to review 'broad principles'. In reply, it offered not only principles, but a formula which was translated into a cash award for the constable at the maximum of his scale equivalent to a pay rise of some 40 per cent.

In justification, the Commission observed that the maintenance of law and order ranks with defence as a primary task of government, yet the police were lamentably short of strength at a time when crime was mounting and the demands made on them were constantly growing. 'Our survey of the manning of the police forces of Great Britain has led us to conclusions which can only be described as grave. In conditions which demand a standard of policing as high as that required at any time in this country's history, we have found a shortage of police manpower seriously affecting nearly half the country's population; a resort to methods of patrolling which, making all allowances for the technical advances of recent years, have the appearance of an expedient rather than a policy. . . . '[14] The Commission found that the service was short of some 13,500 men, representing a deficiency of 14 per cent, and strength had actually declined during the time that it had been sitting. The shortage was particularly acute in London, the Home Counties, the West Midlands, and the industrial North, but in these areas were concentrated between 40 and 50 per cent of the population. Here the beat system of prewar days had largely broken down. The Commission instanced towns with a population of from 40,000 to 50,000 where only two or three policemen were on the streets at any given time during the day or night; in one town with a population of 111,000 only three men, all probationers, had been on the beat on the day before their visit. The decline in strength was due less to the inadequacy of recruitment than to the heavy rate of premature retirement.

The gravity of the situation was underlined, in the Commission's view, by the alarming increase in crime and in the volume of road traffic, mention of which was made in the last chapter; and, to add to the strain on the police, they seemed to be working in an increasingly adverse social environment. 'The policeman represents a stable element in society at a time of rapid social and economic change. The decline in religious observance, a general lowering of moral standards, a restless, turbulent age—it is against this shifting background that the policeman is expected to set an example of old fashioned virtues. We accept that these conditions can easily foster a hostile current of opinion which increases the difficulty of the constable's task.' The Oaksey Committee, the Commission recalled, had declared in 1948 that police responsibilities were more exacting then than when the Desborough Committee had been impressed by them in 1919; now, in 1960, they had further increased in their range and variety since Oaksey. The case for recommending a substantial increase in pay was summed up as follows: 'The police are expected to know more than was necessary twenty, even ten years ago; the public expect them to achieve higher standards in the application of their knowledge; their duties have increased; and they are required to discharge these duties in circumstances which are probably as difficult as at any time since the police were first established during the last century.'[15]

With this sombre statement of the problem, the Commission went on to analyse the reasons why the police service had lost the attraction it had held before the war: the sharp fall in the value of police pay; the erosion of the pre-war attractions of security and a good pension, since these had become common to other workers; and the liability of a policeman to work while others enjoyed leisure at week-ends, Bank holidays, and in the evenings. Moreover, he was subjected to strict discipline, sometimes exposed to danger, often to unfair criticism, and occasionally to social ostracism.

What 'broad principles', then, should govern police remuneration? The starting-point, in the Commission's view, should be the 'paramount importance' of morale, which was bound to suffer if the level of pay fell substantially below what either members of the service or the general public regarded as fair. The aim should be 'the maintenance of an efficient service fully up to strength and based on conditions recognised by the police themselves and by the public as fair and reasonable'. The Commission rejected the principle of fair comparison, recently adopted for the Civil Service and other groups of public employees, because it could find no duty comparable with that of the constable's. It rejected the principle of supply and demand, because the test of the market alone would have led to a degree of instability in police pay which the Commission considered to be unacceptable; moreover, it would not have produced the 'fair' rate of pay to which it attached importance as a means of restoring police morale and encouraging recruitment. Instead, the Commission argued the case for a tailor-made pay formula designed to take account of the social and industrial changes since the war, which had led to the worsening of the policeman's relative position. Aware of the depressing history of police pay during the previous decade, it took the view that principles alone would not form a satisfactory basis on which the negotiating body would be able to construct a new scale. It therefore interpreted its own formula in a manner which raised the maximum of the constable's pay from £695 to £910, with two long-service supplements to raise it to £970. The jubilation of the police will be understood when they learned that the Commission had virtually met their own claim, powerfully presented in evidence on their behalf by the adviser to the Police Federation, Mr. (later the Rt. Hon.) James Callaghan, M.P.

Indignant as they were that the Commission had usurped the function of the negotiating body, the local authorities nevertheless agreed with the Government that the recommended pay scale should be introduced immediately. The effect was impressive in two ways. During the year just before the Commission presented their report the police service lost a net total of 500 men. In the following two and a half years there was a net gain of 7,000.[16] As to the effect on morale, the Commissioner of the Metropolitan Police said in his annual report for 1960: 'Throughout 1960 members of the Force awaited the publication of the Interim Report of the Royal Commission with a feeling of tension, and at times they were clearly unsettled. . . . Immediate acceptance and implementation of the major recommendations was greatly appreciated, and senior officers report a marked relief of tension among the rank and file of the Force, restoring that atmosphere of contentment which is essential for the proper discharge of police duty.'

The wage-fixing formula proposed by the Commission was rejected, but the negotiating body subsequently (in November, 1962) signed an Agreement providing for biennial reviews of police pay on principles embodied in the Agreement. The general objective was declared to be to maintain the value of the Commission's award, consistently with changes in the wages index and with the general economic state of the country.

Further evidence

The Commission turned to its main terms of reference. Who should control and administer the police in the modern State? It is impossible here to give an adequate survey of the wealth of evidence that poured in, now occupying more than 1,000 printed pages, ranging, as a recent writer has observed, from reflections on dynamic democracy and the nature of happiness to the depth of kitchen sinks in police houses—extremes which, however, met only in Scottish evidence. Only the more important lines of argument bearing on the central issue can be examined.

It soon became apparent that the Commission was being invited to choose between two conflicting points of view on the cardinal question of the control of the police outside London. Most witnesses who represented the central and local government saw little wrong with existing arrangements. Ill-defined as they were, they had in most cases

278

established an efficient, enlightened, and well-understood local relationship which worked admirably in the interests of the police and the public, and also of strong local government. The majority of the chief constables also thought that mutual aid between forces, and the co-operative agencies described in earlier chapters, had resulted in a flexible organisation which gave all the advantages of a nationalised police structure without the drawbacks. Local administration and local contacts were invaluable. Frankpledge, after all, had been a localised device, and so had parish constables. The way ahead lay in developing more common police services under a flag of quasi-independence emblazoned with a motif from *Fisher* v. *Oldham Corporation*. However, the Chief Constable of Lancashire led a radical faction of chief constables. To him the requirement was 'local association, but not local control', and the question had to be asked: How local is local? The needs of 1960 were not those of 1835, and there was a strong case for nationalising the police, or at least for creating a regional organisation; as a minimum, almost all the county borough forces should disappear.[17] The Police Federation also sided with the radicals: local control over the police was 'not always conducive to efficiency', and local forces should be grouped into large regional units with executive and operational functions.

The local authorities, as is to be expected, and in particular the Association of Municipal Corporations, shared the chief constables' attachment to local policing. Views of respectable antiquity were expressed about the danger to democracy if a 'Minister of the Interior on Continental lines' were able to instruct the police, and examples of twentieth-century dictatorships were cited as modern warnings. The Desborough Committee, whom the authorities had been anxious for other reasons to disown in 1920, was now favourably quoted as declaring that central control of the police would be foreign to the 'constitutional principle' of local law enforcement.[18] When it came to Fisher, however, the Association of Municipal Corporations parted company with the chief constables. Too much had been read into the case, they held: on a judgment concerning an issue of civil liability had been built a whole doctrine of police independence which owed nothing to the law, to common sense, or to political wisdom. The chief constable had a special status in local government which precluded a police authority from giving him orders on individual cases of law enforcement, but beyond this, 'the delegation by the watch committee of executive control to the chief constable is a matter, as we see it, not of law, but of good administrative practice'. There was nothing, on this view, to stop a watch committee from giving its chief constable instructions on matters of policy, and in some circumstances it might well have a duty to do so.[19]

So far the Commission had been invited to consider two issues: (*a*) the proposition that policing should remain a local function, and (*b*) the extent to which a chief constable should enjoy independence in exercising it. But there now came a strong body of evidence in opposition to any kind of locally provided policing at all. The Law Society and the Inns of Court Conservative and Unionist Society (between them embracing a large and authoritative section of the legal profession, including several Members of Parliament) argued for some form of nationalisation of the police which would make the Home Secretary accountable to Parliament when things went wrong locally.* It was the first time for very many years that nationalisation had been favoured by any responsible body of opinion, and it is not without interest that its advocates argued the case on the same principal grounds that Rowan and Chadwick had done in the report of the Royal Commission of 1839: that a centrally controlled force would be constitutionally preferable, as being ultimately under Parliamentary supervision, and that it would also be operationally more efficient. The Inns of Court memorandum of evidence, in particular, is an admirably written and cogently argued document in the academic tradition of Bentham, Colquhoun, and Chadwick. It makes full allowance for the conflicting principles at stake, the English fear of arbitrary police power, and the empirical way in which the system had grown up, but argues that the shifting social scene and the need for better leaders and better organisation powerfully support the constitutional grounds for radical change.[20]

Had these arguments prevailed the Commission would have had no need to try to resolve the riddles of local policing. Any theory of the independence of chief constables would have been extinguished when their office was brought within a single police hierarchy stemming from the Home Secretary. As it was, however, the Commission sought academic aid in solving the conundrum. They put four fundamental questions to Professor E. C. S. Wade, Professor of Constitutional Law at Cambridge. Two of them were: Is a constable in keeping the Queen's peace carrying out primarily a national or a local function? What degree of independence does a chief constable have in enforcing

* Both societies claimed that their proposals did not amount to 'nationalisation', but, as the Royal Commission observed, it is difficult to reconcile this view with the changes they advocated.

the law? Professor Wade replied to the first question that only 'a long historical tradition in the nature of the office' required a purely local jurisdiction, and there was nothing but local prestige standing in the way of the amalgamation of police forces or 'other rationalisation of the structure of the police service'; and he developed the proposals put forward by the Inns of Court Conservative and Unionist Society. The answer to the second question he found difficult and obscure, but he drew an interesting distinction between the *judicial* function of the police, which demanded freedom from outside interference, and the *executive* function of maintaining law and order, which was a responsibility shared by all citizens alike; on the basis of this distinction, a chief constable should be open to direction on a limited range of 'executive' matters.[21] These, however, were very deep waters, and the argument about what was, is, and ought to be the control over chief constables continues to the present day.[22]

The Commission, meanwhile, had heard similarly divergent views about the best means of dealing with complaints against the police, and on this subject also the lawyers found themselves at odds with the local and central government witnesses and the police associations. The latter were, in general, satisfied that the disciplinary powers of chief constables were adequate to deal with complaints, and that these powers were fairly and impartially exercised to protect the interests of both police and complainant. The lawyers, on the other hand, regarded it as intolerable that a body such as the police should be free to investigate complaints against their own members. Justice, they claimed, might be done, but it could not be seen to be done, for a man ought never to be judge in his own cause. They acknowledged that discipline in a police force, as in the armed services, must be administered by the commanding officer; but this principle ought not to rule out means for an aggrieved citizen to appeal against the decision of a chief constable. A series of tribunals ought to be set up, or an Ombudsman on the lines of the Scandinavian institution, to hear complaints against the police.

Views were also divided on what must always be largely a matter for subjective assessment—namely, the state of relations between the police and the public. Some witnesses claimed that these relations were excellent; others maintained that they were very bad. The Commission accordingly sought the most objective assessment it could command, by commissioning a special social survey by the Central Office of Information.

Faced with all this confusing evidence (and much more), the

Commission spent twelve months preparing a report the publication of which all who had given evidence awaited with keen interest. The occasion was, indeed, historic, for the wide-ranging review was the first of its kind since modern police forces had been set up in the nineteenth century. Some felt that the Commission faced a unique opportunity to recommend outright nationalisation of the police; others were concerned lest they should take it, as the 1839 Commission had done.

Final Report of the Royal Commission: nationalisation rejected

The Commission presented its final report in May, 1962.[23] Not surprisingly, it discovered a great deal that was out of date. Both the structure and the legal basis of the police system echoed 'not only the requirements of policing a century ago, but also the fears and prejudices, as well as the political wisdom, of the Victorian age'. Were the police, then, to be nationalised? The Commission came near to the brink. The organisation would be more logical, and 'there remains in the minds of a number of us a clear impression that a single centrally directed force would prove to be a more effective instrument for fighting crime and for handling road traffic than the present large number of local forces, each possessing a greater degree of autonomy than we think should be preserved. . . . A long tradition of association between the police and local justices is today no more than an historical survival without practical significance. This has given way to a relatively new association between the police and local government: but this, in our opinion, should have no greater sanctity if it impedes progress towards the development of a police service matched to the requirements of the second half of the twentieth century. That there is a strong case for bringing the police of this country under complete central control is undeniable. Such a step might well enable the service more effectively to fulfil its purposes and, at the same time, would put it under effective Parliamentary supervision.'

This Commission, like the only other Royal Commission which had ever examined the constitutional position of the police—in 1839—dismissed the danger that a national police force might lead to a police state: 'British liberty does not depend, and never has depended, upon the dispersal of police power. It has never depended upon any particular form of police organisation. It depends on the supremacy of Parliament and on the rule of law. . . . To place the

282

police under the control of a well-disposed government would be neither constitutionally objectionable nor politically dangerous; and if an ill-disposed government were to come into office it would without doubt seize control of the police however they might be organised. If reasons are to be found for continuing a system of local police forces, therefore, they must be found elsewhere.'[24]

These reasons were set out. The idea of partnership between central and local government in the administration of public services was of 'immense practical value', and admirably suited the British temperament, with its opportunities for promoting an enlightened and mature public opinion and a sense of civic responsibility. Moreover, the present system 'has not failed, and its development under the guidance of the central departments has achieved much that is of the highest quality. The advantages of local administration by lay persons familiar with the character and needs of the communities they live in are important . . . the trend towards enhanced authority in the central departments continues, and there is scope for readjusting the present balance of responsibility for the police without doing violence to the idea of partnership between central and local government for their administration.' The improvements sought by those who urged nationalisation could, the Commission thought, 'be achieved without seriously disturbing the local basis on which the present police system rests, and thus sacrificing much that is valuable'. Nevertheless, the somewhat ambivalent attitude was underlined a few sentences later: relations between the police and the public were good—'we think that they can best be maintained by accelerating the pace at which the police service moves towards greater unity, than by any abrupt and radical change which might not be readily understood'.[25]

One member of the Commission, Dr. A. L. Goodhart, had no such reservations. In a spirited memorandum of dissent, he attacked the findings of the majority, and urged the creation of a 'centrally controlled police force, administered on a regional basis', to be entitled, 'The Royal English and Welsh Police'. The danger in a democracy did not lie in a central police that is too strong, but in local police forces that are too weak: it was the private gangs of the Fascists and Nazis that had enabled Mussolini and Hitler to establish their dictatorships when the legitimate police proved impotent. Dr. Goodhart disputed the Commission's reading of the history of the English police, and observed drily that an attempt had been made, 'especially by the Association of Chief Police Officers of England and

Wales, to claim the honour of having the parish constable as an ancestor, but this ambition seems an odd one, as his contemporaries had nothing but evil to speak of him'. The majority, he suggested, having deluded themselves in their reading of the history of the police, had extracted false principles from that reading, and these principles, in turn, had led them into the deeper error of recommending the continuance of a system of separate local police forces instead of a unified, national system. Thus they had blinded themselves to the logic both of the history of the police and to the urgent needs of the time.

The dispute over the history of the police—a dispute over its lessons rather than its facts—is of interest to the historian, but seems of scant relevance to the opposing findings, for each side appears to have prayed in aid its own version of history to support conclusions which, however, owe more to differing assessments of contemporary requirements. The argument turned on five historical features identified by the majority of the Commission as having moulded the development of the police system, and having survived to invest it with its modern character.

The first of these features was the local character of the office of constable, which, the Commission noted, helped to explain why there were still so many separate local police forces. Dr. Goodhart carried the point further by insisting on the distinction between a local force and a locally controlled force: the former would exist under any system of police organisation; it was the latter that was objectionable. The second feature was the common-law origin of the office and powers of the constable, from which, in the view of the majority of the Commission (a view supported by the judgments quoted earlier in this chapter) had emerged the modern concept of the independence of the police in enforcing the law, and also the acceptance of the police as a force indistinct from the general body of citizens, and possessing few powers not enjoyed by others. Dr. Goodhart rejected both theses. He maintained (as some local authority witnesses had done) that the judgments which allegedly supported the doctrine of the independence of the police in law enforcement were really founded on a much narrower issue—namely, whether a constable was technically a servant of the local police authority or the Crown in such a way as to permit an action for the loss of his services; and that these judgments were in any case irrelevant to the position in the Metropolitan Police. Moreover, it was not until the Metropolitan Police had proved that they could maintain law and order that they gained first the respect, and then the affection, of the people by emerging as an efficient force, distinct from the public, in whom people could have confidence.

The third historical feature which the majority of the Commission recognised was the subordination of the constable to justices. They argued that, because this form of control had fallen into disuse, chief constables had assumed authority and powers which their predecessors would formerly have sought from justices—powers for which police authorities were now rival residuary legatees. The question was: Who should take over the control of the police forces now that the justices had opted out? To which the Commission replied that control should continue to be divided between the three-fold partnership of Home Secretary, police authority, and chief constable. Dr. Goodhart did not dispute the Commission's view of the historical role of the justices or the crucial nature of the question posed, but he found a different answer to it, preferring with Colquhoun, Bentham, Peel, and Chadwick a hierarchy of control leading directly to the Home Secretary. Finally, the Commission observed that the three foregoing historical features originated from pre-Tudor times, but there were two others embodied in nineteenth-century legislation which had given modern police forces their dominant character. These were the embodiment of constables into police forces, and the subjection of these forces to a degree of democratic supervision. Dr. Goodhart agreed, but regarded these changes as the decisive ones, for it was the formation of the Metropolitan Police in 1829, under the control of the Home Secretary, which was the only historical event of any lasting significance: if the history of the police had any lesson, it was in the bitter opposition that tended to be aroused whenever attempts were made to strengthen the police and to increase their efficiency.

The earlier chapters of this book are perhaps a sufficient commentary on this interesting exchange.

However, it would be an over-simplification to regard the conclusions of the majority and the minority of the Commission as being in total opposition, for all agreed, at all events in principle, on the logic of the case for nationalising the police: as constitutionally preferable to a system of local forces, in that the Home Secretary would be accountable to Parliament for the activities of the police in the same way that other Ministers are accountable for the public services for which they are responsible; and as operationally preferable, in permitting greater economy and efficiency in the deployment of ideas, men, and resources. The conflict centred on an assessment of the countervailing advantage of preserving some kind of local link. No doubt it also turned to some extent, not so much on what might ultimately be desirable as on what was immediately practicable; and if Dr. Goodhart showed greater boldness and a clearer sense of logic, the majority of the Commission, in adopting the principle of acceleration towards greater unity in the police service, must be given credit for greater political realism, for within the relatively short space of two years their views were accepted by the Government and by Parliament, and embodied in the Police Act, 1964.

The Commission's proposals

How did the majority of the Commission think the police service should move towards greater unity? First, there should be stronger central control. The Home Secretary himself should be given additional powers. He should be made statutorily responsible for police efficiency.* He should have new powers to call for reports from chief constables, and to compel the retirement of a chief constable on grounds of inefficiency. His power to approve (or disapprove) the appointment of a chief constable (available in the counties since 1839 and in the boroughs since 1920) should be extended to the appointment of deputy and assistant chief constables as well. He should be empowered to make compulsory schemes for the co-operation of police forces—for example, in setting up crime and traffic squads. He should have power to set up local inquiries into matters concerning the policing of an area. A fresh assault should be made on the small police forces. The Home Secretary's power to compel the amalgamation of police areas should cease to be fettered by the limit of 100,000 population imposed by the Police Act of 1946. 'Forces numbering less than 200 suffer considerable handicaps . . . the retention of forces numbering less than 350 in strength is justifiable only by special circumstances

---

* The particular recommendation was made in this form, but was later shown to have been misconceived. It was first criticised by Dr. Goodhart, quoting Sir Ivor Jennings: 'General language has to be understood in the context of the specific powers granted by legislation.' The Home Secretary, speaking in the House of Commons in the debate on the Royal Commission's report, took the same point: 'A Minister ought not to have responsibility without power. My responsibility would be determined, defined, and limited by any specific powers that Parliament might confer' (*Hansard*, Vol. 677, No. 110, col. 689).

... the optimum size of force is much greater than this—probably 500 or upwards.'

The Commission acknowledged that much had already been done to promote uniformity throughout the police service, but thought that the process had been too empirical and haphazard. Initiatives might come from the Home Office, the Police Council, or the Central Conference of Chief Constables, but planning had suffered through not being the clear responsibility of any single component of the service. A chief inspector of constabulary should be appointed, with a responsibility for strategic planning.* He would be the senior professional adviser to the Home Secretary on police matters, and should be given charge of a central police research and planning unit, which, aided by scientists, would have a duty to plan police methods, develop new equipment and study new techniques.

Under the chief inspector, the corps of inspectors should be strengthened so as to allot one to each of the eight police areas into which England and Wales were divided for police purposes. The role of the inspectors themselves should be broadened. They should no longer confine themselves (as they were still legally bound to do by the Act of 1856) to the merely regulative functions of inquiring into the state of efficiency of each particular force and the conditions of the cells and lock-ups. They should expand the constructive side of their work, the importance of which had grown in recent years. They should be concerned 'with the efficient collaboration of neighbouring forces, with the promotion of co-ordinating machinery between them, and with the development of services best handled on the basis of a district rather than within a single force. . . . It is in our opinion essential that the inspectors should lose no time in planning and developing these arrangements. Within the framework of a unified police service under the exclusive control of the Government, they would have been provided as a matter of course; and the continuance of separate forces must not, as has been the case until now, be allowed to impede their proper development.' By all these means the Commission hoped to secure 'most of the advantages of a unified service without losing the valuable link with local government'. The administrative attitude of the central departments towards police affairs would become positive. 'Their responsibility will be not merely to

---

* The County and Borough Police Act, 1856, had limited the number of inspectors to three, but this limit had been removed, and authority given to appoint a chief inspector, by the Police (His Majesty's Inspectors of Constabulary) Act, 1945.

287

correct inefficiency, but to promote efficiency . . . they will for the first time be in a position to raise standards of equipment and of policing uniformly throughout the country.'[26]

Cumulatively, all these recommendations pointed to a very definite shift of the balance from local to central responsibility for the police. Yet there was to be no central 'control' in the dictionary meaning of the word—namely, a power to direct or command. Was there, then, to be local control? The main functions of police authorities, under the Commission's plan, were restricted to four: to provide, pay, equip, and house a police force; to give advice and guidance to the chief constable about local problems;* to appoint, discipline, and remove the senior officers (subject to the Home Secretary's overriding authority); and to foster good relations with the public. Thus the idea of local control, too, was set aside in a way that would have been totally incomprehensible to most nineteenth-century watch committees and county justices.

The Commission acknowledged the fundamental importance of this central question of control, which had been so prominent an issue in the chain of events leading to its appointment, and its report analyses the matter with anxious care: 'The problem of controlling the police can be restated as the problem of controlling chief constables'—since officers below that rank composed a disciplined hierarchy. And over a wide range of his duties, a chief constable was virtually uncontrolled: 'Thus he is accountable to no one, and subject to no one's orders, for the way in which, for example, he settles his general policies in regard to law enforcement over the area covered by his force, the disposition of his force, the concentration of his resources on any particular type of crime or area, the manner in which he handles political demonstrations or processions and allocates and instructs his men when preventing breaches of the peace arising from industrial disputes, the methods he employs in dealing with an outbreak of violence or of passive resistance to authority, his policy in enforcing the traffic laws and in dealing with parked vehicles, and so on.'[27] The Commission maintained that a chief constable ought, as a matter of principle, to be exposed to criticism in matters of this kind,

---

* But Dr. Goodhart doubted whether the knowledge which members of a watch committee might have concerning local conditions would add greatly to the efficiency of the police in dealing with crime. 'More information concerning local crime can probably be obtained from public-house-keepers than from members of a watch committee, but it does not follow that the former should become a police authority.' Many of them of course, had been members of police authorities in earlier times.

and it pointed out that in London the Commissioner of Police was liable to have his decisions challenged in Parliament, in virtue of the Home Secretary's role as police authority for the Metropolitan area. The position of provincial chief constables, in this respect, ought to be similar to that of the Commissioner.

The practical expression of this view, and the Commission's substitute for direct control over the police, either centrally or locally— both of which it found equally distasteful—was as follows: The chain of command would stop at the level of the chief constable. No one should have power to give him orders, even on broad matters of policy. The chief constable should be free, within the limits of his duties, to act as he saw fit both in enforcing the criminal law in individual cases, and also on questions of policy. But just as the Home Secretary called for reports from the Metropolitan Police Commissioner and the Commissioner was thus indirectly exposed to Parliamentary criticism, so provincial chief constables should in future be required to submit reports to police authorities and also to the Home Secretary, with a similar liability to criticism *ex post facto*. By these means the Home Secretary's answerability to Parliament would be extended. However, in order to protect a chief constable against an ill-advised request for a report (no doubt the Commission had in mind the demand made to Captain Popkess by the Nottingham Watch Committee), he should be entitled to refer any doubtful request to the Home Secretary, whose decision, though final, would itself be open to Parliamentary criticism. In effect, therefore, while no one was to be able to tell a chief constable what he was to do, he would be liable to be called to report to the police authority and to the Home Secretary on what he had done, and to expect criticism if either of these authorities thought that he had acted unreasonably. 'This novel method of government through reports, without power to do anything', Dr. Goodhart commented caustically, 'is a new development in the science of politics.' On another view, it was arguable that a chief constable's conduct would be markedly constrained by the knowledge that he was fully accountable for all his decisions, and this constraint was heavily underlined by a further recommendation of the Commission that both the Home Secretary and the police authority (acting with the approval of the Home Secretary) would have power to retire a chief constable on grounds of inefficiency if he had lost their confidence. Moreover, an augmented corps of inspectors of constabulary would in future exercise closer supervision over the whole area of the chief constable's command.

To the local authorities, and particularly to the Association of Municipal Corporations, most of these recommendations were, naturally, unwelcome. The practical result in the counties was likely to be slight, but the watch committees faced an undoubted emasculation of their powers, for whatever might be said of their claim to be able to give directions to chief constables, they had always had an undisputed legal power to appoint, discipline, and promote the junior ranks of the force. The Commission now proposed (as both the Desborough and Oaksey Committees had done) to transfer this power to the chief constable. And ill-defined as the watch committees' former control over chief constables themselves had been, long usage had given it a very real substance which was now in jeopardy. To some in local government circles the prospect seemed bleak. It might even be preferable to nationalise the police and transfer the whole cost to the Exchequer, than to expect local government to continue to share half the cost while stripping police authorities of their former powers. In the event, these first reactions proved to be unduly pessimistic.

Other recommendations of the Commission

The final report of the Commission ranged widely. Among its other proposals were a review of the status of police cadets and new arrangements for recruiting policemen, and the Commission attached great importance to the need to attract more men with higher education. It proposed that standing joint committees, the police authorities in counties since the inception of county councils in 1888, should lose the financial autonomy they had enjoyed for seventy-five years, and that in future they, like the watch committees in boroughs, should submit their annual estimates to the council. In future, too, the composition of watch committees and standing joint committees should be assimilated: each should contain one-third magistrates and two-thirds elected councillors. Thus the watch committees were to lose the identity they had enjoyed ever since they were created by the Municipal Corporations Act, 1835. The case for appointing magistrates was argued on the grounds that their familiarity with police problems placed them in a specially favourable position to administer police forces, and that they constituted a body of public-spirited citizens whose services could not be enlisted through the normal machinery of local government. The Commission overlooked, or perhaps disregarded, the sustained efforts made during the nineteenth century to oust magistrates from control of the police, nor did it refer to the evidently temporary nature of the compromise by which they were admitted to standing joint committees in 1888, at a time when county councils had not been 'educated in the science of government'.*

Finally, the Commission dealt with relations between the police and the public. Their fundamental importance was acknowledged: in Britain, 'the police cannot successfully carry out their task of maintaining law and order without the support and confidence of the people . . . they act for the community in the enforcement of the law and it is on the law and on its enforcement that the liberties of the community rest'. From the start, when the Metropolitan Police were founded by Peel, the police had been obliged to rely on the sympathetic and active co-operation of the community, and to the early pioneers was due the credit for inspiring great traditions of public service. Peel's first instructions to the Metropolitan Police, part of which the Commission quoted, remained as valid as when they were issued 130 years earlier. To the surprise of many (and the disbelief of some) the present state of relations between the police and the public was declared, on the evidence of the specially commissioned social survey, to be very good. While recommending some ways in which relations could be further improved, notably by trying to secure more uniform policies of traffic-law enforcement, the Commission dismissed by a majority the idea of establishing an independent system of investigating complaints against the police. A further series of recommendations were designed to improve disciplinary procedures and to encourage public confidence in the arrangements for handling complaints within police forces. Three members of the Commission, however, in a note of reservation, recommended the appointment of a Commissioner of Rights, on the lines of the Scandinavian Ombudsman, to hear complaints against the police.

Reception of the Report

Describing Dr. Goodhart's minority views as a formidable piece of virtuosity, *The Times* commented: 'There can be few reports of this

* This point was taken by Mr. Chuter Ede during the Committee stage of what is now the Police Act, 1964. (An attempt was made to dislodge magistrates from standing joint committees in 1914, when the Home Office prepared a Bill to give the police function to county councils. The Bill did not reach the Statute Book, and a Home Office witness before the Desborough Committee turned right about, and argued that watch committees should be composed as to half councillors and half magistrates.)

stature which have seen the light of day burdened with such an embarrassing built-in essay of self-destruction.'[28] The *New Statesman* put the point more picturesquely: 'The majority point out the only road to the future: Dr. A. L. Goodhart alone takes it. . . . The best view of this report is to regard it as 22 pages by Dr. Goodhart, with a preface seven times as long by a faintly admiring syndicate of diplomats.'[29] Other responsible journals took a similar line—the *Economist* was disappointed that the Commission had not followed 'the sensible Dr. Goodhart' in recommending the creation of regional police forces.[30]

The Government soon made its position clear. Addressing a conference of chief police officers a few weeks after the report had been published, the Home Secretary, Mr. R. A. Butler, announced that the Government had no intention of proposing legislation to nationalise the police, and that he did not share the Commission's view that there was no danger in a national force: 'I am quite convinced that it would be wrong for one man or one government to be in charge directly of the whole police of this country. Our constitution is based on checks and balances. This has kept our liberty through the generations.'[31] He undertook to discuss the Commission's report with the local authority and police associations. The local authorities, meanwhile, fortified by these views, briefed Members of Parliament on both sides of the House for the coming struggle.

By May, 1963, when the report was debated in the House of Commons,[32] a Chief Inspector of Constabulary had been appointed, the inspectorate had been increased to seven, and a police Research and Planning Branch was being set up in the Home Office to give top priority to the grave problem of serious and unsolved crime. Outlining these achievements, the Home Secretary (now Mr. Henry Brooke) said there should be a stronger initiative from the Home Office in the future, and that he was inclined to agree with many of the Commission's specific recommendations, which would extend his powers and hence his accountability to Parliament. Moreover, the time had come to take a further major step forward in the process which had gone on for the past eighty years, of reducing the number of separate police forces, and he proposed to ask the inspectors of constabulary to review police areas in the wake of the reports of the Local Government Commission, which was in process of reviewing local government boundaries. He agreed with the Royal Commission that his powers to compel amalgamations should be strengthened.

Fourteen Members spoke in the ensuing debate, and discussion cut across party lines. Almost all favoured stronger Home Office control over the police. Four Members (one Labour and three Conservative) opted for outright nationalisation, as against five (three Labour and two Conservatives) who opposed it. Seven Members (four Labour and three Conservative) wanted more amalgamations, and only two (one from each side of the House) wanted none. The greatest concensus of opinion was on the question whether there should be some form of independent means of hearing complaints against the police. Eight out of nine Members who expressed an opinion on this (four on each side of the House) thought that there should be.

The Parliamentary Under-Secretary of State for the Home Office, winding up the debate, said that he had asked Dr. Goodhart how it came about that he reached diametrically opposite conclusions on the same evidence, and Dr. Goodhart had reminded him in reply of the Lord of Appeal who, being in disagreement with his two colleagues, said, when asked to give judgment, 'I dissent from my learned colleagues for the reasons they have given.' He was struck by the fact that there were more Tory than Socialist supporters of nationalisation. (There always had been—notably Peel in 1829 and Lord Salisbury in 1888.) The Government would weigh all that had been said before introducing legislation.

The Police Act, 1964

In November, 1963, eighteen months after the Royal Commission had reported, the Government introduced its Police Bill. The Bill contained no surprises, and it was evident that the local authority associations had had as little success in their campaign to persuade the Government to drop the Commission's more radical proposals as the nationalisers had had in urging the Government to go further. The Bill comprehensively revised and re-enacted the whole general law on provincial police administration, and it provided for the complete or partial repeal of sixty-one Acts of Parliament dating back to 1801; thus all the familiar nineteenth-century statutes, many of which had long outlived their usefulness, were swept away. For the rest, the Bill followed very closely the Commission's recommendations. Counties and county boroughs were preserved as the standard police areas, and the Bill formally recognised the many changes in the organisation of the police service that had been effected without specific statutory authority during the preceding thirty years.

For the first time in the history of the police, the Bill attempted to define the respective functions of the Home Secretary, police authorities, and chief constables. The Home Secretary was to be given a new duty to take initiatives to promote the efficiency of the police, and powers to discharge the duty. These powers were of two kinds: those directed to promoting the efficiency of each individual police force (the power to call for reports from chief constables, to approve the appointment of the senior officers and compel the retirement of an inefficient chief constable, and to set up a local inquiry into the policing of an area); and those directed to promoting the efficient policing of wider areas by developing co-operation between forces, providing common service arrangements, and amalgamating police areas. The main functions of every police authority (to be composed as to two-thirds councillors and one-third magistrates) were defined as the maintenance of an adequate and efficient force, properly housed and equipped, and the appointment, and if necessary removal, of the chief constable. A police authority, like the Home Secretary, had power to call for reports from its chief constable and—although this could not, of course be written into the Bill—its scope for influencing the morale and efficiency of the force was unimpaired. Each police force was explicitly placed under the control and direction of its chief constable, and chief constables in boroughs, as well as in counties, were to have powers of appointment, discipline, and promotion over the subordinate ranks. The scope of the duties of the inspectors of constabulary was enlarged for the first time since their office was created in 1856, and the Home Secretary was empowered to appoint assistant inspectors and staff officers to help them to carry out their wider duties.

Other provisions of the Bill gave statutory recognition to the many agencies that had been developed under local or central initiatives in the past decades; these included the common service arrangements, the Police College, district police training centres, forensic science laboratories, wireless depots, and the negotiating machinery. The Police Council, set up by the Police Act, 1919, was replaced by a Police Advisory Board to advise the Home Secretary on general questions affecting the service, and the Police Council for Great Britain was recognised as the negotiating body. The area of jurisdiction of a constable was no longer to be restricted to that of his own locality and neighbouring forces: he was to have the powers and privileges of a constable throughout England and Wales. Authority was given for chief officers to enter into collaboration agreements, for example, to set up traffic or crime squads; police authorities were likewise empowered to make agreements for the joint use of premises, equipment, or other facilities by police forces. The Bill formally authorised the establishment of the Research and Planning Branch in the Home Office, and it cleared up the anomalous status of the many police officers seconded from their home forces to serve in establishments provided by the Home Secretary; these officers were declared to be engaged in temporary service under the Crown. The effect of this was that they remained police officers, but ceased for the time being to be members of their forces except for purposes of pay, pension, promotion, and discipline.*

The Bill proposed improved arrangements for dealing with complaints against the police by empowering a chief officer of police to call upon an officer of another police force to investigate complaints, and enabling the Home Secretary to direct that this should be done. Unless the investigation then showed conclusively that no criminal offence had been committed, the report of the investigating officer was to be sent to the Director of Public Prosecutions. A new duty was placed on police authorities and inspectors of constabulary to keep themselves informed as to the manner in which complaints against the police were dealt with.

The Bill was given an unopposed Second Reading, occupied a standing committee for no less than forty-four hours, and passed with little controversy through the House of Lords. It received the Royal Assent in June, 1964, and came into force in stages during the ensuing twelve months. The local authority lobby fought the Bill hard during its passage through Parliament, and vigorously opposed the introduction of magistrates to watch committees, but later made it clear that the newly formed police authorities would co-operate to the full in making the new arrangements work. Thus another milestone in police history, comparable in magnitude to the events of 1919 and 1920, had been passed.

* At the end of 1966 the number of officers (excluding the Metropolitan Police) engaged on central service or otherwise seconded from their parent forces was 876. They included detectives serving with crime squads.

Chapter Ten

Forward from the Royal Commission

Recent and contemporary events can only be recorded for what they are, not for what they signify; and assessment is doubly hazardous at a time of swift change. For five years after 1960 the police service was under close scrutiny, first by a Royal Commission and then by Parliament. Never in all its history had it suffered so prolonged and critical a review. The times were unsettled for policemen of all ranks; and even in the later nineteen-sixties, the nation's vigilance over its police force was still not relaxed.

On June 1st, 1965, the whole of the new Police Act came into force, with the reconstitution on that date of police authorities containing two-thirds councillors and one-third magistrates; most provisions had been brought into operation much earlier. It was an opportunity to assess what had been accomplished, and the dominant feature was the substantial fulfilment of the trend started by Desborough: by a process of quite extraordinary complexity, there had emerged a sort of national police service, comprising a loose federation of local units, each preserving its own loyalties and affiliations, but conscious also of a sense of national purpose and unity. It may be (the view is not universally shared) that out of this prolonged clash and compromise between local and central interests the country now possesses a flexible police structure matched to its current challenges, and that all that is lacking are adequate resources of manpower and equipment. The functions of local police authorities were not, after all, greatly attenuated. In evidence given to a Select Committee of Parliament in 1966, the Association of Municipal Corporations was still able to claim: 'Such is the relationship of confidence between most police authorities and chief constables that consultation on operations does commonly take place. . . . Even if the position of the watch committee is one of influence with, rather than control over, the chief constable, their existence is still justified as regards operational matters as a sounding board sensitive to public opinion.'[1]

In other ways, too, the extent of change was perhaps less apparent than the degree of sameness that persisted. Many old police stations continued to be overcrowded, ill-adapted to modern usage, ill-painted and forbidding—though some new buildings provided a startling contrast, with their modern architectural styles, first-class amenities and bright offices and canteens. The traditions and ways of some middle-aged policemen would be proof against innovation of any kind. In some areas the life of the man on the beat differed little from that of his predecessor of half a century earlier. The occasional black sheep still gave the police an unjustifiably bad name. The legislative reforms had barely touched the Metropolitan Police, and Peel's Act of 1829 remained on the Statute Book. A partnership of central and local government continued to administer a system of local police forces outside London, and chief constables still enjoyed a measure of independent discretion in carrying out their duties that marked them off from other chief officers of a local authority. The joint agencies and common services set up during the last thirty years had likewise been steadily developed, rather than changed in their essentials.

Yet it is not necessary to look far beneath the surface to recognise that, cumulatively, the round of reforms first started by the Royal Commission may eventually be seen to have constituted as radical a mutation of the English police system as that which resulted from the reforms of the Desborough Committee forty years earlier; and in its new Research and Planning organisation the Home Office has fashioned an instrument, to serve the course of further adaptation, which has opened up exciting new prospects in the way of applying Britain's technological resources to police work. A momentum of reform was generated, and with it a willingness within the police service itself to accept the need for further changes.

Police work in modern times

The duties of the Metropolitan Police were laid down by Peel, and his early instructions were widely copied in other forces. The only attempt to describe the duties of the police in modern times seems to have been that of the last Royal Commission, as follows:

'First, the police have a duty to maintain law and order and to protect persons and property.

'Secondly, they have a duty to prevent crime.

'Thirdly, they are responsible for the detection of criminals and, in the course of interrogating suspected persons, they have a part to play in the early stages of the judicial process, acting under judicial restraint.

'Fourthly, the police in England and Wales (but not in Scotland) have the responsibility of deciding whether or not to prosecute persons suspected of criminal offences.

'Fifthly, in England and Wales (but not in Scotland) the police themselves conduct many prosecutions for the less serious offences.

'Sixthly, the police have the duty of controlling road traffic and advising local authorities on traffic questions.

'Seventhly, the police carry out certain duties on behalf of Government departments—for example, they conduct inquiries into applications made by persons who wish to be granted British nationality.

'Eighthly, they have by long tradition a duty to befriend anyone who needs their help, and they may at any time be called upon to cope with minor or major emergencies.'[2]*

Unhappily, the police can claim only modest success in discharging the more important of these duties in recent years. The rise in the postwar level of crime up to the time of the appointment of the Royal Commission was reviewed in Chapter Eight. From 1954, when the increase resumed after a temporary abatement, it continued unchecked; and by 1964 the number of indictable offences known to the police, which had stood at less than half a million ten years earlier, exceeded 1 million. It has continued to rise ever since, and although the rate of increase has fallen slightly in recent years, the rise in the numbers of offences involving violence has been disturbing. The police have faced—and continue to face—the greatest challenge in their whole history. Detectives more highly trained than their predecessors, and with forensic science laboratories, criminal record offices and crime squads to help them, have been working longer

* That report was published in 1962. Ten years later the police were recognising yet another duty, and to many it seemed to be one of growing importance: a duty to go out and foster good working relations with the public, and especially with those groups in the community, such as young people and coloured immigrants, whose support could not be taken for granted. This recent development is touched on later in this chapter.

hours than ever before. It is heartening that in these adverse circumstances the proportion of known indictable offences cleared up by the
police has actually been rising—in 1970 it stood at just under fifty
per cent.

Particularly serious were increases in crimes of violence against the
person and robbery. More criminals were carrying firearms and,
ominously, no less than half the indictable crimes were committed by
young people under twenty-one. The police feared that a large
number of these crimes by young people, especially larcenies and
breaking-in offences, were remaining undetected, so that their
perpetrators were emboldened to embark on a criminal career. It was
in the cities and large conurbations that crime was most prevalent,
and these were the areas where the shortage of police, so acute a
decade earlier, still persisted, despite the Royal Commission's pay
award.

Anxious as they were to discover in what way police techniques
were apparently failing to check the growth in crime, the inspectors of
constabulary nevertheless insisted that the police could not meet the
challenge unaided. National prosperity and improved social conditions had, contrary to earlier assumptions, led to a situation in
which crime appeared to flourish.* The ready availability of more cash
and valuable property, and the ease with which it could be stolen and
rapidly transported, was a constant attraction, not only to persistent
criminals, but to amateurs of all ages in a wide range of society. The
cure for society's ills, the inspectors of constabulary concluded, lay
beyond the resources of the police. Not only would they need the
support of the public, but continued research would be necessary into
such subjects as criminology, scientific aids, juvenile delinquency, the
causes of crime and the treatment of offenders, the criminal law and
rules of evidence, and much else.[3]

For several years senior police officers had expressed concern about
the growth in the numbers of well-organised attacks on cash and goods

* Much has been written in recent years about the increase of crime in an
affluent society, and surprise has often been expressed that prosperity
should encourage crime rather than deter it. But this discovery was made as
long ago as 1839 by the Royal Commission which recommended a centralised police system for the counties of England and Wales. 'Having investigated the general causes of depredation, of vagrancy, and mendicancy,
as developed by examination of the previous lives of criminals and of
vagrants in the gaols, we find that in scarcely any cases is it ascribable to the
pressure of unavoidable want or destitution; and that in the great mass of
cases it arises from the temptation of obtaining property with a less degree
of labour than by regular industry. . . . '

in transit and on banks, post offices, and business houses. These culminated in the Great Train Robbery, which occurred in the early hours of the morning of August 8th, 1963. The Glasgow to London mail train was held up by a gang of men in Buckinghamshire, and mail-bags containing over £2½ million were stolen. This, unquestionably the most serious robbery in the history of the country, shocked many law-abiding people into a realisation of the desperate character of the war against criminals which the police were waging on their behalf. The police arrested a number of men concerned in the robbery, but the amount of money recovered was relatively small. One result of the crime was a full inquiry into the lessons to be learned to see what changes in police techniques might be desirable to deal with any comparable crime in the future. An incidental result was that, seemingly for the first time in police history, soldiers with fixed bayonets and automatic rifles were summoned to guard the prison in which three of the men convicted of the crime were serving long sentences of imprisonment.[4]

Concerned as they were about the volume of crime in the 1960s, the police were scarcely less anxious about the congested state of the roads and the rising number of traffic accidents. Here again the affluent society had created more, not less, police problems. The Great Train Robbery forced people's attention on the formidable nature of the challenge presented to society by criminals, but a year later the inspectors of constabulary were still concerned that the social conscience of the nation had not yet awakened to the appalling problem of road accidents, with its tragedy of so many lives cruelly ended.

The number of registered motor vehicles doubled in the ten years from 1954 to 1964, and in that year the number of people killed on the roads annually had risen by nearly 3,000; in 1966 the total was about 8,000, but in subsequent years it has fallen—largely, perhaps, on account of the enactment of new laws to discourage motorists from driving after drinking alcohol. As with crime, the solution of the traffic problem lay beyond police resources. They could hope to limit its size, not to solve it, for its solution must depend on a combination of many factors—better roads, improved street lighting, vehicle-testing, speed limits, limitations on street parking, and much else. Nevertheless, a strong body of enforcement officers patrolling the highways has always been regarded as one of the most effective contributions to road safety. Traditionally this duty has been carried out by uniformed police officers, but there has in recent years been a body of opinion in favour of setting up a separate corps of traffic police, possibly working under the authority of ordinary police officers.* This course was rejected by the Royal Commission on the Police and by the Government, and the police found it necessary to divert an increasing proportion of their manpower to traffic duties. In 1963 about 10 per cent of the police outside London, or some 6,000 policemen, were engaged solely on this work, and it was estimated that, in addition, a uniformed foot constable devoted three hours out of an eight-hour tour of duty to road traffic duties, such as dealing with accidents and reporting traffic offences, but excluding point duty. About 160 police officers were employed full-time on accident-prevention work, and many others were giving lectures on road safety to schoolchildren and others. In 1970 about 1 million persons were prosecuted for motoring offences, and many others were given written warnings. Nearly two-thirds of offences of all kinds dealt with by the police were traffic offences. Complaints were made of lack of uniformity between one force and another in enforcing traffic laws, and chief constables have combined to standardise their policies. Meanwhile, the traffic warden system has been developed as an important means of providing relief to the police and the functions and powers of wardens have been expanded.

The difficulties of the police have been further aggravated by sustained resistance to authority on the part of political demonstrators critical of the Government's defence policies, and by some large-scale outbreaks of hooliganism.

The campaign for nuclear disarmament will have its footnote in the history of our times; its purpose and policy are no concern of this book. Nor, so long as it remained a legitimate political movement employing the accepted democratic processes of persuasion, was it any concern of the police, except for the need to control the large number of people who for several years took part in marches from Aldermaston to London, and afterwards conducted meetings, attended by some 20,000 people, in Trafalgar Square. But during the late 1950s a splinter group, known as the Committee of 100, advocated passive resistance to authority as a means of pursuing their aims. Severe clashes with the police resulted, and it became evident in the

* An early protagonist of this view was Captain Sant, the Chief Constable of Surrey from 1899 to 1931, who tried unsuccessfully to persuade his brother chief constables that a separate body of 'road wardens' should be set up, so as to free the police 'for their proper job of preventing and detecting serious crime' (*Surrey Constabulary, 1851–1951*, p. 52).

early 1960s that a campaign of mass civil disobedience had been mounted with the object of disrupting the normal machinery of law enforcement to an extent that would overwhelm the police and the courts. Several major clashes occurred, in the course of one of which, in April, 1961, a force of no fewer than 3,000 policemen engaged a crowd of 2,000 demonstrators and arrested over 800 of them. These demonstrations culminated in a mass meeting held in Trafalgar Square in September, 1961, when it became necessary to invoke some elderly statutes against the demonstrators. The Commissioner of Police made directions under the Metropolitan Police Act, 1839, the effect of which was to prevent access to Trafalgar Square and streets in its vicinity. These directions were widely disregarded, and proceedings were subsequently taken under the Justices of the Peace Act, 1361, against thirty-eight demonstrators. Most of them (including the philosopher Bertrand Russell) refused to be bound over to keep the peace, and so were committed to prison. Over 4,000 policemen were employed on this occasion, and they made over 1,300 arrests. The number of demonstrators seems to have been only slightly in excess of the number of policemen. Later in the year activity centred on American air-bases outside London. The demonstrations revived in intensity at the time of the Cuban crisis in October, 1962, but in the following year Parliament passed a Public Order Act which strengthened the powers of the courts to deal with persons who caused or provoked disorder at public meetings. In the meantime, the police had obtained and executed warrants for the arrest of some of the leading members of the Committee of 100, who were subsequently charged with offences under the Official Secrets Act and sentenced to terms of imprisonment.

It seems probable that these clashes with the public, many of whom were young people acting through what they regarded as the highest motives, led to a deterioration in relations between the police and the public as a result of criticism of the police in the Press and through broadcasting media, which the police were unable effectively to rebut —not because they accepted it as just, but because they themselves investigated complaints against their colleagues and so were unable to convince some of the public that the investigations had been impartial. It was, of course, open to complainants to take civil or criminal proceedings against policemen, and it is perhaps significant that nobody seems to have done so. At all events it is clear that when they faced the next serious threat to law and order in 1964, the police enjoyed the full support of all law-abiding sections of the community.

This was the occasion of 'mods and rockers' disturbances which broke out at several seaside resorts and in various parts of London. Major disturbances involved between 3,000 and 5,000 young people, and there were times when the disorders began to resemble gang warfare between opposing factions. The publicity given to each incident encouraged others, and local police forces were reinforced by contingents brought in from elsewhere. A large reserve of police was available in London, and arrangements were made for men to be flown to trouble-spots by the Royal Air Force. The first of the airborne policemen were sent to Hastings in August, 1964. These outbreaks of disorder were greeted with public hostility to the demonstrators, widespread support for the police, and firm action by the courts, whose powers to deal with vandalism were strengthened by Parliament by the Malicious Damage Act, 1964.

In recent years tendencies in Britain (as in other countries) towards anti-authoritarianism, coupled with a new readiness to espouse, and demonstrate for, international causes—reinforced, even, among some sections of young people, by a belief in anarchy as a form of society preferable to the smug legitimacy of the ordered 'establishment'—all these forces have further imperilled the traditionally close relationship between police and public, for it is the police who stand in the front line, on the streets, as emblems of resistance to change by 'authority'. A major confrontation between the police and the public rich in lessons for the student of British police history, occurred in London in 1968, a year that witnessed severe civil disorders in the streets of Paris, Berlin, Chicago and Tokyo. A great demonstration, involving some 30,000 people, marched through the streets of London on October 27th, 1968. The issues were various, but the most prominent was protest against the war in Vietnam. Banners were held high, flags waved, and the chanting grew in volume. Many feared severe riots, and some even talked of revolution. In the event there was virtually no violence, and the great occasion ended at about midnight with a few demonstrators singing *Auld Lang Syne* with a handful of tired police. Did it mean that the British were effete, had lost the will to protest and to press the logic of their convictions to inevitable violence? Or was it the good temper of the police, their refusal to be provoked, their reliance on good humour and on using no more force than was necessary, that saved the day? The chief London correspondent of the *Washington Post* took the broad view: 'What did not happen, quite simply, was something that has occurred in every other major western country this year, a truly violent confron-

303

tation between angry students and sadistic police. . . . British experience in building a non-violent relatively gentle society seems of paramount importance to a world beset by police brutality and student nihilism.' A sharper comment, perhaps more timely, came from home. 'Anything which makes the British more complacent than they are already,' declared the *New Statesman* of the events of October, 1968, 'is a minor national disaster.'

The police continue to tackle these vast problems with inadequate strength. Recruitment has continued to be fairly buoyant in consequence of the stabilisation of the value of police pay—the average gain in total strength in the ten years from 1961 to 1970 was of the order of 2,000—but there has remained a persistently high rate of premature retirements. In 1970 England and Wales had over 90,000 policemen, about one for every 500 inhabitants and more than ever before in peacetime, but the increased numbers scarcely kept pace with the growth of police duties and a reduction in their working hours, so that there remained a substantial gap between the authorised establishments of some forces and their actual strength. The total deficiency in 1970 was of the order of 14,000, and many people were beginning to wonder whether it was ever likely to be made good. A more realistic approach seemed to be to relieve the police of duties which do not require their special skill and training by building up an effective civilian support structure. At the same time a sustained effort has been directed to equipping and training each policeman so as to improve his efficiency up to the limit of the individual's capacity.

Training, and the Police College

The growing professionalism of the police service is reflected in the fact that policemen now spend an annual average of about fourteen days on training courses of one kind or another. In 1970 the four detective-training centres set up before the war, with a fifth, in Liverpool, which had subsequently been added, trained over 1,700 officers, and twelve driving schools maintained by the larger forces provided driving courses for over 7,000 others. Instruction was given to crime-prevention officers, under the auspices of the Home Office, at the headquarters of the Staffordshire Constabulary; courses were offered by Manchester University on immigrant problems; and the directors of forensic science laboratories encouraged the training in police forces of specialist officers in scene-of-crime work. These officers, some of them policewomen, are sent to the scene of a crime at the earliest possible moment so as to search for scientific clues, often combining their technique with fingerprint and photographic work, and so releasing the detective officer in charge of the case to pursue his side of the investigation without delay. During 1971 a Home Office working party was studying ways in which this service could be developed as a major aid to the C.I.D.

Training can achieve much, but only within the limits of the available raw material. The Royal Commission had expressed concern at the lack of well-educated recruits to the police. Although rather more than 40 per cent were educated at grammar schools, only about 1 per cent had two or more G.C.E. passes at advanced level; a further 10 per cent had five or more subjects at ordinary level, and some 20 per cent had one to four subjects at ordinary level; the Commission found no recent instance of a university graduate entering the police.* The service was failing to attract its fair share of the educated section of the community, although boys entering as police cadets tended to possess rather higher educational qualifications than those recruited in the ordinary way at the age of nineteen. The Commission expressed particular concern that the police were failing to attract enough recruits of the quality to make the senior officers of the future. Thus it echoed what its predecessor had said in 1929, and Trenchard more vehemently in 1932. Since 1948, however, a Police College acceptable to all ranks of the service had been in existence, and it was evident that its role, academic standing, and curriculum could play a major part in solving the problem.

For the first ten years and more of its life the College offered the bulk of its courses to middle-aged sergeants and inspectors; but the Government's White Paper of 1947 had made it clear that the original arrangements were not to be regarded as the last word, and that the possibility of providing a course open to young constables would be examined in the light of experience. By 1961 over 3,000 policemen had attended the basic courses at the College, and in that year the Government announced the introduction of two new courses.[5] The first was a special course, lasting twelve months, for constables who obtained a high enough place in the qualifying examination for promotion to sergeant. Policemen who successfully completed the course received automatic promotion. The second was a senior staff course of six

---

* In fact, 25 out of half a million graduates entered the police between 1945 and 1965. The effect of more recent efforts to attract graduates is described later in this chapter.

months. This was of a primarily professional character designed to equip officers of the rank of inspector or above for the highest posts in the service. These proposals, and particularly the availability of accelerated promotion for exceptionally able young men, marked a notable change from the past: they would undoubtedly have been very strongly resisted by many policemen had they been brought forward when the postwar Police College was first established, but now they were accepted without demur. The Government explained their limited purposes as follows: first, to enable the service to produce its own leaders by giving early training to those who had demonstrated their suitability for higher rank; and, second, to offer attractive prospects for the recruit of good quality so that he would feel that he would be given the opportunity to use his talents to the best advantage.

The first of the new special courses, for thirty-six young constables, opened in October, 1962. Their average age was twenty-seven; half were those who had obtained the highest aggregate of marks in the promotion examination conducted by the Civil Service Commission, and half were chosen after extended interviews from among those next in order of merit. All but one of these pioneers successfully passed the course and returned to their forces as sergeants, but experience of this first group had proved the superiority of the extended-interview system over a purely academic basis of selection, and this arrangement, occupying about two days, with intelligence tests, group exercises, and interviews, has been adopted for selecting candidates for subsequent courses. The average age of students on the special course in 1970 had dropped to twenty-six. In the meantime, partly in an effort to attract more sixth-form school-leavers and graduates into the police, important changes had been made in the qualifications for admission to the course. The minimum period of service required of a recruit before he could sit for the examination for promotion from constable to sergeant was reduced from four to three years, and later to two years, so that the able recruit of nineteen might aspire to go to the College as a sergeant at the age of about twenty-two or twenty-three. A further change in the arrangements provided that, if he successfully passed the year's special course, the officer would then be automatically promoted to the rank of inspector after a further year's satisfactory experience in the normal duties of sergeant. Thus the way is now open for first-class young men to obtain very rapid promotion in the British police.

These new arrangements have been widely advertised in schools and universities, and they were accompanied by the introduction, in

306

1967, of a scheme designed to attract up to twenty graduates into the police service every year. Candidates were invited to attend extended interviews to assess their character, intelligence and potential, and those selected were given to understand that, having passed the promotion examination, they would be admitted to the special course after a minimum of two years' service. This scheme, opposed from the outset by the Police Federation, proved less attractive than had been hoped, and the twenty extra places allotted at the Police College for these additional prospective special-course students have never been filled. Leaders of the service feared that not enough had been done to replace Trenchard's controversial Police College at Hendon (pp. 207–9) as an instrument for attracting men of the calibre to lead the police in the years ahead—the Chief Inspector of Constabulary noted in his report for 1968 that the then Commissioner of the Metropolitan Police, the President of the Association of Chief Police Officers, the Commandant of the Police College, the chief constables of five forces and he himself had all been direct entrants from Hendon. This, however, implies too gloomy a view. The police service had long recognised a responsibility to spot the talent within its own ranks, and in 1964 a scheme was started by which 'Bramshill scholarships' were granted to outstanding students from the special course to enable them to study full-time at British universities. This scheme has been highly successful, and by the end of 1970 about one hundred scholarships had been awarded to officers to study law, history, economics and other subjects. At that time there were some two hundred graduates in the police, about forty of whom had graduated as Bramshill scholars.

The senior course at the College,* started in 1963 as a means of training carefully selected officers for the highest posts in the service, has in the meantime been adapted and modernised with the aid of a team of specialist inspectors from the Department of Education and Science. The review is important for two reasons. In the first place it marked a recognition that the senior police officer of today requires a thorough grounding in management and scientific studies, as well as the training in police duties and the liberal studies that were

* Starting as a Senior *Staff* Course, it was subsequently termed a Senior *Command* Course; and a shorter course for intermediate command was introduced. The original College course for training sergeants to become inspectors was replaced, in 1967, by a course for newly promoted inspectors. All the courses at the College (except the special course) welcome students from overseas, whose presence, and special contributions, greatly enrich the corporate life of the College.

Forward from the Royal Commission

thought to be adequate ten years ago. In the second place the review heralded the start of an association between the police and academic educationists which is bound to affect many concepts of police training that have hitherto owed more to tradition and practical common sense than to educational theory. This association was formalised, in 1971, by the creation of a Police Training Council with a duty to keep under review all aspects of police training. Judged by the first two reports received by the Council soon after its formation, the influence of its academic members, and that of the academics who had already been appointed to working parties which the Council later adopted, is likely to be profound. One of these working parties studied the training of police recruits; the other, the training of police in race relations.

The arrangements for training recruits, standardised soon after the Second World War (pp. 245-6), had been modified from time to time to keep pace with changes in the law and in educational theory (for example by developing more practical training at the expense of lectures), but they had not been re-examined from first principles for twenty years. It seemed fair to ask, for example, whether the police were being trained for the demands of the law rather than the real needs of the community. In 1970 a working party consisting of Home Office officials and representatives of the local authorities and the police, together with academic advisers, was set up to undertake a fresh review. Strongly influenced by the academic members, it proceeded to appoint a team of three experts. These, a research psychologist, a training officer with experience in industry, and a police superintendent familiar with traditional methods of police training, embarked on an original study based on well-established principles known as Instructional System Design. They first drew up a job specification for a recruit (having carried out extensive interviews with samples of recruits and their supervising officers) by analysing the knowledge, skills and attitudes he required. From this they deduced a scheme of priorities by identifying areas where the objective evidence showed the existing training to be inadequate—for example in enabling a police recruit to deal effectively with such common situations as domestic disputes, traffic accidents, fights, and encounters with juveniles. Next the team of experts drew up a model syllabus designed to rectify the particular weaknesses they had found, and they recommended how best the instruction should be given, placing particular emphasis on practical training, and on placing the trainee in realistic, role-playing situations from which he

308

would be motivated, from an immediate realisation of his mistakes, to learn for himself. The team of experts found much in the existing training syllabus that they considered to be unnecessary at this initial stage of a recruit's training, and they were satisfied that the new syllabus could provide in ten weeks a more relevant and hence more valuable course than the traditional syllabus had provided in thirteen.

The working party as a whole adopted this report and welcomed the originality of its approach—chief constables, studying the existing syllabus independently, had themselves reached the conclusion that a number of subjects, particularly in the field of criminal law, might well be dropped. Commending the report to the Police Training Council, the working party defined the four main objects of a recruit's training as follows: first, to provide him with at least the minimum skills and knowledge he needs to equip him for operational work; second, to build up his self-confidence and practical common sense; third, to give him a sound understanding of the role of the police in British society; and fourth, to provide a firm base for further training in the recruit's own force. Arrangements were being made to run the first experimental courses on the new lines during 1972; they are then to be evaluated in the light of experience. In the meantime the working party has turned its attention to the later stages of a recruit's training.

The study of the arrangements for training the police in race relations was undertaken at the same time as that concerned with recruit training, and again the working party included members with specialist knowledge of the subject. They heard evidence from leaders of immigrant communities, noted that the absorption of coloured people into Britain was being accompanied, and to some extent hampered, by social tensions, and recognised that the situation created problems for the police which were not at present fully understood. Encounters between police and coloured citizens were liable to lead to a degree of friction not to be expected in encounters between people of the same colour. The working party considered that much more attention should be given to these problems in police training at all levels, but thought that training in race relations should be placed in the broader context of relations between the police and the community generally. They proposed several ways in which this wider training should be given, and suggested that suitable policemen should be encouraged to undertake study tours to the countries of origin of immigrants. The working party also sponsored a programme of research into the kinds of situation that involved coloured people with the police, so as to identify the skills the policeman needs to develop if he is to handle these situations successfully.

Police cadets

The Royal Commission noted that youths recruited to the police as cadets had a higher average level of education than direct entrants.

The idea of police cadets was slow to develop. The system had its origin long before the Second World War, when it was customary to employ 'boy clerks' in police offices on clerical duties. By 1939 about half the police forces in the country were offering employment of this kind, and many of the youths received instruction in physical training, law, and police duties, so that they would be ripe for appointment as constables when they reached the minimum age of nineteen. About 600 youths were employed in this way on the outbreak of war, but most of them were not provided with a uniform. During the war a Police Auxiliary Messenger Service was created for young men between the ages of sixteen and eighteen, who were employed on clerical, telephone, and other duties, some of them for part-time only. This body lapsed at the end of the war, and the further development of cadet schemes was left to local initiative. The Oaksey Committee accepted them as an ancillary, but not a major, source of recruitment, and the Home Office recommended the lines on which their training might be conducted.

Police cadets were given statutory recognition in the Police Act, 1964, where they were described as persons appointed to 'undergo training with a view to becoming members' of a police force. In 1965 a Home Office working party endorsed their value as a major source of recruitment, and recommended that ex-cadets should form 30 to 40 per cent of the recruit intake.[6] This marked a major break with the past. Ever since regular police forces were created recruits had generally brought with them experience derived from some other employment. They had to: when most boys left school at the age of fourteen or earlier, a substantial gap had to be filled before a youth reached the minimum age for enrolment as a policeman, and the average age of entry in Victorian times was nearer thirty than twenty. Virtue had been made of this necessity, and it had long been held, no doubt correctly, that the wealth and variety of background experience brought into the police service in this way, together with the broadening of sympathies and understanding of other ways of life, greatly enriched it. The Royal Commission had noted the danger that a youth immersed too early and too completely in the police atmosphere could be harmfully cut off from the normal stream of civilian life, and the Home Office working party underlined the point by recommending arrangements for training police cadets which would not only give an adequate understanding of police work, but would at the same time broaden the cadet's general education with social and liberal studies, and give opportunities for participation in voluntary community work: 'A cadet's training should be designed to make him a good citizen first; and thereby provide the makings of a good police officer, with some insight into the social roots of police work.' In 1970 there were about 3,600 cadets in provincial forces and a further 700 in London, the annual intake being over 1,000. By this time an early and extremely valuable initiative by the Metropolitan Police in developing a co-ordinated system of training, extending over a period of three years, had begun to yield a flow of recruits without whom the problem of manning the force would have been virtually insoluble.

The role of the Home Office

How has the Royal Commission's insistence on a stronger lead from the Home Office worked out in practice? It is too early to attempt any conclusive answer, but a brief account may be given of some of the ways in which the Home Office has become increasingly involved in the management of the police service in recent years.

Central arrangements now govern the qualifying examinations for the promotion of policemen and the bulk of their training, and the Home Office has ultimate control over the appointment of all senior officers. Local forces continue to enlist their men, but a national plan has been drawn up for developing the cadet system as a major source of recruitment, and some £300,000 is being spent annually on national advertising campaigns. The common services fund, under Home Office management, pays for forensic science laboratories, wireless depots, training centres, promotion examinations, recruiting publicity, the provision of a national co-ordinator for regional crime squads, the Police College, and a proportion of the cost of the Police Council for Great Britain. The machinery of central and district conferences of chief constables has grown a long way from its early

311

origins in the First World War, and there is now a regular series of meetings of the inspectors of constabulary and Home Office administrators which provide a forum for discussion of operational and other matters which affect the whole police service.

In the meantime the Home Office inspectorate has been re-organised. Since 1970 there have been, under the Chief Inspector of Constabulary, one inspector for each of the four regions (Northern, Eastern, Midlands, and Wales and South-west) into which the country is divided for police purposes, and two so-called 'functional' inspectors, responsible for matters concerning crime and traffic respectively; these latter also shared the responsibility for inspecting the forces in South-east England. In addition, there was a woman assistant Inspector of Constabulary and a staff officer with special responsibility for police training. In effect, there is now a headquarters for each regional group of forces, and this headquarters has under its surveillance not only the efficiency of each force, but also the joint agencies which serve the needs of groups of forces. The inspector in each region also has a duty to promote the development of collaboration between forces, and he acts as the chairman of a committee of chief constables which supervises the operation of the regional crime squad. The inspectors continue, as they have done since 1856, to report on the efficiency of each force, but now their reports are submitted in the first place to the chief inspector. Shortcomings are drawn to the attention of the police authority and the chief constable, and occasionally the Home Office finds it necessary to bring pressure to bear to ensure that recommended improvements are effected.

It will be seen that much of this activity has evolved naturally and easily out of earlier processes that, for fifty years, had been transforming the English pattern of separate local police forces into a national public service, still nourished by the local roots and loyalties the Royal Commission was reluctant to sever. The activity, and the change which has accompanied it, has been evolutionary, not revolutionary. The same may be said of the way in which the old Police Council, set up by the Police Act, 1919, was replaced by the new Police Advisory Board. The Council, it will be recalled, had lost much of its early vigour by the time the Royal Commission was appointed, and its eclipse in the 1950s coincided with a faltering of Home Office initiative. The phoenix that rose from its ashes, the Police Advisory Board, winged its way through 1966 trailing three working parties, whose combined reports span vast areas of police activity, and nicely complement much of the work of the Royal Commission and the Police Act that followed it.[7]

The origin of these working parties lay in the discontent of the Police Federation, who in February, 1965, published a paper entitled *The Problem*. In it they argued that the main problem which faced the police service was lack of manpower, and that means had to be found of reducing the heavy rate of wastage. They proposed a large increase in pay, with a supplement for the undermanned areas, together with much more attention to man-management, better equipment, and the more widespread employment of civilians and traffic wardens. These views were considered by each of the components of the police service separately, and then at its first meeting in January, 1966, the new Police Advisory Board set up three working parties on manpower, equipment, and operational efficiency and management. Each comprised representatives of all ranks of the police service and of the local authorities, together with outside experts brought in for the special contribution they were able to make; and each sat under a Home Office chairman. Thus the police embarked on a process of self-examination which probably has no parallel in any other public service. Each of the working parties was requested to complete its work within a year, and in December, 1966, the Police Advisory Board met to receive the reports of all three. 'This has been a most encouraging day,' declared the Home Secretary after the meeting. 'I believe that the working parties' reports . . . point the way to far-reaching reforms which will make an important contribution to success in the fight against crime. We intend to act vigorously on these recommendations.'

The .reports set the pattern for a further round of extensive reforms. They deal with the way in which scientific discoveries and technological advances can be applied to police work, and with the development of more flexible systems of policing which may well replace the traditional system of foot-patrolling in urban areas. Means are discussed of relieving the regular police of all work which does not require the special qualifications and training of a constable, and the exercise of authority, by handing many duties over to a strengthened civilian support structure and an expanded corps of traffic wardens. Much is said about the introduction of general training in man-management in the police service, and the need to examine the human relationships, and discover the causes that lower a policeman's morale to the point at which he resigns. Stress is laid on the way in which the status of the ordinary constable should be

313

enhanced so as to develop his sense of personal responsibility. The reports also seize on a few still-surviving relics of Victorian times which had escaped the notice of all earlier inquiries, such as the manner of parading and briefing men for beat patrol duties, which in some areas still seemed to be based on the assumption that constables were illiterate.

These early results suggest that the Police Advisory Board, whose Chairman is the Home Secretary, is likely to play an important part in strengthening the central control and leadership of the police service to which the Royal Commission attached so much importance. And while these results were fructifying the Home Secretary himself had, in May, 1966, taken another important initiative, in the form of yet a further attack on the smaller police forces. This time the assault was on a scale even bigger than Chuter Ede's achievement in the Act of 1946, and it greatly outmatched the ill-fated efforts of Palmerston in 1854.

Further amalgamations

Hitherto the policy had been that announced by the Home Secretary to Parliament when the report of the Royal Commission was debated. This was to review police areas in the light of changes in local government boundaries resulting from the work of the Local Government Commissions, which were then reviewing the whole of England and Wales. While, therefore, the Royal Commission's insistence on the need to abolish the smaller police forces had been accepted by Parliament and by successive governments, the progress of amalgamations was necessarily slow.

Soon after the Police Act, 1964, removed the limit of 100,000 population beyond which the Home Secretary's compulsory powers were not exercisable, the Home Secretary secured the agreement of five police authorities in the Fen country to set up a single combined force. This, known as the Mid-Anglia Constabulary, came into being on April 1st, 1965; an important voluntary amalgamation of five police areas in the West Midlands, together with the first compulsory scheme under the Act, combining the police areas of Northampton and Northamptonshire, came into force a year later. Luton, meanwhile, was acting out a historic role in the tussle between local and central government. As long ago as 1920 the Town Clerk of Luton had led his colleagues in other non-county boroughs in protest

314

against the Desborough Committee's proposal to abolish the smaller police forces, but Luton lost its force in 1947 as a result of the Police Act of 1946. For many years this expanding town strove to achieve the status of a county borough, and it eventually did so on April 1st, 1964. Under the law as it then stood, it became entitled to re-establish its own police force, which it did. Three months later the Police Act received the Royal Assent, and the Home Secretary told Luton that unless it chose voluntarily to amalgamate its newly formed force with the surrounding Bedfordshire Constabulary, he would exercise his strengthened powers to compel it to do so. Luton resisted the pressure, and a public inquiry was held early in 1965. This concluded that, although the amalgamation of the two police areas was clearly in the interests of efficiency, nevertheless, in view of Luton's passionate desire to have its own force, its civic pride, and the history of bad relations between the two neighbouring constabularies, the separate force should be allowed to remain for a trial period. The Home Secretary, however, rejected this view and a separate Luton force was abolished for the second time on April 1st, 1966.

By then much bigger events were pending. The Local Government Commissions were wound up, and the Government announced its intention to set up a Royal Commission on Local Government. Thus it was clear that no further changes in local government boundaries would be made for some years. The problems of crime and road traffic, however, would not wait; and on May 18th, 1966, the Home Secretary announced a nation-wide programme of amalgamations, to be enforced if necessary by compulsion, the effect of which would be to reduce the number of separate police forces in England and Wales from 117 to forty-nine. Their strength would range from about 700 to nearly 7,000, the majority being in the range of 1,000 to 2,500.*

This programme was tackled vigorously, and by the end of 1967 two-thirds of it had been accomplished; the whole programme was in operation in 1969. Predictable misgivings were expressed in some quarters about the effect which such wholesale slaughter of small forces would have on local influences over the police, and on the men's morale. But at the end of it all the Home Office was well satisfied: 'Benefits in the shape of improved efficiency, greater flexibility and increased resources are widely acknowledged by those

---

* The programme provided for the amalgamation of existing local authority areas. The Home Secretary rejected suggestions that he should promote legislation to empower him to carve the country up into areas more convenient from the police point of view.

Forward from the Royal Commission

involved, including many who were firmly opposed to the amalgamation proposals,' declared the Chief Inspector of Constabulary in his report for 1969.

Even now, however, the pattern of police areas had not been finally settled. Successive Governments had been studying the report of the Royal Commission on Local Government that had been set up in 1966, and early in 1971 firm proposals were at last announced for the reform of local government in Britain. Outside London, England and Wales were to be divided into 44 new counties, six of which, covering the main urban conglomerations, were designated 'metropolitan counties'. Policing was stated to be a responsibility of each of these counties, and the Home Secretary announced that, so far as possible, each new county would have its own police force— although the forces of some of the new counties would be amalgamated, either in order to preserve existing combined forces or because the individual counties concerned would have insufficient resources to secure efficient policing on modern standards. The Police Federation protested. They argued that it would be wrong to make further changes so soon, and that existing forces should be allowed to continue. They should be grouped in regional units of administration, the Federation suggested; but the Home Secretary was adamant. As this book went to press the future pattern of local government areas and consequently of police areas in England and Wales was still not settled in every detail.

Research, planning, and scientific aids

The appointment of a Chief Inspector of Constabulary, with responsibility for a new Research and Planning Branch in the Home Office, was one of the early fruits of the Royal Commission's report. The Branch was set up in August, 1963, under the immediate direction of an assistant chief constable. It then consisted of four chief superintendents and two scientists; four years later it had been expanded into a unit comprising twenty-one scientists and seven senior police officers, with full supporting staff, all under the direction of one of the inspectors of constabulary.

The Branch was at first asked to study methods of dealing with serious and unsolved crime, and to see how best the police could utilise their limited resources in enforcing the traffic laws. The first task, involving the application of operational research techniques, was quickly

316

Research, planning, and scientific aids

recognised to be incapable of any quick and final answer. The Branch
set about seeking information about methods of criminal investigation employed in many police forces in England and Wales, and
further research was undertaken in America. It also studied the
effectiveness of the regional crime squads which had already been set
up under local arrangements. They had grown up in a piecemeal
manner and there were gaps between the areas they covered; these
gaps occurred in some sensitive parts of the country, including areas
where motorways were being extended. Within twelve months the
Branch had confirmed the value of crime squads, and it drew up a
blueprint for nine regional squads to cover the whole country. These
came into operation on April 1st, 1965, each being composed of a
mobile team of experienced detectives, under the command of an
assistant chief constable, which was immediately available to help the
local force concerned. In all, some 600 detectives were seconded to
these squads. A committee of chief constables supervised the operation
of each squad, and the police authorities concerned housed and
equipped it. To co-ordinate the work of the nine regional squads, a
national co-ordinator was appointed with an office in Scotland Yard,
and he in turn was answerable to a committee of chief constables
under the chairmanship of the chief inspector of constabulary. As a
means of providing crime squads with information about organised
crime and notable criminals, a series of criminal intelligence bureaux
was established, and experiments were conducted with multi-channel
radio sets for use on the vehicles operated by the squads. Latterly the
squads have devoted much attention to the known criminals in their
areas as well as to crime; they have been busily employed on serious
criminal activities generally, including the investigation of cases of
murder.

While these developments were going forward, the Police Research
and Planning Branch was also studying its other urgent task, the
policing of motorways and arrangements for dealing with long
distance traffic problems. Large-scale trials were undertaken on long
stretches of motorway, and a major experiment was conducted on the
M6 in the summer of 1964, when three forces responsible for policing
the motorway, the Cheshire, Lancashire, and Staffordshire Constabularies, established a joint command post. Helicopter patrols
were superimposed on ground patrols, and experiments were conducted with closed-circuit television.

During 1966 some forty research projects were being pursued by
the Branch, and plans were far advanced to expand it a stage further

317

by giving it responsibility for the field-testing of items of equipment, thus enabling it to help to formulate the requirements of the police, and act as a channel of communication between the police, manufacturers, and scientists in promoting research and development. To aid this process, the Home Secretary, in January, 1966, set up a Scientific Advisory Council, composed of distinguished scientists, to advise him on the scientific aspects of research for the police, including forensic science, and a Central Research Laboratory was opened at Aldermaston later in the year. A small expert committee (whose work is not confined to the police) has also been set up to advise on longer-term developments, and on research, in the whole field of electronics and communications. By all these means it has been possible to apply the results of scientific discoveries and technological advances to police work in a way, and to an extent, that has never been possible in this country before, and that has few, if any, parallels in other countries.

In the meantime, the Police Research and Planning Branch embarked on potentially far-reaching studies of the greatest interest, which involved the application of operational research techniques to the method of policing an area. Some attempt was made in Chapter Eight to show how the shortage of policemen was partially overcome by the adoption of new methods, and by placing an increasing reliance on police mobility. Sustained experiments with flexible systems of policing had been undertaken in many police forces for some years before the Research and Planning Branch was set up in 1963, and they have continued since: the Lancashire Constabulary, in particular, attracted attention by their application, in selected urban areas, of experience gained in Chicago and elsewhere in the use of mobile police patrols equipped with two-way radio; and the annual reports of the Metropolitan Police Commissioner describe interesting experiments in 'neighbourhood' policing in the outer areas of London. The availability of new equipment, in particular small personal radio sets which link a policeman constantly with his section headquarters, opened up the possibility of introducing these new methods of policing on a wide scale, and the application of operational research techniques enabled them to be scientifically evaluated.

One such method, introduced in the course of 1966, is known as 'unit beat policing'. Its aims are described in the publication, *Police Manpower, Equipment, and Efficiency*.[8] Briefly, they are to provide a more efficient system of policing, closer contact between

318

the police and the public, a better flow of information to the centre, a more worthwhile and interesting job for the ordinary policeman than traditional beat patrolling had been able to offer, and a significant saving in the demand for police manpower. Thus in one town in the north of England where unit beat policing was first tried out, the town centre continues to be patrolled in the traditional way, but the remainder of the town has been divided into eight areas. In each of these is one constable, equipped with a personal radio, with a general twenty-four-hour responsibility for the area. It is his own patch, and he is expected to get to know the people in it, just as the village constable knows his fellow villagers; and he enjoys a measure of discretion over when to turn out for duty. Superimposed on every two such areas is a motor-car patrol (the cars quickly and affectionately became known as 'panda' cars, because of their appearance) on constant duty for twenty-four hours; and a detective constable is also appointed to each of these car beats. Thus small local teams have been built up, the flow of information from which is fed to, and collated by, a detective constable at the centre. This new system of policing was popular, and it spread rapidly: by the end of 1968 some 30 million people (60 per cent of the population) were covered by it, and experiments were being made into extending its principles into rural areas. The system was not, however, without its critics. There were fears that the increasing mobility of policemen in 'panda' cars was removing them dangerously far from that close contact with the public which has always been of inestimable value in Britain; and many people in rural areas complained bitterly at the loss of their village 'bobby' as Home Office scientists, attempting to measure the cost-effectiveness of that hallowed British institution, concluded that it was very low. By 1970 the quiet revolution in ways of patrolling rural England was far advanced, as men were being grouped into mobile teams that covered wide areas and, with rapid communications at their disposal, were able to give a more efficient (if less personal) service to the community than had ever been possible under the old system.

The Home Office Police Research and Development Branch, meanwhile, was itself being reshaped to serve wider and more ambitious purposes. In 1969, six years after its formation, it was transformed into a new organisation, comprising three sections: a Scientific Development Branch, headed by a senior scientist; a Police Research Services Branch, under an assistant chief constable; and a Management and Planning Group under a recently appointed Economic Adviser to the Home Office. The object of the change was to expand and strengthen earlier work undertaken for the police by the Home Office in scientific research and the development of new methods and equipment, and, in particular, to carry forward pioneer work to provide forces with a financial planning and accounting system based on the planning–programming–budgeting (P.P.B.) approach to public expenditure.

Here there is no space to describe the wide-ranging programme of work that was being undertaken within the organisation in the late 1960s and 1970s. Among the more important projects have been an evaluation of the role of regional crime squads; an assessment of value scales applied to the work of the C.I.D.; research into the best use of limited manpower resources; and the application of optics, electronics and even psychology to serve the purposes of the police. Attention has also been directed to major traffic problems, including a study of the effectiveness of different levels of motorway patrolling; the allocation of traffic policing resources; vehicle management; and the value of helicopters in police work. In the application of computer technology, systems have been developed to collate, store and retrieve criminal intelligence data and to automate the processes of storing and comparing fingermarks. A major piece of research was inaugurated in 1971 in Birmingham, where a purpose-designed computerised command and control system, linked to the city's twelve sub-stations by means of an advanced system of communications, was brought into operation in February, 1972—the first of its kind in the country, or, indeed, in Europe. A principal object of this system is to provide instant information about the availability of all foot and mobile patrols throughout the city.

The largest and potentially most important application of technology to the police service, however, is a police national computer project, due to become operational in 1973. This scheme, which is being planned centrally, is designed to store in a central computer at Hendon (on the northern outskirts of London) information held in the central criminal record office, and to provide instant access to it to all police forces in the country over a high-speed network with terminals in all the principal police stations. Among the first records to be made available will be the main fingerprint collection, lists of stolen vehicles and of wanted and missing persons, and the index of the names of known criminals.

Little has been said in this book about either the triumphs of the police or their failures. As, however, the subject of complaints against the police was one of the matters expressly referred to the recent Royal Commission, and is likely to be the subject of public discussion for some years, brief mention must be made of some incidents which placed the police in an unfavourable light after the Commission had reported.

The Commission, on the evidence of a social survey, stated that no less than 83 per cent of people interviewed professed great respect for the police, 16 per cent had mixed feelings, and only 1 per cent had little or no respect for them. These findings were greeted with scepticism in some quarters, and this was subsequently heightened when, as a result of several incidents, a fresh round of public discussion started up about the state of the relations between the police and the public, in which misgivings were voiced about the arrangements for dealing with complaints against the police. In particular, the view was widely expressed that a system under which the police inquire into complaints against their own colleagues is intrinsically defective, since justice cannot then be seen to be done.

Only one of these incidents reflected seriously on the conduct of the police officers concerned. This was a case in Sheffield in 1963, in which two policemen were found guilty of seriously assaulting prisoners in their custody. The officers were dismissed, and appealed to the Home Secretary against their punishment. A subsequent inquiry established beyond doubt not only that they had been guilty of violence, but that the inquiry into the allegations against them, which had been conducted by senior members of the force, had not been searching enough to uncover the truth. In the event, the Chief Constable and other officers of the force resigned. Inevitably, incidents of this kind undermine the self-confidence of the police to an extent wholly out of proportion to their frequency, but it is doubtful whether they shake public confidence. As one newspaper put it: 'The sense of sadness felt at the revelations is in an odd kind of way a compliment to the force. If we thought less highly of it the sense of being let down would not be so acute; it is rather like catching Father cheating.'[9]

Soon after this the Home Secretary set up an inquiry into allegations made against members of the Metropolitan Police. The allegations related to incidents which had occurred a number of years

321

earlier, when it was said that the police had ill-treated some prisoners, and that senior officers, in reporting on the matter to the Home Secretary, had covered up for their subordinates by suppressing damaging police reports. The inquiry showed that these particular allegations were unfounded, but it disclosed that a police investigation into other allegations which had been made at about the same time had been superficial.

In the meantime a major inquiry had been started into incidents in which a Metropolitan detective-sergeant named Challenor had been involved. It was the first inquiry to be set up under the Police Act, 1964, and its terms of reference were to inquire into the circumstances in which it had been possible for this officer to continue on duty at a time when he may have been affected by the onset of mental illness. The events leading up to the inquiry started on the occasion of a visit to this country in July, 1963, by the King and Queen of Greece. In the course of a political demonstration against the visitors, Challenor arrested a man who subsequently acknowledged at the public inquiry that he had been 'consciously playing the brinkmanship game with the police'. The man was charged with carrying an offensive weapon consisting of part of a brick, which Challenor alleged in evidence that he had found in his pocket. The accused, however, maintained that the brick had been 'planted' on him by Challenor. He was acquitted, issued a writ against the police, and was paid a sum of £500 in settlement of his claims for damages for false imprisonment, malicious prosecution, and assault. By this time Challenor had been removed to a mental hospital, and there had been a series of further complaints about cases in which he had been involved, including some on behalf of other people arrested by Challenor, or other officers, and similarly charged with possessing bricks. An inquiry by a Chief Superintendent of the Metropolitan Police was instituted into all these matters, and as a result of this Challenor and three police constables who had been under his control at the West End police station were charged, in June, 1964, with conspiring to pervert the course of justice by planting bricks on innocent persons. Challenor was found unfit to plead, but the other three police officers were convicted.

These events inevitably shook public confidence in the integrity of the police, and several professional criminals exploited the situation by coming forward with allegations that they, too, had suffered miscarriages of justice. Meanwhile, rumours of corruption among some of the police officers who had the unpleasant duty of dealing with members of the underworld in the West End of London were also rife, a situation very similar to the one which had caused the appointment of the Royal Commission in 1906. In July 1964, the Home Secretary announced the appointment of two inquiries: one under the Police Act, and a second into the additional rumours and allegations, which was to be conducted by the Chief Constable of a large Midlands police force. At the same time he announced that he had recommended the grant of free pardons to the persons convicted in the 'bricks' cases, and to two other men who had been convicted as a result of evidence given by Challenor at a time when he may have been mentally ill. The statutory inquiry eventually found that Challenor had continued on duty for a period of some three months after the onset of mental illness, in circumstances which cast no blame on any members of the Metropolitan Police or on any of the doctors who examined him; and it made some recommendations designed to ensure that if ever another similar case occurred incipient symptoms of mental illness would be brought to notice without delay. Both it and the report of the Chief Constable who had undertaken the other inquiry dismissed allegations of corruption as unfounded, and established that some of these allegations had been inspired by malice.[10]

Apart from the evidence of inexcusable behaviour by a few policemen in Sheffield, these incidents reflected little discredit on the police. Nevertheless, the vast publicity, which continued for months before the findings of impartial inquiries could vindicate the men concerned, inevitably did a certain amount of harm. Criticism of police activities often persists simply because it relates to matters which are *sub judice*, and on which the police cannot therefore comment. These conditions readily lend themselves to the malicious and criminally disposed, who, relying on public credulity, not infrequently base their defence in the courts on an unscrupulous attack on the integrity of the police.

These incidents, occurring in fairly rapid succession, threw into relief the problem of the best means of dealing with complaints.* The arrangements in the Police Act were criticised by the police on the ground that a great deal of valuable police time was being wasted in investigating malicious or unfounded allegations, and that the scales were always tilted against them—C. H. Rolph has written of the 'saddest example' of despotic disciplinary power in 'the grim, burrowing determination of senior police officers accumulating evidence and

* Statistically, the problem is relatively small. In 1964 there were about one and a half complaints per 100 police officers per year.

323

working out charges against a fallen colleague'.[11] At the same time, sections of opinion which for a number of years had pressed for an independent system of investigating complaints remained equally dissatisfied. It seems unlikely, however, that any radical change in the arrangements is to be expected in the foreseeable future. An entirely acceptable answer to the question, '*Quis custodiet ipsos custodes?*' remains as elusive as when it was first asked in Roman times.

Police and public in the 1970s

It has been stressed throughout this book that the success of the police in this country has always depended on public approval. This was first recognised as long ago as 1829 in the original instructions to the Metropolitan Police. If public support were to be withdrawn, the police would have to be armed with additional powers, which they have never sought and do not seek now. The heritage of English freedom would not be lost, but it could easily be tarnished. The relationship between the police and the public in England is sensitively balanced, and must never be taken for granted. It is no accident that four out of the five Royal Commissions that have been appointed to consider police affairs originated out of concern on this account. There is certainly no room for complacency in 1972. Professor Banton, a pioneer sociologist in undertaking an academic study of the place of the policeman in the community, has concluded without hesitation: 'There can be no question that police–public relations have changed since the end of the Second World War, and are continuing to change.'[12]

There has probably never been any time in their history when the police have stood so much in need of public support as they do today. Criticism of the police is as legitimate as it is necessary, but scandal is noisier than virtue and the many tend to be censured for the faults of the few. Yet the censure itself is a perverse thing, and perhaps little more than an unworthy 'holier than thou' reaction instinctive to Englishmen who dislike authority, did not want police in the first place, and would gladly dispense with them now if they could. The truer undercurrent is in the vast tide of sympathy that flowed out to the police when, as happened on a tragic afternoon in August, 1966, three of their members were cruelly murdered in a London street by armed criminals. The Memorial Service in Westminster Abbey and the public subscription for the policemen's dependants were in a

324

sense the contrition of a nation expressing its deepest feelings of gratitude and honour towards the public servants to whom it owes most.

The relations between the English police and public cannot be summed up in a sentence, or fully analysed in a book. Nearly half a century ago, in 1908, a leading article in *The Times* perhaps came near to the heart of the matter as it was then: 'The police are a body who, though distinctive in their character from all others, as the members of any public service must necessarily be, are yet related to the people whom they serve by ties of intimate personal association which are not to be found in any other country in the world. The policeman in London is not merely guardian of the peace; he is an integral part of its social life. In many a back street and slum he not merely stands for law and order; he is the true handyman of our streets, the best friend of a mass of people who have no other counsellor or protector.'[13] How much of this is left in the age of mass motoring and the Welfare State? A former policeman, writing of 'the ambivalent attitude which is the relationship of the police and the working-class public', has recently commented, 'the feeling that the men are only chatting to keep on the right side, and are really wondering what the bleedinell you want there anyway, sticks out like a sore thumb'.[14]

It is sometimes overlooked that the police are used for different purposes from one generation to another. In the nineteenth century the main problems were poaching, vagrancy, and petty crime; during the first three decades of the twentieth, public order constituted a major problem; now the challenge is from crime of all kinds, and road traffic. The utility man of fifty years ago helped to run the ambulance and fire brigade, and in these and other ways he was seen to be rendering services to the community. If discipline in the force was harsh, social adjustment outside it was easier. Now it is the other way about: police discipline has been tempered, but the social environment is hostile. When the English upper and middle classes successfully resisted the idea of professional police for three-quarters of a century after Fielding had pointed the way, it was because some feared the loss of liberty and most objected to the expense. Today the cost (of the order of £300 million a year) is accepted, but the issue of personal freedom against the restraints of the community is again wide open, and the policeman stands at the storm centre round which many of the tensions of modern society are working themselves out. He tries to exercise a stabilising influence at a bewildering period of our national life, when almost everything is in a state of change. He

325

lives in the midst of an upheaval in ideas, morals, religious beliefs, and all the old-fashioned values. Crime is rampant, and the changing values and changing standards affect the policeman, for he is much more deeply involved in society than most. At its humdrum least, he is spending his time getting to know and understand people. At its highest, the police, being so closely in touch with the public, and therefore so responsive to current trends and aspirations, can themselves contribute to the quality of society of the future.

Is the English police system adaptable enough, and is it being adapted, to sustain our changing civilisation? (Merely to ask the question is to emphasise the weight of responsibility the police bear, and their dependence on a satisfactory rapport with the public.) A partial answer may perhaps be attempted. The police have always been a stable body, conservative in outlook, and slow to accept innovation. Many of them in former times were recruited from the slow, dependable agricultural classes. Their purpose, of bringing the security without which civilisation is impossible, breeds the need for security in themselves. History shows how this reluctance to accept change has been reinforced by vested interests. Radical proposals for reform of the police system, such as were put to the recent Royal Commission, are exciting not so much on account of intrinsic merit as for their rarity. For most of the 140 years of professional policing in this country change has been forced from without by pressure of circumstances, not willed from within.

But now there are signs that all this is changing. A questing spirit is abroad that is unlikely to be stifled. In the bars and common-rooms of the Police College, in the conference-rooms in the Home Office, in many police headquarters, and in hundreds of canteens and mess-rooms throughout the country, there is an eagerness to discuss the future of the police, and their place in the community; and public interest in them is intense. A police service recruited largely from townsfolk with a high proportion of ex-cadets is itself a very different sociological group from the one that relied predominantly on the changeless qualities of a vanishing rural England. What it loses in stability it is likely to gain in adaptability.

Outstanding in its deep concern about the role of the police in British society is the Police Federation, which celebrated its Golden Jubilee in 1969. That year it sponsored the first of a series of week-end seminars to discuss relationships between the police, Parliament, the Press, immigrants and students, at which distinguished speakers were drawn from numerous backgrounds. At the latest such seminar, in 1971, leaders of students and immigrant communities were cordially invited to tell the police what in their opinion was wrong with them. The spirit at such gatherings, where the talk flows long past midnight, augurs well for the future of the police–public relationship in this country.

But there is, as I have said, no room for complacency. The alienation from authority of many young people is beyond dispute, and it is equally clear that many members of immigrant communities, with experience of very different police systems in their countries of origin, and lacking insight into British ways, fail to understand that our police, in dealing with law-abiding citizens, are essentially benevolent. The policeman may be seen by the young as a tool of the establishment, by the immigrant as a representative of prejudiced authority. Both need reassuring; so, too, do the police themselves, now that the social forces that have traditionally supported the constable have been weakened, and that his right of intervention is constantly being challenged in new ways. If the police were to lose public support and goodwill on any significant scale it seems clear that their traditional character could not long survive. Britain could then expect what she has so long resisted—a tougher, more authoritarian, more oppressive system of police; and public confidence, once lost, would be hard to regain. Apprehension of this danger lay behind a remarkable initiative taken by the Church of England's Board for Social Responsibility in organising courses for police officers, school teachers, clergy of all denominations and social workers. These have provided opportunities for inter-disciplinary study and discussion of many aspects of the role of the police in society, and they have resulted in the appointment of local police liaison officers to work with representatives of the church and other local bodies. Such arrangements seem well calculated to help in the destruction of professional barriers between the social services which is vital to the well-being of the community. In recent years, too, the police have appointed full-time community relations officers with a particular concern for young people and immigrant communities. The Metropolitan Police, which led the way for so many reforms in policing Britain, now have a whole Community Relations Branch, under a commander, the significance of which was underlined by the Commissioner in his report for 1968. The formation of the Branch, he declared, indicated 'a new and very different approach to what is basically an old problem. Police can no longer afford to remain withdrawn and play a waiting game, but must be extrovert and

327

prepared to go more than half-way to make contact with sections of the public in a manner which would have been unheard of only a few years ago.'

So the experiments, the research, the questioning, go on. Probably no other nation has ever devoted so sustained an effort, over so long a period, to the overhaul of one of its foremost public services. It is true that the 'science of policing' which Colquhoun discovered more than 150 years ago to be so little understood has advanced only slowly as an academic study: no chair of policing yet exists in any British university. But the prolonged re-examination from first principles of the relation of the police to the State and to the public, and of the operational efficiency and needs of the police, has stimulated a public discussion which is likely to go on. It may in time lead to the formulation of a science of policing that will vindicate British empirical methods; more probably, perhaps, it will show that we have things to learn from other countries as well as much to teach them from our experience, on the whole not unsuccessful, in the art of reconciling order with liberty.

References
and
Bibliography

References

Chapter One

[1] 'The King's peace' is the legal name for the normal state of society, according to Stephen: *A History of the Criminal Law of England* (1883). A modern definition is 'the maintenance of conditions under which the normal functions of civilised government can be carried on, where obedience to the law is adequately secured, and the people are free to pursue their lawful ends without threat of interference': *The Home Office*, by Sir Frank Newsam (1954), p. 29.

[2] *A History of English Law*, by W. S. Holdsworth (7th edn., 1956), Vol. 1, Introductory Essay, p. 9.

[3] *The Medieval Foundations of England*, by G. O. Sayles (1948), p. 188.

[4] *Ibid.*, p. 188.

[5] *The Frankpledge System*, by W. A. Morris. The term is derived from *fri-borg*=full security. The system did not operate in the northern and western parts of England.

[6] Holdsworth, *op. cit.*, Vol. I, pp. 76–81.

[7] *Oxford Studies in Social and Legal History*, Preface to Vol. VII.

[8] *Eirenarcha*, by Lambard (1602).

[9] Holdsworth, *op. cit.*, Vol. IV, pp. 125 and 158.

[10] Sir Thomas Smith, quoted in the First Report of the Constabulary Commissioners, 1839, p. 179, and Harrison, quoted in *ibid.*, p. 380.

[11] *Justices of the Peace, 1361–1848*, by Bertram Osborne (1960), p. 87.

[12] *A History of the Criminal Law of England*, by Sir James Stephen (1883), Vol. I, p. 190.

[13] From presentments of Essex constables during the early years of Elizabeth, quoted by Osborne, *op. cit.*, p. 21.

[14] *English Local Government*, by S. and B. Webb (1906), Vol. I, pp. 463–73.

[15] *Ibid.*, p. 473.

[16] 34 & 35 Hen. VIII, c. 26.

[17] Lambard, *op. cit.*: the reference appears to be to a *high* constable, who was appointed by the *royal* hundred court and not the manorial court.

[18] Osborne, *op. cit.*, p. 87.

[19] 13 & 14 Chs. II, c. 12.

[20] 'The Office of Constable', by H. B. Simpson, article in the *English Historical Review*, October, 1895.

[21] *Commentaries*, Book 1, Ch. 9, IV.

[22] *Parochial Tyranny*, by Andrew Moreton (Defoe), p. 17, quoted by Webb, *op. cit.*, p. 62.

[23] S. and B. Webb, *op. cit.*, pp. 328–9.

[24] *Ibid.*, p. 340.

[25] *Ibid.*, Vol. IV (1922), p. 408.

[26] *Ibid.*, pp. 351–2.

[27] S. and B. Webb, *op. cit.*, Vol. 3 (1908), pp. 474, 476, and 484, and *English Municipal Institutions*,

References

1835–1879, by J. R. Somers Vine (1879), pp. 185–91.
28 S. and B. Webb, *op. cit.*, Vol. 4, p. 355.
29 Select Committee on Police, 1852–3, Qn. 506.

30 *English Municipal Institutions, 1835–1879,* by J. R. S. Vine (1879), pp. 185–91.
31 S. and B. Webb, *op. cit.*, Vol. 4, pp. 268–9.
32 *Ibid.*, pp. 235–6.

Chapter Two

1 *A Treatise on the Police of the Metropolis,* by Patrick Colquhoun, 5th edn. (1797), p. 213.
2 *A History of English Criminal Law,* by L. Radzinowicz, Vol. 3 (1956), p. 14.
3 *Ibid.*, p. 374.
4 *History of England in the Eighteenth Century,* by W. E. H. Lecky (1892 edn.), Vol. 4, p. 320.
5 *English Local Government,* by S. and B. Webb, Vol. 1 (1906), p. 576.
6 *Justice and Police,* by F. W. Maitland (1885), p. 108.
7 *Observations on a Late Publication, intituled, A Treatise on the Police of the Metropolis, by P. Colquhoun, Esq.,* by a Citizen of London: but no Magistrate (1800).
8 *Op. cit.*, Vol. 2 (1956), p. 263.
9 A comprehensive statement, 'Working Arrangements of Police Units in the Metropolis about 1828', is at Appendix 10 to Radzinowicz, *op. cit.*, Vol. 2.
10 *Crimes and Punishments* (translated by J. A. Farrer, 1880) pp. 242–3, quoted by Radzinowicz, *op. cit.*, Vol. 3, p. 426.

11 *Parl. Deb.*, Vol. VII (June 4th, 1822), c. 803, quoted by Radzinowicz, *op. cit.*, Vol. 3, p. 362, note 7.
12 *Mr. Secretary Peel,* by Norman Gash (1961), p. 492.
13 *Ibid.*, p. 493.
14 *Parl. Deb.*, N. S., Vol. XVIII February 28th, 1828), cols. 784–816.
15 Radzinowicz, *op. cit.*, Vol. 3, p. 449.
16 *P.P.* (1828), Vol. VI, 'Police of the Metropolis'.
17 *Parl. Deb.*, N.S., Vol. XXI (April 15th, 1829), cols. 872–7.
18 Gash, *op. cit.*, p. 496.
19 See, particularly, *British Police and the Democratic Ideal* (1943), and *A New Study of Police History* (1956), both by Charles Reith. In these valuable accounts Mr. Reith has made extensive use of Home Office papers in the Public Record Office and the commissioners' papers in the library of New Scotland Yard.
20 *A History of Police in England,* by W. Melville Lee (1901), p. 249.
21 Gash, *op cit.*, p. 502.
22 *Ibid.*, pp. 503 and 507.

Chapter Three

1 Evidence óf Mr. E. Corbett to the Select Committee on Police, *P.P.*, Vol. XXXVI, Session 1852–3, Qn. 2,231.
2 10 Geo. IV, c. 97, 'An Act to enable the Magistrates of the County Palatine of Chester to appoint Special High Constables for the several Hundreds or Divisions, and Assistant Petty Constables for the several Townships of that county'.
3 Quoted by S. and B. Webb, *English Local Government,* Vol. 1, p. 502.
4 *Parl. Deb.*, 3rd Ser., Vol. X (1832), col. 1,234.
5 3 and 4 Will. IV, c. 90.

6 S. and B. Webb, *op. cit.*, pp. 604–5.
7 *English Social History*, by G. M. Trevelyan (1942), p. 527.
8 First Report of the Constabulary Commissioners, pp. 1,080 (1839), para. 122.
9 For the primitive pre-1835 arrangements for policing Bristol see S. and B. Webb, *op. cit.*, Vol. 3 (1908), p. 474.
10 'Reform of the Borough Police, 1835–1856', by Jenifer Hart, *English Historical Review*, July, 1955.
11 *Ibid.*
12 See *The Life and Times of Sir Edwin Chadwick*, by S. E. Finer (1952), pp. 126–7; also Chadwick's Evidence to the Select Committee on Police, 1853.
13 *H.O.*, 43/49 and 51, letters of July 29th and August 24th, 1836.
14 *H.O.*, 43/51. The 'country gentleman' nominated by Russell was Charles Shaw Lefevre, who later became Speaker of the House of Commons.
15 *H.O.*, 43/51, letter of August 24th, 1836. A set of rules for one of these associations, the 'Rochdale Association for the Prosecution of Felons', is at Appendix III to *Cuffs and Handcuffs*, by Stanley Waller.
16 Hart, *op. cit.*
17 *History of England*, by G. M. Trevelyan (1956 edn.), p. 642.
18 *Chartism*, by Thomas Carlyle (1839).
19 *H.O.*, 41/13.
20 G. J. Harvey's *London Democrat*, April 27th, 1839.
21 Quoted by Hart, *op. cit.*, from the *Life and Opinions of General Sir Charles James Napier*, by Lieut. General Sir W. Napier (1857), ii, 15–56.
22 Circular letter addressed by Lord John Russell to the Chairman of Quarter Sessions, February 2nd, 1839. *P.P.* (1839), xlvii.

23 *Parl. Deb.*, 3rd ser., Vol. XLIX, July 24th, 1839, cols. 727–30.
24 *Ibid.*, 3rd. ser., Vol. XLIX, July 23rd, 1839, cols. 691–702.
25 Peel is thus quoted in the *History of the Corporation of Birmingham* by J. T. Bunce (1878), Vol. 1., p. 195, presumably from a local newspaper report of the proceedings in the House of Commons. The report in *Parl. Deb.* (3rd ser., XLIX, July 29th, 1839, col. 945) is similar in sense, but less forthrightly expressed.
26 *Parl. Deb.*, 3rd ser., Vol. L, August 8th, 1839, col. 116.
27 *H.O.*, 45/249 C.
28 *Parl. Deb.*, 3rd ser., Vol. L, August 8th, 1839, col. 116.
29 *Ibid.*, 3rd ser., Vol. L, August 15th, 1839, col. 357.
30 *H.O.*, 65/13.
31 *H.O.*, 40/50.
32 *Ibid.* Perhaps Coleridge's derisory remarks about the Alfoxden spy still rankled.
33 *H.O.*, 65/4.
34 *Ibid.*, letter of March 17th, 1840.
35 *Ibid.*, Letter of November 7th, 1839.
36 'Returns of Police Establishment in each county or division of a County', *P.P.*, Vol. XXXII (1842).
37 *A History of Police in England*, by W. Melville Lee (1901), pp. 295–6.
38 County Police Act, 1840 (3 & 4 Vict., c. 88).
39 Evidence given to Select Committee on Police, 1852–3. Qns. 2,639 and 2,954.
40 Quoted in *Cuffs and Handcuffs*, by Stanley Waller, p. 22.
41 *The Times*, January 10th, 1842.
42 *Justice and Police*, by F. W. Maitland (1885) p. 106.
43 5 & 6 Vict., c. 109.
44 *To Guard my People: A History of the Swansea Police Force*, by W. W. Hunt, p. 39.
45 *The History of the Anglesey Constabulary*, by Hugh Owen, p. 89.

References

[46] *A People's History of England,* by A. L. Moreton, p. 423.

[47] *H.O.,* 45/260, letter of August 3rd, 1842.

[48] *Ibid.,* letters of July 29th, August 3rd, and August 13th, 1842.

[49] *Ibid.,* letters of September 2nd and 3rd, 1842.

[50] *Ibid.,* letter of August 13th, 1842.

[51] *Ibid.,* minutes on letter of September 3rd, 1842.

[52] *Ibid.,* letter of September 23rd, 1842.

[53] *H.O.,* 43/63, letter of January 31st, 1843.

[54] *H.O.,* 43/49.

[55] Minutes by Sir George Grey in *H.O.,* 45/3,308, 3,760 and 3,798 (1850–1).

Chapter Four

[1] Evidence of Mr. J. R. Beddome to the Select Committee on Police, 1853.

[2] *H.O.,* 45/O.S., 4,609. The writer Lord Fortescue, became a member of the first police authority of Devonshire on the formation of a county constabulary three years later—a few months before the Act of 1856 came into force.

[3] *P.P.,* Vol. XXXVI (Police), Session 1852-3.

[4] e.g. evidence of a member of the Bath Watch Committee, *Ibid.,* Qns. 2,280–96. Some county forces were also reduced. Thus in 1842 the strength of the Lancashire Constabulary was cut from 500 to 350. Severe outbreaks of Chartist rioting occurred a few weeks later, of which Edwin Chadwick was an eyewitness. The incident left him in no doubt that, had the Lancashire police been a unified force, properly up to strength, it would have been unnecessary to call in the military once more—as in fact was done (Qn. 3,642).

[5] *Ibid.,* Qn. 3,498.

[6] *Ibid.,* Qn. 767. Another witness thought the swearing-in of specials created disorder and 'did more harm than good' (Qn. 2,058).

[7] Evidence of Captain W. C. Harris, Chief Constable of Hampshire.

[8] *Ibid.,* Qn. 3,644.

[9] The Committee called six county and three borough chief constables of forces in England— Durham, Essex, Lancashire, Hampshire, Wiltshire, East Sussex, Bath, Norwich and Manchester.

[10] *Ibid.,* Qns. 1,299–1,304 and 2,368 *et seq.*

[11] *Ibid.,* See, for example, the evidence of a Bath magistrate who recalled a member of the Bath Watch Committee who canvassed a policeman and told him, 'If you will support me as a member of the town council, I will do what I can to get you promoted when I get into the Council' (Qn. 2,127).

[12] *Ibid.,* Evidence of Mr. J. Dunne, Chief Constable of Norwich, who claimed that divided control tended to make effectual action impossible: 'In many instances the watch committee lay down instructions, and give orders which the magistrates countermand' (Qn. 1,949; see also Qn. 1,993).

[13] *Ibid.* Evidence of Mr. W. H. S. Stanley, (Qns. 299–301). A magistrate for several counties in the West Country took a similar line (Qn. 2,086).

[14] *Ibid.,* Qns. 2,963–64.

[15] *Ibid.,* Qns. 2,757–60 and 2,903.

[16] *Ibid.,* Qns. 1,555–76.

[17] Often after initial hostility and

prejudice: see, e.g., the evidence of Captain McHardy, Chief Constable of Essex, and Colonel J. Woodford, Chief Constable of Lancashire (Qns. 816 and 1,644–5).

[18] *Ibid.*, Qn. 1,874.

[19] *Ibid.*, Qns. 1,929–37 and 1,951–3.

[20] *Ibid.*, Qn. 2,842.

[21] *Ibid.*, Qns. 1,846–51.

[22] *H.O.*, 45/O.S., 4,777, which incidentally gives a revealing glimpse of the working of the machinery of government at the higher levels in the Permanent Secretary's state of unawareness betrayed by the question, 'Has the government decided upon bringing in a Bill founded upon the Report of the Committee of last Session?'

[23] *H.O.*, 45/O.S., 5,800, Minute of March 15th, 1854.

[24] *H.O.*, 45/O.S., 5,477.

[25] Speech by Mr. Forster, the Member for Walsall, on March 10th, 1856 (*Parl. Deb.*, 3rd ser., Vol. CXL, col. 2,149).

[26] *H.O.*, O.S., 5,276. Cobden and Bright were among those appointed to form a deputation to the Home Secretary.

[27] *Parl. Deb.*, 3rd Ser., Vol. CXXXIII (June 2nd, 1854), col. 1,267.

[28] The text of the Bill is printed in *P.P.*, 1854, Vol. V. This summary has been taken from an article entitled 'The County and Borough Police Act, 1856', by Jenifer Hart, in *Public Administration*, Winter, 1956.

[29] *Parl. Deb.*, 3rd Ser., Vol. CXXXIV, June 27th, 1854, cols. 750–1, June 30th, 1854, cols. 957–8, July 3rd, 1854, cols. 1,073–5.

[30] *H.O.*, 45/O.S., 6,266A.

[31] *Parl. Deb.*, 3rd Ser., Vol. CXL (March 10th, 1856), col. 2,130.

[32] The original suggestion that the Exchequer grant should be assessed in this way can be traced to a letter to Palmerston from Captain McHardy, the energetic Chief Constable of Essex (letter of February 20th, 1854, in *H.O.*, 45/O.S., 5,276).

[33] *Parl. Deb.*, 3rd Ser., Vol. CXL (February 13th, 1856), col. 690. Formally, however, the Association of Municipal Corporations does not seem to have been constituted until March, 1873: see the *Yorkshire Gazette*, March 29th, 1873. (For this information I am indebted to the present Secretary of the Association, Mr. J. C. Swaffield.)

[34] *The Times*, February 21st and 22nd, 1856.

[35] Circular letter of July 24th, 1856, in *H.O.*, 65/5.

[36] *Parl. Deb.*, 3rd Ser., Vol. CXL (March 10th, 1856), col. 2,181. Mrs. Hart has shown that, despite the organised opposition of the boroughs, support for the Bill cut across party lines, and, even more surprisingly, that eighty-three Members for English and Welsh boroughs entitled to maintain their own police forces voted for the Bill, as contrasted with only sixty-nine against.

[37] For this, and a number of other useful facts about the early activities of the inspectorate, I am indebted to an article, 'The Home Office and the Provincial Police in England and Wales, 1856–1870', by Henry Parris, *Public Law*, 1961, p. 230.

[38] Letter to Woodford of August 27th, 1856, in *H.O.*, 65/5.

[39] Colonel Woodford's report for 1856–7.

[40] *H.O.*, 45, O.S., 6,641 (1858).

[41] Letter of December 10th, 1841, in *H.O.*, 65/4.

[42] Parris, *op. cit.*, p. 241.

[43] *Ibid.*, p. 242: also Hart, *Public Administration*, Winter, 1956, p. 412.

[44] See e.g. a report of 1857 of the newly formed Rochdale Town Council, quoted in *Cuffs and*

References

Handcuffs, by Stanley Waller, p. 24.

[45] See Parris, *op. cit.*, where the pros and cons of consolidation, as seen at the time, are well discussed; also Cartwright's report for 1858–9, who opined, correctly, that legislation would eventually be necessary to deal with the smaller forces.

[46] Letter to Woodford in *H.O.*, 65/3, dated October 21st, 1856, quoted by Parris, *op. cit.*

[47] *Short History of the Berkshire Constabulary*, p. 28.

[48] Birkenhead, Leamington, Ramsgate, Tunbridge Wells, and Hove ('Provincial Police Establishments', Memorandum by Sir Godfrey Lushington, in *Home Office Printed Memoranda*, etc., Vol. III).

[49] Hart, *op. cit.*, p. 413.

[50] These minor changes, dealing with such matters as the administration of detached parts of the counties, the appointment of a chief constable for adjoining counties, the powers and duties of county chief constables and other matters, are summarised in *Home Office Printed Papers*, Vol. III.

[51] The Police (Expenses) Act, 1874. By an Act of 1890, the conditions on which grant was payable were broadened to include management and efficiency as well as the earlier criteria of numbers and discipline. A summary of the somewhat involved history of the police grant is given by Mrs. Hart in *The British Police*, 1951, pp. 36–8. A more detailed

account is contained in *The Home Office and the Police between the Two World Wars*, by Sir Arthur Dixon (1966), Chapter 11 (unpublished).

[52] Memorandum of April 27th, 1874, in *H.O.*, O.S., 19,774.

[53] *H.O.*, O.S., 19,774.

[54] *Home Office Printed Papers*, Vol. III, memorandum dated May 1st, 1876, where the list of consolidated boroughs is set out.

[55] Parris, *op. cit.*, p. 255.

[56] Quoted by Hart, *op. cit.*

[57] Minutes of March, 1883, quoted in *ibid.*

[58] *History of the Corporation of Birmingham*, by J. T. Bunce, Vol. 2, pp. 284–7. The Chief Constable was soon afterwards at loggerheads with both the magistrates and the Watch Committee on another matter, and was required to resign under the threat of dismissal.

[59] *Kent Police, 1857–1957*, p. 151.

[60] *Parl. Deb.*, 3rd Ser., Vols. CCCXXIII–CCCXXX.

[61] Vol. CCCXXIII, col. 1,645.

[62] See, e.g., the speech of Mr. Long, Vol. CCCXXIV, col. 1,282.

[63] Vol. CCCXXVII, col. 525.

[64] Vol. CCCXXVIII, cols. 797–861.

[65] Vol. CCCXXVII, col. 1,053.

[66] Vol. CCCXXIX, col. 1,653.

[67] Vol. CCCXXX, col. 1,174.

[68] Cmd. 1728, para. 82.

[69] *Justice and Police*, by F. W. Maitland (1885), p. 107.

[70] See, e.g., *Lincolnshire Constabulary, 1857–1957*, p. 32. The Parish Constables Act, 1842, was repealed by the Police Act, 1964.

Chapter Five

[1] *Interim Report of the Royal Commission on the Police*, Cmnd. 1,222 (November, 1960), para. 61.

[2] *The Kent Police Centenary*, ed. R. L. Thomas (1957).

[3] Letters in *The Times* of December 27th, 1855, and of September 17th, 20th, 23rd, and 26th, 1856.

[4] Select Committee on the Police Forces Weekly Rest-Day, *P.P.*

(1908), Vol. IX, evidence given by the Editor of the *Police Review*.

[5] *Fifty-two Years a Policeman*, by Sir William Nott-Bower (1926) p. 41. The author secured the appointment at Leeds, afterwards became Head Constable of Liverpool, and completed his career as Commissioner of the City of London Police.

[6] Memorandum of October 29th, 1858, in *H.O.*, 45/19,774.

[7] Select Committee on Police Superannuation Funds, *P.P.*, Vol. XV, Session 1877. Evidence of Mr. W. Farr. Qn. 71.

[8] *History of the Cheshire Constabulary*, by R. W. James, p. 34.

[9] For the loan of this document, only one copy of which has been traced, I am indebted to the Chief Constable of Liverpool.

[10] *To Guard my People: A History of the Swansea Police Force*, by W. W. Hunt (1957), p. 40. One signatory, unable to write his name, made his mark.

[11] *P.P.* (1908), Vol. IX. Evidence of Mr. G. H. Tripp.

[12] *Monmouthshire Constabulary Centenary, 1857*, pp. 17–18. Some interesting examples of the way in which discipline was administered towards the end of the century are cited in *The History of the Anglesey Constabulary*, by Hugh Owen, p. 38, and *The History of the Newport Police Force*, pp. 90–1.

[13] Select Committee on Police Superannuation Funds, *op. cit.*, Appendix, Tables XLVI and XLVII, which were deduced from the experience of the Metropolitan Police, 1829–60, of the county police from 1840 to 1874, and of the borough police from 1836 to 1874.

[14] *Monmouth Constabulary Centenary, 1857–1957*, p. 16.

[15] *Police!*, by Clarkson and

[16] Richardson (1889), pp. 142–5.

[16] *Ibid.*, pp. 145–6.

[17] Thomas, *op. cit.*, pp. 34 and 104.

[18] *P.P.*, Vol. IX, *op. cit.*, evidence of Dr. Little, Qn. 866.

[19] See, e.g., *History of the Caernarvon Constabulary*, p. 34, and *Dorset Constabulary, 1856–1956*, p. 13.

[20] H.O. Reports and Memoranda regarding various strikes, Tithe Disturbances, Riotous Proceedings, and Unlawful Assemblies, 1886–1912.

[21] *News from Nowhere*, by William Morris, Chapter VII.

[22] Clarkson and Richardson, *op. cit.*, p. 205.

[23] The Police Disabilities Removal Acts, 1887 and 1893.

[24] *P.P.* (1908), Vol. IX, Appendix XIX.

[25] *Ibid.*, Qn. 1,783.

[26] A full and authoritative account of the history of police pensions up to 1886, which usefully supplements the report of the select committee of 1875–7, is contained in *Home Office Printed Memoranda, etc.*, Vol. III.

[27] 3 & 4 Vict., c. 88.

[28] *Dorset Constabulary, 1856–1956*, p. 24.

[29] *A History of the Caernarvonshire Constabulary*, p. 31.

[30] 11 & 12 Vict., c. 14.

[31] 22 & 23 Vict., c. 32.

[32] See, e.g., letters of August, 1869, in *H.O.*, O.S., 45/19,774.

[33] *P.P.* (1877), Vol. XV.

[34] *P.P.* (1908), Vol. IX, Qn. 1,756.

[35] *Ibid.*, Qn. 2,012.

[36] *Ibid.*, Qns. 144–67.

[37] *Ibid.*, Qns. 2,670 and 2,984.

[38] *Ibid.*, Qn. 1,093.

[39] *Ibid.*, Qn. 830.

[40] *Ibid.*, Qn. 1,266.

[41] *Ibid.*, Qn. 1,093.

[42] *Ibid.*, Qns. 1,455–6.

[43] *Surrey Constabulary, 1851–1951*, p. 27.

[44] *P.P.* (1908), Vol. IX, Qn. 2,640.

Chapter Six

[1] These facts about the early relations between police and motorists are drawn from *The Golden Milestone, 50 years of the A.A.*, by David Keir and Bryan Morgan (1955), and *A Short Centenary History of the Surrey Constabulary* (1951).

[2] *Report of the Royal Commission upon the Duties of the Metropolitan Police*, Cd. 4,156 (1908). The quotations are from pp. 56–7 and 101.

[3] *The Times*, December 24th, 1908.

[4] 'Report of the Select Committee on the Employment of Military in Cases of Disturbances', *P.P.* (1908), 236.

[5] The correspondence between the Home Secretary and the authorities in South Wales is quoted from 'Colliery Strike Disturbances in South Wales—Correspondence: November, 1910', in *Miscellaneous Home Office Reports and Memoranda (Strikes, etc.), 1886–1912* (unpublished).

[6] Quoted by Sir Arthur Dixon, *The Emergency Work of the Police Forces in the Second World War* (unpublished, 1963), p. 4.

[7] *The Home Office*, by Sir Frank Newsam (1954), p. 40.

[8] *The Times*, August 31st and September 2nd, 1918.

[9] *The Times*, August 4th, 1919.

[10] *The Home Office and the Police between the Two World Wars*, by Sir Arthur Dixon (unpublished, 1966), p. 22.

[11] *Committee on the Police Service, Minutes of Evidence*, Cmd. 874 (1920), Qn. 3,563.

[12] *Ibid., Report*, paras. 28–9.

[13] *Ibid., Evidence*, Qns. 47, 63 and 64.

[14] *Ibid., Evidence* of Mr. H. B. Simpson.

[15] *Ibid., Report*, para. 14.

[16] Cmd. 574.

[17] *Home Office Memorandum of Evidence to the Oaksey Committee* (1949).

[18] Dixon, *op. cit.*, p. 42.

[19] *Ibid.*, pp. 48–9.

[20] Cmd. 3,297, paras. 16–17.

[21] *Mr. Punch and the Police*, by Christopher Pulling (1964).

[22] Dixon, *op. cit.*, p. 57.

[23] Cmd. 3,297, para. 52.

[24] Dixon, *op. cit.*, p. 206.

[25] Cmd. 4,294.

[26] Cmd. 4,320.

[27] *Home Office Memorandum of Evidence to the Oaksey Committee* (1949), p. 72.

[28] *The British Police*, by Jenifer Hart (1951), p. 135.

[29] Cmd. 877.

[30] Cmd. 2,224.

[31] Cmd. 3,297, paras. 256–7.

[32] *A Woman at Scotland Yard*, by Lilian Wyles (1952), p. 44.

Chapter Seven

[1] Quoted by H. M. Howgrave-Graham, *The Metropolitan Police at War* (1947).

[2] The first Police War Reserve to be set up was in the Metropolitan Police in May, 1938. It was followed soon afterwards by similar organisations in the City of London and in numerous county and borough forces. The Reserve was finally disbanded on December 31st, 1948.

[3] The composition of the wartime police service is fully and authoritatively set out in Sir Arthur Dixon's unpublished work, *The Emergency Work of the Police Forces in the Second World War*

(1963), from which many of the facts in this chapter have been drawn.
4 The regional reinforcement scheme was given statutory force by Defence Regulation 39.
5 Report of H.M. Inspectors of Constabulary for 1939.
6 T. H. O'Brien, *Civil Defence,* Volume 3 of the *Official Histories of the War.* (Other persons appointed as controllers were county and town clerks (about one-half of the total) or aldermen or councillors.)

7 Howgrave-Graham, *op. cit.*
8 Report of H.M. Inspectors of Constabulary for 1940–5.
9 Quoted by Dixon, *op. cit.,* p. 224–5. General Eisenhower, Supreme Commander of the Allied Expeditionary Force, sent a message to the Home Secretary on June 20th, 1944, expressing 'the deep gratitude of myself, my commanders and staff for the great assistance which the Police Forces have given to us in all the various stages which have led up to the Allied landings in France.'

Chapter Eight

1 *Royal Commission on the Police, Minutes of Evidence,* Vol. 3, p. 92.
2 The Economy (Miscellaneous Provisions) Bill, 1922.
3 *P.P.* (1932), 106.
4 The Defence (Amalgamation of Police Forces) Regulations, 1942, made on July 23rd, 1942.
5 *H.C. Deb.,* October 14th, 1942, col. 1,734.
6 *Police Training in England and Wales,* Cmd. 1,450 (1961). The arrangements were subsequently modified in detail.
7 *Higher Training for the Police Service in England and Wales,* Cmd. 7,070 (March, 1947). The proposals were first discussed with representatives of the local authorities and all ranks of the police service.
8 *Interim Report of the Royal Commission on the Police* (November, 1960), Cmd. 1,222, para. 21.
9 *Ibid.,* para. 22. Lord Trenchard, however, had not been impressed by the quality of the recruits, at all events up to 1931 (p. 206).

10 Cmd. 7,674 and 7,831.
11 Cmd. 7,321 (January, 1948).
12 Conducted (in 1951) by Sir Malcolm Trustram Eve and two assessors.
13 *P.P.,* 30, *Select Committee on Estimates* (Session 1957–8), Police.
14 Cmd. 1,222, para. 31 and fn. 8. A graph comparing movements in the constable's pay with average industrial earnings is at Appendix III to the Royal Commission's Interim Report.
15 *Report of the Commissioner of Police of the Metropolis,* Cmd. 9,786 (June, 1956).
16 Report of H.M. Inspectors of Constabulary for the year ending September 30th, 1958, para. 62.
17 Home Office Memorandum of Evidence to the Oaksey Committee, 1949.
18 Inspectors of Constabulary Report for the year ending December 31st, 1959, para. 19.
19 *Report of the Commissioner of Police of the Metropolis,* Cmnd. 1,106 (July, 1960).
20 Cmd. 645 (February, 1959).

References

Chapter Nine

[1] 330, *H.C. Deb.*, 3rd Ser. col. 1,174.
[2] Erskine May, *Parliamentary Procedure* (16th ed.) pp. 356 and 360—quoted by the Clerk of the House of Commons in evidence to the Royal Commission on the Police, 1962: Appendix II to the *Minutes of Evidence*.
[3] *Parl. Deb.* (1905) 150, cols. 1,184–5.
[4] 93, *H.C. Deb.*, 5th Ser., col. 1,613.
[5] 314, *H.C. Deb.*, 5th Ser., col. 1,625.
[6] 586, *H.C. Deb.*, 5th Ser., col. 1,294.
[7] *The Allegation of Assault on John Waters* (April, 1959), Cmnd. 718.
[8] *The Times*, July 9th, 1959.
[9] [1930] 2 K.B. 364 and [1955] A.C. 477.
[10] *Enever* v. *The King* [1906] 3 Commonwealth L.R. 969.
[11] See, e.g., articles on 'The Independence of Chief Constables' and 'Police Responsibility', in the Spring and Autumn issues for 1960 of *Public Administration*, and *Police and Government*, by Geoffrey Marshall (1965).
[12] 613, *H.C. Deb.*, 5th Ser., cols. 1,239–1,303.
[13] Cmd. 1,222 (November, 1960).
[14] *Ibid.*, para. 79.
[15] *Ibid.*, paras. 61–2.
[16] 677, *H.C. Deb.* 5th Ser., col. 682.
[17] *Minutes of Evidence*, pp. 921–40.
[18] *Ibid.*, pp. 626, 654–5, and 983.
[19] *Ibid.*, p. 631.
[20] *Ibid.*, pp. 683–723.
[21] *Ibid.*, Appendix II to the *Minutes of Evidence*, pp. 28–35.
[22] See particularly *Police and Government*, by Geoffrey Marshall (1965).
[23] Cmd. 1,728 (May, 1962).
[24] *Ibid.*, paras. 128, 135–9 and 147.
[25] *Ibid.*, paras. 142 and 148–50.
[26] *Ibid.*, paras, 324–5.
[27] *Ibid.*, paras. 89.
[28] *The Times*, June 1st, 1962.
[29] C. H. Rolph, *New Statesman*, June 8th, 1962.
[30] *The Economist*, June 2nd, 1962.
[31] *The Times*, June 27th, 1962.
[32] 677, *H.C. Deb.*, 5th Ser., cols. 680–799.

Chapter Ten

[1] First Report from the Estimates Committee (Session 1966–7), Police, *P.P.* 145, August, 1966, p. 180.
[2] Cmd. 1,728 (May, 1962) p. 22.
[3] *Report of H.M. Chief Inspector of Constabulary for 1965*, p. 37.
[4] *The Times*, November 24th, 1965.
[5] Cmd, 1,450 (August, 1961).
[6] *Report of a Working Party on Police Cadets* (H.M.S.O.), 1965.
[7] *Police Manpower, Equipment, and Efficiency* (H.M.S.O.), 1967.
[8] *Ibid.*, pp. 117–18.
[9] Quoted in the report of H.M. Chief Inspector of Constabulary for 1963, p. 73.
[10] Report of Inquiry by Mr. A. E. James, Q.C., Cmnd. 2,735 (August, 1965), and *Parl. Deb.*, Vol. 718, col. 1,203 (November 4th, 1965).
[11] *The Police and the Public*, by C. H. Rolph (1962), p. 184.
[12] *The Policeman in the Community*, by Michael Banton (1964), p. ix.
[13] *The Times*, December 24th, 1908.
[14] Rolph, *op. cit.*, p. 121.

Select Bibliography of Printed Sources

Histories of law, constitution, and local government

Burn, R., *Justice of the Peace and Parish Officer* (13th edn., 1869).
Cam, Helen, M., *The Hundred and the Hundred Rolls* (1930).
Holdsworth, W. S., *A History of English Law*, Vol. 1 (7th edn., 1956), and Vols. 2–13 (1909–52).
Lambard, W., *Eirenarcha* (1602).
Maitland, F. W., *Justice and Police* (1885).
Maitland, F. W., *Constitutional History of England* (1919).
Marshall, Geoffrey, *Police and Government*, (1965).
Morris, W. A., *The Frankpledge System*.
Osborne, Bertram, *Justices of the Peace, 1361–1848* (1960).
Radzinowicz, L., *A History of English Criminal Law*, Vols. 1–4 (1948–68).
Sayles, G. O., *The Medieval Foundations of England* (1948).
Simpson, H. B., 'The Office of Constable', in *The English Historical Review*, October, 1895.
Stephen, Sir James, *A History of the Criminal Law of England* (1883).
Webb, Sidney and Beatrice, *English Local Government* (Vols. 1–4, 1906–22).

A selection from reports of royal commissions and other official inquiries, parliamentary papers, and other documents published by H.M. Stationery Office

P.P. (1828), Vol. VI, *Police of the Metropolis.*
P.P. (1839), 1,080, *First Report of the Constabulary Commissioners.*
P.P., Vol. XXXVI (Police), Session 1852–3, *Report of Select Committee on Police, and Minutes of Evidence.*
P.P., Vol. XV, Session 1877, *Report of Select Committee on Police Superannuation Funds and Minutes of Evidence.*
P.P., Vol. IX (1908), *Report of Select Committee on the Police Forces Weekly Rest-Day and Minutes of Evidence.*
Cmd. 4,156 (1908), *Report of the Royal Commission upon the Duties of the Metropolitan Police and Minutes of Evidence.*
Cmd. 874 and Cmd. 574, *Reports of the Committee on the Police Service (The Desborough Committee)*, 1920.
Cmd. 3,297, *Report of the Royal Commission on Police Powers and Procedure* (1929).
Police Postwar Committee (Four Reports, 1946–7).

Select bibliography of printed sources

Cmd. 7,070, *Higher Training for the Police Service in England and Wales* (March, 1947).
Cmd. 7,674 and 7,831, *Reports of the Committee on Police Conditions of Service*, Parts 1 and 2 (1949).
P.P. 30, *Select Committee on Estimates* (Session 1957–8), Police.
Cmd. 1,222, *Interim Report of the Royal Commission on the Police* (November, 1960).
Cmd. 1,450 *Police Training in England and Wales* (1961).
Cmd. 1,728, *Final Report of the Royal Commission on the Police* (May, 1962).
Royal Commission on the Police, 1960–2, Minutes of Evidence.
Report of a Working Party on Police Cadets (1965).
P.P. 145, *First Report from the Select Committee on Estimates, Session 1966–7* (August, 1966).
Reports of H.M. Inspectors of Constabulary from 1856–1966.
Reports of the Commissioner of Police of the Metropolis.
Police Manpower, Equipment and Efficiency (1967).

Police: general

Banton, Michael, *The Police in the Community* (1964).
Browne, Douglas G., *The Rise of Scotland Yard* (1956).
Clarkson, C. T., and Richardson, J. H., *Police!* (1889).
Colquhoun, Patrick, *A Treatise on the Police of the Metropolis* (7th edn., 1806; reprinted 1969).
Dilnot, George, *The Story of Scotland Yard* (1926).
Fielding, John, *An account of the origin and effects of a police set on foot . . . in the year 1753 upon a plan . . . by the late Henry Fielding (1758).*
Hart, J. M., *The British Police* (1951).
Hart, J. M., 'Reform of the Borough Police, 1835–1856', in *The English Historical Review*, July, 1955.
Hart, J. M., 'The County and Borough Police Act, 1856', in *Public Administration*, Winter, 1956.
Howgrave-Graham, H. M. *The Metropolitan Police at War*, (1947).
Howgrave-Graham, H. M., *Light and Shade at Scotland Yard* (1947).
Lambert, J. R., *Crime, Police and Race Relations* (1970).
Lee, W. L. Melville, *A History of Police in England* (1901; reprinted 1971).
Martin, J. P., and Wilson, G., *The Police: A Study in Manpower* (1969).
Moylan, Sir John, *Scotland Yard* (1934).
Newsam, Sir Frank, *The Home Office* (1954).
Nott-Bower, Sir William, *Fifty-two Years a Policeman* (1926).
Pringle, Patrick, *Hue and Cry* (1955).
Pulling, Christopher, *Mr. Punch and the Police* (1964).
Parris, Henry, 'The Home Office and the Provincial Police in England and Wales, 1856–1870', in *Public Law*, 1961.
Reith, Charles, *The Police Idea: Its History and Evolution in England in the Eighteenth century and After* (1938).
Reith, Charles, *British Police and the Democratic Ideal* (1943).
Reith, Charles, *A Short History of the British Police* (1948).
Reith, Charles, *A New Study of Police History* (1956).
Rolph, C. H. (Ed.), *The Police and the Public: An Enquiry* (1962).
Scott, Sir Harold, *Scotland Yard* (1954).

Whitaker, Ben, *The Police* (1964).
Wyles, Lilian, *A Woman at Scotland Yard* (1952).

Local police force histories

Histories of the following police forces are known to exist at the present time (in a number of cases the county history deals also with the histories of borough forces within the geographical county).

County histories

Anglesey, Berkshire, Buckinghamshire, Caernarvonshire, Cheshire, Cornwall, Denbighshire, Devonshire, Dorset, County Durham, Essex, Flintshire, Gloucestershire, Gwent, Hampshire, Herefordshire, Hertfordshire, Huntingdonshire, Kent, Lancashire, Leicestershire, Lincolnshire, Monmouthshire, Norfolk, Northumberland, Oxfordshire, Pembrokeshire, Radnorshire, Somerset, Surrey, Sussex (East), Sussex (West), Warwickshire, Yorkshire (East Riding), Yorkshire (North Riding), Yorkshire (West Riding).

Borough histories

Birkenhead, Birmingham, Bolton, Bournemouth, Brighton, Bristol, Derby, Dudley, Gateshead, Godalming, Grimsby, Hull, Ipswich, Leeds, Liverpool, Macclesfield, Newport, Northampton, Nottingham, Oldham, Peterborough, Preston, Portsmouth, Reading, Rochdale, Southampton, Southend-on-Sea, Southport, Swansea, Tynemouth, Wakefield, Wallasey, Walsall, Wolverhampton, Worcester.

Index

Index

The interested reader
is referred to the
Patterson Smith Reprint Series
in Criminology, Law Enforcement, and Social Problems
which is listed
on the following pages

PATTERSON SMITH REPRINT SERIES IN
CRIMINOLOGY, LAW ENFORCEMENT, AND SOCIAL PROBLEMS

* new material added

PATTERSON SMITH REPRINT SERIES IN
CRIMINOLOGY, LAW ENFORCEMENT, AND SOCIAL PROBLEMS

* new material added   † new edition, revised or enlarged

PATTERSON SMITH REPRINT SERIES IN
CRIMINOLOGY, LAW ENFORCEMENT, AND SOCIAL PROBLEMS

* new material added † new edition, revised or enlarged